Reviews of *The Power of Centre* Edition

'The Power of Centre' reminds me that Britain was once a Holy Land, where towns and villages have a long and mythic history. What books we had were burned, what songs and stories pertaining to places were su[illegible]sed, as our indigenous language was outlawed, and we were [illegible]beys and churches, a history book of Jewish sacred la[illegible]n and the total disconnect that most people d[illegible]ct. This book is part of the recovery, [illegible]ystery once more in the groves, the [illegible]

[illegible] 102)

'As ever, the author's prose is r[illegible]imes, almost addictive. They hardly waste a [illegible] paragraph, without relating some fascinating fact or c[illegible]ept. It's a surefire sign of any good book that you are left wonde[illegible]g why you never noticed the content and the significance of the text for yourself. The premise is that all places have a Centre. Some of these are essentially geopolitical but, as often as not, they are also the critical core location of a community. Among the Centres considered are those pivotal to every section and region of Greater Britain, and to the Celtic fringes in particular. *The Power of Centre* will have you scratching around for OS maps you never knew you needed, and trawling the internet for places you've never heard of. Yet, for UK readers, we are never far from our own Centres - and even those from further afield are always close to a compassionate consideration of an inner sense of place.'

Nigel Twinn (Author of Dowsing and Earth Mysteries)

'Reading this book takes one on a series of pilgrimages that cannot fail to get the travel bug itching. History, of both conventional and less attested and esoteric varieties, gives a background to the sites, and is threaded through with personal biographical memories - the reader can easily share their excitement as fate brings them the kind of experience that affirms the sense of being guided on the path of discovery.

John Billingsley (Northern Earth book review issue 153 June 2018)

'Another masterly work by the authors of *The Spine of Albion*, (reviewed in a previous Newsletter), *The Power of Centre*, carries on the work of understanding the landscape in terms of Sacred Geometry. As *The Spine of Albion* looked at the longest and most important ley in Britain, so *The Power of Centre*, as the name suggests, looks at the concept of 'centrality' in earth mysteries. All-in-all, this is one of the most fascinating and well-researched books of its ilk that is out there.'

Liza Llewellyn (The Network of Ley Hunters review Issue 28 Lughnasadh 2018)

Monument in Girja, Lithuania marking the centre of the European landmass, calculated by the French National Geographic Institute in 1989.

Monument in Kyzyl, Tuva, Russia marking the Geographical centre of Asia.

Monument in Belle Fourche, South Dakota marking the Geographical centre of the United States of America.

Centres of Power
in Britain and Ireland
Uncovering the Secrets of the Hidden Omphalos and the Ancient Celtic Goddess

Gary Biltcliffe
and
Caroline Hoare

As the individual's spirit is centralised in the body
And the body has a physical location
So the world's spirit was thought of as centralised at a fixed point.
This point acted as a centre,
A pivot about which everything else revolved.

(Nigel Pennick)

Sacred Lands Publishing

The Power of Centre first published in 2018 by Sacred Lands Publishing
This revised and retitled edition published in 2025 by Sacred Lands Publishing.

© Gary Biltcliffe & Caroline Hoare 2025

Published by
Sacred Lands Publishing
Weymouth
Dorset
www.belinusline.com

The rights of the authors to be identified as the Authors of this Work have been asserted in accordance with the Copyright, Designs and Patents Act 1988.

All rights reserved. No part of this publication may be reproduced, stored in a retrieval system or transmitted, in any form or by any means, electronic, mechanical, photocopying or otherwise, without the prior permission of the publisher.

Every effort has been made to trace the copyright holders, and the publishers will be happy to correct any mistakes or omissions in future editions.

The quote on the title page is from *The Ancient Science of Geomancy* by Nigel Pennick, a prolific writer on European mystery traditions.

ISBN: 978-0-9572382-3-7

British Library Cataloguing in Publication Data
A catalogue record for this book is available from the British Library.

All photographs, line drawings and maps are by Gary Biltcliffe and Caroline Hoare unless otherwise stated.
Front cover artwork by Yuri Leitch. Design by Yuri Leitch and Gary Biltcliffe.
Back cover artwork by Caroline Hoare and Gary Biltcliffe.

Set in 11.5/13.5 pt

Contents

Preface

It was a beautiful warm summers evening in July 1998 when my mother and I attended a talk in Shaftesbury, in the county of Dorset, by Colin Bloy founder of the Fountain International Organisation. Afterwards, as we strolled along Park Walk, we stopped to watch the setting sun cast shadows across the valley, and I could still hear Colin's powerful words reverberating in my head. His notion of healing a town or community with focused love using visualisation at specific and relative centres of power was inspirational. He also used the principles of metaphysical science to explain that the brain produces alpha rhythms during meditation of a frequency around 8 Hz, which is the same as the pulse of the Earth and the feeling of unconditional love. He believed that visualising a surge of pure energy or light towards the 'navel' or 'omphalos' of a given area that needs healing, significantly alters the vibration of the ambient energy field of the whole.

My first encounter with centography (the search for geographical centres) was thanks to my late friend John from Dorset, who was very spiritual and had a connection with the land and animals like a true aboriginal. On one occasion he took me to a field of wilting crops and told me that it had a history of poor growth probably caused by geopathic stress – even his dog would not venture into the field. He asked if I could help him with a healing meditation to balance the energy. It was such a large field I wondered where to stand to perform the ceremony. John said 'the centre is always the best place to perform healing.' But how do we find the centre,' I said. 'With dowsing or a detailed map,' he replied. John did not know why but whenever he asked for the healing point of an area, his dowsing rods always led him to its central point.

Many years later I discovered through the study of *feng shui* with Caroline that the same procedure is used to heal a house by finding its centre and working from that point. We soon realised that this concept might work with towns and cities and after discovering their centres, there was occasionally something sacred or symbolic already in place. We were also amazed to find that some of the oldest cities had quartering cosmology in their layout surveyed from a central point at a crossroads.

On a grander scale, many of the old Celtic nations, shires and countries also had a centre-point, many having a connection to the Celtic goddess, which led to the writing of *The Power of Centre,* the first edition of this book.

Standing on one of these centre-points of power with an open mind and heart will allow a connection to higher levels of consciousness, and invite inspiration and communication. The great philosopher, antiquarian, artist and writer John Michell is often credited with the discovery of the St Michael Line – a long-distance alignment of St Michael sanctuaries from Cornwall to the Norfolk coast. His moment of inspiration came on a sacred hill called Burrow Mump in Somerset, when he saw that the axis of the hill pointed towards Glastonbury Tor in the distance, and he had a sense that the alignment continues further to the Avebury Stone Circle. Later, on a map he discovered that all three sites were indeed aligned, and further observations led to the discovery of the line.

During the writing of this book, we discovered that Burrow Mump is the geographical centre of Somerset and therefore a place of inspiration. We have included a list of English county centre-points which reveal some amazing places. For instance, in Hampshire the centre is Winchester Cathedral – the very place where a young William Wykeham in the 14th century was inspired to create a new educational system during masses to the Virgin Mary.

How can there be power at geographical centres? What is this energy that pervades the omphalos of any given area? This book will begin by introducing the reader to the concept of particle entanglement to gain an insight into this mystery and reveal why this information has been the source of forbidden knowledge throughout the ages.

Today, every country in the world has calculated its geographic centre, marking them with a feature such as a monument or a tree or the raising of a pillar. The obsession with centography remains strong even in the European Union, which is always erecting new monuments when countries enter or leave. This new revised edition goes deeper into the mystery of why geographical centres are important on a psychospiritual level to both early and modern cultures.

Gary Biltcliffe March Equinox 2025

Chapter 1

Pathways to the Centre

Our Spiral Galaxy (ESA/Hubble & NASA)

Plasma, Entanglement and the Axis Mundi

Everything is born from a centre. We are created in the centre of our mother in the womb, and after birth, we are fed from her navel via the umbilical cord to the centre of our body. Everything that exists on this Earth in all its wonderful forms started its molecular journey from the middle of our galaxy, the 'true mother', and according to 'quantum entanglement', we are still connected to her, for subatomic particles can be in communication even when separated by vast distances.

Old scientific paradigms used to view the Universe as inert matter, fragmented and void of life except for planet Earth. This misconception may have influenced humanity to a sense of self-importance and uniqueness, eventually bringing rampant materialism, consumerism and environmental disasters. The theory that a black hole and its massive gravitational forces are responsible for holding the Universe together is also outdated. Today, scientists are proposing that instead of gravity, it is electricity or electromagnetism that holds the galaxy together called the 'Electric Universe' theory. Rather than a dark void between the stars and planets, there is a matrix of electrical strands weaving everything together made from self-organising ionised gas or a higher form of intelligent matter called 'plasma'.

The Earth and the Sun are positioned on one of the arms of our spiral galaxy and a long way from the centre, which appears as a bulge of light when observed from our planet. Recently with the use of thousands of hours of powerful radio telescope observations, a more accurate picture of the core can be revealed as a place of massive energy – a portal where plasma enters the Universe and the birthplace of life, as opposed to a black hole that sucks everything into oblivion.

Plasma is a form of superheated, highly electromagnetic ionised gas and is one of the fundamental and dynamic components of everything that exists and the highest known state of matter. The Sun and many giant gaseous planets are all made of plasma – in reality, 99 per cent of what we see from our telescopes is plasma.

The atom is at the root of everything that exists and has within its nucleus positively charged protons, neutrons with no charge and negatively charged electromagnetically bound electrons orbiting outside the nucleus. Therefore, the force of creation on Earth is tripart at its very core, existing in positive, negative and neutral charges. Atoms then bond with others to become molecules and earthly matter, such as solids, liquids and gases.

Under a microscope, solids are molecules bound in a structured way, but when energy is applied to them, they start to move around each other to become liquid and when more power is applied, they separate and become gas. But when more energy is used, something incredible happens – the negatively charged electrons that orbit the neutral atoms break free and become positively charged, causing the atom to magically change its state, or evolve, to become a positively charged ion. This process is called ionisation.

The planet Earth consists of matter in its lowest atomic state, unlike other planets made of plasma – though it still manifests naturally on Earth in the form of lightning and the Arora Borealis or Northern Lights. Plasma is also released from the immense pressures of gas within the Earth's crust and will find its way to the surface through cracks or fissures in certain rocks. Many people have witnessed plasma lights in earthquake areas and around fault lines, particularly near many sacred sites called 'earth lights'. Some of the lights are often seen floating over lakes and marshes and behave peculiarly as if they have intelligence. Plasma acts unlike any other type of matter because it has evolved and broken free from its atomic state and can pass through matter like a ghost.

The recent experiments with subatomic particles have given us a new understanding of the mystery of interconnectedness. When one particle splits from another, they continue to know about the states of the others instantaneously, even though the particles may be at opposite ends of the galaxy, travelling at different speeds and even entering alternate realities.

Quantum physics views time not as a constant but as a figure-of-eight or loop – the future, present and past flowing continuously together. However, particle entanglement operates outside of our known time and space continuum and therefore, on some minuscule level, we are connected to everything in the past, present and future.

But why do we not sense this connectedness? Well, for one thing, humanity would become insane with massive information overload. But we can carefully tap into this stream of consciousness with meditation and focused thoughts – this is why many sensitive individuals can psychically see into the past, have premonitions of the future and pick up the present thoughts of another person on the other side of the world.

Plasma can change form and move in and out of this dimension, and like a computer linked to the web, it is tuned to the collective 'Universal Mind' and, therefore, knows everything about us and how we can be influenced here on Earth. Many have interpreted these plasma forms as gods, aliens, guardian angels, fairies or spirits. Even our soul is plasma in substance, and the afterlife is likely to be a plasma world.[1]

Many believe we are in essence, highly evolved plasma beings who have agreed to experience lower atomic states to physically play out emotional scenarios to help us grow spiritually. Often these roles we experience are challenging, with much hardship, isolation and lack of love. But the love and beauty of nature and the Earth, with all its varied landscapes, can be the healer through the harshest times. I believe the various recognised centre-points around the world have nourishing and curative powers, as the fundamental experience of being born and fed from the centre of our mother perhaps transfers symbolically to our existence here on Earth.

When our ancient ancestors chose a territory or island to settle, they first sought to locate the geographic midpoints of their new realm to create an omphalos or focal point to honour, control and connect with spirits of the higher worlds and the Earth Mother to bring about harmony and balance within themselves and the land in which they were to live, but also give them the power to influence.

For many cultures, a stone or wooden pillar is a common object used to mark a midpoint site, symbolic of the upper, middle and lower worlds denoting a vertical column called the 'axis mundi' or 'world pillar'. This central pillar can be developed with the setting up of roads radiating out to the cardinal points to attract the energy of the cosmos, creating an omphalos of spiritual influence. Examples of this cosmology can still be seen in many ancient and modern towns and cities around the world, as we will reveal in later chapters.

Other representations of a central shrine can be a mound, hill, mountain, holy well or tree. The tree is another perception of the axis mundi and is symbolic of the planes that influence us here on Earth, for its roots run deep underground, connecting with the underworld and symbolic of our past – its trunk represents our present reality, and the upper branches express the heavenly planes and our future. Many trees worldwide represent the middle of a territory or sacred landscape, and in Britain, the Midland Oak, the Whiteleaved Oak and the Fortingall yew were three such trees as were the great ash tree on the Hill of Uisneach at the navel of Ireland. When I was a child, I was constantly climbing trees reaching for the top branches where I would find peace, beauty and inspiration away from the 'trunk' of the present and the roots of the underworld.

Nordic world tree called the Yggdrasil by Olfusen Bagge 1847

In Norse cosmology, the 'world tree' was the great mythical ash tree of Odin that grows at the centre of the world called *Yggdrasill*, where gods, humans, animals and nature were nourished. It was also the point of communication between heaven and Earth and all phases of existence to all living things.[2] It plays a central role in almost every major world religion because it represents the archetype for the human psyche to attain self-fulfilment as both an earthly and a divine being. In other words, it represents humanity's spiritual journey through the different planes or dimensions of existence and communication between the higher or lower realms, depending on our desires. The tree is nourished by its roots that spread to sacred wells, which feed the rivers, bringing life to the world. The tree also suffers from entwined dragons that gnaw at its roots, because they are held in place to keep stability in the lower realms.

Our ancient nonmaterialistic ancestors, who were more at 'one' with the 'universal mind', became aware of the importance of this journey from the navel outwards and carved the spiral and concentric rings into their stone monuments and burial places representing the unwinding spiritual quest

World Mountains and Omphalos Stones

According to Greek and Egyptian legends, the earliest city on Earth was on the island of Atlantis, a great landmass in the middle of the Atlantic Ocean destroyed by a tsunami. This great kingdom became the home of Poseidon, the God of the Sea, who fathered five sets of male twins. Its central hill was called Mount Meru and was the source of the main rivers through the island. Poseidon sculpted the mountain into a series of concentric walls and canals radiating out from the centre, where he built a temple in his name. He then divided the land into ten provinces, each ruled by one of his sons.

Although the legendary Atlantis was supposedly destroyed around 9000 BCE, its cosmology of honouring a 'world mountain' later spread to ancient Sumer, the Indus Valley, Greece, Egypt, Peru and the Middle East, where we find Mount Ararat, considered the 'roof of the world' and the source of the Rivers Tigris and Euphrates, its valleys becoming the cradle of civilisation. In the East, Mount Fuji, Japan's highest mountain and Mount Kunlun in China are viewed as the centre of the world. But the pyramidal-shaped Mount Kailash in the Himalayas has a unique quality and is highly revered by many religions as the Earth's navel. It is the source of four of India's major rivers at the meeting of four continents and is said to be highly magnetic and possess great supernatural power. Even today, it is one of the most forbidden places on Earth to climb, although many have tried and failed.[3]

The world's five main religions, Judaism, Christianity, Buddhism, Hinduism and Islam, have all attached themselves to a symbolic 'world mountain'. Interestingly, Christianity, Judaism and Islam revere the same iconic Mount Sinai in Egypt, where Moses received the Ten Commandments. Mount Olympus, the highest mountain peak in Greece, is the holy mountain of the ancient Greek civilisation and was once regarded as the home of their gods, who were adept at calculating the centre of the world's landmass. In Greek mythology,

Mount Kailash by Jean-Marie Hullot.

Cronos, the first of the Titan deities, devoured his offspring as soon as they were born in fear of his mother's prophesy that his children would overthrow him. Although Cronos managed to swallow his first five children, his wife Rhea sought the help of Gaia, the Earth Mother, to save the sixth child, Zeus, by concealing him in a cave on Mount Ida in Crete. Meanwhile, Rhea wrapped a stone in swaddling clothes and gave it to her husband, who promptly swallowed it, believing it to be his youngest son. When Zeus grew to be a man, he forced his father to disgorge the contents of his stomach, which first produced the stone, followed by all of Zeus' five siblings. With their help, Zeus defeated the Titans and became the new king of the gods.

Zeus decided to search for the centre of the world and place an oracle there to commune with the 'axis mundi' so that he would know the future. He did this by releasing two eagles at Mount Olympus in opposite directions, and after encircling the Earth, they finally met at Delphi in Greece. Here Zeus placed the stone that Cronos swallowed under the glens of Mount Parnassus as a sign to humanity. Today, tourists are shown a dome-shaped circular replica stone carved with serpents called the 'Omphalos of Delphi' now housed in the museum.

In Greek, the word 'omphalos' means 'navel' and today, this name refers to any divined geomantic centre. The original cone-shaped stone was set into the ground at Delphi on the hillside where it is said Apollo speared the dragon, now the site of the Temple of Apollo. The original stone is now lost, but legend says it was a large meteorite that fell from the sky in deepest antiquity, and the first physical object to emerge on dry land after the waters of 'the deluge' had settled.

The name 'Delphi' derives from the Greek *Delphus* meaning 'hollow' or 'womb' or possibly 'vagina', and in a cleft-shaped cave the legendary Oracle (a gifted psychic) would communicate a message from the 'womb' of the Earth Mother on the seventh day of each of the seven warmer months of the year. Omphalos sites became pilgrim destinations to honour the goddess of fertility and regeneration and to receive advice from the Oracle through collective unconsciousness. In the Late Classical period (4th–5th century BCE), Delphi transferred its worship from the Earth Mother to the male god Apollo, although the oracle priestess was allowed to remain. This displacement of the feminine to a masculine deity at these centres coincided with the rise of the later Greeks and Romans, whose patriarchal religion spread throughout Europe to Britain in the 1st century CE.

Another spiritual centre in Greece is a tiny rocky island called Delos, which lies at the centre of the Aegean Sea. Here, mythology tells us that Apollo and his sister Artemis were born. In the first millennium BCE, the island became known as the main cult centre of Apollo, with an egg-shaped stone carved with coiled serpents at its omphalos. Such is the sacredness of this island that, even today, visiting times are limited, and no one is permitted to dwell or spend a night there except for the antiquity guards, archaeologists and conservators who attend to the archaeological site.

As the ancient world's population grew, cities were established using cosmological principles, by divining a central point by a geomancer and then laying out the roads to the cardinal points. A well-known example is the augur or priest geomancer of the Etruscans, the pre-Roman civilisation of central Italy, who wore a conical hat and held a rod, just as today's bishops wear a mitre and carry a crook. He would first survey the land by determining the position of the stars and planets in conjunction with the landscape topography. He also used divination by observing visible signs in nature, such as where a bird takes sudden flight or a specific location that has attracted an animal to linger there. Weather portents such as lightning strikes, claps of thunder, sudden rain, or hail were also scrutinised.

Once the augur identified the centre it was marked with a mound or a pit called a 'mundus', then standing on the spot at night to observe the pole star, he marked a line towards this fixed northernmost star on the ground with his rod. The Latin name of this north-south axis is 'cardo'. An east-west line was also laid out, called 'decumanus', at right angles to the cardo, creating a cross on the ground. Symbolically, this crossroads to the cardinal points acts as a conduit for the cosmological powers that radiate out from the axis mundi at the centre. The priest then faced the south and recited the words: 'This is my front and this my back, this my left and this my right.' (see Fig. 1) Honouring the South was an ancient custom in many cultures around the world, but this sacred direction changed to the East in Christian times.[4] The ancient practice of city foundation by an augur may however originate in Mesopotamia or the Indus Valley.

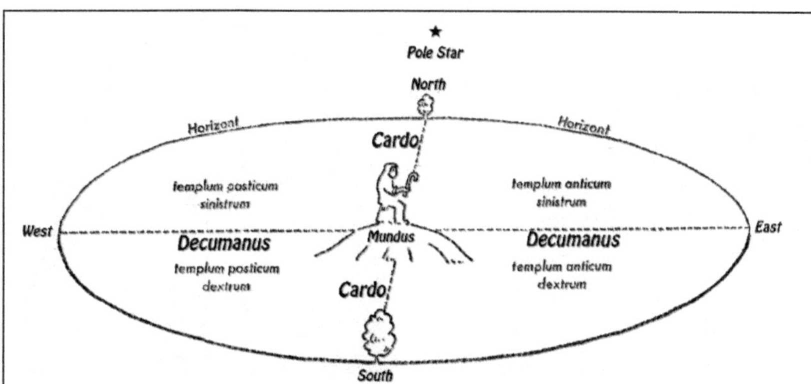

Figure 1. Etruscan or Roman Augur. Courtesy of Erdmann Barbara

Babylon in Mesopotamia is one of the world's most ancient cities, constructed around 3000 BCE and the largest during the period 1770–1670 BCE. It would become one of the greatest centres of learning in the world under Nebuchadnezzar II (604–562 BCE). Plans of the layout of ancient Babylon discovered on clay tablets are remarkably similar to the legendary descriptions of the great city of Atlantis. Its central temple complex, where great festivals took place, included the royal palace, the great Ziggurat (stepped pyramid) and at its core the Temple of Marduk (also called the Esagila). According to the ancient creation myths of the Babylonians called the *Enûma Eliš*, the temple has divine form and location, for it was the spot chosen by the gods for their king's residence, where all life ultimately originated and where humans were created and Marduk himself was born.[5]

The Ziggurat next to the Esagila represented the world mountain, connecting the three cosmic realms of the heavens, the surface world and the underworld. The *Enûma Eliš* also records that here Marduk created the world from the corpse of Tiamat, the dragon-shaped primeval mother, and fastened her tail to the world axis to wedge her lower abdomen onto the heavens, thereby lending eternal permanence to his work of creation.

At the focal point within the Temple of Marduk was a cone-shaped meteoritic stone carved with a serpent coiling around it exactly like the Delos omphalos, representing the earthly dragon power of Tiamat. Marduk, also called Bel, later the Celtic Belinus, has similar traits to other mythical characters such as St Michael, St George, Beowulf, Sigurd, Cadmus and Apollo, all legendary dragon slayers who control the Earth's energies and are associated with judgement, magic and holy places.

Babylonian omphalos stone with coiled serpent by George Rawlinson (1880)

The Harappan culture of the Indus Valley also built great cities around 2600 BCE and worshipped sacred stones at their central shrines called *baetylus*, which is Semitic for *bet el* meaning 'house of God', a word denoting sacred stones that were supposedly talismans endowed with life.

According to their legends, the mysterious baetylus stones fell from the heavenly realms and held inherent powers of prophesy that could be translated through a psychic or oracle. Meteorites were the most precious stones to early man and were often revered at the centre of their kingdoms. In one of India's most historical epic poems called the *Mahābhārata*, the city of Prayag, now Allahabad in northern India, is listed as the last and most important of two hundred and seventy ancient holy places and the mythical creation point of the Universe. The major cult sanctuaries at Prayag were situated on an island with a shrine dedicated to the primordial serpent that protected the eternal tree or 'world tree' at its centre.[6]

The foundation myths of ancient Egypt, say their land evolved from a 'primordial mound' or 'island of creation' that rose from the floodwaters of the Nile. Here raised upon a pillar they worshipped a black metallic stone called the Benben, a meteorite that fell from the realm of the sky gods and revered as a cosmic seed of first creation.[7]

Many ancient cultures focused their spiritual or religious identity on a sacred stone in the belief that it was the true centre of their world and therefore connected to the three cosmic realms. For example, the holiest shrine of Islam is Mecca in Saudi Arabia and its focal point is the cube-shaped temple called the Kaaba, which houses a black meteoritic stone at its eastern corner. For the early Christians and Jews, Jerusalem was the centre of the world and the focus of their religion was the Temple Mount and the rock beneath the temple, a place also sacred to Islam. In *Ezekiel* 5:5, Jeremiah quotes God as saying, 'This is Jerusalem; I have set her at the centre of the nations.'

The Dragon Lines and Serpent Currents

Another feature of the omphalos in myth and legend is the hidden dragon or serpent force within the land. Across the world, many indigenous cultures refer to the importance of taming or slaying the dragon or serpent. The name dragon derives from the Latin *draconem* and the Greek *drakon* meaning 'serpent'. Today, researchers believe that these unseen creatures are purely mythical and symbolic of the fertility force of nature. The serpent is associated with the omphalos in many cultures. The Nordic world tree has serpents gnawing at its roots – The Greek Apollo speared the dragon at Delphi – the Delos stone has coiled serpents around it – Marduk of Mesopotamia created the world from the corpse of a dragon-shaped primaeval mother, who fastened her tail to the world axis and at Prayag in Northern India they worshipped the serpent that protected the tree of life.

The serpent is depicted entwined around the omphalos stone on ancient coins, said to be symbolic of the control of the serpent power at the navel. Delphi's omphalos stone also has coiled interlaced patterns that may represent the serpent force, similar to Celtic designs seen on many standing crosses. A later legend states that the Greek god Apollo slayed or controlled the great serpent or dragon Python so that he could establish his oracular temple at Delphi, utilising the power of the serpent beneath it.[8]

Dragon slaying is a popular theme in many religions. In the East, the serpent or dragon energies are considered rampant and untamed, necessitating some kind of control, such as staking to the ground. In England, St George slayed a dragon on a conical flat-topped mound called Dragon Hill below the Uffington White Horse in Oxfordshire that many believe represents a dragon. However, only sensitive individuals such as psychics and dowsers can detect these hidden serpents or dragon energies and without scientific approval it is conjectural. Those who have seen these invisible lines of power say they are like beams of light that weave across the Earth in the manner of a snake or serpent. They connect with special places of telluric power in the landscape such as mountains, hills, caves, lakes and springs and certain manmade temples, standing stones or earthen enclosures.

A replica of Delphi's omphalos stone (Delphi Archaeological Museum)

Throughout the world, folklore and legend refer to dragons and serpents as mysterious reptilian creatures that haunt the countryside and protect treasure in a 'dragon's den'. They would repeatedly terrorise the local population from their lair, often located in peculiarly shaped hills, mounds, lakes or springs. In British legends, the dragon consumed virgin maidens offered by the locals to appease its hunger or wrath until a brave knight rescues them and slays the dragon.

The earliest example of this depiction comes from the ancient Greek tale of Perseus rescuing Andromeda from the sea dragon. In many cultures, the dragon represents God's wrath or the destructive force of nature. In the Americas, the ancient tribes of the Toltecs and Aztecs sacrificed their people to the earth serpent to regenerate the fertility in the land.

In the past, Beltane, the Celtic festival celebrated on 1 May, was a time when towns and villages across Europe paraded the effigy of a dragon through the streets to welcome or draw the fertility force into their environs to precipitate a good harvest. Thus, slaying the dragon was not the killing of the beast but the fixing of its fertile qualities at a sacred place when it rises to its full power in the spring. There are many Christian images of the dragon slayers St George, St Michael and St Margaret, which depict them pinning the dragon to the ground without piercing their skin.

The St Michael Line is one of the most famous long-distance alignments and the longest east-west land route in Britain, stretching from the western extreme of Cornwall near Land's End to Hopton-on-Sea in Norfolk. A great number of St Michael churches and many historic and prehistoric religious sites are situated on this line, including St Michael's Mount in Cornwall, Glastonbury, Avebury and Bury St Edmunds.

As mentioned in the Preface, John Michell, a pioneer of the Earth mysteries movement, first recognised the geomantic importance of the St Michael Line in the early 1990s when standing on a hill called the Mump near Burrowbridge located at the centre of Somerset. He noticed that its elongated shape points towards the Tor, a prominent hill in Glastonbury 16 km away and envisioned that it extends eastwards to pass through the great southern entrance stones of the Avebury Stone Circle in Wiltshire.[9]

Michell also writes that 'As astronomers and astrologers, the Celts and their priesthood, the Druids, continued this tradition of tracing the emergence of the dragon force, manipulating and animating its fertilising power required in the land. Ceremonial processions along these energetic paths created straight tracks, similar to those walked by later pilgrims visiting holy shrines.'[10]

The challenge of dowsing the St Michael Line was undertaken by the dowser Hamish Miller and researcher Paul Broadhurst in the 1980s. However, instead of detecting a straight line, Hamish dowsed a sinuous path of masculine solar energy that weaved across the landscape, visiting prehistoric sites and Christian sanctuaries on either side of the St Michael Line. Hamish also discovered that at certain secret places of power, the line narrowed down to a point in the ground and reappeared a little further away in precisely the same manner. He realised that this unusual behaviour was the result of another flow of energy crossing with it to form what Hamish called a 'node'. He found himself having to de-tune to follow this other line for, although similar in width and strength, it had a gentler and softer nature, which he later determined to be of opposite polarity or a lunar feminine current of energy.

They named these energy lines Michael and Mary and their research was published in the book *The Sun and the Serpent* in 1989, which has motivated generations of Earth Mystery enthusiasts around the world to rediscover and re-examine their own sacred sites.[11]

The Chinese geomancers call these winding earth energies *lung mei* (translated as dragon or serpent veins) – the dragon being a symbol of this divine force – containing either male (yang) or female (yin) properties. Geomancers were trained in the art of astrology and the divination of the land, and were skilled in finding the most auspicious places to build shrines and temples for the Chinese emperors. They understood the life-giving qualities of the earth serpents or dragons, and in certain places shaped their landscape to harness their energy, inducing spiritual harmony and aiding fertility within the land. The emperor's palaces and tombs were the only structures permitted on the dragon paths, thus ensuring the imperial leader's power in life and death and the future success of his dynasty.

The male current, or 'White Tiger' as the Chinese refer to it, follows the high places across the country such as mountain-tops, while the female current, or 'Blue Dragon', visits caves, lakes, rivers and springs deep in the valleys. With the aid of divining rods, a compass and a vast knowledge of the celestial influences, the Chinese geomancer detected these paths of the dragon, constructing buildings so as not to interfere with or block their natural flow. The sole purpose of this practice of feng shui was to bring order and beauty to the landscape. The geomancers were also skilled in channelling and directing the dragon lines of earth energy to the imperial seat of the emperor.

Modern researchers claim that the dragon energy lines are linked to a grid or network of magnetic lines that circumnavigate the Earth. Moreover, for centuries, those initiated into the underground stream of esoteric knowledge believed that the point where they crossed to form a 'node' was regarded as a fortuitous place of yin and yang power. Similar to Chinese practices, numerous temples and churches in Europe were built over these node points. In the course of dowsing the Michael and Mary lines of the St Michael alignment, Miller and Broadhurst uncovered evidence that our ancestors had at one time manipulated these currents or lines of dragon force, to exert greater control or authority over certain places of power.[12]

Chinese Dragons male (gold) and female (violet) by Ccyyrree

When the dragon force is out of balance, the resulting negative energy can be detrimental to our health. The practice of driving a stake in the ground to cure imbalanced earth energies, called by dowsers 'black streams', is a modern version of the dragon-slaying act.

When plasma is released from the Earth, the electrically charged particles encounter the least resistance by following magnetic lines of force known as field-aligned current filaments and can follow already established natural lines of geomagnetic force.[13] In space these plasma lines are known as Birkeland currents containing streams of positive and negative energy constricted within magnetic fields like the energy lines tracked by the dowser. The crossing points in space or 'pinch points' are akin in microcosm to the node points found along energy lines on the Earth. These currents also contain positive and negative lines like the male and female dragon lines found weaving around the straight alignment of the St Michael Line. The concept of two currents around a central pole like the caduceus is seen in plasma cosmology and within the famous St Michael Line.

I later discovered that another long-distance alignment called the Belinus Line is the north-south equivalent of the famous St Michael Line, forming the longest through-route, from the Isle of Wight at the southern base of Britain to the tip of Scotland near Durness. This line

Figure 2. The Belinus Line

connects Winchester, the old capital of England, with the old Scottish capital of Dunfermline and Lairg, the capital of Sutherland. The line connects six cities in all, including Carlisle, the old Roman capital of the north, Manchester and Birmingham the industrial capitals of the 19th and early 20th centuries, and Inverness the capital of the Highlands (see Fig. 2). While dowsing the Belinus Line through Britain, Caroline and I discovered yin and yang energy flows similar to the Michael and Mary dragon lines dowsed by Hamish Miller. The investigation of this line started in the early 1990s and was finally completed in 2012 with our self-published book *The Spine of Albion.*[14] We also noted that the Belinus Line connects with the geographical midpoints of Britain and Scotland which also inspired the writing of *The Power of Centre*.

The Goddess and the Navel

Many omphalos or axis mundi sites are historically linked to the mother goddess at many places around the world, for it is here that she nourishes us. The ancient British goddess Brigantia is often depicted in carvings on ancient stones standing next to a cone-shaped omphalos stone or baetylus. On later British coins, Brigantia becomes Britannia, ruler of the seas, and appears as a seated warrior wearing a helmet and holding a shield and spear. There is also a lighthouse in the background, its appearance symbolically representing both fire and the omphalos. In earlier depictions, she holds a round cross-shield that represents the cross-quarter wheel of the heavens, the four elements and the four cardinal directions. The trident, like the spear held by Brigantia, refers to the axis mundi, a connector rod between the realms of mortals and spirits.

The ancient British and Irish goddess archetype called variously Brig, Bride or Brigid is associated with many navel sites around Britain and Ireland. According to legend, the Irish pagan goddess Brigid had her main sanctuary at Kildare, where she guarded a perpetual flame along with nineteen virgin maidens during a 20-day cycle. Her flame was honoured at every hearth, or fireplace, in every home and at the smithy, where fires create the utensils and tools of life and death. A statue of her at a nearby holy well on the outskirts of Kildare is remarkably similar to the Roman goddess Vesta who is also connected to omphalos sites.

In Ireland, the three or four-armed Brigid cross was pinned above the hearth as a protective amulet at the sacred 'centre' of the home. Today, many houses are built without fireplaces and many chimneys in older houses are being blocked up, its occupants preferring oil or gas central heating. As the focus switched from the hearth to the television or computer, we lost the ancient practice of honouring and blessing the centre of our home, which I believe has left us 'un-centred' and disconnected from our core being and our heart centre.

The Great Mother and her sacred flame represent the flame or light within us, the spiritual energy that ignites our soul at the core of our being and all things. She is the protector at the heart of our home, goddess of sovereignty and guardian of many of the centre or navel points around Europe. We also observed in our investigations that the navel sites were associated with springs and wells, the life-giving waters of Mother Earth, or a mystical lake or pond whose waters gave birth to major rivers that feed the oceans and seas. Water sites such as

British goddess Brigantia found at Birrens, Scotland. Courtesy of Yuri Leitch

these are the haunt of spirits as well as places of healing, with many of the wells known to cure skin diseases and eye complaints. The veneration of lakes and ponds dates back thousands of years through the offerings of swords, rings and coins thrown into the still waters on a certain sacred day of the year to appease the spirits. Many of the old omphalos sites revered by our ancient ancestors have survived and become popular tourist destinations, while others remain neglected and forgotten, consigned to folk memory or destroyed due to modern development.

According to the principles of Chinese feng shui, where centres of countries, towns or cities remain intact and are still honoured and nourished in the right way, there is a harmonious balance of energies, but if they have suffered neglect or destruction there will be imbalance and disharmony. This may harm the fortunes and prosperity of these towns and cities and entire kingdoms, undermining the psyche of its inhabitants, and keeping them unmotivated and uncaring of their environment. Likewise, through the blocking up of holy wells and springs and the changing of river courses without care and love, this stifles, stagnates and causes imbalance to the life-giving force within the land and a disconnection from the cosmic realms.

There is evidence that these divined centres of power became the target of one culture attempting to overthrow the other. Charlemagne (747–814 CE), king of the Franks, was the first recognised emperor in Western Europe since the fall of the Western Roman Empire. His destruction of the *Irminsul*, meaning 'great or mighty pillar', the chief seat of Saxon religion for the Germanic people, was an attempt to break their power and ensure the continuance of his kingdom.

The Benedictine monk Rudolf of Fulda (d. 865 CE) describes an Irminsul in his Latin work *De miraculis sancti Alexandri*: 'The Irminsul was a great wooden pillar erected and worshipped beneath the open sky, its name signifying the universal all-sustaining pillar.'[15] The destruction of a nation's omphalos site and the eradication of its history has taken place all over the world and today many of these important places lie forgotten, with just a fragment of folklore to give us a clue as to their past significance.

Calculating the Centre

There are two ways in which to determine the physical or geographical midpoint of a country, island or continent. The gravitational method uses the suspension of a two-dimensional cut-out model of a region, its centre located through its balancing point or centre of gravity when placed on the point of a needle. The other is the boundary method using maps, with lines or circles drawn between the extreme points of a country to define the centre, also, finding the longest north-south line is a popular practice. Using the Google Earth line or measurement tool gives the boundary method more accuracy due to its three-dimensional mapping program; the use of the global positioning system (GPS) will also add accuracy to the calculation.

In the search for the omphalos of a continent, country or island, both methods can only show an approximate point for the centre. However, we have discovered that it is often the nearest natural or manmade feature at these centres that receives the power – which become more powerful over time from the projected thoughts and prayers of pilgrims. According to Plato's Laws, the city had to be built at the centre of the kingdom, at a spot that has all the conveniences a city requires; therefore, not necessarily at the exact centre.

In ancient times, the task of finding the centre of a territory was the work of highly trained surveyors, similar to the Etruscan augurs mentioned earlier. In Britain and Ireland, ancient writers ascribed such skills to the Celtic Druids, whose height of power was between 1000 BCE and 70 CE. The Roman general Caesar stated during his campaign to conquer Britain that the Druids were skilled in astronomy, astrology, geodesy and land measurement,[16] all the attributes required for the task of finding a sacred centre. The Celts and early Britons perceived the order of the Universe as a wheel, symbolic of the constant spinning of the stars in the night sky and the turning of the seasons over a year. The belief that the pole star was the axle of the giant wheel, which represented the point where souls ascended to the otherworld is also fundamental in Celtic cosmology.

Like Plato, who sought the old methods of sacred planning to help rebalance the land and reverse his country's desire for war and materialism, it was our aim during the course of researching the old centres of our ancient lands to help heal our environment and its peoples. In our work with feng shui for homes and businesses, we have discovered that by working with the sacred centre or axis mundi, the healing is more profound and links us to the whole, whether it be the centre of a room, a house, a park, a county or an entire country.

In the human body, the navel is the remnant of the umbilical cord, a footing for a bridge that makes our development possible in the physical world and gives us a foundation upon which we can flourish. Similarly, each ancient civilisation nurtured the navel of their landmass to ensure growth and prosperity.

Esoteric practices require one to focus on the solar plexus or navel to find one's power centre. This is true within the landscape, and by finding its centre we find the focal place of power and therefore the most effective place to perform ceremony and healing. This we can also adapt to towns and cities. Taking from the old practices of worshipping the mother goddess Bride or Brigid and the elemental spirit of the land, we feel that by honouring and nourishing the centres of our nations, towns and cities, harmony and balance to the land and its people can be restored, promoting good fortune, health and wellbeing.

As we began our research of the centres of the British Isles and Ireland, we discovered that within each kingdom, country, district, city or town there are still remnants of a revered centre, with evidence of Earth goddess worship and kingship ceremonies, often within the shadow of a holy mountain or hill and near a forgotten holy well.

The following chapters record many remarkable accounts of our adventures as we embarked on a quest to rediscover the mystical Celtic centres of the British Isles and Ireland.

References:

1. Temple R (2022) *The New Science of Heaven*. Coronet, an imprint of Hodder & Stoughton, London.
2. Pennick N (1979) *The Ancient Science of Geomancy: Man in Harmony with the Earth*. Thames & Hudson, London.
3. https://www.youtube.com/watch?v=VwAG-y0sTjc.
4. Etruscan Religion http://www.mysteriousetruscans.com/religion.html.
5. Enuma Elish. http:www.sacred-texts.com/ane-enuma.htm
6. Earth Navels. http://www.ancient-wisdom.com/earthnavels.htm.
7. https://robertbauval.co.uk/articles/articles/DE14.html.
8. Graves R (2011) *The Greek Myths: The Complete and Definitive Edition*. Penguin, London.
9. Michell J (1983) *The New View Over Atlantis*. Thames & Hudson, London.
10. Ibid.
11. Miller H & Broadhurst P (1989) *The Sun and the Serpent.* Pendragon Press, Launceston.
12. Ibid.
13. Temple R (2022) *The New Science of Heaven*. Coronet, an imprint of Hodder & Stoughton, London.
14. Biltcliffe G & Hoare C (2012) *The Spine of Albion: An Exploration of Earth Energies and Landscape Mysteries along the Belinus Line*. Sacred Lands Publishing, Weymouth.
15. Pennick N (1973) *Geomancy*. Cokaygne Publishing, Cambridge.
16. Caesar, Julius (100–44 BC) *De Bello Gallico. Book VI.*

Chapter 2

The Ancient Royal Centres of the Emerald Isle

Ireland is a Celtic realm unmolested by the Romans, Saxons and Normans, and its ancient landscapes still feature the most remarkable example of the reverence of a national omphalos. The Emerald Isle also presents 'as above so below' cosmology in the arrangement or division of its ancient territorial provinces and kingship sites around a geographical middle kingdom ruled by a High King where the island's most important national games and parliament assemblies took place. Celtic Ireland also held sacred an east-west middle route, like a belt dividing the island into two halves. The route follows natural banks of gravel left over from the Ice Age called *eskers*. This central causeway became one of the earliest thoroughfares, along which Celtic Christian missionaries founded their first monastic schools, later to influence many parts of Britain and Europe.

The division of Ireland happened in more recent history, becoming two self-governing bodies – Northern and Southern Ireland in 1921 with Northern Ireland remaining in the UK and Southern Ireland becoming a Republic. The British colonisation of Ireland began when Oliver Cromwell came to power and sent his Parliamentarian soldiers there in 1649 to crush the resistance, inflicting brutal punishment on the people and the country. Therefore, Northern Ireland and the Republic of Ireland have very recent centre-points, but for most of its history, it has always been one nation with a national omphalos.

As we set out to explore and research the history of Ireland's centre-point, we soon encountered the conflicting views of historians, medieval and modern political propaganda, exaggeration, pseudohistory, a lack of archaeological excavations, and limited documented evidence, but worst of all, the wanton destruction of sacred places. However, there is a rich source of oral history and small publications, including local myths and legends, allowing us a glimpse of the past. Because the Romans never conquered Ireland, its surviving folk memory recalls a distant world of warrior gods, which inspired authors such as J.R.R. Tolkien and the early Celts who survived here longer than any other European society.

Irish storytellers and orators have recited their island's numerous invasions for thousands of years with fantastic tales of gods, goddesses, warrior kings, and queens woven into the history of the landscape recalled in its place names and stories of certain rocks, stones, mountains, mounds, rivers and holy wells.

According to the *Lebor Gabála Érenn* (The Book of the Takings), seven races occupied Ireland before Christian times. The first to arrive was Cessair, daughter of Noah, who stepped foot on these virgin shores with fifty women and three men before the Biblical Flood. After the floods subsided, there came a group of settlers called the Formorians, a race of hunter-gatherers, often referred to as giants, who wielded great supernatural powers, including nature's most harmful and destructive influences. The Partholón followed them and worked the land as the first farmers, clearing four plains and mining for gold. Stories say they perished in a plague created through supernatural means by the Formorians. When the People of Nemed arrived, they supposedly cleared twelve plains for agricultural use, but they too succumbed to the evil and tenacious Formorians, and only thirty managed to escape the country by boat.

Descendants of these survivors would return, calling themselves the 'Fir Bolg', or Firbholg, who were responsible for the establishment of 'High Kingship' and instituted the political division of Ireland into five provinces around a ritual ceremonial centre. They were also replaced, not by the Formorians, but by settlers seeking Ireland as their new home called the Tuatha Dé Danann, translated as 'the followers of the goddess Danu'. They brought with them four treasures – the Stone of Destiny or *Lia Fáil*, an inauguration stone for their kings; the Spear of Lugh, which ensured their victory; the Sword of Nuadha, which spared no one and the Cauldron of Dagda, from which no company ever went away unsatisfied.

This elemental-like race successfully defeated the Formorians and reigned supreme for many centuries, until the arrival of the last invaders of Ireland known as the Milesian Gaels. They supposedly sailed to these western shores from either Iberia or Portugal, with some legends relating that they originally came from Egypt. Eventually, the Danann retreated into the underworld and became the gods, goddesses and fairy folk of later Irish folklore and legend.

Noah's daughter Cessair, the Partholón and the Tuatha Dé Danann all arrived at the same auspicious time of year, Beltane. At each successive invasion, the new arrivals formed a higher social order above that of their predecessors, while integrating their ritual magic traditions.[1]

This also reflects in the divisions of the country, first into two, then four and five, and eventually twelve. This corresponds to Plato's cosmological ideals of creation, beginning with the separation of light from darkness, the polarity of yin and yang, and the principle of 'as above and so below'. The quartering of the land mirrors the four seasons, cardinal directions and elements, which then progresses to four around a core central fifth, from which the four 'are anchored and revolve.' This also symbolises the evolution of man requiring a permanent central authority. The last race subdivided each of the four provinces into three, which created twelve sectors around the central thirteenth. This supposedly corresponded to the twelve races of man, the classical pantheon of gods, the signs of the zodiac, the hours in a day, and months in a year. The same number in mythology could symbolise King Arthur and his twelve knights, his Irish counterpart being Finn and his twelve warriors called the Fianna.

The four ancient provinces of Ireland still exist today as the counties of Leinster in the east, Munster in the south, Connacht in the west and Ulster in the north (see Fig. 3). A smaller fifth province called Midhe was at the centre of the four provinces, now part of West Meath in Leinster. The names Midhe and Meath are similar to other named centre places around Europe including Meon Hill, in Warwickshire, Myon in France, Milan in Italy, anciently known as Mediolanum, and Meonenim a Biblical central place in the Holy Land said to be the 'oak of the sorcerers'.[2]

Within the fifth province, history, myth and legend point to the Hill of Uisneach as the navel or omphalos of Ireland and this hill is still revered as such today. Each of the four provinces had its royal sites, traditionally places of assembly, religion and politics where Celtic kings ruled over the land and its people, similar to King Arthur in his Camelot. The four royal centres are Dún Ailinne in Leinster, Cnoc Áine in Munster, Rathcroghan (Ráth Crúachan) in Connacht, and Emain Macha (Navan Fort) in Ulster. However, as regards Cnoc Aine, the so-called royal centre of the Munster kings, we were later to discover that nearby Lough Gur was the actual sacred ritual assembly place of this ancient kingdom, aligned exactly with the Hill of Uisneach and Emain Macha.

These important places of state survived up until Roman Christianity usurped their power. There are a great many smaller royal enclosures all over Ireland, which for some historians hold as much significance as the four main sites, such as the Hill of Tara in Meath. However, these additional places of sovereignty may have indeed been important during a time when the Milesians divided the four

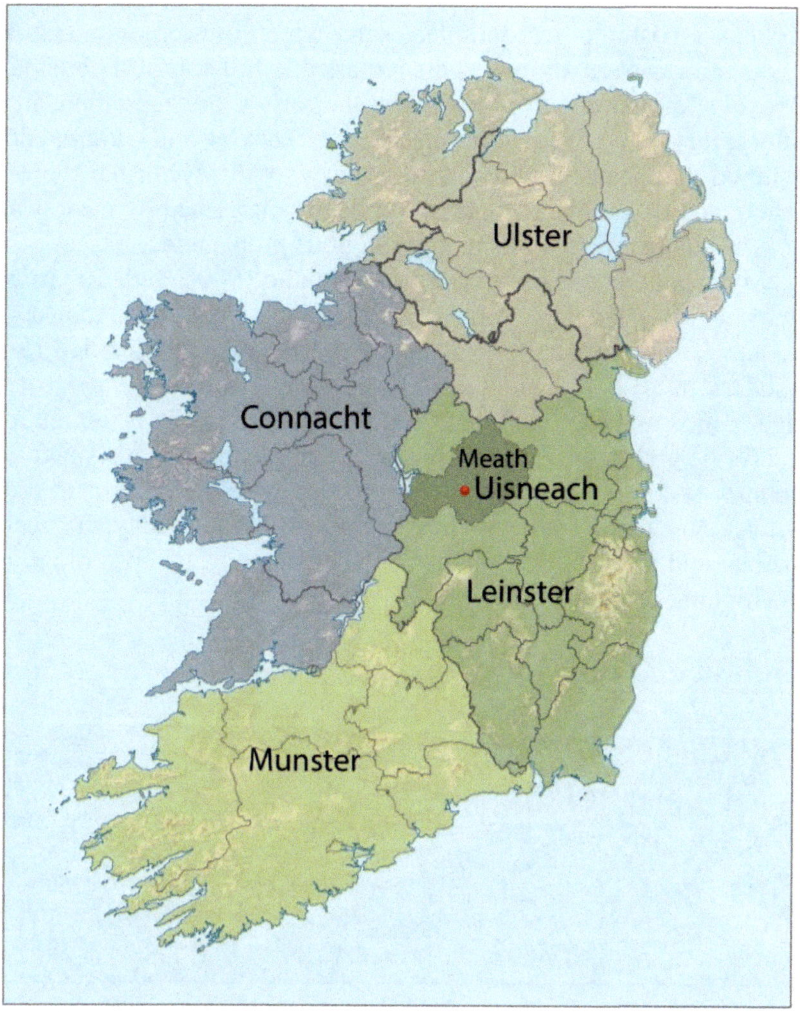

Figure 3. The Ancient Divisions of Ireland

provinces into seven, each having their own royal enclosures.

Authors such as Michael Dames in *Mythic Ireland* and Graham Robb in *The Ancient Paths* have shown that the four main royal sites are exactly aligned to the Hill of Uisneach. Dames proved the incredible accuracy of the early Celts in their arrangement of temples over great distances with his plotted wheel of solsticial sun risings and settings seen from Uisneach at the hub.[3] On a map, Robb also plotted the alignments between the four royal enclosures and found that they form a remarkable, near-perfect diamond-shaped geometry across Ireland.[4] Both authors point out that Uisneach is indeed the navel of Ireland, a cosmological template from which other monuments and royal centres were aligned. This remarkable hill was still considered a royal site right up until the time of the early Celtic Christians in the 5th century when the great monasteries of Durrow and Clonmacnoise usurped its pagan influence. However, we will reveal that there are other candidates for the centre of Ireland determined by cataclysmic coastal changes and political and religious propaganda.

My many visits to Ireland in the 1980s and 1990s seeded a growing interest in cosmology and goddess/saint worship amongst the country's old stones, holy wells and earthworks. Reverence to the goddess in all her various guises can be found in the names of the rivers, hills and sacred shrines. Dublin's River Liffey is named after the Celtic goddess Lif yeh – its ancient inhabitants even shaped their country according to our worldly existence and the cosmos to create heaven on earth. Many sensitives who visit Ireland today still feel its special and ethereal energy - perhaps unaware of its cosmology and positioning of its sacred centres.

Dublin and the Holy Way

Figure 4. Colm Ó Lochlainn's map of the east-west route of An Slí Mhór from Dublin to Galway Bay

Caroline and I began our investigations in the capital city of Dublin with a visit to the famous National Museum of Ireland – Archaeology, where we experienced the incredible artefacts of a once highly cultured Celtic race that lived at one with the land. Later, during our walk around some of the city's historic sites, we found ourselves distracted by the discovery of an ancient east-west route that divides the country into two almost equal halves, called the Esker Riada. Its name derives from *eiscir* meaning 'ridge' and *riada* meaning 'road', although the road is a series of raised gravel causeways. These sinuous ridges or eskers were formed naturally when loose rock and sand deposits churned up beneath a glacier became exposed after the rapid melting at the end of the last Ice Age.

For the first humans, these eskers provided a perfect overland route, resembling today's disused railway embankments, through the impenetrable boglands of central Ireland between Dublin Bay on the east coast and Galway Bay to the west. Where there were gaps between the eskers in the bog, tracks were laid using tree trunks arranged end to end to bridge them, like the Neolithic 'sweet tracks' in Somerset, England. Latest research shows that the early Celts used this road, known then as An Slí Mhór, meaning 'the Great Way' (see Fig. 4). It would later become a pilgrim route, walked by many of the early Irish saints, who incorporated sections of the Esker Riada along its course from Dublin Bay and the Hill of Howth to Inishmore, the largest of the Aran Islands, via a boat crossing. These Islands, situated off the west coast at Galway Bay, were deemed the spiritual realms of the dead from prehistoric times, and Inishmore was as sacred to Ireland as the Isle of Iona is to Scotland and Lindisfarne to England.

There are differing opinions concerning the exact route of An Slí Mhór, as some believe that the legendary road began at the great kingship site of Tara in Co Meath and ran to Clonard before joining the Dublin to Galway Esker Riada. This may be due to the dubious legend of Tara's 'Five Royal Roads'. According to *The Annals of the Four Masters*, 'The night of Conn's birth was discovered five principal roads leading to Teamhair [Tara], which were never observed till then.'[5] However, as we were soon to discover, there were at least two further ancient sites called Tara in Ireland, including one near Durrow, which had evidence of five ancient trackways meeting right in the middle of An Slí Mhór.

We were fortunate to find a book referring to this old pilgrim route by researcher Hermann Geissel. In *A Road on the Long Ridge: In Search of the Ancient Highway on the Esker Riada*, Geissel studies old maps, local knowledge, geology, history and the 'lay of the land' to make a solid case for the Dublin-Galway route being the Celtic An Slí Mhór.[6] We also consulted Colm Ó Lochlainn's map from *Roadways in Ancient Ireland* and, sure enough, it again shows a detailed network of ancient roads, including his projection of An Slí Mhór from Dublin to Galway Bay.[7]

Furthermore, many authorities agree that Clonmacnoise was founded at an important central junction of the Esker Riada with the north-south River Shannon. This important monastic centre was built by St Ciaran in 548 CE and became one of the greatest pilgrimage centres in Europe. The majestic River Shannon is Ireland's largest waterway and provided the earliest settlers an easy means of travelling north and south through the country, its crossing with the Esker Riada creating a natural 'crossroads' right at the heart of Ireland.

There is also a popular belief recited by earth mysteries author John Michell in *At the Centre of the World* that the actual geographical centre of Ireland is halfway between Dublin and Galway to the east of Athlone.[8] After checking Lochlainn's map, we discovered that halfway along An Slí Mhór, east of Athlone, five ancient roads meet exactly at the spot where the famous monastic school and abbey at Durrow was founded by St Columba in 553 CE. From here, another line of eskers leads north to the Hill of Uisneach, the ancient mythological centre of Ireland, which led us to believe that the Esker Riada and An Slí Mhór served as a road to the royal centres of Ireland.

Sadly, this old east-west route is fast disappearing due to modern development and the construction of new roads, but also because the sand and gravel eskers have become a valued source of building material. Nevertheless, awareness of the ridge's natural beauty and its significance in Ireland's history is now being realised and has led to new measures to make it an important feature of Ireland's ancient history. Indeed, Co Offaly County Council has moved to protect the ridge through their region and the Irish Geological Heritage Programme has pressed for the Esker Riada to be recognised as a World Heritage site.[9]

Apart from Geissel's book, there is at present no proper guide to this ancient east-west route, but there are modern roads and lanes that still trace its original course. We first learned of An Slí Mhór while visiting a lesser-known tourist destination called St Audoen's Church at Cornmarket, possibly the oldest site of Christianity in Dublin. The grand gothic church blackened with age received its dedication to the 7th-century St Ouen or Audoen of Rouen from the first church on this site. The next rebuilding in 1181 saw a dedication to St Colmcille or St Columba and was incorporated within the medieval walls of the old city opposite Newgate. This may be where St Columba stopped before journeying to his monastery at Durrow.

St Audoen's Church houses the 'Lucky Stone', also referred to as the 'Traveller's Luck Stone'. This round-headed Celtic cross stone was used as a charm, whereby rubbing the stone was meant to bring pilgrims, merchants and traders good fortune or luck. Many of them would stop here before journeying across An Slí Mhór, having prayed for safe passage. Although the stone has been inside the church since before 1309, its original site was outside by the edge of the road at the traditional starting point of An Slí Mhór. This stone rich in quartzite mica-schist is said to have a supernatural guardian, for despite being removed from the church on several occasions, it somehow always found its way back.

Traveller's Luck Stone, St Audoen's Church, Dublin

The first recorded mention of the stone was when Jon Le Decer, Mayor of Dublin, erected a marble cistern in Cornmarket in 1309 and placed this stone against it, so that all who drank of the waters may have good fortune. In 1826, however, it disappeared, until 20 years later when it was found at the front of the newly erected Catholic Church in High Street. It was said that on one occasion, while it was being driven away in a horse and cart, the stone became heavier and heavier until the horse collapsed under its weight. The thieves promptly dumped it on waste ground, where it was eventually found. When workers attempted to smash it up, they witnessed the stone moaning and rolling over; this is a common folktale concerning certain megaliths in Britain that stubbornly refuse to be moved.[10]

Walking down the aisle of this ancient church towards the front porch, we soon found the Lucky Stone tucked away in a corner, secured in a recess halfway up the wall. As we approached it, we could physically sense the power of this mysterious stone, which seemed to be almost electric to the touch. We rubbed the stone and asked the guardian for guidance during our explorations of Ireland.

On our way out, I felt drawn to approach an attendant at the reception desk to inquire further about the Lucky Stone. He informed us that there were two other similar crosshead stones in Dublin roughly the same age, one of which was inside St Patrick's Cathedral and another in Merrion Square in the southeast of the city. He concluded that these stones defined a sacred boundary in Saxon times or even before.

He then enthusiastically started to tell us about An Slí Mhór and produced an old map showing where it originally started, close to the church by an old fording of the River Liffey, and its journey across Dublin to the monastic site at Clondalkin. The map shows the route passing straight through a site that is now occupied by an Ibis Hotel on the western outskirts of the city, located next to the Red Cow Roundabout on Dublin's orbital motorway – incredibly, the very hotel we were staying in. We could not believe that we were sleeping on this ancient pilgrim route!

As he was stabbing his finger on the map at other sites along the route, I instantly recognised some of them, particularly Carbury Hill, Croghan Hill, Durrow and Clonmacnoise, important sites featured in much of Ireland's mythology and religious history. We also observed that there are a great many healing wells along this remarkable route.

Although every year thousands of tourists visit Ireland to see such royal centres as Tara, the Neolithic complex of passage mounds called Bru na Boinne, and the famous monastic sanctuary at Kells, I had a sense that this ancient route, probably the oldest road in Northern Europe, may one day be just as famous.

After listening to the fascinating guide in St Audeon's Church and with the help of Geissel's book, we decided to go with our instincts and explore some of the sites along this forgotten sacred middle route to the centre of the country, including Croghan Hill, the source of the River Boyne, Durrow and the religious site of Clonmacnoise.

A Pilgrimage along An Slí Mhór

The ancient course of An Slí Mhór leaves the suburbs of Dublin and passes through Clondalkin, with its ancient round tower, one of the best preserved in the country, at 25.6 m high with its original conical cap. The early Christian settlement here, allegedly founded by St Mochua (b. *c.* 570 CE), is also home to a healing well dedicated to St Brigid, established for baptising pagans in the 5th century. Locals believe in the curative powers of the waters particularly for eye and skin complaints.[11] The traditional ritual for healing was to make the sign of the cross with a piece of cloth over the ailment area and then hang it on the hawthorn tree that stands over the well. This was followed by Seven Hail Marys, Our Fathers and Glory be to the Father, recited every day for seven days.

Like many other important religious sites in Ireland, the town was sacked and burned by the Vikings and also witnessed a famous battle in 1171 when the last High King of Ireland, Ruairi O'Conchúir, failed to hold back the invading Norman army led by Richard de Clare, Third Earl of Hertford.

A few kilometres west of Clondalkin is Celbridge, where An Slí Mhór crosses the River Liffey at a fording place near the old mill. The name of the town derives from a cell or church that stood within a circular enclosed sanctuary; the ruins of a 6th-century church can be seen just under a kilometre away from the Liffey next to An Slí Mhór, also founded by St Mochua, often referred to as Crónán. Mochua's family was of royal descent from Cathair Mór, a famous King of Leinster who reigned in the 2nd century. The only remnant of this saint's Christian site is a holy well located near the mill, used to convert the local pagans. According to folklore, this sacred well once flourished as an important cult centre of the Druids long before Mochua arrived.

The next significant site along this ancient road is Taghadoe, another early monastic settlement with a round tower, founded by an abbot of Clonmacnoise called St Tua in the 8th century. This site is close to Maynooth where a decisive battle took place in 123 CE, fought between King Eoghan, also known as Mug Nuadat, and King Conn. After his defeat, Conn was forced to concede to the division of Ireland into two halves, using what is believed to be the line of the eskers as a boundary: 'Conn's Half' to the north and 'Mugs Half'' to the south. St Mochua continued to establish further churches along An Slí Mhór, at a site between Taghadoe and Donadea, close to Balraheen Crossroads, and at Timahoe, a name meaning 'house of Mochua'.[12]

In our book *The Spine of Albion*, we discovered that early Celtic saints tended to be associated with certain old routes and places of power, and here St Mochua seems to be a guardian of this eastern section of An Slí Mhór as far west as the ancient royal residence of Carbury Hill. This prominent hill, with its Bronze Age barrows, is known in folklore as Sidh Neachtain or the 'Fairy Mound of

Neachtain'. According to the 'Mythological Cycle' in *The Annals of the Four Masters*, Neachtain was a semi-god and leader of the Tuatha Dé Danann who became King of Leinster for one year. Reputedly, he and his brothers were the keepers of a sacred well that stood at the foot of the hill associated with the gift of wisdom.

When Neachtain married the goddess Boann (or Bóinn), she wished to see the sacred well, but her husband denied her request, explaining that its location had to remain hidden and protected. One day, Boann secretly followed Neachtain and, upon finding the well, she allowed herself to taste its forbidden waters. The well suddenly burst forth, and continued to surge round the hill and through the kingdom until it reached the Irish Sea. According to the legend, the curious Boann fell into the rushing waters and eventually drowned, and thus the River Boyne became an embodiment of her spirit.[13] The Boyne is Ireland's most sacred river and its source, now called Trinity Well, is at the foot of the hill on the private grounds of Newberry Hall.

Although the course of the Boyne is relatively short, it has a great number of sacred places lying within its valley, including the Hill of Slane, where St Patrick lit the first Christian fires to break the power of the pagan sun worshippers. Other important places along its course are the Hill of Tara, the former capital of the High King of Ireland, the Bru na Boinne passage tombs, the great monastic centre at Kells, Mellifont Abbey, Trim Castle and the medieval city of Drogheda, where in 1690 the infamous Battle of the Boyne changed the fate of Ireland. This battle was a conflict between the Jacobites, led by the Catholic King James II of England, Ireland and Scotland, and the Williamites, supporters of the Dutch Protestant Prince William of Orange.

The ruins of a castle lie on Carbury Hill, a fortress built by an Anglo-Norman family called the de Berminghams in the 12th century, who also settled in Birmingham, England, having established it as a major centre of trade. These powerful nobles had possession of most of the land around Edenderry, and built their castle close to the site of a fairy mound of the Tuatha Dé Danann, perhaps adhering to a local superstition, or maybe they knew it was a powerful site of telluric energies.

Another de Bermingham stronghold stands a little further along An Slí Mhór at Monasteroris Abbey, just west of the town of Edenderry. The abbey was run by an order of Franciscan monks invited here by its founder John de Birmingham, Earl of Louth, in 1325, a fine example of a castellated monastery. Today, the curious remnants of a dovecote on top of a mound or motte, the ruins of the massive defensive walls of the monastic buildings and a small parish church are all that remains of the abbey.

Croghan Hill and the Brigid Line

Exactly astride An Slí Mhór, 20 km east of Monasteroris Abbey, is the enigmatic Croghan or Crochen Hill. Crochen is the daughter of the sun goddess Etain and the mother of Maebh or Maeve, the goddess queen of the kings of Connacht. The hill is said to be the true navel of Ireland, formed from an extinct volcano that erupted billions of years ago out of the Bog of Allen. It is the place of 'the vessel of the Earth goddess' and a site of burial that extends back to the Bronze Age. According to legend, the hill is an entrance to a magic underworld called *Bri Ele*; 'Ele' represents the sun goddess of great beauty.

I was fascinated by the curious folk memory that refers to this hill as the true Umbilicus Hiberniae or Ireland's bellybutton, rather than the Hill of Uisneach in Co Meath. Although it cannot be said to be the geographical centre of Ireland, it does lie at the centre of the Irish Midlands, once ruled over by the powerful kings of Leinster, like a world mountain with views of the fertile flatlands and the great peat bogs that stretch out from here for miles around. It is said that the mythical giants of Ireland were unearthed in this vast area of bogland, including the 'Old Croghan Man', who measured approximately 2 m tall and was believed to have died sometime between 362 and 175 BCE. The Christians regarded Croghan Hill as the birthplace of the 6th-century St Brigid, where she took the veil and built a monastery, perhaps indicating that it was a place for the ritual and ceremonial honouring of Imbolc, the festival of fire and Brigid's feast day. Another local myth refers to one of three daughters of Dagda, all called Brigid, who works away in her smithy beneath Croghan Hill, creating beautiful cauldrons.[14] The Ulster Cycle of Irish literature mentions Brigid as the triple goddess who represents the waxing, full and waning moon in the form of the Maiden, Mother and Crone. Her symbol is the triple sun spiral, each of which represents the closely wound quasi-helical shape of the sun's path over a three-month cycle, also representative of a woman's nine-month gestation period. In Christian times, the triple goddess symbol became the triskele found in manuscripts and carved on crosses.

There are several holy wells on Croghan Hill, one dedicated to Brigid and another to St Patrick. According to folklore, as St Patrick climbed the hill, his horse jumped halfway up and hit a stone that immediately sprung into a well, the horse having left a knee print on the stone while drinking its waters. Locals believe that if the stone is taken away it will always return to its rightful place. Every St Patrick's Day on 17 March there is a local pilgrimage to the site, where people pray and drink from the holy well. Again, this was originally a place revered by the pagan Druids, where a sacred stone probably stood by the spring, later Christianised by Patrick.

We parked our car in the village of Croghan located at the foot of the hill and soon found the footpath which ascends steeply to its summit. Here we discovered an abandoned graveyard on its eastern slopes, said to be the site of the 5th-century Bishop Macaille's church and St Brigid's first convent. St Macaille of Croghan was a disciple of St Mel. He is said to have assisted in presenting the veil to St Brigid on the hill when he witnessed a flame rising from out of her head. There is no historical evidence to account for these legends of a Christian Brigid at Croghan Hill, but the flame rising from her head may be an allegory alluding to the ancient pagan fire ceremonies performed here. Perhaps the worship of the fire goddess took place on this iconic hill that lies at the centre of the old Kingdom of Leinster.

We encountered St Macaille, also known as Maughold, on the Isle of Man, who was a disciple of St Patrick – a region that marks the centre of the whole of the British Isles and Ireland. Incidentally, the same legend of Brigid receiving the veil is associated with the Hill of Uisneach, where Brigid also built a nunnery.

Croghan Hill has all the qualities of a world mountain standing at the centre of an omphalos landscape. It is pyramidal shaped when seen from a distance with otherworldly legends – it stands next to an ancient east-west route – it has a holy well to a saint/goddess and a sacred stone.

There is also a solar connection with the Hill of Uisneach, the mythological centre of Ireland. Any visitor who stands on the summit of the Hill of Uisneach by the earthen remains of the ancient fire temple can see Croghan Hill rising prominently to the southwest, marking the angle of the midwinter sunrise at the solstice. In calendar terms, this heralds the beginning of the year, an event that the ancients recognised as the rebirth of the sun god emerging from the underworld and fertilising the goddess with solar energy. Remarkably, this midwinter solstice line extends further southwest beyond Croghan Hill to the great healing sanctuary of St Brigid in Kildare, where she became abbess of a nunnery and tended a perpetual flame in a fire temple with her nuns. It is here that St Brigid is said to have died and been buried beneath the high altar of the nunnery church until her bones were removed for safety. Therefore, without Croghan Hill blocking the view, the midwinter sun would have been seen rising out of the Brigid sanctuary from the Hill of Uisneach.

The three Brigids are each associated with a particular skill – poetry representing intellect, smithcraft for creativity and healing expressive of fertility. Uisneach is historically a place of poets or 'Aonachs' who would perform during national assemblies at Beltane, the volcanic Croghan Hill is associated with smithcraft as Brigid had her smithy workshop beneath the hill, and Kildare is a sanctuary of healing.

Therefore, this midwinter alignment from Uisneach to Kildare incorporates the three aspects of the goddess Brigid, activated when the first rays of the midwinter solstice bathe all three sites, symbolically spreading her power across the land to the navel after the longest night of the year. Keating in *The History of Ireland* suggests her name is derived from *breo-shaighead*, which means 'arrow of fire' or the fire of the sun[15] which we could interpret as plasma. Fire is strongly associated with all three sites on this line, represented by beacons and fire temples where virgins tended the sacred flame. This is identical to the worship of perpetual fires in ancient temples dedicated to the Roman goddess Vesta and the Greek goddess Hestia. Uisneach, Croghan Hill and Kildare could all be considered navel sites where the rays of the newborn sun at midwinter ignite the fertility within the land (see Fig. 5).

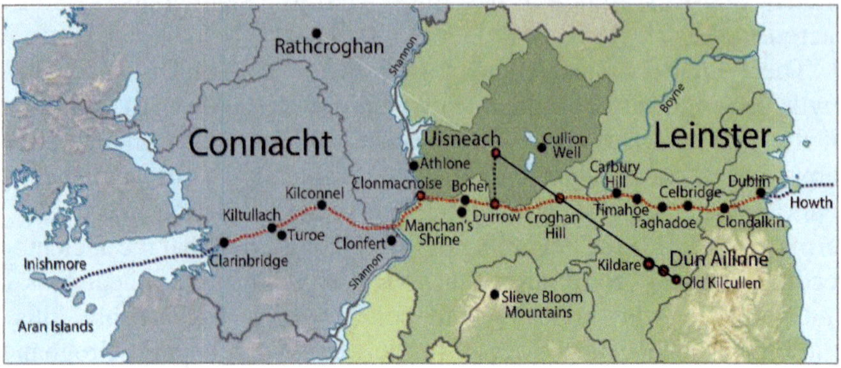

Figure 5. An Slí Mhór and the solar line representing the three Brigids.

Kildare and the Perpetual Flame

From Croghan Hill, we diverted southeast, via Rhode, Clonbulloge and Rathangan, to Brigid's fire temple and cathedral at Kildare. According to legend, in 480 CE, St Brigid arrived in Kildare with her nuns and founded the 'Church of the Oak Grove', having erected it under a large sacred oak tree on Drum Criadh (the 'ridge of clay'). The cathedral we see today is thought to stand over the site of this early church, later renamed Cill Dara meaning the 'Church of the Oak' from which we get the modern name Kildare. However, it is more likely that this was already a Celtic ceremonial site created in the shadow of the royal centre of Dún Ailinne for Irish Druids, who honoured their deities in oak groves – specifically the divine goddess in the land.

Here, within St Brigid's fire temple, a flame was kept burning perpetually right up until the Reformation in the 16th century. According to the writings of the Norman historian Giraldus Cambrensis (*c.* 1146–1223) '[Brigid's fire temple] is surrounded by a hedge, made of stakes and brushwood, and forming a circle, within which no male can enter; and if anyone should presume to enter, which has been sometimes attempted by rash men, he will not escape the divine vengeance.'[16] In 1993 the flame was relit by the Brigidine sisters in Kildare who still tend the flame today at their centre, Solas Bhride.

The goddess Brigid has always been associated with poetry, smithcraft and healing, and later the Christian Bridget inherited her qualities. So great was her fame that soon after Brigid's death in 523 CE a costly shrine was erected in her honour within a new and larger building. For many centuries Kildare maintained a unique order whereby the abbess ruled over a double community of women and men, and the bishop was subordinate in jurisdiction to the abbess.

The foundation flourished from the early 7th century, becoming a centre of learning, attracting pupils from overseas as well as from the sons of the Gaelic Irish nobility. As it grew in importance it also became a significant political and secular centre controlled by the powerful kings of Leinster. It was described in the 7th century by local monk Cogitosus as being long ago 'a vast metropolitan' of streets and stone steps.

St Brigid's Cathedral, Kildare

Between the years 835 and 998, the cathedral was devastated by Viking raids no less than sixteen times. *The Annals of Ireland* record that the invaders destroyed the town of Kildare 'with fire and sword' and carried off the shrines of St Brigid and St Conleth. Fortunately, the relics of St Brigid were removed to Downpatrick in Co Down for safety before her shrine was completely destroyed.[17]

However, her cult continues today at the nearby St Brigid's Garden Well about 1.5 km south of the town, where people still receive her blessing by caressing her statue and leaving offerings. The pagan cult of the well, cult of the fire and cult of the oak were all ancient rituals evolved from the worship of the old Earth goddess Bride or Brigid.

Ireland once had over 3000 holy wells and springs, most of which are now lost or overgrown while others have become tourist attractions where rituals are continued under the banner of Catholic Christianity. Thirty-two holy wells were recorded in the Kildare area alone, bubbling up from an immense aquifer under the flat open plain of the Curragh, only two of which survive today, the most ancient being the 'Wayside Well' on Tully Road. It was once revered as a place of the goddess Brigid and stands a short distance from the more modern St Brigid's Garden Well. The local Catholic clergy transferred their Christian devotion and practices to this newer spring in the 1950s, supposedly out of concern for people's safety in accessing the more ancient well, which was at the bend of a narrow busy road. All the signs and tourist information direct you to the later well, while the Wayside Well goes unnoticed at the rear of the car park of the Japanese Gardens.

St Brigid's Garden Well, Kildare

As we strolled around the interior of the cathedral church at Kildare, we read that it has been restored several times since Norman times and sensed that it had been long deserted by Bride's energy, perhaps due to the devastation and desecration that took place here during numerous raids and battles. We spotted a wonderful and rare carving of a 'green' dragon with a branch of oak coming from its mouth, which to us signified the presence of dragon or serpent energy that the Druids worshipped here in the oak groves. There was also a stained-glass window showing St Bride with the flame over her head and a carving of an equal-armed cross with a spiral at its centre, a curious combination and a clue to later discoveries we made around the British Isles that link this particular goddess with centre-points of the landscape.

On Ptolemy's 1st-century map of Ireland, the mysterious inland city of Laberos is marked where Kildare is situated today. Henry O'Brien and J. Lorenzo Villanueva, authors of the book *Phoenician Ireland*, have translated many of the Phoenician names on the map and referred to Laberos as meaning 'fire cave', which could be a description of the fire temple at Kildare.[18]

Ptolemy's 1st-century map of Ireland

Alternatively, before Christianity, a fire-altar may have been kept at nearby Dún Ailinne, the ancient royal centre of Leinster, and removed to the neighbouring Kildare after the hillfort's power declined.

Dún Ailinne, the Royal Centre of Leinster

While visiting Kildare, we took the short drive to Dún Ailinne or the Hill of Ailinne, also known locally as Knockaulin (the Beautiful Fort), one of the greatest royal sites in Ireland. This remarkably vast hillfort stands 183 m above sea level, with a massive circular 18-ha enclosure, and is similar to the other royal sites of Rathcroghan, Tara and Emain Macha. Dún Ailinne however, is the largest prehistoric earthen enclosure in Ireland, encircled by a 1.8-m-deep internal ditch or 'henge', suggesting it was constructed for ceremonial purposes rather than defensive. Excavations of the interior have revealed a Bronze Age cairn further surrounded by circular enclosures and Iron Age timber structures. On its northern ramparts is an ancient spring, later dedicated to St John; the saint's feast day being 24 June, which may allude to a place of midsummer celebrations as, from here, the summer solstice sun can be seen rising over Uisneach, the cosmological centre.

In folklore, the hill was built by the ancient king and mighty warrior Art Mes Delmonn, a prince of Leinster and associated with the mythical Finn Fail meaning 'Fair Seer', descendant of Nuadha, first king of the Tuatha Dé Danann, whose mother was Boinne and father 'the sun's rays'. It was also the haunt of the goddess Ailinne.

Many see the pagan ceremonial fires that once existed at Dún Ailinne preserved in St Brigid's fire temple at Kildare. Christendom usurped the vital role of the goddess by the Christian archetype Brigid or Bridget at their new centre at Kildare, who according to old Irish poems became the rival of Ailinne. When the newly baptised kings of Leinster abandoned their ceremonial hill around 695 CE, many historians believe that the goddess fire ceremony was transported to Kildare in the form of the perpetual flame. This period also saw the rise of an early Christian settlement at nearby Old Kilcullen, established in the 6th century under the guidance of St Patrick. The atmospheric site of Old Kilcullen is also aligned with Dún Ailinne, Uisneach, and Rathcroghan, probably built there to harness the pagan power of the abandoned royal centre nearby.

Much of Dún Ailinne's ceremonial enclosure has experienced damage and desecration through centuries of farming and quarrying. Like many heritage sites in Ireland, it is on private land, and access is limited to only a few afternoons a week provided there is no livestock grazing there. This is now common practice in Ireland as a result of accidents involving walkers and cattle. Permission to visit the site can be sought through the Kildare Heritage Centre, where you can enquire when and how to access this extremely important and valuable site.

We believe that Dún Ailinne is of great historical significance and if the proposed plans succeed, it will one day be protected by Heritage Ireland and opened to visitors on a more regular basis. Perhaps then, in some glorious future, its mystical power will once again rise like the midsummer sun to sanctify the land and its people.

Durrow, the Lost Monastic Centre

Returning to Croghan Hill, the road west after 8 km coincides with the great Rahugh Ridge, which Geissel argues is one of the most extraordinary features of post-glacial topography to be found in

Ireland and comparable to Northern Ireland's Giant's Causeway and the Cliffs of Moher in Co Clare.[19] Here, a monastery was founded in 537 CE by St Hugh, from which this ridge gets its name. It takes the form of a remarkable surviving esker, once a core section of the prehistoric Esker Riada, along which An Slí Mhór travelled. The road features a motte or mound, the site of the 'Assembly of Rahugh', where in 857, Máel Sechnaill, High King of Tara, declared his political supremacy over the northern half of Ireland at a point where An Slí Mhór crosses an ancient road that linked Tara in the northeast with the ancient kingdom of Munster in the southwest.

Following signs to the town of Clara, we arrive at the ancient monastic site of Durrow, which lies almost exactly halfway along An Slí Mhór. It was one of Ireland's most important Celtic Christian settlements, founded in 553 by a young St Columba or Colmcille as he is also known. Later, Columba would settle in the Western Isles of Scotland among the Dál Riada Irish Scots where eventually he and his twelve followers would establish a Celtic Christian missionary on Iona in 563, formerly the isle of the Druids. Adomnan of Iona (*c.* 624–704), who wrote *Life of St Columba*, tells us that St Columba came to Iona having had a vision of crowning a great king of the Dál Riada Kingdom. At the time, Columba was probably playing the role of a politician rather than a missionary as this strategic action would eventually help to establish the Dál Riada's power over the Picts. It is also said that he fled to Scotland in disgrace after provoking a great battle at Durrow between the northern and southern Irish pagan and Christian tribes.[20]

The Cathach of St Columba, a late-6th-century Irish Psalter said to be the oldest surviving manuscript in Ireland, tells of Columba's exile from Ireland and describes a quarrel with St Finnian of Movilla Abbey over a psalter. Columba is said to have copied the original owned by Finnian and, in the belief that he owned the copyright, Finnian kept Columba's copy for himself. A great dispute erupted between them as to who owned the rights to Columba's facsimile psalter. Finnian raises the issue with Diarmait mac Cerbaill (d. *c.* 565), High King of Ireland, who gave the judgement 'To every cow belongs her calf, and therefore to every book belongs its copy.' Columba disagreed with King Diarmait's ruling against him and reportedly instigated a successful rebellion against the king's forces and the Uí Néill clan of Northern Ireland. The battle was claimed to have caused around 3000 casualties, after which Columba fled to Scotland.[21]

Many of the powerful Uí Néill kings were buried at Durrow and, in 763, Domnall, King of Meath was laid alongside them. This burial site would be later usurped by the rival monastery of Clonmacnoise when a great battle ensued between the two religious houses. Durrow, during Columba's life and for centuries after his death, was a well-known centre of education. The Venerable Bede (672–735) called it *Monasterium nobile in Hiberniâ*, meaning 'the most noble monastery in Ireland', and, alongside Armagh, it was renowned as the 'University of the West'.[22]

The monastery is also famous for the *Book of Durrow*, an illuminated manuscript written here in around 650. Like Clonard, Derry and most other monasteries in the area, Durrow was frequently ravaged by the Vikings, although not totally destroyed. It was only when the Normans invaded led by Hugh de Lacey that this important monastic site was completely demolished to make way for the building of a castle.

As we entered the interior of the restored Durrow Church, we were greeted by a magnificent 10th-century High Cross, one of the finest in Ireland, moved here from the churchyard in 2005. It is carved with scenes from the Bible including Christ holding a sceptre and cross-staff, and a panel depicting snakes intertwined around three human heads, perhaps referring to humanity's connection with the consciousness of the Earth through the serpent energy lines, nature's invisible fertilising power. It is accompanied by another High Cross, although only a fragment remains, carved with spirals and Celtic knot designs.

At one time, this old monastic site was possibly an important place of worship for travellers as they journeyed along An Slí Mhór only a short distance north of the church, which today is bounded by a tree-lined bank. The surrounding terrain appeared to us to be the remains of a flood plain with a causeway linking this site with the ancient highway, perhaps once marked by Columba's High Cross to show the way for Christian pilgrims. The church has been rebuilt many times on this site, which may indicate its importance as a ceremonial enclosure to the pre-Christian folk of Ireland in earlier times.

In Gaelic, Durrow means 'a plain of oaks' and many of the descendants of the old oak wood that once surrounded this site are still noticeable around the church and in the nearby woodlands. Perhaps within this old oak plain there was a Druidic temple within an ancient grove of oaks. Indeed, Columba was well known for his

Druidic practices, having attended a Gorsedd or national meeting of Bards during his religious training as the young son of Prince Fedilmith of the Uí Néill clan. In time, he would plead the case for a new form of Druidism within the teachings of Jesus Christ and declared 'Christ is my Druid, he is my true miracle worker.' These teachings became the mainstay of Celtic Christianity and the order of Culdee monks.[23]

Tenth century High Cross at Durrow Church

From the beautiful and tranquil setting of the church, we followed a narrow footpath leading to a small copse of trees and raised ground known as St Colmcille's Island, where we found at its centre a holy well. It is now protected by a well house, and steps lead you down into its waters. A stone plaque reads 'St Columba used this well when he preached the gospel and built an abbey near it AD 500. The angels shall enjoy my sacred cell, my sloe, my nut, mine apple, and my well.'

While standing at this enchanted spot, we were lulled into a dream-like state by the rustling sounds of the old oaks and the trickling water issuing from the ancient spring. We imagined the old Druids walking in procession through the oak grove to the well, honouring the Earth goddess and nature during a sacred ceremony. Here I sensed the path of dragon energy snaking through the woods to connect with the well, increasing the sanctity of this once epicentre of Celtic Christianity that marked the halfway point on Ireland's east-west road.

Looking at Lochlainn's map, I observed the five ancient roads all meeting An Slí Mhór at Durrow (see Fig. 6). The north road leads straight to the Hill of Uisneach and beyond to the religious capital at Armagh and the ancient royal capital of the Ulster kings at Navan.

Another road links the ancient town of Athlone and Rathcroghan, the inauguration place of the Connacht kings. The northeast road journeys to the monasteries of Clonard and Teltown, where fairs and annual games were held, and onwards to Tara, the capital of the kings of Meath. The southeast road leads to the great earthwork mound at Ardscull and continues to Dind Rig, the Firbolg's ancient capital of Leinster on the banks of the Barrow River. The road south heads to

Holy well, St Colmcille's Island, Durrow

Roscrea, where you can travel south to the Rock of Cashel, a later religious capital of the Munster kings. To the southwest is their more ancient inauguration site at Lough Gur and Cnoc Áine.

The Annals of the Four Masters mentions five royal roads leading from Teamhair, a common name that translates as 'eminence or hill' or 'pleasant hill', deriving from *Tea Mhur* meaning 'Tea's ground', which in time became Tara.[24] Through studying early local maps I discovered that adjoining the old Durrow Abbey estate is a district or township called Tara exactly where five roads come together; this name has existed here since at least 900 CE.

No written records remain of the early years of Durrow's monastic community or the site's earliest beginnings, but the oak trees and the ancient well, combined with the hub of ancient roads halfway along An Slí Mhór, may suggest that it was an important religious site of the Druids long before Columba and no doubt the reason for the siting of his first monastery here. Marc Alexander in *Enchanted Britain* wrote that the Celtic Christians were renowned for building their religious houses over ancient sacred sites, including Druidic colleges.[25]

Durrow's landscape features and topography suggest it may have at one time been an important omphalos. It is situated at a great crossroads halfway along the middle belt of Ireland with an ancient holy well and a magnificent carved standing cross. This charming area certainly has a lost history that reaches out to the enquiring mind, and as Caroline and I wandered through the oaks and placed our offering at the sacred well, the spirit of this place left a powerful impression on us. The Revd A. Coghan when writing about Durrow in *The Diocese of Meath: Ancient and Modern (Volume 2)* captures this feeling beautifully:

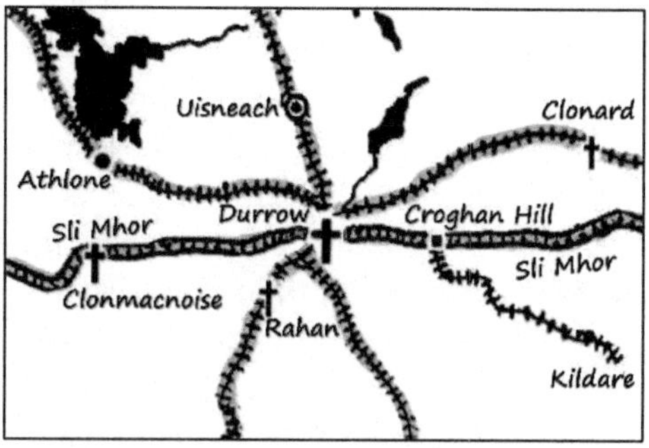

Figure 6. Lochlainn's Map showing the five ancient roads meeting An Slí Mhór at Durrow

> 'Yet in its ruin, and loneliness, there is a charm, a holy spell around the hallowed site and the surrounding scenery, which no earthly power can uproot, and which speaking to the heart in a language not to be mistaken, that here undoubtedly was one of the ancient sanctuaries of Ireland.'[26]

Uisneach, the Navel of Ireland

The present geographical centre of the combined countries of Eire and Northern Ireland is roughly somewhere within a 20-m radius of the historic town of Athlone, built around an important fording of the River Shannon that has existed here since the Bronze Age, which could be rightly called Ireland's most central town. However, as we later found with many geographical centres, villages and towns within proximity of these places often compete for the honour of being the omphalos of Ireland, putting forward their evidence using historical records, local traditions and mythology. The exact point is always hugely debatable, but the National Ordnance Survey, using the gravitational method, places the centre of old Ireland 8 km north of Athlone, on the western shore of Loch Lee opposite the Cribby Islands.

However, for thousands of years, the Hill of Uisneach, lying just 16 km north of An Slí Mhór from Durrow, was the traditional national centre. The gently sloping feminine-shaped hill of this legendary kingship site is spread over 2 km and is not immediately noticeable from a distance. It lies in a remote rural area surrounded by narrow country lanes between the villages of Loughanavally and Ballymore on the road from Mullingar-to-Athlone in County Westmeath.

The sacredness of this place is not immediately apparent, but amongst the green fields and hedgerows lie scattered numerous circular and linear earthworks, barrows, cairns, a shallow lake and two holy wells. Furthermore, despite it being only modestly high at 183 m above sea level, it is said that twenty Irish counties can be seen from the summit of the hill on a clear day.

In ancient times, claimants to the high throne of Ireland would 'marry' Ireland's founder goddess at Uisneach. She was the mother goddess of the land: 'the rocks formed her bones, the earth her flesh, the rivers her veins.' Also known as the 'Great Rite', this ancient marriage tradition originally took the form of the king 'marrying the land' to exercise his sovereignty over the nation.[27] In some cases it involved the symbolic act of plunging a sacred knife, representing the male, into a cup or chalice filled with wine held by the high priestess, signifying the female. This powerful act would also have the potent effect of harmonising the earth's energies within the land to ensure fertility.

Cary Meehan writes that the five sons of Deala of the Firbolg, who settled after the Nemedians, each ruled over the five provinces they had created. They took responsibility for their nation's prosperity, providing order and justice for all. They allowed their people to attend assemblies once a year at the palace of the High King at Uisneach. Here the regional kings had to wear a ring or armband of red gold, which they would leave as a tribute on the chair of the High King, a ritual that forms the basis of sacral kingship.[28]

Although the later Tuatha Dé Danann settlers preferred to rule from the Hill of Tara, they first set up their royal centre at Uisneach; the Hill of Tara was considered a sister site, and remains of an ancient road have been uncovered which connected the two places. On the

Hill of Uisneach, High King Dagda kept his legendary stable of 'solar horses'. Dagda had three daughters, all called Brigid, who as mentioned earlier, represented, poetry, healing, and smithcraft.

The hilltop lake known as Lough Lugh was named after Lugh Lamfháda or 'Lugh of the long arm', another hero of the race of Danu. Lugh was said to have drowned in the lake at the summit of Uisneach and then buried beneath a cairn beside it. Beltane fires were lit at Uisneach and at Lughnasa, associated with the harvest god also called Lugh. In ancient times the Lughnasa celebration would commence at Uisneach and from there people would process several miles south to Árd Éireann, the highest point of Slieve Bloom which was seen as the 'birth mountain' and where supposedly the first gods of Ireland landed.

In legend, the hero warrior Lugh came to Uisneach to save his mother's people from the heavy taxes exacted by the demonic giants, the Formorians. Having survived the great Biblical Flood, he defeated this evil race and ruled from the hill, where he reputedly ended his days. Great assemblies continued at Uisneach where Druids and kings administered their political and fiscal power.

In 1927, excavations by archaeologists R. A. S. Macalister and R. Lloyd Praeger discovered a substantial layer of ash at the most important goddess-shaped enclosure on the summit of Uisneach known as the 'fire temple'. The ash is thought to be remnants from a 'perpetual fire' or a 'great bonfire lit at frequent intervals.'[29] Between these fires, cattle were driven to be cleansed of disease by the smoke, cattle being in ancient times a token of people's wealth. 'Great ceremonies took place on the hill, and as well as continuing to feature a giant bonfire, goods were exchanged and sacrifices offered to gods. It was often the first chance of the year for neighbours to greet each other after a long and often-times bitter winter, and great celebrations ensued, not only at Uisneach but throughout the country. Feasting, dancing, music, tournaments and lovemaking were all avidly partaken as the festival proceeded.'[30] In fact, the great fire ceremony at Uisneach was such an important tradition that it continues to the present day.

The concept of the fire-altar at the navel or the centre of the Earth is a tradition in many cosmologies throughout the world. Pythagoreans believe in the idea of a 'fire' or continual flame at the centre of the Universe. The Vedas, the oldest scriptures of Hinduism, saw the gods as descending to an altar at the centre of the Earth. Indo-

Aryans who lived in India during the Vedic period (*c.* 1500–500 BCE) believed that when the gods first arrived on Earth they erected a fire-altar as a symbolic act to gain possession of the land and secure their legal claim over it.[31]

The sons of Mil or Milesians were the last race to invade Ireland and may be the ancestors of many Gaelic Irishmen today. Led by Miledh, they defeated the Tuatha Dé Danann, claiming their right to the kingship of Ireland on the Hill of Uisneach. Like the gods of the Vedas, they lit a fire affirming their sovereignty that burned for seven years, the fire from which all other fires were lit throughout the country. Dames states: 'From Midhe, the array of distant hills and mountains, and the solar and lunar risings and settings which coincided with their summits, were the stuff of a god-given mandala. This served to reveal sacred Ireland in its entirety, and set it within the orb of a divine Universe, rendered synonymous with the eyeball of the human worshipper.'[32]

On one of my early visits to the hill in the 1990s, I found St Patrick's Well surrounded by iron railings and a little further north Finnleaseach's Well, the latter being a spring that according to folklore marks the true navel of Ireland as well as being the source of twelve rivers.[33] Interestingly, in chapter 4, we refer to a Welsh mountain called Plynlimon or Pumlumon that lies at the centre of Wales, its slopes having given birth to five great rivers including the Severn and the Wye.

Water is an ancient symbol of the flowing energy of the divine feminine within the land and was often seen by the early Celts as a gateway to the unseen realms, or 'otherworld'. Often these wells and springs were divinely created at the centre of their kingdom to harness the feminine energy of Mother Earth, inducing spiritual harmony and aiding fertility. From ancient times, natural wells and springs have been venerated and adorned with offerings. Many sacred sites were built next to the Earth's naturally flowing springs, having been birthed by the underground streams of potent energy encircling the site. This power given freely by Mother Earth ebbs and flows according to the lunar phases, its life-giving magnetic force keeping the land healthy and balanced. Standing stones and thorn trees are often situated above streams, which can amplify these energies to a positive effect.

The feminine presence associated with wells, streams, rivers and lakes is often represented in folklore by the water nymph or fairy, which the old pagans would communicate with through blessings and ritual offerings. Many holy springs and wells throughout the British Isles were visited during Beltane to celebrate the fertility of spring. For the ancients, as well as appeasing the water spirits, the purity of the water was of utmost importance if the land and its people were to thrive. For if the springs become blocked, contaminated, neglected and forgotten, the magnetic field becomes distorted and out of harmony with the natural frequencies of the Earth, the waters no longer having the life-giving powers to balance the land and maintain health for its people.

On the southern slopes of Uisneach is a glacial erratic limestone boulder standing 6 m tall called the Cat Stone. The unusual-shaped stone weighs around 30 tons and was deposited on the hill during the last Ice Age and some even say it arrived from the Biblical Flood. Once known as *Ail na Mirean* or 'Stone of Divisions', it supposedly marked the traditional centre-point, the Umbilicus Hiberniae or 'navel of Ireland'. It was also where, during the Irish War of Independence in the early 20th century, a flag was inserted in the top of the boulder around which political meetings were held.

Locals called the stone in the 1930s *Carraig a' chait*, meaning the 'rock of the cat' because of its similarity to a crouching cat.[34] However, John O'Donovan (1806–1861) who translated *The Annals of the Four Masters* believes the name arose out of the corruption of Carraig Choithrigi, found in the *Book of Armagh*, which translates as 'Rock of the Divisions of Sovereignty'.[35] Its common name *Ail na Míreann* is derived from *aill* meaning 'cliff or rock' and *mireann* meaning 'a portion or share'. *Aille* also translates as 'the act of praising or giving thanks'. So perhaps it was a stone where people ritually gave thanks for the fertility of the land. The Cat Stone was the most impressive of the sites on Uisneach that, according to some researchers, was once surrounded by a ring of stones.

These may have been the stones mentioned by historian and monk Geoffrey of Monmouth in *The History of the Kings of Britain*, written in the 12th century. He wrote that in honour of all the great British warriors who had died during the many conflicts with the Saxon invader Hengist, Ambrosius Aurelianus asked all the stonemasons and carpenters in the land to find him a fitting memorial. It was not until Merlin was sent for that he was informed of the existence of a stone monument known as the Giant's Ring at Mount Killarus (Hill of Killare) in Ireland, supposedly having originally come from Africa and placed there by the giants, possibly the Formorians. It is said that over one of the stones, water was spilt to run into a bath for healing, each stone having a different cure.

Monmouth writes: 'Their design in this was to make baths in them, when they should be taken with any illness. For their method was to wash the stones and put their sick into the water which infallibility cured them .... There is not a stone there which has not some healing virtue.' Fifteen-thousand men journeyed to Ireland from Britain to fetch the stones, led by the king's brother Uther Pendragon who reputedly took the Irish by surprise and seized the stones.[36]

The stones mentioned by Monmouth were 'blue' stones similar to those found today within the inner sanctum of Stonehenge. Although these particular blue-spotted dolerite stones have been proved without doubt to be from the Preseli Hills in Wales, the stones referred to by Monmouth may have been another set of blue stones that were set up as a memorial elsewhere, a place yet to be identified.

The Cat Stone is also associated in Irish mythology with the seer Fintan, 'the Ancient White One', who came to Ireland before the Biblical deluge as one of the first settlers accompanied by Noah's daughter Cessair. He survived the Flood by transforming into a salmon and lived in the lake on the summit of Uisneach. He fed on the nuts from the nine enchanted hazel trees that fell into the lake, and thus the lake acquired his knowledge. He transformed into an eagle, before finally resuming his human form. Fintan then planted on the hill the 'Branching Ash Tree of Uisneach', also known as the 'Tree of Enchantment'. The ash trees that still grow around the hill today are perhaps descendants of Fintan's tree. These sacred trees are associated with rebirth, divination, protection, wisdom and spiritual knowledge, and Druids would make magical wands from their branches. The ash is also renowned as the world tree of Norse mythology, symbolic of an omphalos site and the axis mundi at which Odin achieved enlightenment.

According to a medieval Irish manuscript called the *Yellow Book of Lecan*, Fintan returns to the 'Stone of Divisions', declaring 'It is a long time since I drank a drink of the Deluge over the navel of Uisneach.'[37] Fintan's mission was to re-establish this navel Stone of Divisions 'at the core of national life.' The rock is composed of five segments along fissures that symbolically relate to the five provinces, and its position is supposedly where the old borders of these provinces once met. Today, only four of the old provinces remain: the ancient middle province of Midhe is now incorporated into the counties of

Leinster, Meath and Westmeath. From the central province, Fintan bestowed upon the other four divisions of Ireland the qualities of

The Stone of Divisions or Cat Stone, Uisneach

'Knowledge in the West, Battle in the North, Prosperity in the East, Music in the South with Royalty representing the Centre.'[38]

There are still traces of a ditch and bank earthwork with a saucer-shaped hollow surrounding the stone, indicating its importance as a ceremonial site. A split in the rock has formed a tunnel at its base where people may have crawled through during 'rebirth' ceremonies. Dames sees the act of Fintan drinking the water of the deluge over the navel stone as partaking of the Flood's prenatal waters at the centre over Ireland's 'mother stone'. He further writes: 'Even in countries like Israel, from which the great mother had been expelled, birth symbolism persisted around the omphalos. A Rabbinical text states: "As an embryo proceeds from the navel onward, so God began the creation of the world from its navel onwards and from thence it spread in different directions."'[39]

Eriu, the great mother goddess of Ireland, is said to be buried under this great stone, after whom the Milesians named Ireland, 'the rocks forming her bones, the earth her flesh, the rivers her veins.' I took out my dowsing rod and walked around the stone in an attempt to locate any earth energy or dragon lines connecting with it, and found several wide lines all shrinking to a point under the stone. This sacred stone possibly represents a major power point or junction box of earth energy, tapping into perhaps a powerful natural force beneath it such as a fault line or spring.

Modern researchers claim that long-distance alignments, such as those that link Uisneach with Ireland's four Celtic royal centres, are connected to a grid or network of earth energy lines that circumnavigate the Earth, their powerful crossing point utilised for religious or occult practices. Druid legends speak of twelve great dragon lines that encircle the globe.[40] Likewise, a Hopi creation myth describes how 'the creator Tiowa assigned Spider Grandmother Woman to send sound and cosmic energy to the crystal at the centre of the Earth to bounce back to the surface to create "spots of the fawn", or sacred power centres joined together by a lattice of energy.'[41]

Our ancient ancestors, including the Druids, understood how to utilise this energy to regenerate the land and cleanse it of any negative forces, similar to the work of modern geomancers who heal areas affected by geopathic stress. Quarrying and mining are known to disrupt earth energies, as well as battles, traumatic events and general dishonouring of sacred sites.

The Staff of Dagda, Killare and the Royal Alignments

As mentioned in Chapter 1, the most important alignment for the ancient surveyors when creating divisions of cosmology is the north-south line or meridian, which the Etruscans called the 'cardo'. At night, using the pole star Polaris as a guide, the augur could mark an alignment towards this stationary star, around which all other stars revolve (see Fig. 1). Dames and Robb suggested the most likely meridian in Ireland runs from Malin Head, the most northerly point of land, to Ardmore on the south coast. This line passes through Uisneach and the ancient dry-stone circular amphitheatre of Grianán Ailigh or Grianán of Aileach, Co Donegal in Northern Ireland. This was one of the most important royal sites of the Northern Uí Néill kings. Grianán of Aileach translates as 'stone fortress of the sun'. Grianán is also thought to derive from the sun goddess Gráinne, sister of Aine.

In legend, around 1700 BCE, the great sun god Dagda of the Tuatha Dé Danann ordered Grianán Ailigh to be built as a sun temple around the grave of his son Aedh, who had been killed in a fit of jealousy by a Connacht chieftain. Garbhan, the Tuatha Dé Danann's best mason, dressed and cut the stones for the construction and Imcheall, his fellow mason, proceeded to assemble them to form a high-walled stone fort. Ptolemy distinguishes this rath (circular enclosure) as a royal residence on his map and many poems refer to it as the oldest and greatest building in Ireland, describing it as the 'Tara' of the north.[42]

The structure is thought to date to the time of the northern Uí Néill dynasty who made it their capital from 789 to about 1050 CE. However, drystone walling is notoriously difficult to date, with many experts agreeing that this construction may be much older. Using geophysics, surveyors have identified several ring ditches around the monument that date from the Bronze Age, the very period that the Tuatha Dé Danann supposedly ruled over Ireland. Legend also states that the giants of Inishowen (warriors of Aileach) lie sleeping within, but when the sacred sword is removed they will spring to life, reclaiming their ancient lands.

In *The Tripartite Life of Patrick*, it is written that St Patrick blessed the fortress and baptised the local chieftain, leaving a symbolic flagstone there, prophesying 'that many kings and clerics would come from the place.'[43] This 2-m^2 flagstone is possibly an inauguration stone carved with the impressions of two feet. Today, the stone supposedly resides at Belmont House School in Derry and is called St Columb's Stone. Between the two outer banks on the south side of the fortress is a holy spring later dedicated to St Patrick, said to have healing powers.

South of Uisneach, the meridian passes through the Slieve Bloom Mountains, its highest point being Árd Éireann, meaning 'the height of Ireland' and revered as the 'birth mountain.' According to folklore, the sun god Finn grew up in the woods on Slieve Bloom after being birthed there by the sun goddess; the solar festival at Lughnasa continued on the summit up until 1940. Ard Eireann also stands directly south of the central east-west highway of the Esker Riada, with Uisneach situated directly north. The meridian then continues through the medieval walled town of Clonmel in Co Tipperary, where one of the finest sheela-na-gigs was found, now in the National Museum of Ireland - Archaeology, Dublin. On the south coast, the meridian passes through the cathedral of Ardmore, the oldest Christian monastic settlement in Ireland.

There was once a magic stone used during fertility rituals in Ardmore called the Cloch-Daha or 'stone of Dagda', but owing to its sexual nature it was removed and buried by the clergy. The stone took the form of an ancient 'bullaun', a hollowed-out stone that either collected rainwater for healing or held pebbles that could be turned for divination. In the folklore of Ardmore, there is a tradition whereby the young unmarried men of the village would insert a pole into the hole of the Cloch-Daha before fixing a rope onto the top of the pole. Young maidens would then dance around the stone, holding the rope to make the pole spin. The act of placing a pole in this stone is symbolic of the axis mundi, and the turning of the pole represents its connection to the goddess. Perhaps this is an early interpretation of the maypole dance, the maypole being yet another concept of the world tree or axis mundi, often placed at the omphalos of a village or town on the green.

The sun god Dagda also built Grianan of Aileach, the great stone fort, and lived at Uisneach, where his three daughters, all named Brigid, were born. He is 'father-time', linked with Druidry and wisdom, and holds a magic staff that has control over life and death as well as time and the seasons, symbolic of the meridian itself. Interestingly, the meridian or 'Dagda Line' fails to pass through the centre of the Hill of Uisneach but instead marks St Brigid's holy well at the base of the hill within an area once known as Killare.

Revd Coghan wrote that a monastery was built at Killare just west of the Hill of Uisneach in the middle of the 6th century, founded by St Aedh or Hugh who died there in 588 CE. He also says that there were three churches at Killare, the first dedicated to St Aid, the next was called Temple Brigid and the third, the Court of St Brigid. There were also three wells recorded there – one to St Aedh, the next to St Brigid and St Conran.[44]

In 1111, Killare was chosen as the meeting place for an important synod that divided Ireland into several dioceses which still exist today. This was an important event and I believe it significant that the year 1111 was chosen. The number eleven represents both a gateway and sacrifice, the 11th of November being the festival of Martinmas when animals were sacrificed for the coming winter. It is perhaps no coincidence that an Armistice was signed after the First World War between the Allies and Germany on this day in 1918 ending possibly the greatest sacrifice of all, leaving 17 million men dead, ranking this war among the deadliest conflicts in human history.

In *The Annals of Westmeath, Ancient and Modern*, James Woods, a native and local historian of Mullingar, cited William Camden (1551–1623), a leading member of the Society of Antiquaries, who believed Killare to be the Laberos on Ptolemy's map and the centre of Ireland, rather than Kildare (a similar name) as proposed by O'Brien.[45]

Using the Google Earth 'path' tool, I drew in the alignments between the royal sites of Rathcroghan and Dún Ailinne and likewise between Emain Macha and Lough Gur (see Fig. 7). To my surprise they crossed with the meridian at Killare only a few metres north of St Brigid's Well. The field in question shows a great number of earthworks and mounds, and after some research, I found that it was the site of Temple Brigid and St Aedh's monastery with the remnants of a Norman castle just to the north.

Today, Killare's illustrious past has been lost to the annals of myth and legend, many of its houses long gone, apart from a church, a school and the Uisneach Inn, with its worn painted image of the Cat Stone on its signboard. The castle is one of three built on the same site, the first erected in 1182 as part of Norman Hugh de Lacy's plan to take over Ireland. This strategic site had great psychological significance for the French invaders, for they could control the major highways through the middle of Ireland and take over their national icon, the place of National Assembly.

We parked at the Uisneach Inn car park and made our way along the road to the entrance gate of St Brigid's Well made of wrought iron with an arch that reads 'St Brigid's'. From here, a footpath leads you along a marshy causeway to the edge of an enclosure of trees. As Caroline and I entered the sanctity of the well, it felt like we were stepping over a magical threshold into a realm of enchantment, the elementals luring us into their otherworld. As our eyes adjusted to the dimmed light, a stone shrine came into view containing a regal statue of Brigid. She overlooks a large heart-shaped pool with an outlet of trickling water inviting you to partake of the curative waters.

An old ash tree draped with clootie overlooks the well and stands as its symbolic guardian protecting the ancient shrine. Traditionally, clootie is an old custom of tying strips of cloth or 'cloot' belonging to sick people to the branches of sacred trees in the belief that as the cloth rots the illness will disappear. In recent times, clootie is left as an offering, honouring the sacred place, particularly at the Celtic festival of Beltane. Brigid or Bride was also the pagan goddess of water, her instrument of healing, hence the numerous wells and springs named after her, particularly in northern Britain, Scotland and Ireland. Ancient pilgrims would visit them at Imbolc, lighting candles and leaving offerings.

Many wells face east to receive the potent rays of the early morning sun to amplify the magnetic force within the water, enhancing its curative power. People would seek the waters for their magical qualities to heal illnesses of various kinds. Often, rituals would be performed to 'activate' the power of the water.

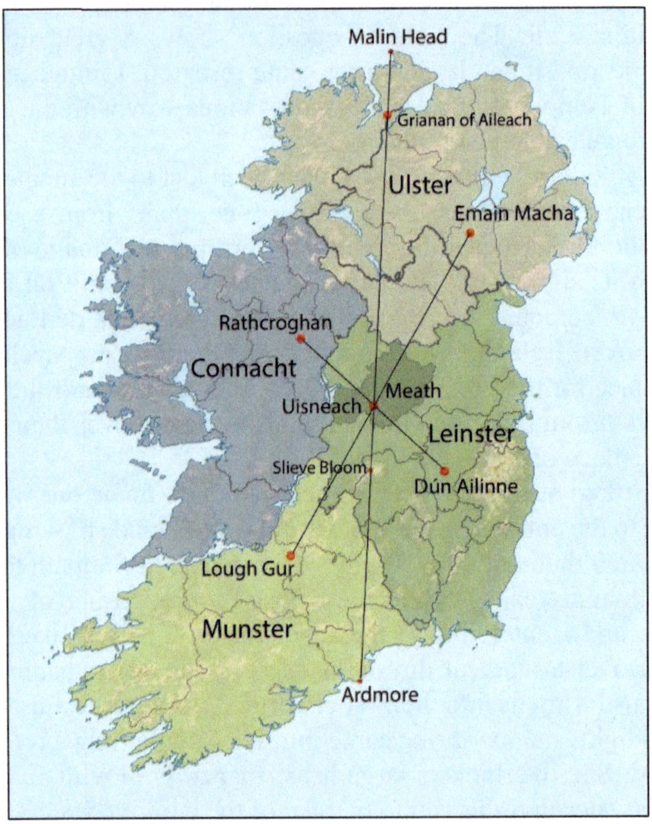

Figure 7. Solar and lunar lines and the meridian or 'Dagda Line', linking the royal sites of Ireland with Uisneach

Over time, people lost the ability to absorb the curative energy of the wells, and the knowledge of how the minerals and stones within the earth could positively affect the spring water as it filtered its way through them to the surface was forgotten. To the Christians, the pagan goddess Brigid or Bride became the 'devil' and those who sought her wisdom became vilified as witches. Honouring the goddess and the spirits of the well was replaced by the act of praying to a statue of Mary, the Holy Virgin, erected next to the wells and springs. Many holy wells disappeared under the high altars of churches and cathedrals, the telluric power used to amplify the influence of bishops and kings.

This silent place exudes peace and serenity and connects us to the sustaining and nourishing womb of the great mother within its protective veil of trees. We sat by the well beneath the sacred ash tree, symbolic of the guardian world tree growing at the omphalos of Ireland. Here we reminded ourselves of the world tree myth in the old cosmology of the bards, having three planes of existence viewed as concentric circles. The lower plane at the base of the tree represents the underworld, the Annwn or 'abyss'. The middle plane is the earthly realm in which we live and strive through good and evil. The upper level equates to the heavenly realm of enlightened beings, having transcended the cycle of earthly lives.[46]

We placed a green healing stone collected from the shores of Iona in the well, imbued with the energy of the great Earth Mother herself.

St Brigid's Holy Well, Killare, below the Hill of Uisneach

We then visualised sending love and transformative golden healing light into the water and to the sacred tree, permeating the energy here with love, joy, harmony and balance. We continued to see this cleansing and healing light flowing through the watery veins of Ireland, including the great rivers of the Boyne and the Shannon, which flow through the important religious site of Clonmacnoise. We then connected the light to the sacred kingship sanctuaries of Dún Ailinne, Lough Gur/Cnoc Áine, Rathcroghan and Emain Macha and through the Rivers Iffey, Camoge, Seramoge and Callan that flow beneath them, transforming the collective energy of the past from one of conflict and division to an atmosphere of peace and unity.

Through the trees, we could just make out raised earthworks in the field beyond, perhaps the remains of Brigid's monastic settlement founded by St Aedh, and the exact spot where the Line that links important places associated with Dagda intersects with the royal site alignments.

Clonmacnoise, the Celtic Christian Centre of Ireland

Returning to An Slí Mhór at Durrow, we headed east to Clara along a historic pilgrim route to one of the most famous monastic settlements in medieval Europe. The 6th-century religious settlement of Clonmacnoise was founded by St Ciaran in 544 CE. Looking at a map of Ireland, the monastery is geographically central to the extreme east-west and the north-south points of land, as shown in Fig. 7.

There are very few early Christian sites in Western Europe that can boast the ruins of a cathedral, seven medieval churches, two round towers, three elaborately carved high crosses and the largest collection of early Christian grave slabs in the British Isles. This vast complex, 24 km south of the town of Athlone, captures the spirit of the old Irish saints and scholars, their story frozen within the beautifully built and carved stone buildings and crosses.

Clonmacnoise is surrounded by glorious water meadows next to the longest river in Ireland where the east-west An Slí Mhór meets the north-south River Shannon, forming a symbolic natural cross at the very centre of Ireland.

The name Shannon derives from the old Irish words *sean* (old) and *abhann* (river), or as some believe from the Celtic goddess Sionna, the name meaning 'possessor of wisdom'. This gentle meandering 360-km-long river weaves its way through the heart of Ireland from its source called the Shannon Pot in northwest Co Cavan to the Shannon estuary at Limerick. The monastery of Clonmacnoise, once one of Europe's great seats of learning, was built on a fertile meadow surrounded by impenetrable bog, which could only be reached by a line of eskers that now form a section of the Esker Riada on which lies An Slí Mhór. This allowed for greater control of access by land but still left it vulnerable to attack by water.

Since early Christian times, pilgrims have stopped at this central crossroads either to visit the great monastery or to continue across the ford by horse or ferry to Galway Bay, where they took a sailing to the monastic school on the Aran Islands founded by St Enda. Despite this route and crossroads being much older than the founding of Clonmacnoise, there is no evidence of a former site of importance here.

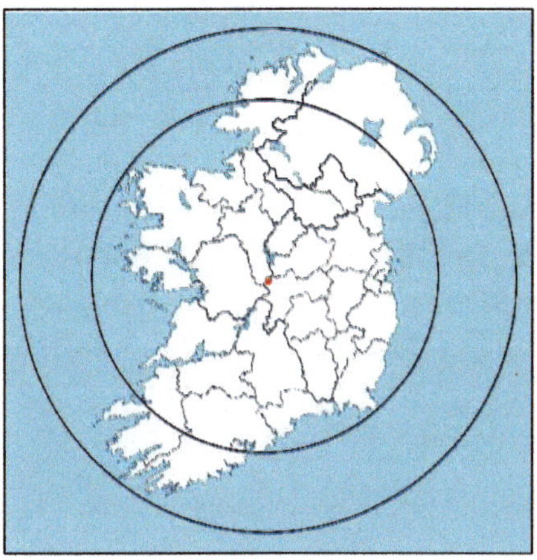

Figure 8. Clonmacnoise Monastery, at the centre of Ireland

Clonmacnoise has been translated as 'meadow of the sons of Nóis', who according to some sources were descendants of the Milesian royal family, the last legendary invaders of Ireland.

When using extreme points of land in both Northern and Southern Ireland to calculate the geographical centre of Ireland, it indicates the area around Clonmacnoise as the omphalos. (see Fig. 8). Perhaps it is no coincidence therefore that the River Shannon as it flows through this central area of Ireland marks the ancient borders of four of the old provinces as it continues north to the fifth at Ulster; the Esker Riada also formed the old border between Leinster and Meath.

Arriving at this historic crossroads in these ancient borderlands on a sunny day, we marvelled at the stunning landscape before us. The rippling waters of the Shannon were glistening in the sunlight, cows lazily grazed its fertile banks as swans glided by, and the air above was filled with the sound of lapwings. Suddenly we were jolted back into the present as a line of tourist buses arrived beside us. We waited until the hordes of people disappeared through the visitor entrance before venturing ourselves towards the ticket office. The museum inside the visitor centre helped us understand the story of this hallowed place, having often found that the key to unlocking the secrets of any sacred place is to research their foundation myths, which in this case involved a character called St Ciaran.

Ciaran is recorded as being born in 516 CE to a carpenter and chariot-maker near the ancient seat of the Connacht kings at Rathcroghan. He studied under St Enda at Inishmore, one of the Aran Islands, and then became a student of St Finian at Clonard. After returning to Inishmore he had a vision:

> 'of a great fruitful tree, beside a stream, in the middle of Ireland, and it protected the island of Ireland, and its fruit went forth over the sea that surrounded the island, and the birds of the world came to carry off somewhat of its fruit.'[47]

Enda explained to Ciaran that he represented the fruitful tree and was destined to locate and protect this middle of Ireland from where knowledge would spread far and wide.

This story of a dream or vision is often associated with Christian saints especially when spending time at sacred places. These special sites often have an atmosphere of otherworldliness conducive to receiving visions during higher states of consciousness. The geology of Inishmore being crystalline rock on top of a major fault line creates a subtle energy that becomes stronger at certain times of year when the magnetic field of the Earth fluctuates due to solar flares or the magnetic pull of the full moon.

Armed with the memory of his vision and his monastic training, Ciaran returned to the mainland and headed for a monastery at Isel, said to have been near Clonmacnoise, or on an island on Lough Ree in the middle of Ireland. This mysterious religious centre was undoubtedly the place he had dreamed of, but its whereabouts today is a mystery. However, his stay here was brief due to his unpopularity with the other monks, who envied his fame as a scholar and resented his excessive charity to the poor. After being asked to leave, he was then 'led by a stag to Inis Aingin', or Hare Island, also in Lough Ree. Here, he lived for three years and three months, attracting brothers from all over Ireland to study with him and where miracles were witnessed attesting 'to his holiness.'

When Ciaran finally departed this remote island, he took with him eight monastic brothers and sailed south along the Shannon, eventually finding the perfect spot to build a religious community on the east bank of the river, accessible by water and road, where An Slí Mhór meets the River Shannon. At the time, this place was called *Ard Tiprait* or 'height of the spring well' within the Kingdom of Osraige.[48]

The foundation story of the new holy site at Clonmacnoise is interesting. The nature of his vision is also significant whereby the 'fruit' of the tree' seen by Enda spreads over the whole of Ireland, its roots anchored at the middle or navel. The fruits represent the knowledge and wisdom that Ciaran issues forth across the country and the seas. This indeed came true, with Clonmacnoise becoming a major European centre of spirituality, learning, craftsmanship and trade by the 9th century. The Norse peoples believed that the great ash tree of Odin was the symbolic axis mundi or 'world axis' where gods, humans and animals were nourished. This was the point of communication between heaven and earth and all phases of existence for all living things. This idea of a tree marking the centre of a kingdom can be found in many cultures throughout the world.

The final phase of Ciaran's journey took him to certain places along the Shannon, which included the monastery at Isel and Hare Island, both close to the central town of Athlone and both renowned as marking the centre of Ireland at the time. Remarkably, the Ordnance Survey's computerised modern calculation of the centre of Ireland is only 2.5 km west of Hare Island. However, Ciaran perhaps realised over time that these sites did not quite match the criteria of his vision, as they both lacked a stream and good access for pilgrims.

The name Clonmacnoise is also believed by some authorities to mean a 'place of pigs'. In legend, pigs are often associated with the locating of sacred centres, such as Binsey near Oxford said to be at one time the sacred centre of England (see Chapter 9). Such was the future importance of this site at Clonmacnoise that before the buildings could be constructed, a special foundation ceremony had to be observed which included the presence of Prince Diarmait, son of Ceerball, High King of Osraige, a kingdom that once lay between Munster and Leinster.

The *Book of Lismore* records the interesting meeting between the two that heralded the foundation of Clonmacnoise. During Diarmait's banishment to Lough Ree on the Shannon, he encountered Ciaran at the chosen spot of his new monastery. As Diarmait approached by boat, he observed that the monks were gathered around a ceremonial fire, which, according to Diarmait's wizards or druids, would never be quenched. The prince encountered Ciaran in the act of marking the site of the church with a wooden pole and asked him 'What is the work thou doest?' 'To build a little church,' Ciaran replied. 'That might as well be its name: eglais bheg,' declared Diarmait. Ciaran invited the prince to: 'Thrust in the upright with me and suffer my hand to be put over thine so that your hand and royal rule will after tomorrow be imposed upon the men of Ireland.'[49]

This legend is a fascinating insight into the foundation ceremony of Ireland's most powerful monastery, which includes a sacred flame lit by the monks at their chosen site, sanctioned by the Druids as a perpetual fire that can never be quenched. The prophesy Ciaran utters during the foundation ceremony comes true as, shortly afterwards, Diarmait becomes the first Christian High King of Ireland. The new king offers every assistance in the building of the monastery, with the endowment of large amounts of land for the use of the whole community.

Adomnan's biography of St Columba mentions that the saint also experienced the oracular power of the new omphalos. He wrote that St Columba visited Clonmacnoise while founding the monastery at Durrow. While there, he prophesied the future debates in the churches of Ireland concerning the dating of Easter and claimed 'that angels had visited the monastery at Clonmacnoise.'[50] Staking the ground at a special spot is also reminiscent of controlling the dragon force in the local landscape. Perhaps this location was divined by dowsing.

After Diarmait was proclaimed king, an Aonach or National Assembly was held at Uisneach over the Beltane period and Ciaran was invited to attend for a fortnight of celebrations and rituals of kingship and honouring the dead. However, during that time a mighty drought caused great suffering to the people, their animals and the land. So the king asked Ciaran to pray for the suffering to end. While praying on the Hill of Uisneach, Ciaran uttered certain words of power that conjured up such rain that it miraculously created the twelve main streams in Ireland. According to *The Annals of Clonmacnoise*, King Diarmait awarded Ciaran a share in a general tax throughout Ireland and 'settled on him his own service and his children's forever.'[51]

It is perhaps significant that after founding the Christian omphalos at Clonmacnoise with the future king, they then together attended the ceremonies at Uisneach, the old pagan omphalos, at what was probably the very last Aonach there. The shift in power from the old omphalos at Uisneach to Clonmacnoise was recorded in *The Life of Colman Ela*, which mentions Clonmacnoise as holding the greatest of the three main Aonach celebrations held every three years, the others being at Tara and the monastery at Teltown.[52]

Most founders of important religious sites at the time, such as Columba, were of royal blood, so it would have been most unusual for a simple monk such as Ciaran who was merely a son of a carpenter to be chosen for such a role. Some historians believe his ancestry is fictitious and see parallels between his father's profession with the Biblical Joseph, father of Jesus. However, it may well have been his remarkable abilities as a psychic visionary that elevated him to this lofty position within the ecclesiastical world at the time. Columba, a great visionary and miracle worker himself, said of Ciaran, 'He was a lamp, blazing with the light of wisdom.'[53]

St Ciaran and King Diarmait performing the foundation ceremony at Clonmacnoise. Courtesy of Ali Isaac, author and blogger

Seven months after the foundation of Clonmacnoise, in 544, Ciaran died of the 'yellow peril', a plague that had been raging throughout Europe since 540, killing over half the population of Ireland including the High King Diarmait. Ciaran's last dying words were 'He who perseveres till the end will be saved.' He was buried under the original wooden church at Clonmacnoise, now the site of the 9th-century stone oratory called Temple Ciaran. His ghostly apparition has been witnessed several times over the centuries, which according to The *Annals of Clonmacnoise* saved the monastery from disaster and plunder.[54]

Pupils and pilgrims continued to throng to Clonmacnoise from all parts of the British Isles and Europe to sample 'the fruits of its knowledge.' It was also favoured from its very beginnings by the High Kings as well as the provincial kings and princes of Ireland, including the Uí Néills of Tara and the O'Conor chieftains of Connacht, many of whom were buried here.

The wealth accrued from successful trade transformed the monastic site into a great city that stretched far beyond the walls we see today. This was no doubt aided by the building of a large wooden bridge across the Shannon, providing easier access from all directions. Remains of this bridge were discovered in 1998, making it the oldest and possibly the largest wooden bridge in Ireland. According to Annette Kehnel in her book *Clonmacnoise: The Church and the Lands of St. Ciaran*, Clonmacnoise was known at one time as 'the shining city', holding vast estates and considerable numbers of tenants.[55]

However, its prosperity attracted the interest of the Norse raiders and pagan clans from Munster who attacked the monastery numerous times, resulting in the destruction of many of its buildings and the looting of important artefacts.

In 1111, it became the cathedral church of West Meath, but by the end of the century, Clonmacnoise was in decline, mainly due to people migrating north to the nearby town of Athlone, by now a growing trading centre for the Midlands of Ireland. Athlone also provided a better route for crossing the Shannon, as well as the best-defended settlement in the region. The declining population could no longer sustain this sizable religious complex and its influence over the area soon diminished. During the same time, new religious orders started to arrive from France, such as the Franciscans, Augustinians and Benedictines, setting up their religious sites throughout Ireland.[56]

Another reason for its decline was due to the new incoming Anglo-Norman de Burgo family who erected a castle nearby in the early 12th century. Their growing ambitions for wealth and power soon saw them enforcing their claim over the lands by curtailing the rights of the local inhabitants and those of the monastery itself, causing more people to leave the area. Although it had a few brief resurgences of fortune, by the 16th century Clonmacnoise was abandoned and became derelict, until the Church of Ireland restored a small church on the site in the late 18th century for local services.

As we strolled around this historic sacred sanctuary, we noticed the many fine carvings that adorn several of the buildings. The old monastic site stands within a circular walled enclosure, with twelve angles or corners creating twelve segments spanning out from the centre. Some researchers believe this style of division conforms to the plan of the Holy City of Jerusalem with King Solomon's Temple and its holy of holies (high altar) at its heart. This sacred plan of building cities in this way stretches back to much earlier times, replicated in the Etruscan cities in Italy, constructed from around 700 BCE to honour the ancient principle of 'as above, so below'.

St Ciaran's Shrine at the centre of the walled settlement measures 2.8 m by 3.8 m, appearing as a small stone oratory or tomb chapel built between the 8th and 9th century and is said to be the oldest stone church in Ireland. As well as marking the very centre of the monastic complex, this chapel is the traditional place of Ciaran's burial. The original shrine was a *dairthech* or 'oak house', a replica of which is on view in the on-site museum. From around the year 606, 'pilgrims have been coming to this site to pay homage to St Ciaran's relics and take soil from his grave to protect their crops and as a cure for ailments, such was the power of this holy man.'[57]

Unfortunately, the taking of soil has undermined its foundations, so much so that the walls of the roofless shrine now lean inwards. During the last few centuries, a chalice and abbot's crozier were discovered buried inside the shrine and are now housed in the National Museum of Ireland - Archaeology, Dublin.

St Ciaran's Shrine at the centre of Clonmacnoise.

After entering the shrine, we sat by what would have been the high altar. As we fell silent, the power of this place began to affect our senses, amplified by its highly magnetic stone that has been the focus of tens of thousands of pilgrims over a period of 1400 years. I had a strong feeling that the builder of this stone chapel had great knowledge of sacred measure, possibly using the exact foundations of Ciaran's original wooden church, thereby creating a truly divine place of power, similar to King Solomon's Temple in Jerusalem, at the sacred navel of Ireland. According to an account of a raid on Clonmacnoise in 1129, a model replica of Solomon's Temple was stolen, along with other gold and silver bejewelled artefacts. I believe the religious symbolism of Clonmacnoise and its myths associated with cosmic order are reflected in the orientation and the ground plan of Ciaran's church.

In his book *Ancient Mysteries, Modern Visions*, Dr Philip Callahan considers that the round towers of Ireland, in their arrangement in the landscape, correspond to the shape of the constellations in the sky. In creating a 'mirror of the heavens', he places Clonmacnoise at the centre reflecting the pole star Polaris and Armagh, the second most important ecclesiastic settlement, corresponding to the ecliptic pole. Although his round tower star map proved to be a little inaccurate, he did identify Clonmacnoise as the geographical centre of Ireland.[58]

King Flann and Abbot Colmán first built the cathedral that stands to the southwest of St Ciaran's shrine in 909. Ruaidrí Ua Conchobair (Rory O'Conor), the last High King of Ireland, was buried there in 1198 near the high altar, joining his father Turlough Mór O'Conor. Its great archway is referred to as 'the whispering arch' as it is said that two people standing on either side of the arch facing away from one another, can hear each other's whispers. We noticed that the foundation stones of some of the other churches were much larger than those above them, suggesting that after the many destructions that occurred here, later masons were unable to reconstruct the monastic buildings using the earlier sophisticated style of masonry. Few places in Ireland can boast two standing round towers and there may have been more on this site, similar to the religious complex at Glendalough in Co Wicklow, one of them incorporated as the tower of a church.

The site also has many fine examples of 9th and 10th-century High Crosses, some with the triskele symbol of the triple goddess. The so-called North Cross is the oldest of the three extant crosses, dated *c.* 800; only the limestone shaft and sandstone base (a former millstone) survive. On one of its panels is the pagan image of Cernunnos, the Celtic god of hunting and fertility, displayed on the east face of the shaft. This, and two similar crosses, all marked the north, south and west ends of the monastic settlement, the Cross of the Scriptures standing opposite the west entrance of the cathedral. However, more significantly, the Cross of the Scriptures includes a carved panel depicting King Diarmait and Ciaran performing the foundation ritual as they together hold 'the foundation post' while placing it in the ground. This image is common in other cultures concerning the foundation of either a city or a temple. Here we see Ciaran with the High King of Ireland staking not only the centre of the future monastic site but also the new navel of Ireland.

There were also hundreds of elaborately carved pre-Norman cross slabs uncovered here, one of which shows a perfect representation of the four kingship centres of Ireland connected to the symbolic centre in the form of a spiral. Perhaps it marked the grave of one of the nobles of Clann Chuinn of the Kingdom of Midhe or one of the many other royal kings and princes of Ireland who were buried here.

A 14th-century poem by Aongus Ó'Giolláin called *The Dead at Clonmacnoise*, translated into English by T. W. Rolleston, reads:

'In a quiet water'd land, a land of roses,
Stands Saint Kieran's city fair;
And the warriors of Erin in their famous generations
Slumber there.

There beneath the dewy hillside sleep the noblest
Of the clan of Conn,
Each below his stone with name in branching Ogham
And the sacred knot thereon.

There they laid to rest the seven Kings of Tara,
There the sons of Cairbre sleep –
Battle-banners of the Gael that in Kieran's plain of crosses
Now their final hosting keep.

And in Clonmacnois they laid the men of Teffia,
And right many a lord of Breagh;
Deep the sod above Clan Creide and Clan Conaill,
Kind in hall and fierce in fray.

Many and many a son of Conn the Hundred-Fighter
In the red earth lies at rest;
Many a blue eye of Clan Colman the turf covers,
Many a swan-white breast.'[59]

The Nun's Church and St Ciaran's Well

As we exited the east gate of the monastic site towards the Nun's Church, we found ourselves walking along a section of An Slí Mhór that coincides with the Esker Riada. We instantly fell in love with this atmospheric ruin and sensed a shift in vibration from a very masculine energy within the main complex to a more feminine frequency, the swirling energy having a mesmerising effect on us. The Irish-Romanesque chancel arch and doorway retain much of their wonderfully ornate carvings, possibly one of the finest examples of this type of architecture in Ireland. Some of the carvings are of beak-head and geometric design, but also hidden among the various carved human and animal heads are two rather interesting images, one of a female figure believed to be a sheela-na-gig and another of a dragon's head, perhaps alluding to a female dragon or serpent energy line flowing through the site.

Ruins of the Nun's Church, Clonmacnoise

The old nunnery was built in 1167 under the patronage of the infamous Derbforgaill or Dervorgilla, the wife of Tighearnan O'Rourke, King of Breifne. Dervorgilla, also known as 'Helen of Ireland', is a reference to Helen of Troy. She was abducted by Dermot MacMurrough Kavanagh, said to be one of the events that led to the Norman invasion of Ireland.

According to the Irish Annals, Dervorgilla was the beautiful daughter of Murchad Ua Maeleachlainn, King of Meath, and had a passionate affair with Dermot, King of Leinster. The 'abduction' occurred in 1152 when Dermot was at war with Dervorgilla's husband Tiernan. She was supposedly carried off willingly, having taken her cattle and chattels with her. A year later, High King Turlough O'Conor returned her to her family and then confined her to Clonmacnoise, where she died in 1193. However, most historians suggest there was no romance involved and that she was simply a willing pawn used as part of dynastic politics.[60]

We found it hard to leave this important centre of Ireland but knew it was time to make our way to St Ciaran's Well, located a short distance to the south of the main complex. A few nights before setting off on this trip, Caroline had a dream that we were to place our special healing stones, collected from various key power places around Britain, including Cornwall and Iona, in the well. As it transpired, our healing was needed as to our dismay we found the spring had completely dried up.

The well has attracted pilgrims since the 7th century and *The Annals of Tigernach* record the death here of an Irish chieftain named Aedh who had been making his way to Clonmacnoise for pilgrimage.[61] According to a tale told in *The Tripartite Life of Patrick*, a leper passing by Clonmacnoise sat beneath an elm tree and asked a man to pull up some rushes. When he did so, water seeped from the earth and produced a spring, which would later become St Ciaran's Well.[62] A large and impressive whitethorn bush once grew beside this well, now replaced by a smaller, younger version. Within its precincts are various carved stones, including an early Christian cross slab, the stump of a stone cross and one carved with a figure with outstretched arms. A fourth, said to include the image of St Colman, was stolen many years ago.

Sadly, the well now lies neglected and almost forgotten, and unfortunately, without any real importance assigned to this precious holy site at the centre of Ireland, damage and theft will continue unhindered. Nowhere, too, is this site mentioned in the visitor's centre at Clonmacnoise, but as one commentator wrote, 'it is still something of a miracle that this site has survived at all.' It once formed part of a pilgrimage route, where pilgrims would stop to encircle the well barefoot three times before kissing the carved stones surrounding it and very likely leaving a votive offering. The pilgrims would then proceed to the monastic settlement and the Nun's Church and from there head north along the Esker Riada as far as they were able. Before leaving, we felt compelled to place some of our healing stones within the dry well, sensing that the curative energy emanating from this once-sacred spring was still a potent force.

Here we reflected on the centres of Ireland we had visited so far and remarked on how they differed in polarity. Clonmacnoise has a gentle but masculine energy, influenced by the power wielded from there by the Celtic community of monks and the High Kings of Ireland. The ancient centre of Uisneach is set within a softer feminine landscape, where the mother goddess resides in its hidden wells and lakes. Croghan Hill radiates a balance of both male and female, in its masculine pyramid-shaped hill and its associations with the goddess Brigid, while Durrow at the meeting of five ancient routes, retains the feminine power within the land through the sacred water of St Columba's Well.

St Ciaran's Well, Clonmacnoise

Lost Lands and the Plagues

Although Uisneach is not the geographical centre of Ireland today, it may have been before a cataclysm changed the shape of the coastline. Around 1159 BCE a great tsunami hit the northern coasts of Ireland due to the massive explosion of the 'Hekla 3' volcano in Iceland. The blast caused by this particular explosion was much larger than that of the Greek island of Santorini (Thera) volcano in the Aegean Sea, which ended the Minoan civilisation on Crete around 1600 BCE.

In the 1980s, Professor Mike Baillie, a leading authority on dendrochronology (tree-ring dating), was instrumental in building a year-by-year chronology of tree-ring growth reaching 7400 years into the past. Annual growth rings in trees vary from year to year depending on the prevailing growing conditions, and by lining up overlapping sequences of growth patterns in oak timbers, it has been possible to reconstruct the climatic variations in Ireland over the past. Definite areas of disturbed growth or very narrow or damaged rings are apparent in 1628 BCE, 1159 BCE, 207 BCE and 540 CE. Baillie believes these anomalies were caused by either comets or volcanic ash blocking out the sun and causing very poor growth. Such catastrophic conditions would also cause widespread famine and the collapse of civilisation.[63]

The dramatic effects of the 1159 BCE event triggered 18 years of climatic worsening across Europe and the Mediterranean, including ancient Egypt, which led to the eventual downfall of the New Kingdom and the start of the Trojan Wars. The mention of flooding and lakes overflowing in Irish folktales may have been associated with this event. The tsunami and volcanic ash created by the explosion of Hekla 3 would have not only altered the shape of Ireland's coastline but also changed the fate of many of Ireland's kingdoms and rulers.

For Uisneach to mark the exact geographical centre today, the land would have to extend further out to sea on the eastern and northeastern coasts. Interestingly, recent archaeological evidence of lost lands along the northeast coast has come to light, lands that would have flourished during the Neolithic and Bronze Age periods. Folklore also tells of a land bridge in the north of Ireland that reached across to Scotland, fragments of which may have survived in the Bronze Age when Uisneach was at its height of power. In *Lost Cities and Sunken Lands*, author Nigel Pennick notes that many places around the British Isles lost coastline in the past, most of which was around Ireland.[64]

Ice core samples from Antarctica and Greenland show evidence of substantial sulphate deposits around 533–534 CE which is evidence of an extensive acidic dust veil. This may have been the result of several comet impacts or a large planetary asteroid brushing its tail of debris into the path of Earth's orbit. An event such as this would have brought widescale chaos, leaving the inhabitants of Ireland with spoiled crops and lake and pond water polluted by toxic dust. A Byzantine scribe called Procopius wrote in *History of Wars*, 'And it came about during this year that a most dread portent took place. For the sun gave forth its light without brightness, like the moon, during the whole year, and it seemed exceedingly like the sun in eclipse, for the beams it shed were not clear nor such as it is accustomed to shed.'[65]

The Annals of Ulster report a lack of bread in 536 and other reports speak of crop failures from 536 to 539.[66] People would have had to rely upon stored food or grain and join gangs of raiders pillaging the rich stores of the royal centres. This may explain the downfall of certain kingdoms and their royal pagan palaces and the subsequent rise of the Christian monasteries.

Perhaps, it is no coincidence that in 544, after many years of suffering in Ireland, Ciaran founded Europe's greatest monastic centre at the newly founded true omphalos of Ireland – thus paving the way for the new Christian religion and amplifying its powerful influence over the whole country. Perhaps the early saints saw this disaster as a judgement from God against the Irish people to change their pagan ways and convert to Christianity. Unfortunately, for the Christians, years of crop failure and contaminated water brought about the 'yellow peril', a plague that had spread from the British Isles and struck during the founding of Clonmacnoise, killing Ciaran and King Diarmait. During this turbulent time, many wealthy families avoided the plague by migrating across the Channel to Gaul. In *The Life of St Samson of Dol*, the biographer refers to the Welsh saint leaving the country after a pestilence to join a British colony called 'New Britain' or Brittany, set up as a refuge by a King of Gaul.[67]

Turoe, the Lost Royal Capital

We headed back to An Slí Mhór to complete our journey across the middle of Ireland to the village of Shannonbridge, where we crossed one of the oldest Irish bridges to Ballinasloe at an ancient fording place of the River Suck. The eskers continue south of the town to Knockglass and on to Kilconnell with its 14th-century Franciscan friary. At Kiltullagh in Co Galway, where it converges with other ancient roads, the Great Way passes through what was, according to some researchers, a prehistoric capital of Ireland. A finely carved stone called the 'Turoe Stone', its shape very similar to Delphi's omphalos stone, recently displayed just south of here at the nearby Turoe Pet Farm near the village of Bullaun, stood at the centre of the now forgotten royal complex.

For centuries this elaborately carved granite monument had largely gone unnoticed until local historian Father Tom O'Connor began to uncover the hidden history of the area in the hope of finding out more about this enigmatic stone. His book, *Turoe and Athenry, Ancient Capitals of Celtic Ireland*, is the culmination of 40 years of research that included looking through ancient manuscripts, old maps, archaeological evidence, the etymology of towns and villages and local legends and folklore. His discoveries revealed the existence of a

Celtic oppidum (town or settlement) that consisted of a vast network of linear ditches surrounding a royal ceremonial enclosure.

This sacred area included the hill of Knocknadala, derived from *Cnoc na nDál* meaning 'Hill of Parliament', and Turoe Hill, which marked the ceremonial centre where the Turoe Stone once stood and was the focal point of the whole complex. Also on the hill, within folk memory, were several standing stones and circles, now destroyed, except for one hidden in woodland. O'Connor believes that the earthen remains around the royal enclosure have 'all the hallmarks and definitive layout of a Celtic royal acropolis with a necropolis burial site which held 150 large tombs, some bearing the names of legendary Irish kings.' Remarkably, these ditch and bank earthworks, if they had survived, would have formed the largest Celtic defence system ever built in Europe.[68]

Due to modern farming and rural development, there is little to see of it today, with the recent building of the M6 motorway causing further destruction, having cut right through the heart of this ancient site, taking a slice out of Knocknadala Hill. Unless major archaeological excavations take place here, its future as an important historical monument is uncertain. The Turoe Stone that once stood for all to see within the grounds of the Pet Farm has now been removed to Galway City Museum for restoration and is yet to be returned as of 2024. It is a mystery why one of Europe's finest examples of early Celtic stone art was left unpreserved for so many years, first in a field, then on the grounds of a private house, and finally at the pet farm.

This omphalos stone once stood just beyond the entrance of an Iron Age hillfort on Turoe Hill known as Rath Ferach Mhor or Rath of Feerwore, but due to the fort's destruction, the original position of the stone has been lost. Farming activities over the centuries have also destroyed most of this Celtic settlement, its earthwork ditches and banks filled in or quarried away for gravel, although some fragments can still be traced in and around the area.

The Turoe Stone dates from 250 BCE and stands 1.68 m high, its decoration sculpted in low relief to a depth of about 2.5 cm, consisting of curvilinear swirling patterns, triskeles and a Greek key border. The triskele in its Christian form represents the triple goddess and is an important symbol of the fertilising power within the land. The stone is carved in the Celtic La Tène style, its size, shape and carvings being remarkably similar to the phallic-shaped Delphi omphalos stone in Greece. The La Tène culture dates from the mid-5th century BCE and originated in Switzerland, where the Celts came into contact with Greek and Etruscan influences from south of the Alps. The Etruscans may have heavily influenced La Tène style on their migration into central Europe, to escape the threat of the growing Roman Empire, which eventually usurped them.

They probably journeyed along the Rhine Valley to the ports of the North Sea and then sailed along the south coast of Britain to Ireland. One of the most important seaports along the east coast of Ireland during the Iron Age was *Ath Cliath Magh Ri*, known today as Clarinbridge, Co Galway. This historic harbour is also known as the 'Port of the Gaels', in other words, the landing place of a race of people who spoke Gaelic, and it is here that the La Tène Celts landed. The port also marked the western terminus of An Slí Mhór/the Esker Riada and, according to ancient records, it was used by early Christians to visit the Aran Islands.[69]

Two other similar granite stones carved with Le Tène art exist in Ireland, one located in the grounds of the derelict Castlestrange House near Athleague in Co Roscommon, moved there in the 19th century by the owner of this estate to provide the grounds with a landscape feature. The other is on display at the Ballyjamesduff Cavan Museum

The Turoe Stone, Co Galway

in Co Cavan, having stood at one time near the stone circle at Killycluggin and reported to have been covered in gold designs representing the fertility god Crom Cruaich or Crom Dubh.

The Castlestrange Stone, as it is known, is contemporary with the Turoe Stone with similar elegant patterns, although slightly smaller. One wonders whether such carvings gave the stone power, similar to those found on so-called prehistoric cup-and-ring-marked stones found predominantly at sacred sites in Cumbria, Northumberland and Scotland.

It is often thought that moving such ritual stones from their original place of power can cause ill luck, which may account for the dilapidated state of the ruined Castlestrange mansion further up the driveway, now covered in brambles. The Killycluggin stone was originally about 1.5 m tall before St Patrick damaged its top half when he overturned it to destroy Crom Dubh's hold over the local pagans.

Early references to Turoe's royal capital came from Greek geographer and cartographer Ptolemy of Alexandria (100–170 CE). He recorded two capitals in Ireland: one called Emain Macha near Armagh in the northeast of Ireland, and the other roughly at the centre of Co Galway, precisely where Turoe is today, naming it *Regia E Tera* which in Old Irish is 'Royal Teamhair,' or Turoe. According to O'Connor, Ptolemy named the lost royal enclosure of Cnoc na nDál as 'the most illustrious city in all Britannia and the most extensive in size, located in the western part of Ireland.'[70]

From Kiltullagh the eskers lead to Clarinbridge, the ancient port of the Gaels or *Ath Cliath Magh Ri*, lying south of Oranmore on the Galway to Gort Road. The name Clarinbridge refers to the ancient plank bridge across the River Clarin, built to replace the original hurdle crossing. This area is littered with earthworks and ringforts with motte and bailey mounds, perhaps remnants of the many tribes that settled and battled here when first landing in Ireland centuries ago. It is also from here that Ciaran would have sailed to Inishmore, where he experienced his vision that would change the course of Irish religious and political history. However, this was not the only encounter we had with Ciaran, for he is also associated with other centres of the British Isles, referred to in later chapters.

The essence of the great goddesses of Ireland also still lingers at the ceremonial centres of Dún Ailinne, Emain Macha, Cnoc Áine and Rathcroghan, although now somewhat veiled and remote. However, as our experiences at Uisneach prove, in her various guises as Brigid,

Ailinne, Aine, Maebh and Macha she is ready to greet those who are willing to seek her. The warrior goddess queen still survives in our psyche, albeit unconsciously in the modern-day female spiritual warrior who strives for equality, freedom and independence.

Like the Celtic queens of old, who ruled their lands and had control over whomever and whatever they desired, modern women of today can choose their destiny. In sharp contrast, medieval stories tell of sad and lonely princesses who wait in the hope of being rescued by a handsome prince from either a dragon or a remote tower.

However, the male deities must not be forgotten either, for the honouring of Lugh, Finn and Crom Cruaich was also essential to the balance and harmony of the Earth. Therefore, we need to honour and celebrate both the healing power and wisdom of the male gods and the female goddesses at their important ceremonial places and connect them all with the nurturing spirit of Ireland's great mother Eriu at the navel.

Nearing the end of our Emerald Isle journey, we stood on an ancient mound where the Saint's Way reaches the western shore looking across Galway Bay to Inishmore, the 'Avalon of Ireland' and the final destination for the early pilgrims. Here we said a blessing in honour of Eriu and all of Ireland's male and female deities, seeing healing light radiate through the mound and across the land to all the centres we had visited, clearing and transforming the battle energy and asking for unity and peace to reign once more across the whole of Northern and Southern Ireland.

The Centre of Northern Ireland

The O'Neill's Stone of Destiny at the centre of Northern Ireland

The territory of Northern Ireland encompasses the ancient province of Ulster although losing three of its nine counties – Monaghan, Cavan and Donegal to the Republic of Ireland. The centre-point of this recently formed country lies 3 miles southeast of Cookstown and about a mile southeast of Tullyhoque Fort which has a fascinating history.

The banked circular ráth of Tullyhoque was a site of ceremonial importance for hundreds of years, but it is most famous today as the old inauguration site of the O'Neill dynasty, who had their own Stone of Destiny called *Leac na Rí*, meaning 'the flagstone of the kings'. This large boulder was incorporated as the seat of a ceremonial stone chair or throne in the 16th century, with the addition of three flat stone slabs forming the back and arm rests. However, it was smashed to pieces during the Elizabethan invasion of Ireland by Lord Mountjoy to quell a rebellion led by Hugh O'Neill king of Ulster. The desecration of the stone was an attempt to symbolically end O'Neill's sovereignty over the land. A reproduction of the 'throne' is located near the car parking area close to the spot indicated by Richard Barthelet in his 1602 map of Tullyhogue, now in the National Library of Ireland.

The Leac na Rí was possibly a much earlier pagan stone of power as it was blessed by St. Patrick himself. The current chief guardian of the ancient clan O'Neill of Tyrone is Dan Ó Néill who states that the surname O'Neill is more of a title of guardianship of the old Celtic ways.

The Centre of the Republic of Ireland

Today the centre of the Republic of Ireland is in the south-eastern region of county Galway, at a point 3km (2 miles) south-west of the village of Eyrecourt and six miles southwest of Clonfert Cathedral. This remote area has little history and the nearest sacred site is 3.5 miles to the southeast at one of the most strategic river crossings of the River Shannon. Here stands the Church of St Francis at the village of Meelick, one of the oldest places of worship still in use in Ireland for Catholic services. It was first established as a small Franciscan friary in 1414 within sight of the Anglo-Norman Meelick Castle. It also served as the ancestral burial place for many of the most prominent landholding families of the area.

References:

1. Macalister R A S (1938) *Lebor Gabála Érenn: The Book of the Taking of Ireland.* Irish Texts Society.
https://archive.org/details/leborgablare01macauoft.

2. Michell J & Rhone C (1991) *Twelve-Tribe Nations and the Science of Enchanting the Landscape.* Thames & Hudson, London.

3. Dames M (1992) *Mythic Ireland.* Thames & Hudson, London.

4. Robb G (2013) *The Ancient Paths: Discovering the Lost Map of Celtic Europe.* Picador, London.
5. Cunningham B (2010). *The Annals of the Four Masters: Irish History, Kingship and Society in the Early Seventeenth Century*. MS123.2. Four Courts, Dublin.
6. Geissel H (2006) *A Road on the Long Ridge: In Search of the Ancient Highway on the Esker Riada*. CRS Publications, Kildare.
7. *Roadways in Ancient Ireland* MacNeill E (1940) *Feil-sgribhinn Eoin MacNeill: Essays and Studies Presented to Professor Eoin MacNeill on the Occasion of His Seventieth Birthday May 15th, 1938*. At the Sign of the Three Candles, Dublin.
8. Michell J (1994) *At the Centre of the World; Polar Symbolism Discovered in Celtic, Norse and Other Ritualized Landscapes*. Thames & Hudson, London.
9. Geissel H (2006) *A Road on the Long Ridge: In Search of the Ancient Highway on the Esker Riada.* CRS Publications, Kildare.
10. Dames M (1992) *Ireland: A Sacred Journey*. Element Books.
11. St Bridget's Well.
http://www.megalithicireland.com/St%20Brigid%27s%20Well,%20 Clondalkin.html.
12. Geissel H (2006) *A Road on the Long Ridge: In Search of the Ancient Highway on the Esker Riada.* CRS Publications, Kildare.
13. Cunningham B (2010). *The Annals of the Four Masters: Irish History, Kingship and Society in the Early Seventeenth Century*. Four Courts, Dublin.
14. Dames M (1992) *Ireland: A Sacred Journey*. Element Books.
15. Keating G (1908) *The History of Ireland*. Irish Texts Society, London. https://archive.org/ details/historyireland03keatgoog.
16. Cambrensis Giraldus (1187) *The Topography of Ireland*. In *The Historical Works of Giraldus Cambrensis*, Thomas Wright, ed., 1882, p. 97. George Bell and Sons, London.
17. Cunningham B (2010). *The Annals of the Four Masters: Irish History, Kingship and Society in the Early Seventeenth Century*. Four Courts, Dublin.
18. O'Brien H & Villanueva J L (1833) *Phoenician Ireland*. R M Timms, Dublin.
19. Geissel H (2006) *A Road on the Long Ridge: In Search of the Ancient Highway on the Esker Riada*. CRS Publications, Kildare.
20. Sharpe R (translator) (1995) *Adomnan of Iona. Life of St Columba*. Penguin Classics, London.
21. https://en.wikipedia.org/wiki/Cathach_of_St._Columba
22. Dumville D (ed.), Shirley-Price L & Farmer D (translators) (2003) *Bede: Ecclesiastical History of the English People.* Penguin Classics, London.
23. Spence L (1994) *The Mysteries of Britain: Secret Rites and Traditions of Ancient Britain.* New edition. Senate, Rickmansworth (new edition).
24. Cunningham B (2010). *The Annals of the Four Masters: Irish History, Kingship and Society in the Early Seventeenth Century*. MS123.2. Four Courts, Dublin.

25. Alexander M (1981) *Enchanted Britain: Mystical Sites in Rural England, Scotland and Wales*. Book Club Associates, London.
26. Coghan Revd A (1908) *The Diocese of Meath: Ancient and Modern (Volume 2).* John F Fowler, Dublin. https://archive.org/details/dioceseofmeathan01cogaiala.
27. The Great Rite. http://whymenmadegod.com/hierogamy.html.
28. Meehan C (2002) *A Traveller's Guide to Sacred Ireland.* Gothic Image, Glastonbury.
29. Macalister R A S & Lloyd Praeger R. *Report on the Excavation of Uisneach*. Proceedings of the Royal Irish Academy. Section C: Archaeology, Celtic Studies, History, Linguistics, Literature, vol. 38, Royal Irish Academy, 1928, Pl. XVII. https://voicesfromthedawn.com/objects-found-plate-xvii/
30. The Hill of Uisneach and the Festival of the Fires. www.festivalofthefires.com/history.
31. Barker M (2011) *Temple Mysticism: An Introduction*. SPCK Publishing, London.
32. Dames M (1992) *Ireland: A Sacred Journey*. Element Books.
33. Meehan C (2002) *A Traveller's Guide to Sacred Ireland*. Gothic Image, Glastonbury.
34. Dames M (1992) *Ireland: A Sacred Journey*. Element Books.
35. Gwynn J (1913) *Liber Ardmachanus. The Book of Armagh*. Royal Irish Academy, Dublin. https://archive.org/details/cu31924091179337.
36. Thorpe L (Translator) (1966) *Geoffrey of Monmouth: The History of the Kings of Britain*. The Folio Society, London.
37. Strachan John and O'Keefe J. G. (1912*) Yellow Book of Lecan*. Royal Irish Academy, Dublin. https://archive.org/details/tinbcailng00strauoft.
38. O'Donovan John (1856) *Annals of the Kingdom of Ireland.* Hodges, Smith & Co. Dublin. https://archive.org/details/annalsofkingdomo01ocleuoft/annalsofkingdomo01ocleuoft/
39. Mircea Eliade (1991) *Images and Symbols: Studies in Religious Symbolism*. Princeton University Press
40. Michell J (1983) *The New View Over Atlantis*. Thames & Hudson, London.
41. Newman H (2008) *Earth Grids.* Wooden Books, Glastonbury.
42. Dames M (1992) *Ireland: A Sacred Journey*. Element Books.
43. Whitley S (1887) *The Tripartite Life of Patrick*. HMSO, London. https://archive.org/details/ tripartitepatrick00stokuoft
44. Coghan Revd A (1908) *The Diocese of Meath: Ancient and Modern (Volume 2).* John F Fowler, Dublin. https://archive.org/details/dioceseofmeathan03cogaiala
45. Woods J (1907) *Annals of Westmeath, Ancient and Modern*. Sealy, Bryers & Walker, Dublin. https://archive.org/details/annalsofwestmeat00wooduoft.
46. Pennick N (1996) *Celtic Sacred Landscapes*. Thames & Hudson, London.
47. Healy J (1908). *Abbey and School of Clonmacnoise*. In The Catholic Encyclopedia. Robert Appleton Company, New York.

48. O'Carroll B & Felton B (2013) *The Story of Clonmacnoise and Saint Ciaran*. Ely House, Shannonbridge.
49. Stokes W (1890) *Lives of Saints from The Book of Lismore*. Clarendon Press, Oxford. https:// archive.org/details/livessaints00stokuoft.
50. Sharpe R (translator)(1995) *Adomnan of Iona. Life of St Columba*. Penguin Classics, London.
51. Murphy Revd D (1896) *The Annals of Clonmacnoise*. University Press, Dublin. https:// archive.org/details/annalsofclonmacn00royauoft.
52. *The Monastic Life and Miracles of St Colman-Elo*. http://omniumsanctorumhiberniae. blogspot.co.uk/2015/09/the-monastic-life-and-miracles-of-st.html.
53. Sharpe R (translator)(1995) *Adomnan of Iona. Life of St Columba*. Penguin Classics, London.
54. Murphy Revd D (1896) *The Annals of Clonmacnoise*. University Press, Dublin. https:// archive.org/details/annalsofclonmacn00royauoft.
55. Kehnel A (1998) *Clonmacnois: The Church and the Lands of St. Ciaran*. Lit Verlag, Münster.
56. O'Carroll B & Felton B (2013) *The Story of Clonmacnoise and Saint Ciaran*. Ely House, Shannonbridge.
57. ibid.
58. Callahan P S (1984) *Ancient Mysteries, Modern Visions*. Acres, Kansas City.
59. Rolleston T W (1857) *The Dead at Clonmacnoise.* http://www.daypoems.net/poems/797. html.
See also Ricks C (1999) *The Oxford Book of English Verse*. Oxford University Press, Oxford.
60. Cunningham B (2010) *The Annals of the Four Masters*: Irish History, Kingship and Society in the Early Seventeenth Century. Four Courts, Dublin.
61. Stokes W & Tigernach, Abbot of Clonmacnoise (1895) *The Annals of Tigernach*. Librairie Emile Bouilon, Paris. https://archive.org/details/annalsoftigernac00stokuoft.
62. Whitley S (1887) *The Tripartite Life of Patrick*. HMSO, London. https://archive.org/details/ tripartitepatrick00stokuoft.
63. Baillie M (1998) *Exodus to Arthur: Catastrophic Encounters with Comets*. Batsford, London.
64. Pennick N (1997) *Lost Cities and Sunken Lands*. Capall Bann, Taunton.
65. Procopius (2005) *History of the Wars, Books III and IV: The Vandalic War*. Dewing H.B.
66. Mac Airt Sean & Mac Niocaill Gearoid (1983) *The Annals of Ulster* (to A.D. 1131): Text and Translation Pt. 1. Dublin Institute for Advanced Studies, Dublin.
67. Taylor T (2010) *The Life of St. Samson of Dol*. Kessinger, Montana.
68. O'Connor T (2003) *Turoe and Athenry: Ancient Capitals of Celtic Ireland*. Tom O'Connor, Athenry.
69. ibid.
70. ibid

Chapter 3

The Pictish and Celtic Divisions of Alba

We next travelled to the ancient realm of Scotland, settled by the early Celts long, ago to uncover whether it too was divided into cosmological divisions like Ireland, with a recognised omphalos shrine at the mid-point. Unfortunately, much of Scotland's oldest foundation myths and folklore were lost over the centuries with the displacement of its people due to numerous invasions by the Romans, Saxons, Normans and the English. However, we soon found tantalising evidence that the early Picts divided Scotland into six provinces around a central seventh, which the Irish Scots later recreated as four kingdoms around a central fifth.

The Picts as a race are one of the oldest in Scotland, descended from the Neolithic and Bronze Age Beaker people known as the Firbolg, who also settled in Ireland. They held two distinctive kingdoms called North and South Pictland. In the south, the Pictish border stretched from the Rivers Clyde and Forth on which the Romans built the Antonine Wall.

The Roman historian Eumenius first mentions the Picts in the 3rd century CE as the *pictus*, describing them as fierce and skilled in battle. Tacitus, another Roman chronicler, observed them as valiant and fearless noble savages. However, Roman biographers were renowned for documenting their version of British history and the recorded events that followed their invasion were no more than political propaganda to justify their imperial assault on Britain and the subsequent massacre of its people. However, the early races of Scotland were later recorded as highly civilised, cultured and literate, their kinsmen residing in Germany and Gaul. From the moment the Romans set foot on Scottish soil, the Picts formed a confederation with the Dál Riada Scots of Ireland, whose kingdom was the Argyll region, to preserve their independence and freedom and to save their land from exploitation, preferring to fight rather than be enslaved.

According to Irish legend, when the Picts first arrived in Ireland they requested from the Milesian King Heremon a part of his newly conquered lands to settle. However, because no women were accompanying them, he refused, although later he offered them the widows of the recently defeated Tuatha Dé Danann. His willingness to allow them to stay in Ireland was based on the proviso that they accompanied a large number of his forces to Alba (the old name for Scotland north of the Forth) to defeat its inhabitants but remain subservient to the kings of Ireland.[1]

Folklorist Stuart McHardy in *A New History of the Picts* states that the Pictish kings were chosen through matrilineal descent. Dr Emily Lyle of the School of Scottish Studies suggests that there were two dominant female lines: one being in the form of an actual queen who preserved the sovereignty of the land, having succeeded her mother and to whom the candidate of overlord was married before he took office. The other would have preserved a continuum of candidates for that marriage and would effectively be 'a royal line of mothers', which McHardy believes would explain the dual mother/goddess that was so central to their beliefs.[2]

The Pictish King Bridei or Brude mac Maelchon (554–584 CE), who ruled over a huge region of Scotland known in *c.* 600 as Fortriu, was the son of Maelgwn who was chosen by Bridei's mother, a Pictish princess, to be his father. The Pictish princesses had the right to the noblest men available to father a child who would become part of a future dynasty.

Even today, very little is known of the Pictish royal line in Scotland apart from king lists and early chronicles written by their enemies and later Roman Catholic scribes. The only historical writing that may resemble the Pictish version of events is a document known as *The Pictish Chronicle,* compiled during the reign of King Kenneth II of Alba (971–995). The earliest of these chronicles, of which there are seven in all, begins with an account of Scotland's mythical founder and first king, Cruithne, who ruled for 100 years after succeeding his father Cinge, Cruithne divided his kingdom into seven provinces and named them after his seven sons, Fidach, Fib, Foltaig, Fortrenn, Cait, Ce and Cercinn.[3]

According to the Revd A. B. Scott in *The Pictish Nation, its People and its Church*, Scotland is referred to by the *Annals of Ulster* as *Cruithintuait* during the time of the Picts, derived from *Cruithni* meaning 'tribe of the designs'. The P-Celtic-speaking Britons translated Cruithni as 'Pryten', which eventually became Briton in the tongue of the Teutonic invaders.[4] The Romans called these northern lands Caledonia, after the Pictish Caledonii tribe, who fought Agricola at Mons Graupius in 84 CE, a battle that halted the Roman advance into the Highlands.

However, by the beginning of the 10th century, the descendants of Kenneth MacAlpin the King of the Picts and Scots, changed the name of these northern lands to Alba or Alban meaning 'high country'. Alba derives from the pre-Indo-European word alb meaning 'hill' and the Italo-Celtic *alpes* or *alpen* meaning 'mountainous regions', the 'p' and 'b' being interchangeable in the languages of the Britons and Celts.

Foundation myths that tell of a country being divided between the sons of a great king are familiar in many nations including Britain, which in legend was said to have been shared between the sons of the Trojan hero Brutus.

The longevity of such kings as Cruithne is also common. His son Cait, legendary ancestor of the 'Cat' clan, was given Caithness and Sutherland; Cercinn, the regions of Angus and the Mearns, formerly known as *Magh Circinn* or the 'plain of Circinn'; Ce was awarded Mar and Buchan, recalled in the name Bennachie; Fib received Fife; Fidach, Moray and Ross; Foltaig had the central province Atholl; and Fortrenn received Strathearn and Menteith. Anciently, Strathearn (southern Perthshire) was known as Fortrenn, and the royal house of Fortrenn still existed up until the 10th century. Argyll and the area of Kilmartin, once part of the Kingdom of the Dál Riada Scots, was never recorded as a Pictish province, although the Picts of Fortrenn were the region's overlords.[5]

Maps of the seven Pictish kingdoms show Fotla, now called Atholl, as the central province. Fotla or Fodla,[6] the 't' and 'd' being interchangeable, was a Celtic goddess in Ireland, one of the three daughters of the magical race of the Tuatha Dé Dannan and one of the names by which Ireland was known in ancient times. The name Atholl is often claimed to derive from *Ath Fhodhla*, said to mean 'New Ireland'; however, the Gaelic word 'Ath' means 'next', and therefore another translation is 'Next Ireland'.[7]

Royal Sites of the Picts

Our research revealed that the old kingdom of Atholl is indeed a central province like Meath in Ireland, therefore it may have shared features found in other omphalos landscapes such as a world mountain, ancient crossroads, an omphalos stone, a goddess shrine and a holy well.

Atholl may also have a site similar to Uisneach, linked to other royal ceremonial sites and palaces, but unfortunately, many of the Pictish royal centres are now barely earthworks in a field, their history and former importance of little consequence to the archaeologists and historians of old. However, recent excavations may give us a clue to the location of at least four of them.

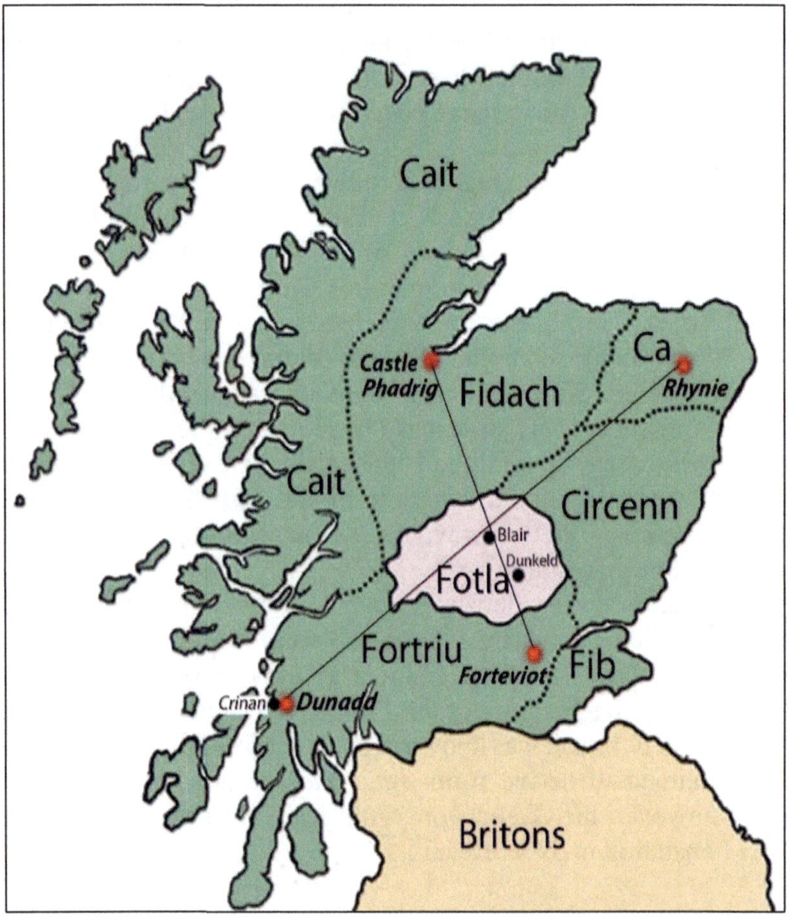

Figure 9. The Divisions of Alba and the four Royal Pictish Sites

The most renowned and documented royal enclosure is located on a rocky knoll just to the west of Inverness called Castle Phadrig, a fort with walls of melted stone. Vitrified forts exist mainly across northern Europe, in particular Scotland, with a few examples in Wales and Northern Ireland. Vitrification is the process through which silica-based stones and mortar are transformed into glass due to exposure to extreme heat. Little is understood about their origins and purpose and even modern attempts at vitrifying walls have only deepened the mystery. To create such high temperatures on top of a hill would require a forest of trees, and even if this is accomplished, the resulting melted wall becomes brittle over time and easier to destroy.

Most of the 200 vitrified forts found across Europe date to 1200 BCE–500 CE. However, many experts agree that the forts were abandoned after vitrification took place, which means that this process was due to either an act of war or some natural disaster probably occurring at the very latest around 500 CE. Theories abound as to the cause, but some agree that it was the result of super-heated plasma from lightning bolts or a comet vaporising in an airburst as it passed through the atmosphere causing the plasma to hit the ground and melt the silica within the walls of the fort. The date seems to fit with the 'yellow peril' plague that swept across the British Isles in 540 CE resulting in tremendous loss of life, including that of St Ciaran and the High King Diarmait in Ireland. Perhaps both events were caused by fragments of a comet? Gildas, a British monk, recorded around 540 AD that the 'island of Britain was on fire from sea to sea .... Until it had burned almost the whole surface of the island and was licking the western ocean with its fierce red tongue.'[8]

Castle Phadrig became the fortress of King Bridei I in the 6th century and the capital of Northern Pictland. The strategic situation of Inverness next to a fording of the Beauly and Moray Firth has attracted people to live here for centuries, and even today, Inverness is still the capital of the Highlands.

According to Adomnan of Iona, Columba visited King Bridei in 565 in an attempt to convert him and his Druids to Christianity. At first, he was received with suspicion as the Picts had recently defeated Columba's kinsmen, the Dál Riada Scots, in a great battle. Columba also had the reputation of having the power to work miracles and magic. At Bridei's stronghold, a former Iron Age fort, legend has it that when Columba arrived, a locked gate rudely confronted him. However, to the king's amazement and alarm, Columba miraculously forced the doors open by making the sign of the cross. From that moment, Bridei revered Columba with 'growing deference and honour.'[9]

Another royal site dating to the 5th or 6th century CE existed in Aberdeenshire among a vast number of Neolithic stone monuments at a place called Rhynie, 48 km east-northeast of Aberdeen. This site boasts eight remarkable carved Pictish standing stones, including the 'Craw Stone', thought to have stood at the centre-point of an elaborate fortified settlement. The name Rhynie derives from *rhynnoid* meaning 'a very royal place', possibly referring to a royal assembly site. Recent excavations to the south of Rhynie at Barflat have uncovered three fortified enclosures, symbolic of a triple sanctuary of the goddess.

There are many Iron Age hillforts around Rhynie including Tap o' Noth, the second-highest fort in Scotland, 2.4 km to the northwest. This oval-shaped enclosure is probably the most famous vitrified fort in Scotland and encloses an area of approximately 100 m by 30 m. Many believe that near here was the scene of the epic battle of Mons Graupius (Mountains of Grampian) that took place in 83–84 CE, the famous last stand between the Romans and the Picts and allegedly the biggest battle ever fought in Scotland. It is well known that the Romans desired Britain's mineral wealth, and close to the huge Pictish royal site was a valuable gold mine within the foothills of the Grampian Mountains.

Other sources place this battle at the vitrified Iron Age sanctuary of Dun Knock near Dunning just north of the beautiful Ochil Hills. Tacitus records the speech made by the great 'fair-haired' Pictish leader Calgacus, meaning 'swordsman', to his warriors as they prepared to do battle with the Romans:

> 'Shielded by nature, we are the men off the edge of the world, the last of the free. Britons are being sold in Roman slavery everyday .... When that happens there will be nothing left that we can call our own: neither farmland, nor mines, nor ports. Even our bravery will count against us, the imperialists dislike that sort of spirit in a subject people. Therefore as we cannot hope for mercy, we must take up arms for what we cherish most. We will be fighting for our freedom.'[10]

Perhaps the most renowned of the Pictish royal centres was Forteviot near Dunning in Perthshire, which according to Nick Aitchison in *Forteviot, A Pictish and Scottish Royal Centre* once stood within the Kingdom of Fortriu, which we first visited when following the male and female serpents through Scotland as part of our investigations of the Belinus Line. This region was reputedly the most powerful of the seven kingdoms of the legendary Alba, its earliest recorded king being King Bridei III, son of Bile (671–692 CE). Some Pictish kings were given the name Bridei, possibly deriving from the British goddess Bride. Recent excavations here have revealed a royal centre consisting of a palace, church, cemetery and assembly place, suggesting that it was a possible focus for ritual ceremony and agricultural production.[11]

Although Forteviot was the capital of South Pictland, which later became the capital of Scotland, many of the Pictish kings had no permanent place of residence. Instead, they would travel around their kingdom, probably sunwise (clockwise), visiting their various royal centres, including Castle Phadrig and Rhynie. Together with their entourage, the kings would engage in such pursuits as hunting expeditions, feasting and ceremonial festivals. This form of royal progress would enable them to exercise royal governance and maintain the king's authority over the land and its inhabitants.[12]

The formidable hillfort of Dunadd in Argyll, located at the southern end of Kilmartin Glen, became the inauguration kingship centre of the Dál Riada kings who settled there from Ireland. A footprint carved into the rock can still be seen at the summit of the fort as a reminder of the old ceremony of the kings symbolically marrying the land while standing on the stone. However, Dunadd, as a place of kingship, has a history dating back long before the Irish Scots, and with the presence of a Pictish carving of a boar symbolising sovereignty, this may well be an important ritual centre of the early Picts long ago.

Most historians place the Irish settlement of Argyll and the Western Isles around 500 CE, led by King Fergus Mór mac Eirc. Many believe that he took the Lia Fáil omphalos stone from Tara with him to use during his inauguration as the first Dál Riada king of Scotland. Eventually, the noble families of the Gaelic Scots intermarried with those of the Picts.

Having been displaced by the powerful Uí Néill clan from their native lands through war, there is no evidence that these new settlers ever fought with the Picts for their right to form their new kingdom in Argyll. Moreover, Scotland has always had close ties with her Irish Celtic neighbours, with many Picts having descended from earlier migrations of the Ulaid of Emain Macha. The earliest migration of the Dál Riada was thought to have taken place sometime in the 3rd century CE, which, according to recent archaeology, kept up the important trade links between the two countries when the Romans closed the doors to England.

There is only 19 km of sea between the western region of Kintyre in Scotland and the northeastern coast of Ireland, which was used as an easy and accessible trading route for thousands of years. The busiest ports between the two regions were further along the Kintyre peninsular at a place called Crinan, named after the Creones tribe who lived in the area in 140 CE. Its earlier name was Port Righ meaning 'King's Port', linked by the River Add to the great Iron Age rock fortress of Dunadd and the Neolithic 'valley of the kings' at Kilmartin. From there, traders could easily travel to the interior of Scotland, evidenced by the number of well-known trade routes that existed through the various valleys that converge at Kilmartin.

This open sea route between the Picts and the Scots and their strong coalition helped to fend off the might of the Roman army who failed to hold on to Pictish lands north of the Antonine Wall, which eventually led to the building of Hadrian's Wall around 122 CE. It also allowed the great Ulster warriors of Emain Macha to fight the elite Roman legions who had thus far been undefeated in their march through England and the Borders. Nevertheless, the Romans were masters of defence and avoided hand-to-hand combat if possible.

It was through the open seaports of Argyll that the later Irish Christian missionaries landed and attempted to convert the Picts, brokering their way towards the unification of the Scots, Picts and Britons under one Christian 'High King'. The Britons of Strathclyde in the Border regions and the Gododdin tribe from Lothian in the west were two Welsh-speaking P-Celtic groups that held territory sandwiched between the Antonine Wall and Hadrian's Wall. They were also kinsmen of the Picts descended from the same Brythonic-speaking Iron Age tribes.

The religion of the Picts focused upon a worship of the goddess inherent within the landscape, revering feminine-shaped hills and sacred wells. Their kings were chosen based upon matrilineal descent and would hold 'cosmic truths' through hereditary rights aided by their Druids. Out of the seven kingdoms of the Picts, Fotla is the only one that has a recognisable name of a goddess and typically forms the central province. Perhaps it had its own ancient place of assembly sacred to the matriarchal Picts, similar to Killare in Ireland beneath the Hill of Uisneach, the site of Brigid's Well and Temple and where Eriu, the great mother goddess of Ireland was honoured at the omphalos.

The Central Plain of Atholl

Interestingly, if you draw a line between Rhynie and Dunadd and another between Castle Phadrig and Forteviot, they cross very close to Blair Castle in the central province of Fotla or Atholl, one of the most visited historical sites in Scotland (see Fig. 9). In Scotland, the Belinus Line, Britain's longest ley line, passes through Pitlochry, the most central town in Scotland, and the grounds of Blair Castle.

Kenneth MacAlpin was the first king of the combined nation of the Picts and the Scots, ruling successfully over a period of 16 years between 843 and 858 CE. Most genealogies refer to his father as Alpin mac Eochaid (839– 841), a king of the Dál Riada, and his mother as Inuistice, a Pictish princess who gave birth to him at Kilmartin. Having proved himself against the Vikings, MacAlpin was considered the founding father of Scotland and was even compared to Alfred the Great of England. He would later move the Celtic church from Iona to Scone, bringing St Columba's relics to the Pictish church at Dunkeld in 849 CE.

MacAlpin's descendants became the Kings of Alba and by the 11th century spawned the longest-living royal family in Britain, which included Malcolm III of the House of Canmore, whose daughter Matilda married Henry I of England, and the Houses of Bruce and Stewart.

There is much debate over the fate of the Picts after this great takeover by the Scots. Having written much of their history, the later Latin scholars and Gaelic Scots allowed them to fade from our memory, renaming their lands and ignoring their oral traditions. McHardy suggests that such a great warrior society as the Picts, who over the centuries successfully fought off the Romans, Angles, Vikings and Danes to retain their freedom and independence, were unlikely to have relinquished their culture and lands lightly. Moreover, MacAlpin was first recorded as the King of the Picts of Fortriu and not of the Scots.

Soon after becoming King of the Picts and the Scots, MacAlpin may have sought the omphalos of this newly acquired territory, copying the tradition of his Irish ancestors in bringing cosmology and harmony to his land and people. He divided his new kingdom into four around a central fifth, which can be observed on old maps of Scotland during and after the reign of MacAlpin. Here we see the named provinces of North and South Pictland and the Dál Riada kingdom including the Outer Hebrides (Brides Isles) and the central province of Fotla – the change of name to Atholl did not appear until much later. Today, the region of Atholl is within the counties of Perth and Kinross, bordering in the south Breadalbane, derived from *Bràghad Albainn* meaning 'the upper part of Alba'.

Finding the exact geographical centre of Scotland is problematic due to the varying methods of calculating the middle of a country with so many outer islands. However, the mid-point according to Ordnance Survey, using the gravitational method, is Atholl Forest, 16 km west of Blair Castle estate and near a marker called the Wade Stone that stands at the side of the A9 in an isolated area of wilderness just south of Loch Garry. General Wade erected this monument in 1729 while constructing a military road to the Highlands, after which it was moved a short distance away with the building of the A9.

Using the boundary method and striking lines between the longest extreme land points in Scotland reveals some interesting results. The longest north-south line in Scotland is from the Mull of Galloway lighthouse to Duncansby Head near John o'Groats, at the extreme northwest point of mainland Scotland. Another boundary line links Gretna Green at the western end of the English Border to the most northerly point of mainland Scotland at Cape Wrath. The southeastern edge of the Scottish border near Berwick on Tweed is linked by another line to the extreme northwest point of the Outer Hebrides at Gallon Head on the Isle of Lewis. The longest east– west line is from Kinnaird Head, Aberdeen, to the southwest tip of the island of Islay at Portnahaven, as shown in Fig. 10.

Remarkably, if not miraculously, all these lines intersect at a point very close to the crossing of the lines that connect all four Pictish royal sites in Atholl, (see Fig. 9). The exact point of this crossing is Colrig Hill close to the Falls of Bruar, 3.8 km west of Blair Atholl. This hill is equidistant from the three extreme geographical points of mainland Scotland – Cape Wrath, Duncansby Head and the Mull of Galloway.

I also discovered that the main axis of Scotland from the Mull of Galloway to Duncansby Head connects with several important sacred sites as it travels through the old kingdom of Atholl, including the village of Fortingall, which has the oldest yew tree in Britain, a symbolic world tree, and the pyramid-shaped Mount Schiehallion representative of a world mountain. With no other sacred mountains within the vicinity of the intersection of the lines near Blair Atholl,

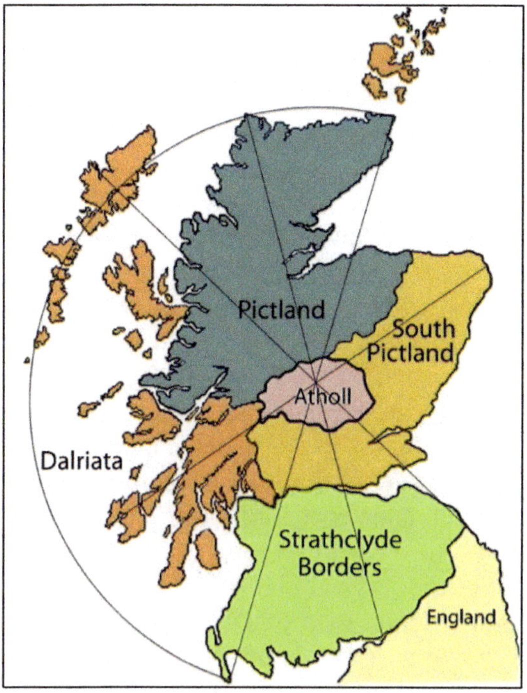

Figure 10. Scotland's Celtic Provinces and Boundary Lines.

Schiehallion, at only 17 km southwest, is the strongest contender for Scotland's 'world mountain'.

There are no sacred sites at the actual crossing point of the lines only the spectacular tumbling waters of the Falls of Bruar, and the modern House of Bruar, acknowledged as Scotland's most prestigious independent country clothing and food stores. However, within this massive tourist outlet centre was one place that fascinated us – a small museum displaying the story of Clan Donnachaidh, thought to be one of the oldest clans in Scotland. The family can trace its origins back to the old Celtic Earls of Atholl, including Abbot Crinan of Dunkeld (d. 1045), the father of King Duncan who was famously murdered by Macbeth.

The Clan Donnachaidh Museum also houses an unusual artefact of a magical nature. The clan, whose name means 'children of Duncan', originated from the joining of the Pictish and Scottish nobility of the kindred of St Columba and their chief clan name is Robertson. Displayed inside is a ball of rock crystal about 5 cm in diameter called the *Clach na Bratach*, considered to be the most precious of the clan's relics, originally brought to Scotland from the Orient.

This rock crystal ball was unearthed in 1315 when the chief's standard pole was pulled from the ground while on the march to Bannockburn. Believing this discovery to be a good omen, the stone was carried into battle within a cage at the top of the standard pole by every Robertson chief thereafter in the hope that it would secure victory over their enemies.

The Clach na Bratach, meaning 'stone of the standard' is said to have mystical powers and could conjure miracles such as the healing of people and animals – it could also imbue water with curative properties. It predicted the future, including the death of a Robertson clan chief. In 1715, Alexander Robertson of Strowan, also known as the Poet Chief, consulted the crystal before heading off to fight in the first Jacobite uprising. When the orb developed a large crack, it unsurprisingly filled the seer with dread, perhaps alerting him to the ill-fortune that he would later encounter during this ill-fated conflict with the British.

It is reminiscent of the 'crystal ball' used by wizards and witches in fairy tales and in particular by the evil wizard Saruman in J. R. R. Tolkien's *Lord of the Rings*. Outside of battle, the stone was kept in a silken purse made by the Countess of Breadalbane. In a letter dated 1702 from the Episcopalian minister in the Highlands, Revd John Fraser, he writes: 'There was a great many fine and precious stones among the Highlanders, many of which they hung about their necks of old, and kept in their standards, and attributed more virtue to them than Albertus Magnus did, and that was too much.'

Only three miles from the crossing of lines, on land suitable for an estate, is one of the grandest castles in Scotland built by the Earls of Atholl. This white stone fortress, next to the confluence of the Rivers Tilt and Garry, with the high mountains to the north and an open aspect to the south, is considered an auspicious or favourable place as regards the ancient Chinese principle of feng shui.

Our ancestors such as the Celtic Druids venerated such fortunate places, building their temples and places of worship close to them. The powerful force generated by the collision of two bodies of running water creates subtle energies the Chinese call 'chi', an unseen energy, like plasma, linking all things in the Universe, finer than the electromagnetic force of the Earth and beneficial to the wellbeing of nature. Indeed, some of our most powerful buildings such as cathedrals and royal palaces stand near the confluence of rivers.

Blair Castle is considered one of the grandest aristocratic seats in Scotland, where the Earls and Dukes of Atholl controlled the main route through the Highlands from medieval times. The Norman Earls of Atholl died out in the early 1300s, but King James II of Scotland reinstated the title in 1457, granting the earldom, the castle and estates to his half-brother Sir John Stewart of Balvenie. After the Fifth Earl died in 1595, his grandson John Murray inherited the title, his descendants becoming the Dukes of Atholl in 1703. Lord George Murray, sixth son of the First Duke of Atholl, commanded Bonnie Prince Charlie's army during the Jacobite Rebellion in 1746, Blair being the last besieged castle in the British Isles. Even today, the Dukes of Atholl still have power, like the old Irish high kings, and they are the only people in the whole of the United Kingdom allowed to raise a private army. Known as the Atholl Highlanders, they undertake largely social and ceremonial duties and primarily consist of workers on the extensive Atholl Estates.

The oldest part of Blair Castle dates from the 12th century, but only the small tower house called Comyn's Tower remains from this early period, constructed of extremely thick walls. Although the castle has been considerably altered over the years, much of what you see today is from the 16th century, the upper storey and battlements having been removed after the Jacobite Rebellion to render it indefensible. It was again restored to great heights during the 19th century and holds some of the finest collections of furniture,

Blair Castle

paintings, historical relics, weapons and hunting trophies in Scotland. The castle's extensive grounds and gardens designed by various family members over the centuries are open to the public.

The Scottish Goddess Bride

We first visited Blair Castle in the summer of 2011 while following the female dragon energy associated with the Belinus Line, which flows through the grounds. We noticed that the design of the gardens incorporated the worship of the old gods and goddesses, including Hercules and Diana, and a ruined church (kirk) dedicated to St Bride is tucked away on a mound predating the castle.

The presence of the Celtic goddess Bride or Brigid is an indication of this site's great antiquity, the church perhaps standing on a former prehistoric burial ground later used by the Earls and Dukes of Atholl. According to various books on local history, there is a tradition that Adomnan of Iona built the first church here, along with several others in the neighbourhood. He was the biographer of St Columba whose relics were housed at Dunkeld, a few miles south of here.

The earliest records of a church here date to 1275, when it contributed tithes or taxes to help fund the crusades. According to legend, the angered spirits of this church nearly caused the death of Angus Og, son of John McDonald II, Lord of Islay, after he attacked

St Bride's Kirk, Blair Castle

and damaged this holy site in 1475. Having experienced the near loss of his ship during a freak storm on his trip home to Islay, he immediately returned to St Bride's to compensate for the damage, seeing the storm as some divine retribution.

The church, set high above the Banvie Burn, is located close to the hamlet of Old Blair, and served both the local congregation and the Norman landowners, the Lords of Badenoch. They were the first to build a tower here and later took the title Earl of Atholl. As well as the sacred burial ground of the Atholls, St Bride's Kirk is the last resting place of the infamous Jacobite John Graham Claverhouse, who died during the Battle of Killiecrankie in 1689.

Many historians believe that the church's location on a mound and its dedication could indicate an early Celtic Christian site. Perhaps, for this reason, the Celtic Dál Riada settlers of Atholl under MacAlpin may have chosen this place to build a shrine to their native Irish goddess on the closest piece of level ground to the exact centre of Scotland.

Typically, the restored church has much older stones incorporated into its foundations, including a large megalith placed in the footings of the north wall, and a cup-marked stone, perhaps further evidence of this site's former importance as a place of pagan worship. In Ireland, many cup-marked stones at prehistoric sanctuaries held the magical powers of a pagan deity. Some of them contained within the circular cavity a smooth rounded or oval quartz pebble, which when turned frequently would create these hollowed-out marks. One such stone is known as the Ballaun Stone, located at Killinagh Church near Blacklion in Co Fermanagh in Northern Ireland, said to have been the site of a 6th-century place of worship founded by St Brigid.

According to folklore, the original and more ancient purpose of these stones was for ritual ceremonial use during certain times of the year such as Imbolc and Beltane. Quartz stones ground sunwise into such a boulder may have had a positive and curative effect on the landscape to help with the fertility and wellbeing of the land. At the Irish omphalos, the goddess Bride had a place of honour beneath the Hill of Uisneach and here at the Scottish omphalos there is evidence that the worship of Bride took place on lands later incorporated into the Blair Atholl Estate.

We also discovered a local legend that mentions miracles associated with relics of the Irish St Bridget once housed in the church. However, many religious houses claimed to have artefacts belonging to famous saints, often with the ability to heal certain health conditions, which drew pilgrims and their purses, from miles around.

Nonetheless, even if this remote church at Blair Castle exaggerated its claim of owning the Irish saint's relics in an attempt to draw pilgrims, it may hint at the fact that this place was indeed a cult centre of Bride.

The early Picts revered the mother goddess at another of their sacred cult centres at Abernethy, just south of Perth on the borders of Atholl. A 6th-century church, built on lands given by Pictish King Nechtan-Mor, later became the site of a 13th-century monastery dedicated to St Brigid of Kildare, and from here her cult reputedly spread throughout Scotland. The seal of St Bridget's Kirk bears an image of the saint holding a pastoral staff with the emblem of the cow. There is also an Irish-styled round tower next to the church, one of only three ever built in Scotland.

Before continuing further into the grounds of Blair Castle, we placed an Iona green stone at the site of the old high altar in honour of Scotland's mother goddess, seeing its power and healing light radiating across the landscape. Very close to Bride's sanctuary stands one of the tallest trees in Britain, a giant redwood on a mound called Mount Strange. The unusual name commemorates James Murray, the Second Duke of Atholl in celebration of taking his seat in parliament in 1737. As the maternal grandson of James Stanley, Seventh Earl of Derby, Murray inherited the mysterious Barony of Strange and the sovereignty of the Isle of Man, an island that incidentally marks the very centre of the combined lands of the British Isles and Ireland.

Cup-marked stone, St Bride's Kirk, Blair Atholl

Such a position as this, with the Duke presiding over two ancient and powerful 'navels', would have made him hugely influential within royal and political circles at the time. His son John, the Third Duke of Atholl, became Grand Master of the Ancient Grand Lodge of England from 1771 until 1774, and Grand Master of the Grand Lodge of Scotland from 1773 to 1774.

So here at the cult centre of Bride in the middle province of Atholl, we have a representation of the world tree on a sacred mound constructed by a powerful duke who was also King of the Isle of Man, the omphalos of the Britain Isles and Ireland.

We then walked a short distance through the woods and encountered a most unusual site, the statue of the goddess Diana within a grove of giant redwoods. The Second Duke of Atholl laid out the grove in the same year as Mount Strange.

Both the statue and the church stand on the flow of the feminine serpent energy current Elen that weaves around the Belinus alignment. She accompanies her male counterpart from the Isle of Wight, similar to the Michael and Mary serpent lines dowsed by Hamish Miller along the St Michael Line. Diana as the goddess of the hunt is associated with animals and woodland, often worshipped in oak groves. She is also a moon goddess, representing the preservation of man through childbirth and is often seen as active in securing the succession of kings.

The Second Duke also created within the grounds the 3.6-ha walled Hercules Garden between 1747 and 1760, which was restored in 1996. A statue of the Greek-Romano god Hercules stands majestically overlooking the garden, having originally been set on a hill overlooking the main western entrance of the castle. Perhaps the Second Duke wished to epitomise this mythical brave and mighty warrior, who defeated many beasts. Alternatively, he may have been alluding to the legendary origins of his illustrious bloodline from Melkart Hercules, the first Phoenician King of Tyre, who defeated Albion to become ruler of Britain. According to Raphael Holinshed's *Chronicles of England, Scotland and Ireland* (a collection of manuscripts and Bardic traditions from around the country during the Tudor and Elizabethan periods), after the Biblical Flood, Hercules took this western realm from a colony of giants in Britain, then known as Albion.[13]

During a tour of the interior of the castle, portraits of the various members of this family certainly allude to an illustrious bloodline, many of them wielding immense power for centuries in both England and Scotland, influencing the decisions of kings and their parliaments. Did the situation of their castle and lands at the very centre of Scotland aid their extraordinary rise to power?

We later discovered that St Bride's Kirk stands by one of the oldest roads through Scotland from Perth to Inverness, formerly called the 'Old North Road', later repaired by General Wade in the early 1770s. Long before Wade created this great feat of engineering, ancient tracks met at the castle, as indicated by William Roy's 1747–1755 Military Survey map. However, as we were soon to discover, there is another ancient crossroads now forgotten within the centre district of Atholl a little south of here.

Pitlochry and Moulin

Just five miles south of Blair Castle is Pitlochry, officially referred to as the most central town in Scotland. Its name alludes to a much earlier settlement derived from the curious name *Pit-clochaire* meaning 'place by the sentinel stone'. This busy tourist resort by the Tummel River soon thrived after the building of the railway in 1863, bringing visitors from all over England and mainland Europe.

We were curious to see whether this sentinel stone may be some sort of omphalos stone, so we ventured into the town in search of information. In *Pitlochry: A History*, Colin Liddell mentions that the place of the sentinel stone was associated with a lookout point of the Picts that later became a Roman encampment. Unfortunately, the stone was blasted to make way for the large Victorian house that now stands on the site called *Tigh Na Cloichlt* or 'house of the sentinel stone'. Thankfully there are numerous megalithic standing stones in the area that survived destruction and many are set in groups of four known as 'Four Posters'. Probably the most impressive were the *Clachan an diridh* or 'stones of the ascent' that once stood as a prominent feature on open moorland south of Pitlochry. Long ago, locals would annually process to this site at Beltane to walk sunwise or clockwise around the stones.[14]

Liddell also mentioned a significant historical place called Moulin that existed long before the Victorians built Pitlochry for tourists, just under a kilometre away. Moulin is centred on an old crossroads of various routes to the Highlands and coasts of Scotland. This now quiet and picturesque village with its old stone cottages and popular 17th-century inn was built over the site of a former Pictish royal fort, thought to be the capital of Atholl or Fotla long before Blair Castle. Here we seemed to be homing in on the true omphalos of Scotland with an important royal centre and historical crossroads within the ancient landscape of Fotla.

Before General Wade built his road through here, the Old North Road connected Dunkeld in the south to Blair Atholl and Kingussie in the north and beyond. Another route through Moulin linked Glen Lyon, Aberfeldy and Strathtay in the west with Kirkmichael, Glen Brerachan and Glen Shee to the east. Liddell shows an old map of Moulin with many roads converging on its centre. This was a highly populated area before the Highland Clearances transformed its landscape into grouse moors and deer forests. The life of the clansman was changed forever, with many of the chieftains being forced to sell their land to the southern gentry.

The Pict's royal fort had great defences consisting of a double circle of outlying hillforts indicating the importance of this settlement, perhaps built to guard the sacred omphalos of the Pictish nation. Many believe Moulin is the ancient settlement of 'Lindum' shown on the north bank of the Tay on Ptolemy's Map of the World of 145 CE. Lindum is Latin for 'fort by the pool', which is similar to the translation of the name Moulin being 'place by the pool'. However, John H. Dixon in *Pitlochry Past and Present* writes that the name may derive from Maoil-inn or 'rounded hill or eminence', referring to Baledmund Hill to the northeast.[15]

Next to the crossroads is Moulin's old church, constructed in 1875, now a Heritage Centre. However, the site is much older and, judging from its circular-shaped churchyard, it may have been the site of a sacred ceremonial enclosure of the Picts. According to local legend, a Pictish chief invited St Colm to establish a church within his fort, although other sources argue that this name referred to St Columba or St Colman of Kilroot, who came to Moulin in 490 CE. However, a market held here on 18 February commemorated St Colm's feast day, called locally *Feill-ma-Chalmaig* meaning 'market of the Blessed Colm'. Several churches were built on this site, two having been destroyed by fire.

St Colm's Church was originally sited on the northern boundaries of the lake or pool, from which Moulin takes its name. This watery expanse that once surrounded this peninsular would have acted as a natural defence for the Pictish fort. In the churchyard are remains of crusader grave slabs, said to be Knights of St John, and a 9-m-tall ash tree, or world tree in Scandinavian lore, revered by the locals as an ancient place of meeting, similar to the symbolic centre at Whitendale near Dunsop Bridge, another important geographical navel. Unfortunately, due to health and safety rules, the council reduced this tree, which had survived the Jacobite wars, to an unsightly stump in 2007.

In 1180, the Earls of Atholl granted the lands and church to Dunfermline Abbey. During the time of Robert the Bruce, it was handed to his faithful brother-in-law Sir Neil Campbell of Lochee.

St Colm's Church, Moulin

His son John succeeded to the Earldom of Atholl and around 1326 built a castle called *Caisteal Dubh* or 'Black Castle' on the site of a crannog (artificial island) in the pool. In a field behind the inn next to the Old North Road is a solitary megalith called the Dane Stane, which some believe was part of a stone circle. According to folklore, this was the site of St Colm's market, encircled by a moat. Each time two farmers struck a deal they clasped hands over the stone.

The *Northern Antiquarian* website refers to a story regarding the present farmer. Apparently, in his grandfather's day, several more stones stood in this field and those saved from demolition are still lying half-buried in the field.[16] Another megalith called the Balnakeilly Stone stands nearby just off the old east road a few metres from the church, set among pine trees next to the entrance to Balnakeilly Estate, once owned by the Stewart family.

With the old ash or world tree now violated, we felt drawn to an elegant copper beech standing at the heart of the village in Moulin Square, placed there to commemorate Queen Elizabeth II's coronation. Here we left one of our precious stones from Iona to honour this old centre of Scotland. Today, no holy well exists at Moulin and despite extensive research, no records remain of its possible whereabouts. However, the inn has now created a micro-brewery from an older brewery, which must have drawn its water from a well.

However, the gentleman manning the Heritage Centre informed us of a holy well less than a kilometre away in Pitlochry, next to where Toberargan Road meets Well Brae opposite a guest house called the Well House. After saying a blessing, we dropped a sacred stone into the well's stone-lined trough, connecting with the water as it continued to trickle forth.

Where the old east-west road from Glen Lyon and Strathtay crosses the River Tummel at the southern end of Pitlochry, in an area once known as Fonab, there existed next to a large outcrop of rock a famous healing well dedicated to St Bride. Here, a passenger ferry would cross the river, now replaced by a suspension bridge. The well had a reputation for aiding cases of lung disease but was filled in at the end of the 19th century when waste began to percolate into it from the nearby sewage treatment plant. This sad loss is typical of the ignorance and lack of respect given to sacred waters during Victorian times.[17]

Traditional Centres of Scotland

Ordnance Survey stone marking the centre of Scotland, Atholl Forest.

According to locals, there are a few places regarded as the Centre of Scotland in the Atholl area. The Macpherson Monument, located high up on Glen Truim Road between the A9 and Catlodge has magnificent views of Creag Dhubh to the north and Upper Strathspey in the west. The monument takes the form of a cairn commemorating the life of Ewan Macpherson of Cluny, chief of the clan from 1746 to 1764. It is made up of local stones contributed by members of Clan Macpherson from around the world.

A short walk from the monument the OS erected a large impressive striped stone at 57°01'12.5"N 4°10'42.0"W with a plaque to mark their calculated centre-point of Scotland, being the most distant point from the North Sea and the Atlantic Ocean. The stone replaced an earlier plaque that was stolen nearby, much to the locals' dismay, who organised a replacement in 2015. In 2017, a tourist decided to chip off a piece of the stone as a souvenir, but when they tried to leave, they found their car had a flat battery. Curiously both the passer-by who stopped to help and the rescue truck that was summoned suffered breakdowns of their own. Even more intriguing is that all three vehicles refused to work until the piece of stone was returned.

A few metres to the east of here is a cross carved into one of the stones of a dry-stone wall said to mark the true centre of Scotland. Recent stories on a local website refer to its power, 'Many years ago, a drunken couple walking home stopped for a romantic midnight rendezvous at the dry-stone wall, at the exact point where the marker stone was. The resulting child grew up to become a famous strongman. More recently, in 2021, two separate couples eloped at the stone, and they've since produced triplets and quadruplets.'[18]

The narrow road alongside the stone was originally built in the early 1700s by General Wade connecting Fort Augustus with Ruthven Barracks in nearby Kingussie. Wade's roads were constructed in an attempt by the British Government to bring order to the wilder parts of Scotland after the Jacobite Rebellion of 1715. This place is mentioned in many guidebooks as 'The Heart of the Highlands'.

Another possible omphalos marker, just south of Blair Castle beyond Killiecrankie near Glen Garry Bridge, is a 19th-century house called Tigh-na-Geat, formerly Tigh-na-teud meaning 'house of the harp string'. This curious name evolved from a local story concerning Mary Queen of Scots, who while passing through here one day on her way to Blair Castle, stopped to replace a damaged harp string. The owner, who was also a ferryman, just happened to be a harp player and offered to repair her instrument.[19]

Continuing further south to Pitlochry we find another locally known centre of Scotland in the private garden of a row of cottages called Green Gates, in the guise of a small circle of seven stones with a diameter of approximately 6.5 m. A report of the 1908 excavation from the *Proceedings of the Society of Antiquities* states:

'In a narrow strip of ground between the Highland Railway on the east and the great main road to the north on the west, is a garden, shielded from observation by a tall hedge on the roadside, and in it there are yet standing in situ the seven stones of this Circle. Never, surely, was the pre-historic past brought so closely into contact with the steam power and motor traffic of the twentieth century. In addition to these more or less disturbing conditions, we are told that, during the most recent government survey, the men of the theodolite arrived at the conclusion that this little circle is really the centre of Scotland.'[20]

Green Gates stone circle, Pitlochry.

Residents of the town of Aberfeldy also refer to certain stones on the hillside above as marking the Centre of Scotland, including one that sits in a local's front garden. Many of these sites lie remarkably close to the Belinus Line, which we discovered links many old middle places of England and Scotland, like an axis mundi. These sites include Meon Hill in Warwickshire near Stratford-upon-Avon, located at the very heart of England. The tiny village of Wall in Staffordshire was once a very important centre of the Druids, located where ancient tracks meet at the centre of the combined nation of England and Wales.

Also on the line is the small Lancashire town of Whalley, which according to OS marks the exact centre of Britain when surveyed without its outer islands. In addition, Middle Knoll in the Forest of Bowland, just north of the tiny village of Dunsop Bridge, is the nearest natural feature to the exact centre of Britain if you include her offshore islands. Shap in Cumbria marks the very centre of the Belinus alignment, once the site of a serpent temple, similar to the prehistoric complex at Avebury before it was almost destroyed by dynamite (see Fig. 2). It also passes through Inverness, the capital of the Highlands, and Lairg, the centre of Sutherland.[21]

Dunkeld, the Royal City

Dunkeld Cathedral by Frank Zweers

To the south of the Old North Road, still within the central province of Atholl, is the picturesque town of Dunkeld beside the River Tay. It was once an important strategic place for the Picts and the site of one of Scotland's most important religious settlements. Here, the High King Kenneth MacAlpin built a monastery on the site of a 6th-century Culdee church, establishing the first ecclesiastical capital of medieval Scotland. Like the central religious complex of Clonmacnoise, it grew in status as one of the most important places of pilgrimage in northern Britain, attracting Christian missionaries such as St Ninian, the mainspring of the northern Celtic church before St Patrick and St Columba.

Early historians describe Dunkeld as the gateway to the Highlands, a frontier town with only mountains and wilderness beyond. The Pictish Kings of Fortriu built a fort here overlooking an important northern trading route where the Rivers Braan and the powerful Tay meet. The Picts controlled this area when the Romans arrived in 84 CE under the command of Agricola. Having penetrated the Tay Valley, they built a camp next to the river, 9.7 km south of Dunkeld at Inchtuthill, their last and most northerly outpost in Britain. The Latin invaders called the tribes here Caledonii meaning 'cunning people', who may have eventually been their undoing, as they never successfully captured many of the strategic Pictish strongholds.

Dunkeld derives its name from two ancient British words: *Dun* and *kaled* meaning 'the stronghold of the rough, mountainous country called Caledonia'. Another source derives it from *Dun Chuildich* or 'stronghold of the Culdees'.

A Culdee Collegiate College is said to have existed in the vicinity around 570 CE. Adomnan of Iona records that St Fintan, a disciple of

St Columba, built a *Muintir Kailli-an-Find* at Dunkeld, meaning 'monastery of St Fintan among the Caledonians'. A Muintir is a family of twelve monks who created a college of education, which produced and copied ancient manuscripts. Each monk was assigned his own circular beehive dwelling constructed of wattle, twigs and mud-plastered walls, very similar to the Culdee community at Glastonbury in Somerset.[22]

MacAlpin enlarged the early church into a monastery to house the relics of St Columba and the Stone of Destiny, the inauguration stone of Irish kings, moved here after the Vikings sacked the Isle of Iona. St Columba was considered 'an indispensable talisman of Gaelic success' and twenty-four of the saint's miracles were said to have been painted over the high altar of the monastery.[23] Legend tells us that St Columba resided at Dunkeld for some time, teaching and preaching to the people of the district who came in great numbers to hear his 'godlie instructions.'[24]

Some sources believe that St Ninian and a contemporary of St Columba called St Colm were the earliest missionaries to the Tay Valley. There was a chapel dedicated to St Ninian in the town and a well on its outskirts dedicated to St Colm. The sacred church of Dunkeld continued as a significant religious centre for hundreds of years, attracting constant strife, particularly from the Danes, who raided the area in the 10th and 11th centuries, plundering the monastery of all its precious relics.

In 1114, King David I of Scotland reorganised the bishoprics in Scotland and appointed a bishop to Dunkeld, building a new cathedral over the site of the monastery. To the northwest of the cathedral stands a long mound called Stanley Hill – its three terraces were created around 1730 by James Murray, the Second Duke of Atholl. This unusual tree-covered sculptured eminence was earlier known as Shiochie Hill and, according to some authorities, was the original sacred seat of Pictish royalty up until 843 CE. Some sources believe this hill or elongated mound may be the Dun or stronghold of the Caledonians from which Dunkeld receives its name.[25] However, without any archaeological evidence as to its origins there is little to suggest that this mound was anything more than a natural geological feature.

Nevertheless, we noticed as we approached the mound the full extent of its steep banks, which seemed reminiscent of a giant Neolithic long barrow. Perhaps it marked an important burial and ceremonial place of kingship for the early Picts, which became MacAlpin's royal residence and religious centre.

Recent excavations revealed that the site was once a very important centre of Pictish power and 'occupied by an elite community who controlled craftwork production and had trade links with continental Europe in the 7th to 9th centuries AD.' Also uncovered was a large mound situated at the highest point of the hill adjacent to a large glacial erratic boulder together with postholes and stones and a low wall enclosing a small upper citadel surrounded by a series of three or four ramparts.[26]

St Colm's Well lies just to the northeast of Dunkeld below the steep banks of a commanding spot set high above the Tay called the King's Seat. The hillfort on the summit has natural rock-faces, precipices and four defensive ramparts, and according to some

Stanley Hill, Dunkeld

sources has traces of an inner walled enclosure, now overrun with rhododendrons. This site may have existed during a time when Dunkeld held a significant position in the early history of Scotland, as a vital stronghold of the Iron Age tribes next to a powerful spring.

The spring is set into a moss-covered rocky escarpment secreted away by nature, the mid-morning sun illuminating the water as it gushes out of the womb-like opening of a dry-stone well house.

It may have existed here over thousands of years but its dedication to St Colm provides us with the only vestige of his presence in Dunkeld, the possible founder of one of the most important early Christian centres in Scotland.

Glen Lyon, the Valley of Lugh and the Earth Goddess

The valley of Glen Lyon is one of the most ancient routes through Scotland, passing south of Mount Schiehallion, and north of Loch Tay. Sir Walter Scott described the valley as the 'longest, loneliest and loveliest glen in Scotland.'[27]

Its Gaelic name, *An Crom Ghleann*, means 'bent glen' and runs for 54 km from the village of Fortingall in the east to Loch Lyon in the west. Some sources say that Glen Lyon is a corruption from the Gaelic *lithe* meaning 'flood', which happens frequently in this valley. The remote Loch Lyon and Loch an Daimh, lie in the wild upper reaches of the glen where hauntingly beautiful remnants of the ancient Caledonian Forest are still visible. Duncan Campbell wrote in 1886:

> 'The hills, rising nearly perpendicular from the bed of the river, give the whole glen its individuality of character; but the surface changes continually from bare rocks to verdant green from woods and purple heath to the rich pasture of the braes, in summer almost white, from the large intermixture of white bed-straw (Galium sexatile) and eye-bright. The patches of arable ground, formed upon the debris washed down by mountain streams, are very fertile, but slow in ripening, as in most places the mountain tops intercept the kindly sunbeams. In some places, indeed, the sun is not seen for upwards of two months.'[28]

Before the English destroyed the life of the Highlanders after the Battle of Culloden in 1746, over 2000 people inhabited the Glen, but today there are fewer than a hundred. The many ancient standing stones, circles and earthen mounds on either side of the river are a testament to the importance given to this Glen in prehistoric times. The early Celtic Christian missionaries came to the valley as early as the 6th century, establishing monastic sites at Dull, Fearnan and Fortingall. It was also the home of the infamous Robert Campbell, Fifth Laird of Glenlyon (1630–1696) of Meggernie Castle, one of the commanding officers responsible for the Glen Coe massacre in 1692. Robert died in disgrace, but his son Iain spent much of his life restoring the family's fortunes, which included the request for the return of the famous *Clach-Buadha* or 'Stone of Victory', now in the possession of the Earls of Breadalbanes of Glenorchy. He believed that its removal from the family home years before had cursed his family, bringing about his father's downfall.[29]

According to another source, the original name of the Glen was *Gleann Lìomhann*, which translates as 'valley of Lugh', after the sun god of Celtic mythology. Philip Coppens, in his article *Glen Lyon: the valley of the Sun God*, believes that the ancient people of this area venerated the old Celtic deities here, 'from the sun god Lugh to the Creator Goddess the Cailleach.'[30]

While the sun god resided at Glen Lyon, the Cailleach's abode was beyond Loch Lyon in Gleann Cailliche. According to folklore, this great goddess had powers to create and destroy akin to the giants of folklore, raising mountains, seas and storms. There is an unusual stone monument to her in the Glen called 'Tigh na Cailliche' or the 'House of the Cailleach'. The site is unique in that it is the oldest and ritually uninterrupted pagan shrine to survive in Britain. The Cailleach was known to only frequent this remote abode from Beltane to Halloween, the Celtic festivals that mark the beginning and end of summer.

Campbell also notes the Glen's numerous traditions associated with the 'Fingalians' led by the warrior hero Fingal. One pertains to a chain of twelve round towers that once existed along the valley called locally *Caistealan nam Fiann* or 'castles of the Fingalians': 'There are five of them at the place called Cashlie (castles), each bearing the name of a known Fingalian chief.' Fingal may also be the legendary Finn MacCool, who has many parallels with the Celtic King Arthur. Stories of Finn and his band of nine warriors known as the Fianna originate in the 3rd century BCE, and probably arrived here with the Irish Scots in the 6th century.[31]

The small village of Fortingall, its name meaning 'stronghold of the Gallic', boasts the oldest living tree in Europe, a massive yew said to be 5000 years old. The tree has been a focus of cult practices since the Iron Age and perhaps even earlier and stands next to the site of an early Christian church dedicated to Coeddi or Cedd, Bishop of Iona (d. 702 CE). Coppens writes that 'the tree is also known as the "Tree of the Resurrection", as the yew begins to "live again" after five hundred years. The present Fortingall Church probably marks an original pagan sanctuary – in which the yew may have played an important role.'[32] Perhaps it was a place where the ancient gods and goddesses were honoured. There is also a local tradition that the yew tree marks the centre of Scotland.

Coppens also mentioned that a church dedicated to St Bran once stood here called *Cille Bhrain,* and later rededicated to St Cedd.[33] In Celtic mythology, Bran is the son of the sea god Lyr, and his brother Manawyddan was Lord and Protector of the Isle of Man. His

The Fortingall yew

grandfather was the sun god Belenos. Bran was also a name given to a Welsh king, father of the great hero warrior King Caractacus (Caradoc), who fought so valiantly against the Roman invasion for the liberty and freedom of the last of the old British tribes in Wales.

Bran was said to be the last Arch Druid of Britain and, according to Barry Dunford in *The Holy Land of Scotland*, married the sister of the Caledonian King Metallanus (d. 35 CE), who resided at a hillfort called Dun Gael (the White Fort), at Fortingall. An oral tradition of the area states that he was uncle to Pontius Pilate, who was born at Fortingall.[34]

The Scottish Chronicles record that King Metallanus had strong ties with the Romans, who at the time were mining the area for iron. Another relative of the king, Mensuteus or Mansuteus, founded a monastic site here during the 1st century CE.[35] Dunford mentions *Achnahanait* as a place name in Glen Lyon, meaning 'field of the Mother Church'. He writes that 'this "Mother Church" was a pre-apostolic Church of Christ established by Druidical Essenes before the birth of Yeshua/Jesus.'[36]

However, as mentioned by Coppens, Glen Lyon and Fortingall in particular were already considered sacred to the prehistoric pagan peoples of this area. The presence of several stone circles and standing stones in the valley and oral traditions of the worship of the sun god Lugh and the mother goddess Cailleach indicate that this heartland of Caledonia was once an important sacred sanctuary that attracted the earliest apostles of Gnostic religion from the Holy Land.

Historically, like the ancient An Slí Mhór or Esker Riada in Ireland, Glen Lyon was an important east-west trading and pilgrim route through Scotland, which possibly explains its many fascinating tales and old legends. To the west, it runs into several valleys that allow access to Loch Awe, Kilmartin Glen, the Western Isles and onwards to Ireland. To the east, the ancient road enters the Tay Valley at Dull, passing through Strathtay near Grandtully and over Fonab Hill to a fording of the River Tummel at the old Pitlochry recreation ground. From here, the road travelled a short distance east to the village of Moulin, where it formed a crossroads with the Old North Road, now the A9 to Inverness. The little village of Dull, east of Fortingall, also has associations with a possible omphalos stone.

The Stones of Destiny, Jacob's Pillar and the Benben

Humanity has been fascinated by magical stones throughout the ages and three of them are said to have found their way to Scotland – the Stone of Destiny, Jacob's Pillar and a meteoritic black stone of the ancient Egyptians.

One of the precious relics brought from Iona to Dunkeld by Kenneth MacAlpin, the new King of the Scots and Picts, was the royal coronation stone or the Lia Fáil (stone of Fate). The Dál Riada originally took the famous stone from Tara when they created their new kingdom in Argyll 300 years before. It later became known as the 'Stone of Scone' or the 'Stone of Destiny'. During the 1990s, I carried out extensive research on this mysterious stone and gave some lectures on the subject in the south of England. It was my fascination for this relic that led me to accept an invitation to see the allegedly 'real' Stone of Destiny held by the Knights Templar in Scotland, close to the central mountain Schiehallion.

During my first visit to the navel of Ireland at Uisneach three decades ago, a local guide pointed to a mound, said to be the original location of the Stone of Destiny, when it was the inauguration stone of the ancient High Kings of Ireland. Symbolically, this stone represented the navel or point of connection between the higher and lower worlds, similar to the renowned omphalos stones mentioned in Chapter 1. The stone is said to have been one of the four treasures brought to Ireland by the Tuatha Dé Danann from an unknown realm, which they erected on the Hill of Uisneach as their coronation stone. It later disappeared, possibly taken by the invading Milesians to their new kingship centre at Tara, or hidden by the defeated Tuatha Dé Danann. Around the beginning of the 6th century, a colony of Irish migrants transported the stone to Scotland, where it became the coronation stone of the Argyll Dál Riada Scots. It would later be the inauguration stone of the High Kings of Scotland at Scone Abbey.

In 1526, Scottish historian Hector Boece called it the 'Stone of Fate', invested with a *mana* or magical power.[37] Others have described it as imbued with the spirit of the ancestors, the newly appointed king receiving the luck or mana from his predecessors through having direct contact with it.[38] When Edward I of England (1272–1307) fought the Scots, he knew the stone at Scone was a powerful symbol of the Scottish nation, and after defeating the Scottish army at Dunbar, he stripped John Balliol of his crown and took the stone to Westminster Abbey.

My favourite version of the stone's history involves the followers of Egyptian princess Scota and her husband Gaythelos, an Amarna royal prince, who brought this stone with them during their long migrations from Egypt to Spain, eventually settling in Ireland around 1350 BCE. This fascinating story says that Gaythelos was a Phoenician or Milesian who fought many successful battles for the Pharaoh, who rewarded him with the hand of one of his daughters in marriage.

Some researchers say that Scota's real name was Meritaten, the eldest daughter of the Egyptian Pharaoh Akhenaten (*c.* 1352–1337 BCE), a heretical king of the 18th dynasty. His mission was to defy the existing worship of a pantheon of gods under Amun by establishing the worship of one god called Aten.[39]

This revolutionary Pharaoh, for want of peace and harmony for his nation, disbanded the Egyptian army and built a great royal city at Tel el Amarna, a remote virgin site, and named it Akhetaton. Incidentally, its situation was exactly halfway between the city of Alexandria in the north and Philae at the edge of the southern border, making it the omphalos of the Upper and Lower Kingdoms of Egypt (see Fig. 11). The city stood on the east bank of the Nile, facing the sunset and laid out to geomantic proportions along a north-south 'royal road', now referred to as 'Sikhet es-Sultan'. The royal residences were to the

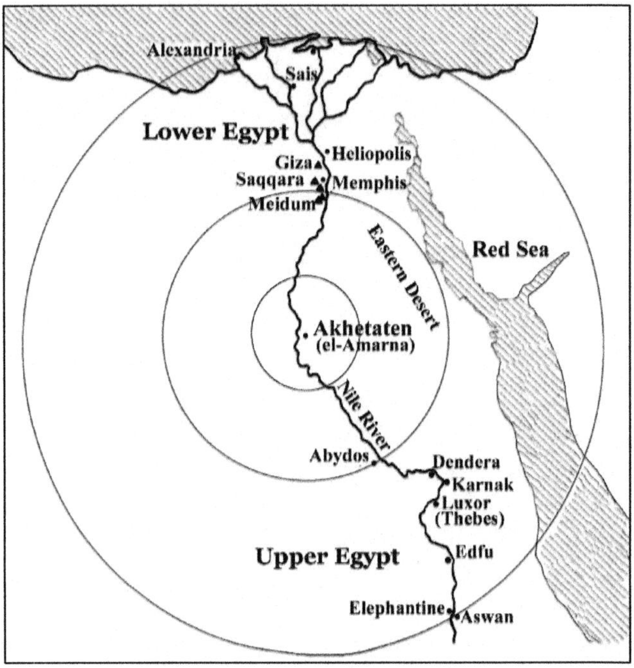

Figure 11. Akhenaten's royal city Akhetaton, marking the omphalos of the Upper and Lower Kingdoms of Egypt

north of the city, the political and religious ceremonial area being placed at the centre, and the residential suburbs constructed in the south.

The geomantic design of the royal city at Tel el Amarna with its north-south 'royal road' has remarkable parallels with the early cities of the Indus Valley culture and the ancient Etruscans, Romans and Greeks, where the streets were laid out around a centre. The name Akhetaton derives from the city's location, meaning 'horizon of Aten', the choice of site having been directly linked to the worship of the sun in the form of the god Aten.

While excavating the ruins of Akhetaton, the archaeologist Cyril Aldred made a remarkable discovery. He observed a saddleback indentation or notch in the western hills that marked the setting sun at the equinox. Aldred believed that this symbolically matched the hieroglyph for 'horizon'.[40] It would seem therefore that Akhenaten deliberately built a city at the centre of the Upper and Lower Kingdoms, exactly where the sun marks the halfway point of its progression through a solar year. For the pharaoh and his people, this must have seemed a very sacred sanctuary of the god Aten, reflecting the same ceremonial practices as the earlier megalithic cultures of northern Europe. However, disastrous plagues soon beset Egypt, which the vengeful priests of Amun at Heliopolis, today a district of Cairo, believed was the result of Akhenaten angering the gods. Soon they set about his downfall, destroying his exciting revolutionary new city of culture and art. Princess Scota escaped with Gaythelos, supposedly taking with them a black marble stone, possibly the Aten stone kept in the holy of holies in the main temple. They migrated by boat through the Mediterranean Sea and eventually settled in Spain. After constant attacks by the local tribes, they decided to seek out new lands, finally arriving on the shores of Ireland.

Having defeated the Tuatha Dé Danann, they placed their marble stone on the sacred Hill of Tara, the royal centre in West Meath, where they inaugurated their future kings, similar to the story of the invading Milesians. A descendant of Gaythelos and Scota was thought to be King Fergus Mór mac Eirc, who settled in the Western Isles of Scotland around 500 CE. Mac Eirc reputedly took this precious stone of Tara with him for his inauguration as the first king of the Dál Riada at Dunadd.

Before the 3rd century CE, there was a strong belief that the Scottish nation took its name from princess Scota. The Venerable Bede claimed that Ireland was known as Scotia Major and Scotland as Scotia Minor.[41] Interestingly, there is a flat stone lying on the coast at a place called Scodaig (Scotaig) near Crinan, the port nearest to the old Pictish fort of Dunadd and the gateway to the prehistoric complex at Kilmartin. It is here, legend says, that Scota landed, her horse having made the hoofprint-shaped depressions on the surface of this stone.[42]

However, the story of Scota mentions that the sacred stone of Aten carried by her followers was made of black metallic stone and carved with hieroglyphs, not the rough Perthshire sandstone from which the Stone of Destiny/Coronation Stone is made.

Another theory put forward by the British Israelites is that the stone now in Edinburgh Castle is the Biblical 'pillow of Jacob' or Bethel Stone mentioned in the *Book of Genesis*, claimed by many historians as the original coronation stone of the Israelites of the Hebrew nation. According to the Bible, 'he rested his head and dreamed … a ladder was set up on the earth, and its top reached to heaven; and there the angels of God were ascending and descending on it.' Jacob rose early in the morning, took the stone that he had used as his pillow, set it up to stand as a pillar, and poured oil upon the top of it, naming that place *Bet-El* or Bethel meaning 'House of God'.

This sounds like the actions of many augurs or geomancers when finding the centre of kingdoms. Was Jacob's pillow a representation of the cosmic axis, a link between the upper and lower worlds and the omphalos stone of the new city of the Israelites? In Germanic and Norse folklore, it was the task of the shaman to venture up and down the world tree to visit the dead in the lower realms and the gods in the upper to unite them as one with the earthly middle plane.

Jacob later takes the stone to Egypt where eventually it came into the possession of Joseph and Moses. During the Biblical Exodus, it was used to crown the kings of Canaan and Sheshem, after which it was kept in Jerusalem, until Jeremiah, a descendant of Moses, rescued it during an invasion by the Babylonians under King Nebuchadnezzar. He then hides the precious relic along with the Ark of the Covenant in a cave on Mount Nebo.[43]

Irish Annals refer to the coming of a great prophet around 583 BCE called 'Brugh', who many believe was Jeremiah, along with his scribe Baruch and the daughter of a king of 'Egypt' called Tea Tepi. The Princess marries the Zarahite King, Eochaidh II, at the capital city of Tara and for some three centuries, their descendants are crowned on the Bethel Stone, which became the Lia Fáil or Stone of Destiny.[44]

Many of the top researchers into the mysterious inauguration stones believe that there were more than one, perhaps up to four different examples existing, held by different races over the centuries in Scotland and Ireland. The stone that King Fergus Mór mac Eirc brought with him from Ireland was supposedly taken around to different sacred places in Scotland, beginning with the fabled city of Evonium (presumed to be Irvine near Kilmarnock) and ending at Scone, north of Perth in Perthshire.

There is evidence of cosmological arrangement in the location of Scone as the axis mundi of eastern central Scotland. The royal centre near Perth lies within the province of Gowrie, which is central to the four Pictish provinces of Atholl, Angus, Strathearn and Fife. This division of four around a central fifth may have been a Scottish/Pictish arrangement within a newly combined kingdom, with Scone as the new royal centre around which revolved inaugurations, assemblies, parliaments and courts. The focus of the ceremonies was on the Moot Hill, also known as Boot Hill, from the alleged practice of Scottish nobles over centuries placing earth from their lands inside their boots and emptying it on the hill after swearing fealty to the king.[45]

We can recall this cosmological concept in the Etruscan practice of new citizens bringing soil from their homeland and emptying it into the mundus pit at the centre of the newly founded city. The Moot Hill then becomes the central 'mound of creation' belonging to a newly combined kingdom of Picts and Scots – a tradition recalled in another of the names of the hill, *Omnis Terra* meaning 'the whole of the land'.

During an earlier visit to Scone Palace, I planned to see the famous Moot Hill and collect information for a talk I was giving on the Egyptian origins of the Stone of Destiny for a local group. After questioning many of the staff at the palace and some of the locals in the nearby town, I discovered there is an alternative story to the one involving the English King Edward I who supposedly took easy possession of it. The monks of Scone Abbey, the 'guardians' of the stone, anticipated the English king's intention to seize their precious relic after the massacre of the Scots at Berwick. Realising that Edward and his officials were unaware of its true likeness, they allegedly switched the stone, handing him instead a fake, said to be a sandstone cesspit cover from the abbey, complete with handles – the original and true inaugural stone now lying in its secret hiding place in the Tay River or Annaty Burn.

Sketch of the original Stone of Destiny

One of the guides at Scone Palace informed me that it took a year for Edward I to realise his embarrassing mistake, so he ordered his English army back to Scone to claim the real Stone of Destiny and punish the monks who had tricked him. Soldiers ransacked the abbey and tortured the abbot, but he refused to inform them of its whereabouts. Recent analyses of the stone by geologists would suggest that this story might be true, having confirmed it to be made from local Perthshire sandstone. Could it be, then, that for centuries, many of the most famous kings and queens of England have been crowned at Westminster Abbey on a cesspit cover?

There is of course another famous story associated with this stone: its abduction from Westminster Abbey by four Scottish University students on Christmas Day 1950. Having successfully removed it from the abbey without detection, they broke the cesspit cover in half as they dragged it to their car. Once repaired, they left the stone wrapped in a St Andrew's flag outside Arbroath Abbey. After members of the British government retrieved it, rumours of its authenticity soon started to circulate, and many believe that, yet again, the British were given a duplicate and the original Coronation Stone was given into the care of the Scottish Knights Templar.

In 1996, John Major of the Conservative Government finally agreed to return it to the Scots and a ceremonial exchange took place on the borders of Scotland between the Home Office and the Scottish government. The stone, possibly a copy of a cesspit cover, is now safely ensconced at Edinburgh Castle and displayed for all to see, receiving thousands of visitors every year.

The whereabouts of the true Lia Fáil or Stone of Destiny and Jacob's Pillar brought by Jerimiah is a mystery, likewise, the black meteoritic stone brought by Princess Scota who gave her name to Scotland.

However, some researchers believe that Scota's stone may have some basis in history as a sacred stone of the Egyptian priests called the Ben-ben. Heliopolis is one of the oldest cities of ancient Egypt, occupied since the Pre-Dynastic Period *c.* 3100 BCE. It was known as the 'city of the sun' and contained one of the most important temples in ancient Egypt, being the cult centre for the worship of the sun gods Atum and Ra. Although there is very little to see today, apart from a garden and obelisk, information boards mention the famous capstone called the Benben Stone, which came from the sacred temple of Ra at Heliopolis.

Pharaoh Senusret or Sesostris I erected the later obelisk over the site of the Benben Stone when restoring the city in 1970 BCE. He ordered an inscription to be carved on a stele that read 'My beauty shall be remembered in his house, my name is the Benben and my name is the lake.' The priesthood here at Heliopolis wielded considerable power during the Old Kingdom and would have influenced the design and positioning of these giant stone needles. Remarkably, the southeast corners of the three great pyramids at Giza are in alignment with the obelisk at Heliopolis, the possible omphalos site of an early Egyptian dynasty.

According to Egyptian folklore, Heliopolis was the site of a sacred mound upon which the first sunrise took place. On top of the mound sat the Benben, receiving the cosmic seeds of life that fell from the heavens. Here within the temple at Heliopolis, the stone was placed in the 'Mansion of the Phoenix' to absorb the first rays of the sun. The rule of the old sun priests of Heliopolis came to an abrupt end when a religious revolution swept the country, and it was during this time that the Benben may have been secreted away.

It occurred to me that the Benben Stone not only represented an omphalos stone to the Pre-Dynastic Egyptians but also marked their 'centre of the world'. As mentioned previously, Heliopolis is aligned to the southeast corners of the Giza pyramids, which are said to be geographically located at the navel of the entire world's landmass. The mound here symbolically represents the site of the first creation, the world mountain, used by many ancient cultures to mark the centre of their world.

Some sources, including Egyptian researcher and author Robert Bauval, suggest that the Benben Stone may have been fashioned from a meteorite that fell to Earth during a meteor shower millions of years ago, bringing with it life-giving bacteria that seeded life on this planet.[46] Perhaps Heliopolis, as the place where the Benben Stone fell to Earth, was forever revered as the site where the very seeding of life originated on Earth. Mecca is the holy centre of the Islamic world where the Kaaba enshrines a black stone also said to be meteoritic. The ancient Mayans in the Americas revered a sacred black stone and at Paphos on Cyprus, the home of Aphrodite, there was venerated within the temple a similar-coloured relic, now placed inside the local museum.

Dull, a Centre of the Culdees

The little chapel in the village of Dull between Aberfeldy and Fortingall was the former property of the Scottish Knights Templar and it was here they displayed the Stone of Destiny claiming it to be the genuine coronation stone. On an earlier visit to Dull, I was invited to view the stone, but I was disappointed when I saw that it was a copy of the sandstone cesspit cover made after it was stolen by students in the 1950s.

Today, Dull is a tiny village in Glen Lyon overlooking the River Tay, made up of a small farming community. However, in the 7th century, it was a highly significant religious centre, with a large monastic community founded by Adomnan of Iona, the biographer of St Columba. A local tradition says Adomnan is buried in the church. However, the monastery was built over an even older Culdee site, said to be the first seat of learning in Scotland long before religion was established at either Dunkeld or Blair Atholl. Dull is derived from its original name *Tulli*, *Tully* or *Tillie* meaning 'mound or hillock'.

In 1997, another Scottish representative of the Knights Templar based at Rosslyn Chapel claimed the Stone of Destiny was hidden within 8 km of Scone. However, one overriding story relating to this stone is that when Scotland regains its sovereignty once more, clues of its whereabouts, held in the hands of the leading families of Scotland for centuries, will be brought together to reveal its true hiding place. However, until that happens, any connection it may have had with ancient Egypt will remain circumspect. Today, the little church at Dull is a private residence, the sandstone 'Stone of Destiny' removed to another secret Templar site and now nothing remains of its early sacred heritage.

The Templar Stone of Destiny once kept at Dull Kirk

Scotland's Central Mountain

All countries have their symbolic world mountain - Ireland has Uisneach, or, as some may suggest, Croghan Hill, in Wales we have Pumlumon (Plynlimon) and in Scotland it is Schiehallion just to the north of Fortingall. The distinctive conical shape of Schiehallion set within a remote landscape makes it visible from many parts of Perthshire, which merits it as Scotland's most iconic central mountain. Many sources confirm this by pointing out that 'the line of latitude midway between the most northerly and southerly points on the Scottish mainland, and the line of longitude midway between the most easterly and westerly points, intersect very near the summit of Schiehallion.' Furthermore, Scotland's longest axis, from the southern tip of the Mull of Galloway to Duncansby Head near John o' Groats, a distance of 460 km, passes through Fortingall and the lower slopes of Schiehallion.[47]

Viewed from Fortingall looking north, the mountain appears pyramidal in shape, whereas its reverse slopes resemble a giant Sphinx. Its Gaelic name is *Sidh Chailleann* meaning 'fairy hill of the Caledonians', perhaps due to the long-held tradition of it being a magical sacred centre. In *A Highland Parish or the History of Fortingall*, Alexander Stewart writes:

> 'Of all the caves in the Parish, the most remarkable is that at Tom a Mhorair, on the south side of Glenmore, near the west shoulder of Schiehallion. It has a fairly wide opening which extends for three or four yards. It then contracts and slants into total darkness in the bowels of the Earth. Some kilometres to the east there is another opening, which tradition holds to be the other end of the cave. According to traditional accounts, this cave was regarded as an abode of fairies and other supernatural beings, rather than a hiding place of mortals. The only men who were supposed to have lived there were believed to have been in league with supernatural powers.'[48]

A former minister of Fortingall, the Revd Robert MacDonald writes of Schiehallion in *A New Statistical Account for Scotland* 'that the inside thereof is full of chambers or separate apartments, and that, as soon as a person advances a few metres, he comes to a door, which, the moment he enters, closes, as it opened, of its own accord, and prevents his returning.'[49]

Further tales refer to an ancient tradition of sleeping warriors lying within one of its caves. On Creag Chionneachan is a cave in which the mythical Scottish Fingal and his warriors are supposed to lie on their elbows awaiting the third blast of the horn to raise them from their slumber. The story is almost identical to those of the mythical Irish Finn MacCool who sleeps in many caves with his followers, the

Schiehallion, Scotland's central mountain. Courtesy of David Cowan

Fianna. Several sleeping warrior traditions occur around Britain, generally associated with Celtic King Arthur and his Knights, who lie in a state of suspended animation until awoken to assist in their country's hour of need. These stories may be an allegory for the dormant telluric power that lies hidden within this enchanted elemental and highly powerful geological site.

Like Uisneach, Schiehallion is also associated with goddess worship. Scottish folklore refers to the *Cailleach*, the winter aspect of the goddess Bride, as haunting Schiehallion from the time of All Hallows, 1 November, to May Day Eve when she transforms back into her summer aspect. On the northern slope of Schiehallion is *Sgrìob na Caillich*, or 'Cailleach's furrow', where linear patterns in the rocks are said to have been caused by Bride's plough. A holy well, called the Maiden Well, on its eastern slopes, faces towards the sunrise. Here, maidens would wash and drink to the health of the coming year at Beltane. Locals also refer to the mountain as 'Maiden's Pap', pap meaning breast.

In *Rambles in Breadalbane*, the author Malcolm Ferguson mentions a link between Schiehallion and the Irish warrior goddess Queen Maebh, Mab or Maeve:

> 'If all the tales one hears related by old natives of Rannoch could be fully relied on, Schiehallion in days of yore used to be a favourite resort of the fairy folks, and more especially once a year, when all the various tribes throughout Glenlyon, Rannoch, Strathtummel, etc. congregated. Here they used to assemble in large numbers and hold their annual convocation, presided over by the beautiful and accomplished Queen Mab, gorgeously arrayed in her favourite green silk robes, with her abundant crop of beautiful golden-yellow hair waving in long ringlets over her shoulder down to her waist. It is said that there are a long series of mysterious caves, extending from one side of the mountain to the other.'[50]

Queen Mab is often referred to as the Queen of the Fairies, but she is also the Cailleach, the mother goddess. Caves were considered literally as entrances to the Otherworld, the abode of fairies. The walls of caves were associated with entrances through which the soul passed, their images often portrayed in artwork on the interiors, similar to the rock faces in the caves of our ancient ancestors in France's Lascaux or Spain's Altimira – or the 'Black Mirrors' of the medieval alchemist, which were seen as portals to the sacred realms of the Otherworld. Similar folklore is associated with Oweynagat or 'Cave of the Cats' located at the royal ceremonial complex of the Connacht kings at Rathcroghan. Here the solstice sunset and Samhain festivals were observed and ceremonially linked to Ireland's omphalos hill at Uisneach. At Schiehallion, Maebh as the fairy queen is seen as the creative force in the land, residing within the cave or womb of Mother Earth at the navel of Scotland.

'Navel' associations around the area of Aberfeldy and Fortingall are symbolically evident in the many traditions of sacred omphalos stones, the presence of a world tree or axis mundi in the form of the largest and oldest sacred yew tree in Europe, and a central mountain where the goddess was worshipped and the greatest warriors of its nation sleep.

The Grail Chapel

Another site on this old east-west Glen Lyon route that extends to Moulin is the exquisite little church of St Mary's at Grandtully, where we previously dowsed the feminine serpent current of the Belinus Line. The foundation of this church is linked with 7th-century St Chad of Mercia, who founded Lichfield Cathedral, which the Venerable Bede once described as the 'Spiritual omphalos of England.' Next to the entrance to Grandtully Castle, the seat of Clan Stewart or Steuart since the late 14th century, is a narrow track that leads to the little gem of St Mary's. The church itself stands on a rocky hilltop and has the unusual appearance of an old barn. Beautifully restored, St Mary's is a rare treat, boasting a well-preserved hand-painted barrelled roof commissioned by Sir William Steuart in 1636. Of main interest to us is the original founding of this church.[51]

According to Liddell, St Chad of Mercia built a church at Grandtully, while his brother St Cedd founded another at nearby Logierait in 650 CE. Ancient stones litter the fields around St Mary's Chapel, indicating that this may have been the former site of a stone circle or Druidic temple. Barry Dunford outlines the various claims by many of the noble Scottish families, including the Stewarts and Sinclairs, that they were descended from the royal Davidic line of Jesus.[52] Jackie Queally notes that descendants of these noble families became members of the Knights Templar who built their churches over the remains of Culdee religious sanctuaries after their destruction by both the Danes and the Normans. The royal dynasties of Scotland intermarried with some of the high priests of the Culdees, who themselves were descended from the royal line of David and that of Jesus. Queally also states that the Stewarts considered themselves 'custodians of the land', so perhaps they realised the significance of this site as possessing feminine dragon energy close to the very centre of Scotland.[53]

One of the paintings on the ceiling inside the church depicts a Grail knight, said to be Percival or Galahad, holding a chalice while a stone appears suspended in midair between his hands. The main mural shows the Judgement (Resurrection) Tarot symbol, but most intriguing is an image of two female angels heavy with a child. If the Stewarts who commissioned this work were keepers of the Grail, was St Mary's their symbolic Grail chapel?

St Ciaran at the Navel of Scotland

Also close to this central glen of Scotland and less than 3 km south of Fortingall, on the north shore of Loch Tay, is a small crofting village called Fearnan. Here to our surprise once stood a church dedicated to St Ciaran, the founder of the new religious omphalos of Ireland at Clonmacnoise. The remnants of the old chapel can be seen on top of a wall next to the road as you arrive at the village in the form of a small hollowed stone with an internal incised cross.

Perhaps it is no coincidence that a monk responsible for founding the ecclesiastical centre of Ireland established a Celtic church close to the centre of Scotland. He must have made an impact in the area, as located in a field above the old farmhouse of Boreland is 'St Ciaran's Seat', also known as *Clach-na-Gruich* or 'Stone of the Measles'. The rock is carved as an unusual chair-shaped boulder with a cavity or recess, which often collects water. In the past, children would drink from this cavity to cure them of measles, hence the latter name. Several cup and ring markings supposedly adorn the rock similar to those found on stones in Northumberland and other parts of Scotland, although difficult to detect today due to weathering. These carvings indicate Clach-na-Gruich was a stone of power used by the prehistoric peoples to invoke fertility in the land.[54]

In folklore, it is an ancient seat of initiation, usurped by the later missionaries as the seat of St Ciaran when the Celtic church Christianised the area. Images from aerial photography show ditched enclosures near the site of the old church that may indicate prehistoric ceremonial enclosures or a large monastic site from the time of Ciaran. We placed our healing stones here to honour the saint, a symbolic male deity at the end of the old western road that radiates out from Scotland's navel at Moulin.

St Ciaran's Seat, Fearnan, Glen Lyon

The central province of Atholl has many symbolic centres such as Schiehallion, the Fortingall Yew, and the centre stone near the A9, but the ancient town of Moulin seems to qualify as the most significant, being the site of a Pictish palace next to an ancient crossroads that links the Old North Road with the magical Glen Lyon east-west route. A little way to the north of Moulin lies Blair Atholl, where once the cult of the goddess Bride flourished, and to the south is Dunkeld, which in earlier times was a highly important monastic centre, similar to Clonmacnoise in Ireland.

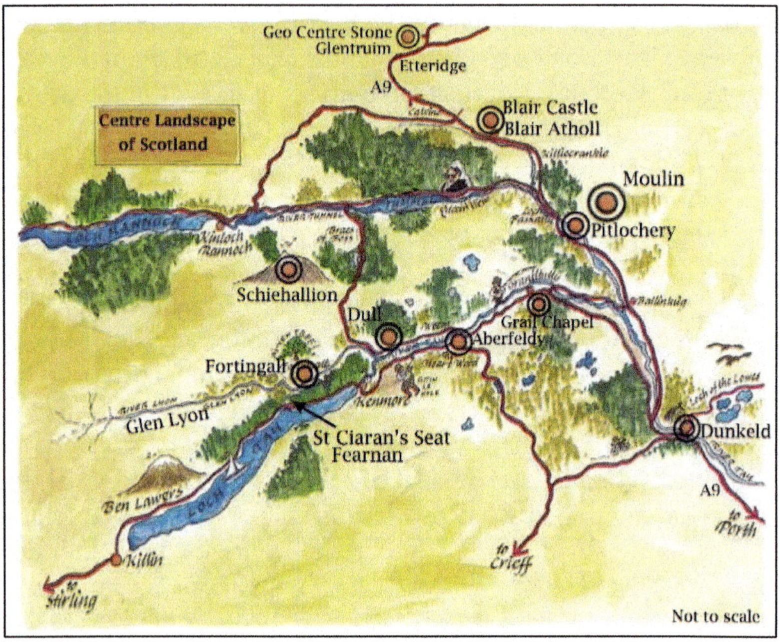

Figure 12. Sacred Landscape at the centre of Scotland

References:

1. *Spain and Scotland: The Ancient Connections* http://halfmoon.tripod.com/Spain.html.
2. McHardy S (2010) *A New History of the Picts*. Luath Press, Edinburgh.
3. Skene W F (1867) *Chronicles of the Picts*. H M General Register House, Edinburgh. https://archive.org/details/chroniclesofpict00sken.
4. Scott A B (1918) *The Pictish Nation: Its People and its Church*. T N Foulis, Edinburgh. https://archive.org/stream/pictishnationits00scotrich/pictishnationits00scotrich_djvu.txt.
5. Skene W F (1867) *Chronicles of the Picts*. H M General Register House, Edinburgh. https://archive.org/details/chroniclesofpict00sken.

6. Approximate location of Pictish kingdoms.
https://en.wikipedia.org/wiki/Picts#/media/
File: Pictish_kingdoms_with_Fidach.png.
7. WordSense. https://www.wordsense.eu/ath/.
8. *De Excidio et Conquestu Britanniae*, section #24. (London, 1568).
https://www.gutenberg.org/cache/epub/1949/pg1949-images.html
9. Sharpe R (translator) (1995) *Adomnan of Iona. Life of St Columba*. Penguin Classics, London.
10. Handford S A (ed.), Mattingly H (translator) (1971) *Tacitus: The Agricola and the Germania*. Penguin Classics, London.
11. Aitchison N (2006) *Forteviot, A Pictish and Scottish Royal Centre*. Tempus Publishing, Stroud.
12. Stewart E (1926, 1979) *Dunkeld, an Ancient City*. Willian Culross & Son, Coupar Angus.
13. Holinshed R (1587) *Chronicles of England, Scotland and Ireland, 6 vols*. Reprinted 1807 for J. Johnson and others, London. Facsimile reprint 1965 by AMS Press, New York.
14. Liddell C (2008) *Pitlochry, a History*. Watermill Books, Aberfeldy.
15. Dixon J H (1925) *Pitlochry Past and Present*. L Mackay, Pitlochry.
16. https://www.thenorthernantiquarian.org/2009/07/28/danes-stone/
17. Liddell C (2008) *Pitlochry, a History*. Watermill Books, Aberfeldy.
18. https://www.visitcairngorms.com/the-centre-of-scotland-stone/
19. Liddell C (2008) *Pitlochry, a History*. Watermill Books, Aberfeldy
20. Faskally – Pitlochry.
http://www.themodernantiquarian.com/site/289/faskally_pitlochry.html.
21. Biltcliffe G & Hoare C (2012) *The Spine of Albion: An Exploration of Earth Energies and Landscape Mysteries along the Belinus Line*. Sacred Lands Publishing, Weymouth.
22. Stewart E (1926, 1979) *Dunkeld, an Ancient City*. Willian Culross & Son, Coupar Angus.
23. Driscoll S T (2002) Alba: *The Gaelic Kingdom of Scotland AD 800–1124 (The Making of Scotland)*. Birlinn, Edinburgh.
24. Scotland's Places. https://scotlandsplaces.gov.uk/digital-volumes/ordnance-survey-name-books/perthshire-os-name-books-1859-1862/perthshire-volume-13/59.
25. Stewart E (1926, 1979) *Dunkeld, an Ancient City*. Willian Culross & Son, Coupar Angus.
26. Powerful finds at King's Seat hillfort. *Current Archaeology* (31 March 2020) 362 https://archaeology.co.uk/articles/news/powerful-finds-at-kings-seat-hillfort.htm
27. Scott W (1904) *The Poetical Works of Sir Walter Scott*. Henry Frowde, London.
28. Campbell D (1886) *The Lairds of Glenlyon*. S Cowan, Perth.
https://archive.org/details/lairdsofglenlyon00campuoft.
29. Clach-Buadha (Stone of Victory).
https://archive.org/details/lairdsofglenlyon00campuoft

30. *Glen Lyon: Valley of the Sun God.* http://philipcoppens.com/glenlyon.html.
31. Campbell D (1886) *The Lairds of Glenlyon.* S Cowan, Perth. https://archive.org/details/lairdsofglenlyon00campuoft.
32. *Glen Lyon: Valley of the Sun God.* http://philipcoppens.com/glenlyon.html.
33. Ibid.
34. Dunford B (2002) *The Holy Land of Scotland.* Sacred Connections, Glen Lyon.
35. Mackenzie J W (1830) *A Chronicle of the Kings of Scotland from Fergus the First, to James the Sixth, in the Year M.DC.XI.* Republished 2008 by Kessinger, Whitefish, MN.
36. Dunford B (2002) *The Holy Land of Scotland.* Sacred Connections, Glenlyon.
37. Boece H (1821) *The History and Chronicles of Scotland.* W and C Tait, Edinburgh. https://archive.org/details/historychronicle01boec.
38 Westwood J (1986) *Albion: A Guide to Legendary Britain.* Book Club Associates, London.
39. Ellis R (2007) *Cleopatra to Christ/Scota: Egyptian Queen of the Scots.* Adventures Unlimited Press, Kempton, IL.
40. Aldred C (1991) *Akhenaten: King of Egypt.* Thames & Hudson, London.
41 Dumville D (ed.), Shirley-Price L & Farmer D (translators) (2003) *Bede: Ecclesiastical History of the English People.* Penguin Classics, London.
42. Westwood J & Kingshill S (2009) *The Lore of Scotland: A Guide to Scottish Legends.* Random House, London.
43. Raymond E (2009) *Jacob's Pillar: Stone of Destiny.* Artisan, Muskogee,
44. Cunningham B (2010). *The Annals of the Four Masters: Irish History, Kingship and Society in the Early Seventeenth Century.* Four Courts, Dublin.
45. Aitchison N (2003) *Scotland's Stone of Destiny.* Tempus, Stroud.
46. *Investigation on the Origins of the Benben Stone.* http://robertbauval.co.uk/articles/articles/DE14.html.
47. Schiehallion Mountain. https://en.wikipedia.org/wiki/Schiehallion
48. Stewart A (1928) *A Highland Parish or the History of Fortingall.* MacLaren & Sons, Glasgow.
49. MacDonald D F (1845) *The New Statistical Account of Scotland.* William Blackwood and Sons, Edinburgh. https://archive.org/details/newstatisticalac01edin.
50. Ferguson M (1891) *Rambles in Breadalbane.* T Murray, Glasgow.
51. Biltcliffe G & Hoare C (2012) *The Spine of Albion: An Exploration of Earth Energies and Landscape Mysteries along the Belinus Line.* Sacred Lands Publishing, Weymouth.
52. Dunford B (2002) *The Holy Land of Scotland.* Sacred Connections, Perthshire.
53. Queally J (2001) *The Culdees, an Ancient Religious Enigma in Scotland.* Celtic Trails, Edinburgh.
54. *Clach-na-Cruich*, Fearnan, Perthshire. https://megalithix.wordpress.com/2008/09/29/clach-na-cruich/

Chapter 4

Cambria, Land of the Britons

Wales is a large western peninsular of Britain jutting out into the Irish Sea – its border with England forms a north-south protective line of marshes and rivers. This ancient landscape once known as Cambria consists of spectacular coastlines, magnificent mountain ranges and luscious river valleys. From the Iron Age to the time of the Saxon invasion it became part of a larger kingdom of Celtic Briton, known in the Welsh language as Cymru.

The Saxon invasions of eastern and southern England and Northumbria pushed the native Britons back and the rugged mountainous Cymru became a refuge and sanctuary. The Saxons later built a great border through the marshes in the late 8th century to restrict their movements called Offa's Dyke, creating two distinctive kingdoms between the Britons and the Germanic Angles and Saxons.

James MacKillop in *Myths and Legends of the Celts* states that in earlier times the people of Wales 'described themselves as living on Ynys Prydain, the Isle of Britain.'[1] They were the most ancient of the Britons, a race that lived throughout the British Isles, speaking the Brythonic language, which survived long after the Roman invasion in Wales, Cornwall, northern England and lowland Scotland.

According to Professor Peter Donnelly of Oxford University, the Welsh are genetically distinct from the rest of mainland Britain, carrying DNA that can be traced back to the last Ice Age, 10,000 years ago.[2]

Until their union with England under the Tudors, they fought hard for their freedom and liberty against the Romans, Saxons and Normans. The name Wales derives from the Germanic word *wealh* or *wealas* meaning 'foreigner' or 'non-Saxon'.

The medieval *Welsh Triads* mention that the earliest peoples of Wales arrived during the Bronze Age from the migrations of a seafaring race called the *Kymry* or *Cymry*, under the leadership of Hu Gadarn.[3] He was described as a 'giant' in stature and never took a territory by 'force of arms but always with justice and in peace.'[4] Gadarn instructed the Kymry on how to manufacture metals and farm the land using the plough.

The later Iron Age Druids regarded him as their founder and a 'fountain of all wisdom'. This enigmatic priesthood survived longer in Wales than in any other region of Britain and the Druids were masters of arcane magic, science and geomancy and clever politicians during the turbulent Roman and Saxon eras. Druidic schools in Britain, Ireland and the Isle of Man taught a variety of subjects including sciences, history and languages, spreading to different parts of Wales including Bangor and Llantwit Major. As in Ireland, students from all over Western Europe were educated in these colleges, including the sons of foreign kings and emperors.

The P-Celtic Welsh, Breton and Cornish languages have a more guttural tone compared to the softer Q-Celtic Gaelic tongue of the Irish and Scottish. Many have observed that Welsh sounds not too dissimilar to Middle Eastern languages; in fact, the *Triads* say that Hu Gadarn originated from Asia Minor between the Black Sea and the Mediterranean.

The Five-Peaked Mountain

Unlike Ireland, the geographical shape of Wales is irregular and less symmetrical, making the exact centre harder to determine because its borders and coastline have changed considerably over the centuries. However, there is an area anciently known as the centre of Wales that has all the ingredients found in other omphalos landscapes along with legends and history indicative of a ceremonial centre. We also discovered to our surprise that Wales like Scotland, was at one point in its history, divided into four regions around a central fifth.

The four main kingdoms of Wales were Gwynedd in the north-west, Powys in the north-east Gwent in the south-east, Deheubarth in the south-west with a central fifth province, like Meath in Ireland, called Gwrtheyrnion, meaning 'place of the Monarch of Men' or 'place of the High King'. This middle region also includes a symbolic world mountain like Uisneach in Ireland and Schiehallion in Scotland.

Alwyn Rees and Brindley Rees in *Celtic Heritage* write: 'In the centre of Wales, near the point where the northwestern, northeastern and southwestern provinces and bishoprics met, is the mountain of Pumlumon ('five peaks [or beacons]'), in which the Wye and the Severn [rivers] have their source.'[5] John Michell and Christine Rhone in *Twelve-Tribe Nations* reveal the accuracy of this ancient tradition by using the boundary method to locate the exact centre of Wales,

Pumlumon, the central mountain of Wales. Courtesy of Steve Hynd

which depicts its extreme land points on a map drawn from a central point marked by the mountain range of Pumlumon. The circle clips the extremities of the country and 'defines its natural geographical borders such as the estuary of the Mersey to the northeast and the course of the Severn to the southeast.'[6]

Pumlumon, anglicised as Plynlimon, is the highest point of the Cambrian Mountains at 609 m, with its five peaks marked by five beacons and a legendary barrow or tomb of a sleeping giant. On its lower plains, many key battles were fought, including those led by Owen Cyfeilog (c. 1130–1197), Prince of Powys, and the Welsh hero Owain Glyndŵr (c.1359–1416). Owain led a revolt against English rule between 1400 and 1415, defeating his enemy on Pumlumon's western slopes at the Battle of Mynydd Hyddgen. Just 150 Welsh archers armed with the newly invented 'six-foot longbow' claimed victory against 1500 well-armed English and Flemish soldiers. This new weapon was capable of firing arrows over a large distance, which the Welsh used to great effect on a slow-moving enemy hampered by the boggy terrain. After the battle, Owain unfurled the banner of Welsh independence on the field of victory, the greatest defeat of the English by a Welsh leader. The victory inspired the rise of Henry Tudor in 1485, concluding in the Battle of Bosworth Field where King

Richard III was killed on the battlefield, which as we would find during this investigation was very close to the navel of England.

In Irish myths, the great rivers of the Shannon and the Boyne were supposedly born from the central mountain of Uisneach; likewise, Pumlumon gives birth to five great rivers in Britain. Although three of them, Rheidol, Llyfnant and the Clywedog, are relatively minor, the River Severn is the longest in Great Britain and the Wye the fifth longest.

> 'On grey Plynlimon's breast,
> Severn, and Wye of pleasant mien,
> And Rheidol rich in great renown.'[7]

Near the source of the Severn, 3 km from the parking area of Eisteddfa Gurig, is Blaen Gwy, where the course of the infant Severn flows beneath Pont-rhyd-galed or 'the hard ford bridge'. Here, there are a large number of barrows and cairns, part of an ancient prehistoric burial ground, no doubt chosen due to its proximity to the source of the longest river in ancient Albion. The name 'Severn' derives from a nymph goddess called by the Welsh *Hafren* and by the Romans Sabrina.

The stunningly beautiful journey of the River Wye from its source on Pumlumon to the Severn Estuary forms the western boundary of England and Wales. Water is in abundance around this central mountain, feeding into several lakes and reservoirs that supply drinking water to the city of Birmingham.

Checking the accuracy with modern computer programs, Pumlumon is indeed centrally placed and conforms in both history and legend as the nation's sacred navel mountain, where High Kings gathered below its slopes for inspiration or empowerment. In Chinese tradition, a five-peaked mountain is considered the 'mother mountain' and the most sacred of all high places. Perhaps Welshmen lit the five beacons on each of Pumlumon's peaks to celebrate a national event or Celtic festival such at Beltane, just as they still do on the Hill of Uisneach in Ireland.

The Lost Commote of the High King

Rees and Rees refer to the fifth province in Wales in more detail: 'To the southeast of Plynlimon, in between the rivers Wye and Severn, is the Commote of Gwrtheyrnion, "the land of Gwrtheyrn" (Vortigern), the ruler of Britain around AD 425 at the time of the Saxon invasion.' Historical experts now believe that the name Vortigern is a title that means 'High King', like the Irish *ard ri*, as there is documentary evidence of more than one leader called Vortigern. Therefore, it would seem reasonable to expect the High King of Wales to reside at Gwrtheyrnion, 'the place of the High King'. In Ireland, the High Kings ceremonially honoured the central mother mountain of Uisneach at certain auspicious times of the year but utilised Tara as the place of masculine kingship rituals and government.[8]

Historia Brittonum, written around 828 CE by the Saxon monk Nennius, has one of the earliest references to Gwrtheyrnion.[9] This middle province became a refuge for the last Welsh king, Llywelyn ap Gruffudd, in 1258, who made it his centre of resistance before being killed by the English at Builth Wells. Like Meath in Ireland and Atholl in Scotland, Gwrtheyrnion is a wild and hilly district that contains many megalithic stone monuments and burial mounds. However, we were interested to know whether there was a special place in this large area that could have once been used for kingship rituals similar to those that took place at Uisneach and Tara.

Michell believed that the theoretic centre was an area in the middle of Gwrtheyrnion anciently called Cwmdauddwr (pronounced 'coombe-ay-ther') meaning 'valley of the two rivers' which today borders the town of Rhayader. He also discovered that lines drawn from here to the cathedrals of the four provinces conform to the same pattern as found in the divisions of ancient Ireland. One of these lines stretches from Llandaff Cathedral in Cardiff, one of the most important early Christian sites in South Wales, to Bangor Cathedral, the ancient ecclesiastical centre of North Wales, passing directly through both Cwmdauddwr and the summit of Pumlumon (see Fig. 13).[10]

Cwmdauddwr's 'two rivers' are the Elan and Wye separated by lush farmland and woodland. It borders the town of Rhayader, the first to be built on the River Wye after its source. Rhayader is also on a long-distance alignment of sites that I discovered back in 2008, outlined in my book *The Spirit of Portland*, called the 'Bran Line'.[11] It starts at the Isle of Portland in Dorset and passes through many important sites in Wales including St Brides Bay, Buith Wells and many of the isles sacred to the Druidic priesthood of Iron Age Britain such as Anglesey, the Isle of Man, Colonsay, the Paps of Jura and Iona, ending at the sacred peninsular of Benbecular.

Ordnance Survey has calculated, using the gravitational method, that the centre of Wales is an uninhabited marshy wetland 12 km south of Pumlumon and 17 km northwest of Cwmdauddwr close to the

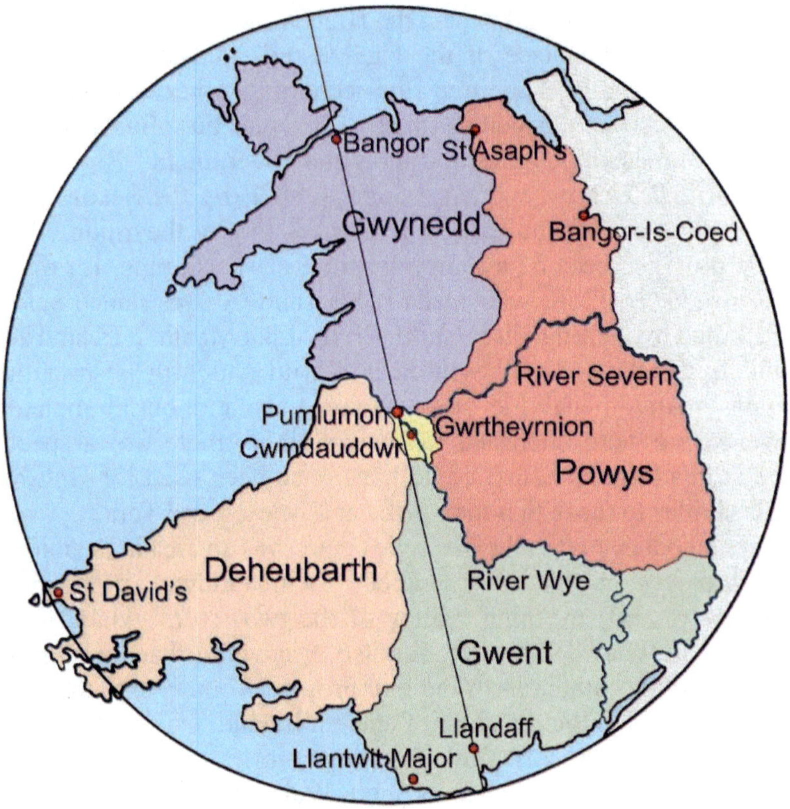

Figure 13. The alignment through the central province of Wales, linking Pumlumon with the cathedrals of Bangor and Llandaff, from a design by Christine Rhone in 'Twelve-Tribe Nations'.

village of Cwmystwyth near Devil's Bridge in Ceredigion. The area is famous for the mining of silver, lead and zinc, extracted from the hills of the River Ystwyth valley since pre-Roman times. Among the earliest gold artefacts ever found in Wales is a curious ritual object named the Banc Ty'nddôl sun-disc, found on the mining site near Cwmystwyth in 2002.

This ancient treasure measuring 4 cm across dates from the Beaker period (*c.* 2000 BCE) and is decorated with three raised concentric circles and dot-work called repoussé on either side of one of the raised circles. At the centre of the inner circle are two rather unusual indentations. The object was found by archaeologists below the Bronze Age copper mine on Copa Hill while investigating the site of Roman and medieval lead-smelting works. It is believed to be part of a funeral garment, possibly from a grave mound, which closely resembles one found in Ireland and on the Isle of Man.[12]

Curiously, its concentric circles draw one's attention to the centre of the sun-disc, perhaps symbolic of an omphalos, the pair of indentations in the middle of the circles referring to ritual ceremonial centres. Despite this extraordinary find, there is very little significant history or folklore relating to this remote spot to indicate that it was ever a place associated with a sacred centre.

Vortigern and Excalibur

Vortigern was a King of Powys who became the overall ruler of the Britons after the death of his brother-in-law King Constantine the Blessed during the 5th century. As High King of Britain, he had within his possession the royal sword that may have later become the legendary Excalibur. Over the years, my late friend John and I went on many quests in search of King Arthur's sword, based on messages from a psychic medium that said the mythical sword lies buried at the junction of two rivers somewhere in Celtic lands. Although its exact location was uncertain, John felt sure it was either in Cornwall or Wales.

Adrian Gilbert's book *The Holy Kingdom* refers to an actual historical sword that once belonged to Roman general Julius Caesar, mentioned by both the Welsh monk Tysilio (548– 640 CE) and Geoffrey of Monmouth, as possibly being a symbol of power for British sovereigns long before the time of Arthur. In 55 BCE, Caesar, with the Roman 10th Legion, made his first attempt to conquer Britain, but after landing on our shores was met by a well-organised British army using archers, skilled swordsmen and chariots led by Prince Nennius, the brother of British King Caswallon. Nennius led the charge and a great battle ensued, during which Nennius fought his way through the lines to face Caesar, the greatest undefeated warrior in the Roman Empire. He engaged Caesar in hand-to-hand combat and the general struck two resounding blows with his sword, the first hit the British prince on the helmet but as Caesar raised his sword to strike a second blow Nennius held up his shield in self-defence. The sword lodged itself so deeply in the shield that, try as he might, Caesar could not withdraw it. As the fierce tide of the battle drew them apart, Caesar was forced to give up his mighty blade.[13]

After freeing Caesar's sword from his shield, Nennius returned to the battle, using it to slay 'many Romans'. The sword proved to be extremely hard and sharp, possibly laden with poison, as anyone cut by it would later die from their wounds, including Nennius himself. There are many so-called magical weapons made from meteoritic iron – there was a dagger made of this sacred metal found in the tomb of Tutankhamun.

The sword now gained the reputation of having magical powers and earned itself the nickname *Mors Crocca* meaning 'red death'. During the great celebrations that followed, the brave warriors who stood up to the might of the Roman Empire paraded the sword around the streets of London, a symbol of the vanquishing of Rome.

After Nennius' death, it was buried with him but remembered in London's coat of arms as a red sword. When London finally fell under Roman rule over a hundred years later, many British warriors retreated to Wales and continued their defiance of the Empire under the leadership of King Caractacus and Arviragus. Eventually, Mors Crocca was handed down through the line of British kings to Vortigern, whose success in battle acclaimed him High King or 'Bretwalda', holding the three crowns of Wales, England and Scotland.

My friend John psychically sensed that Mors Crocca was unearthed during the Saxon invasions and became Excalibur. Although there is no substance to this theory, I did discover that the Welsh name for Excalibur, or its earliest documented name, is *Caledvwlch* meaning 'hard cleft' perhaps referring to the sword of Caesar being wedged deep in a 'cleft' of his shield. The Mors Crocca may have been made from meteoritic iron, enabling it to remain harder and sharper for a lot longer than other swords.

Further research revealed that a description of Excalibur was included in *The Dream of Rhonabwy*, from the *Mabinogion* Tales, describing it as having two entwined chimaeras or dragons on its handle with their fire-breathing heads facing each other at the hilt. This appears to be representative of the Roman god Mercury whose rod was entwined with two serpents. A legend says the rod made Mercury invincible, which perhaps Caesar saw as symbolic during his mission for greatness. Interestingly other elite Roman swords have been found with entwined twin serpents on the handle and hilt.

Monmouth and Tysilio believe the sword was buried with Nennius under the White Mound on which the Tower of London stands today. However, why would such a prize sword taken from one of the world's most revered warriors at the time be left to decay? Perhaps, when the nation was under threat once more, this time by the Saxons, this invincible and magical talisman was unearthed to help the country in its hour of need. *The Welsh Triads* reveal that Arthur removed the head of Bran from the White Mound, perhaps he also removed the sword that once saved the nation.

Vortigern became unpopular towards the end of his reign and according to 6th-century British historian Gildas, who wrote *De Excidio et Conquestu Britanniae*, he inadvertently betrayed his nation after inviting the Saxons into the country led by the mercenaries Hengist and Horsa. This came about after the withdrawal of the Romans, which resulted in a lack of good fighting men to combat the increasing threat from the invading Picts from Scotland.

Hengist and Horsa had other plans, however, and after increasing their fighting force, they turned on the Britons intending to claim lands for themselves. They overwhelmed much of the south and east of England, forcing the local British people to retreat to Devon, Cornwall and Wales.[14]

In *Historia Brittonum* Nennius tells us that Vortigern fled to Wales and attempted to 'build and fortify a city to defend himself' against his people who believed he had betrayed them.[15] He supposedly built a castle on Dinas Emrys in the province of Gwynedd, northwest Wales, overlooking the River Glaslyn, but the structure repeatedly collapsed for no obvious reason.

After consulting the Druids, Vortigern was told to sacrifice a boy born without a father and mix his blood with the mortar to alleviate a curse that was affecting the hillfort. Vortigern's men eventually found such a boy who called himself Myrddin Emrys or Merlin, but before he could be put to death he saved himself through his gift of prophecy and revealed the true cause of the curse. He announced that beneath the castle there were two dragons dwelling in a lake, causing the foundations to crumble.

Vortigern ordered his men to dig and eventually they found the lake mentioned by Merlin. After draining the water, the dragons, one red and the other white, immediately started to fight. After a long and fierce contest, the red dragon said to represent the Welsh nation, overcame the other, representing the Saxons, and so the delighted Welsh adopted the red dragon as their emblem.[16]

However, in Geoffrey of Monmouth's version of events, the red

Illumination of a 15th-century manuscript of Monmouth's 'The History of the Kings of Britain', showing King Vortigern and Ambrosius watching the fight between two dragons.

dragon loses the fight, due perhaps to him having given up any hope of a return to British self-rule after the Norman invasion. Other sources claim that the young boy who prophesied the fighting dragons beneath Vortigern's fortress was Ambrosius Aurelianus who, having returned from exile in Brittany to reclaim his throne, attacked Vortigern's stronghold at Dinas Emrys.[17]

Much of the negative propaganda associated with Vortigern places all the country's ill fortunes at his door after the demise of Britain, forcing him to seek sanctuary in the remote regions of his native country. Gildas surmised that Vortigern was an honourable leader who was simply ill-judged in his trust of the heathen ungodly Saxon leaders.

Vortigern's Castle

According to *The Chronicle of the Kings of Britain* attributed to Tysilio, Vortigern fled from Dinas Emyrs during a siege by the British king Emrys Wledig, also known as Ambrosius Aurelianus, after his castle was burned to the ground. He is said to have escaped to another of his castles in the Welsh province of Gwrtheyrnion by the Wye, where he met his demise around 441 CE.[18] This new information seemed to make sense as to why this middle kingdom received the name 'the land of Gwrtheyrn or Vortigern', to immortalise the place where he died and was buried. The exact location of this castle, however, is still debated so we hoped a visit to Rhayader would reveal more information about its early history.

Rhayader is a historic market town in the county of Radnorshire, lying on a bend of the River Wye at the head of the picturesque Elan Valley at the centre of the middle kingdom of Gwrtheyrnion. It is situated 20 km north of Builth Wells and 48 km east of Aberystwyth and is often referred to as the 'Gateway to the Lakeland of Wales.' Rhayader is the Welsh name for 'waterfall of the Wye', although the waterfall disappeared in the 18th century when the rocks were dynamited to build a new bridge. The town developed around a busy crossroads of two important historic north-south and east-west routes through Wales (see Fig. 14). As a result, it became a vital staging post at a strategic fording place of the River Wye, now marked by the old stone bridge. So here we find the centre crossroads of Wales that equates to those of Durrow in Ireland and Moulin in Scotland.

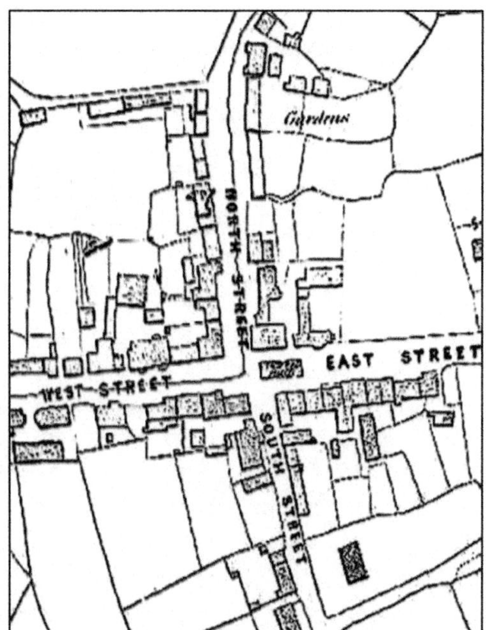

Figure 14. Rhayader's central crossroads (1840)

Marking the crossroads is a freestanding clock tower, symbolically representing the axis mundi. Even the perfectly intersecting North, South, East and West Streets are exactly aligned to the cardinal points. During the 19th century, no fewer than six toll gates were placed on the roads in and out of the town, reflecting the commercial importance of this central settlement.

A visit to the local museum on North Street reveals the historical importance of this area which dates human habitation back to at least 5000 years. The numerous cairns and standing stones in and around the surrounding hills are indicative of an important prehistoric ritual landscape. The Romans built camps to the east and west of the town perhaps to control this strategic area, which may have been a centre of prehistoric routes in Mid Wales going back to at least the Bronze Age. The Romans also constructed or, as some archaeologists now believe, re-paved a road through Rhayader, leading from the lead and silver mines at Cwmystwyth to their fort of Castell Collen at Llandrindod Wells, which continued to the south coast.

Most authorities say the town dates from the 5th century, around the time of Vortigern, and continued in medieval times as an important place for monks to stop as they travelled between Strata Florida Abbey and Abbey Cwm Hir, both major religious houses in the centre province of Gwrtheyrnion.

The Rhayader Hoard. Courtesy of Jonomac4

However, perhaps one of the most interesting items of information in the museum is the local discovery in 1899 of an important 2nd-century Romano-British hoard of gold jewellery, embossed with Celtic-style ornate decoration. Items include a ring set with a carved onyx, a gold armlet and a 22.5-carat gold necklace adorned with sapphires and carnelians. The Rhayader hoard was discovered hidden on a mountaintop half a kilometre south of Rhayader by a local man while out hunting with his dog and is presently housed at the British Museum in London.

Experts believe that the jewellery belonged to a person of high status, perhaps the wife of a Celtic chieftain or a Romano-British leader. Locals call it the 'Vortigern hoard' based on an old legend that after the king fled to this area he hid his treasure in the hills. The four Bronze Age gold torcs unearthed in a field locally may also be part of this treasure, now in the National Museum of Wales in Cardiff. Vortigern's treasure may have included gold from earlier periods, just as wealthy people collect valuable antiques today.

Information in the local library helped confirm Vortigern's connection to Rhayader by the renowned English antiquarian William Camden in 1607. He wrote:

> 'The name Rhayader is Welsh for a waterfall or fall of the water by which stands a castle which Rhys Prince of South Wales repaired under King Richard the First. The surroundings are of a vast and wide wilderness and craggy mountains, a safe place of refuge for a fugitive. Vortigern, the last monarch of the British who withdrew himself here after he was blamed for the Saxon invasions of this land and died here, not from guilt of his so-called wickedness, but from 'fire from heaven'. Vortigern was burnt along with his castle and city which he had built here for his refuge.'[19]

The Welsh Triads or *Trioedd Ynys Prydein*, meaning 'Triads of the Island of Britain', are a group of literary sources in medieval manuscripts which preserve fragments of Welsh folklore, mythology and traditional history in groups of three. In Rachel Bromwich's edition, *Triad 51*, Vortigern is named Gwetheyrn the Thin 'who first gave land to the Saxons in this island, and was the first to enter into an alliance with them … And in the end Uthur [Pendragon] and Myrddin Emrys [Merlin] burned Gwrtheyrn in Castell Gwrtherynyawn beside the Wye, in a single conflagration to avenge their brother.'[20]

The Chronicle of the Kings of Britain also refer to a castle by the Wye where Vortigern met his end [21] and further reading of the *History of Wales* by J. E. Lloyd, actually pointed to the place where it stood in Rhyader.[22] Both Monmouth and Nennius mention a St Garmon or Germanus arriving in the area around the mid-430s or 440s who 'cursed the king [Vortigern] for committing incest and thereafter hounding him to his castle where he died.'[23] [24] A church dedicated to St Garmon stands 5.6 km northeast of Rhayader, which 'is set within an ancient Celtic circular Llan', indicating that its foundation dates to the very beginnings of Christianity.[25]

After visiting the library, we felt drawn to explore the site of Castle Gwrtheyrnion, to the west of the crossroads on the east banks of the Wye. As we stood by the river looking up towards a steep grassy knoll, the sun suddenly broke through the clouds to illuminate a white sandstone outcrop streaked with red layers, creating an unusual and dramatic effect.

We soon discovered that there is little to see of the old castle, except for a natural turf-covered crag or mound with a flagpole in the middle marking the location of its keep. On the north and east sides of the hill, defences can be seen below in the form of rock-cut ditches, with a causeway to the northeast which still provides access today. The bailey was at one time lost beneath brambles and weeds until it was cleared by the council in 1998. The castle keep was well maintained when we arrived and full of picnickers and sunbathers. After settling down on a bench under a group of five young oak trees on the lower section, probably part of the old bailey, we contemplated whether this was indeed the site of Vortigern's last stand against his enemies and the place of his demise.

According to official guidebooks, the first recorded fortress on this site dates from 1177, built by Lord Rhys, one of the most successful and powerful Welsh princes of his generation who ruled the province of Deheubarth. Its function was to repel the Normans who were establishing themselves on the coast of Cardiganshire. Lord Rhys supposedly constructed the castle partly in response to the brutal slaughter of his son-in-law Einion Clyd during a skirmish with the Norman invaders. Although Lord Rhys' castle was over 500 years later than the time of Vortigern, we did find certain sources referring to an earlier castle on this site, which Lord Rhys simply rebuilt. During its long history, the castle fell many times at the hands of both the Welsh and the English. Sadly, we found no sign of Vortigern's castle possibly due to its total destruction by fire.

The present castle grounds extend to the north towards the local parish church at the end of West Street dedicated to St Clement, also standing on a knoll overlooking the Wye. The site was previously occupied by a 5th-century church dedicated to St Cynllo, brother of St Teilo and grandson of Coel Hen, the head of several 5th-century royal families of the Hen Ogledd, a line of kings that included Urien, King of Rheged, in Cumbria.

A 1-m-long thigh bone of a possible 3.6-m-tall giant man was found here during the digging of the foundations of a new tower, along with several skeletons laid neatly in a mass grave. They were thought to be soldiers of the garrison of Rhayader Castle slain by Llywelyn ap Lorwerth (*c.* 1172–1240), also known as Llywelyn the Great. Inside the church, we discovered an early font with well-worn carvings of Celtic-style heads at each corner marking the cardinal points.

Bride and the Land of the Two Rivers

From Rhayader, we crossed the Wye over the old stone bridge to enter the mystical realm of Cwmdauddwr, the ancient Welsh Commote, which Michell believed marked the true ritual centre of Wales at the heart of the ancient fifth province of Gwrtheyrnion. Here we hoped to find some evidence of Vortigern. Unlike the fortified sanctuaries of Ireland, the wide and fast-flowing rivers and mountains in this area create natural boundaries and defences. The village is known today as Llansantffraed-Cwmdauddwr meaning 'church or holy enclosure of St Bride at the confluence of rivers', obviously referring to the Wye and the Elan which meet just over 1.5 km downriver of here.

In many cultures, sacred temples were orientated towards the region's world mountain. Their peaks were considered most sacred, as they reached up towards the heavens and the realm of their gods. The ceremonial centre of a kingdom would often be to the south of the holy mountain, indeed, Pumlumon, the Welsh world mountain, is just a few kilometres to the north of Cwmdauddwr.

A short walk from the bridge we encountered a church dedicated to St Bride, or St Ffraid or Fride as she is known in Wales. During our research in Rhayader library, we discovered that close to the church stood an early Celtic monastery, its boundaries still visible from the air. A church dedicated to St Bride is recorded here as early as 1368. Judging by the style of masonry around one of its windows, it probably stood 200 years before that, as some historians suggest. Records show that Lord Rhys called together a gathering at this spot in 1184 to present the vast area of Plynlimon known as Elynedd to the Cistercian monks of Strata Florida Abbey.

St Bride's was the old mother church, holding ecclesiastical control over the 'Commote of Dauddwr'. Here the monks from Abbey Cwm Hir would rest as they travelled along a pilgrim route called the Monk's Trod to Strata Florida Abbey. Yet again, we find a sacred sanctuary of the ancient British goddess between two rivers near a central crossroads marking the omphalos of a central province.

Although the church was heavily restored during late Victorian times, it stands within an enclosure of great antiquity that according to the information board included a holy well dedicated to St Bride, which stood just outside the churchyard. Locals once celebrated the feast of St Ffraid, Fride, or Bride, here at Imbolc on 1 February with the baking of pies to nourish the villagers. As we walked through the graveyard, we could see the stones of an earlier church or perhaps the Celtic monastery. On the wall of the porch is an ancient water stoup decorated with three female heads, perhaps symbolic of the triple goddess Bride. It was placed here after its discovery in a wall of Neuadd Farm, not far from the confluence of the Elan and Wye, which some believe came from the earlier medieval church.

Unfortunately, the church was locked, but, luckily, phone numbers pinned to the porch wall enabled us to contact one of the local key

St Bride's Church, Llansantffraed-Cwmdauddwr

holders, who very obligingly agreed to let us in. As we waited, I noticed more carved stone female heads high up on the exterior walls of the church depicting the maiden, mother and crone. Inside the church, my attention was immediately drawn to a wonderful stained-glass window of St Bride with flames rising out of the top of her head. It is symbolic of the eternal flame and the cult that recognises Bride as the goddess of the fertility of the land, invoked using fire ceremonies.

The altarpiece also impressed us, in the form of a fine stone carving of Leonardo da Vinci's 'The Last Supper'. In the controversial book, *Templar Revelation*, by Clive Prince and Lynn Picknett, the authors claim that instead of painting John the Evangelist sitting to the left of Jesus, which was the tradition, Leonardo painted Mary Magdalene because one of the lost gospels refers to Mary as Jesus' wife.[26]

Stained-glass window of St Bride

By the side of the altar is the church banner with a remarkable woven image, still carried at the front of processions through the village. Within a circle of foliage and flowers is the figure of St Bride with her head tilted down within a central circle. She appears to be seated, cradling a child with a halo around its head, although to us it looked more reminiscent of a sun emerging from her navel as if Bride is giving birth to it – a perfect image of the goddess Bride, placed here at the omphalos, birthing life to the land.

I started to wonder if the holy well near here was a part of the omphalos landscape, so I asked the churchwarden if she knew of the whereabouts of St Bride's Holy Well mentioned on the information board fixed to the gate of the church. To our surprise and dismay, she confessed to having never known of its existence, despite living in the village most of her life. We had asked several locals the same question but were met with the same response.

Despite a thorough search of the church precincts and the immediate surroundings, we still found no sign of a well. Nevertheless, I felt very strongly that it still existed, so, using a single dowsing rod, I asked the question 'In what direction is the well?' The rod immediately swung towards the edge of a farm, but before we could investigate any further, the heavens suddenly opened. With the rain now falling heavily, we decided to stop for the day and head back to our B & B across the river in Rhayader.

We both sensed that the well was an important site and were saddened that it was now lost and forgotten. So often, churches are built next to ancient springs and holy wells that were once part of a sacred ceremonial landscape of ancient pagan worship. They were often rededicated to male saints and their waters were used for baptism, rather than for their healing and nourishing power.

Font in St Bride's Church carved with the heads of the triple goddess

Druids were renowned for planting avenues of oaks leading to holy wells, which was the main focus of their ceremonies. Perhaps the old Welsh Druids communed with the goddess of Wales at this well, focusing their healing thoughts to balance and harmonise the land through the navel of Wales. Our main mission now was to find a copy of an early map of the area that might show us where the well was located, and that meant returning to the local library the following day.

As we left the churchyard, we spotted a few metres away an extremely old pub next to the church called the Triangle, once a 16th-century drovers inn. We popped in to have a quick look and instantly decided that this was where we would spend our evening. We may even meet a local or two who could provide us with some useful information about the area and the whereabouts of the old spring.

We received a warm welcome when we arrived at the B & B in Rhayader; the proprietor seemed keen to learn about our research into the history of the town and church. I asked him if he knew about St Bride's Well and again I was met with a shake of the head. However, he did know a local man who lived in Cwmdauddwr who may be able to help. He described him as about 70 years old, tall and thin with grey hair. He then said, 'If you are going to the Triangle Inn tonight you'll probably find him propping up the bar.'

That evening we walked back across the bridge over the Wye and entered the tiny pub. While buying our drinks at the bar, we asked the proprietors if they had heard of the well. Again, they had no idea that it even existed but remarked that the man who would know had left just five minutes before. 'You will always see him about though,' they said, 'a tall thin grey-haired man.' We looked at each other disbelievingly, as we were certain we had just passed him on our way here, but as we settled into a table in the corner, we assured ourselves that we would eventually track this elusive man down. Warmed by the open fire we tucked into simple but delicious fare made of locally grown produce. For me, the temptation of home-reared beef pie was just too much to resist and reminded me that I was partaking in an ancient custom unique to Cwmdauddwr where, a long time ago, pies were baked on Bride's feast day, 1 February.

As we sat pondering the day after our meal, I fell silent for a moment almost falling into a meditative state and saw in my mind's eye Vortigern and his sword inside a flaming tower to the north of the pub. I dismissed it and carried on discussing with Caroline whether the stories we had read in the library about this enigmatic king were true. According to early historic accounts of the area, Vortigern was killed by 'a fireball from heaven' that crashed into the castle, and not in a siege at the hands of his enemy Ambrosius Aurelianus.

The next day we returned to the library to look for an old map of the area. Again, we experienced disappointment when the librarian informed us that such a map could only be accessed at the County Archives office in Aberystwyth. We decided to stay and research more of the local history and discovered some new information about the existence of an earthen mound next to the Triangle pub where we had dinner the previous night. Just as we were about to leave, the librarian rushed over, and said, 'Hold on, I think I have found what you need in the back office.' In under a minute, she returned brandishing a large map and said, 'For some reason, we must have overlooked this one, they should all be at the National Library.'

Our spirits lifted as she invited us into the back office to view the rather yellowing and creased map. She left us to study it for a while and before long I spotted a site marked as the well just to the south of the church on the edge of the ancient boundary next to a farm, exactly where my dowsing rod was pointing the day before. Comparing the old plan with our OS map, we marked the location and set off back to the church, this time confident that we would find the well.

On the way, we passed a tall elderly grey-haired man, who gave us a friendly nod. Was he the local who knew about the history of the village that everyone had been telling us about? I stopped and thought about calling out to him, but then realised if we had spoken to him at the pub the previous evening, we would not have obtained the information at the library about the mound.

We took a footpath through the field at the back of the church, set within a timeless landscape, perhaps following in the footsteps of the early pilgrims as they walked to the well to honour this ancient goddess of the Britons. As we reached a country lane, we turned left and continued around a sharp bend in the road where the old map indicated the location of Bride's Well. At first glance, there were no

St Bride's Holy Well, Cwmdauddwr

visible signs of it, but after a few minutes of hunting around in the surrounding hedges, we suddenly heard the trickling of water. We moved towards the sound that seemed to be coming from behind brambles and nettles. Excitedly, we used our boots and hands to pull away the tangled vegetation to reveal a spout pouring spring water into an ancient stone trough. We had found St Bride's Well!

We picked out one of our healing stones, and Caroline, with a blessing, placed it in the well in honour of Bride and the elemental spirits that also dwell at this important centre of the old rulers of the Britons. After a pleasurable time by the well, we had a strong sense to visit the mound mentioned in one of the Rhayader history books in the library, said to be partly hidden in a private garden adjoining the carpark.

The site is said to be a remnant of a motte and bailey castle that was later named *Tommen Llan St Fraed* meaning 'grave of Saint Ffraed'. Camden mentions this mound as being 'two furlongs from Rhayader Castle.'[27]

We discovered that a charter written in the 1180s mentions the castle built by Lord Rhys of Deheubarth in 1177, which he had to rebuild in 1194, located on the west bank of the Wye in Cwmdauddwr, and therefore not the motte and bailey site visited previously near St Clement's Church across the river in Rhayader.[28] It certainly made more sense to us that Vortigern's stronghold would have been in this old region of Cwmdauddwr, said to be at the very centre of Gwrtheyrnion, the middle province of Old Wales and 'the place of the High King'. This means that the mound called *Tommen Llan St Fraed* was all that remains of a tower that overlooked the Wye and Bride's sacred sanctuary – we had found Vortigern's tower!

The mound is now standing half-hidden in a private garden, covered by brambles and enclosed by a low wall that partly surrounds the carpark in front of the church gate. The Triangle Inn stands next to the mound on what was probably the site of the bailey. I then remembered my strange vision of Vortigern and his sword while sitting in the pub the previous evening. Was this mound also his grave?

Fire from Heaven or Earth

An interesting account by Giraldus Cambrensis in *The Journey through Wales*, written in 1188, relates how a delinquent locked up in Rhayader Castle arranged for his wife to smuggle a magic bell into the dungeon. This bell named 'Bangu' is believed to have belonged to St David and was given to the man's gaolers to buy his release. However, his captives duped him, keeping the bell while he remained a prisoner. Giraldus relates how every night since that event 'as if by Divine vengeance' the whole town was consumed by fire except for the wall on which the bell was hung.[29]

The 1180 Charter mentions that Lord Rhys rebuilt a castle in Cwmdauddwr in 1194, only 17 years after his original stronghold was constructed. Could this have been the result of the first castle being completely consumed by fire through some kind of 'divine vengeance?' Vortigern too was supposedly consumed by fire in his castle, which an early source says was from a burning bolt from the sky. Could a falling meteorite or burning debris from a passing comet have caused this fireball? Or was it a thunderbolt of plasma produced by an earlier passing of the 540 CE comet previously mentioned, the fireball that vitrified the silica in the walls of Scottish forts and caused the plagues in Britain and Ireland bringing to an end the power of Uisneach and the rise of Clonmacnoise?

The name Brigit is derived from 'arrow of fire' or 'fiery dart' and the Irish saint of that name is widely assumed to have died around 525 CE, during a period, according to Gildas, that the 'Island of Britain was on fire from sea to sea …. Until it had burned almost the whole surface of the island and was licking the western ocean with its fierce red tongue.'[30]

Mike Baillie in *Exodus to Arthur* claims that 'a climatic downturn became evident during this mysterious period when "narrowest tree-ring" chronologies for AD 536 to 545 were observed.' He also cites the work of Dr Victor Clube, who stated that 'fragments from the debris of a destroyed asteroid might have hit the Earth in the area of northern Europe, causing plague, rising sea levels, tsunamis and tectonic plate movements in the 6th century.'[31] In their book *The Cosmic Winter*, Victor Clube and Bill Napier hypothesise that the Earth occasionally passes through a cloud of meteors caused by the breakup of a massive comet or planet. Moreover, the most dangerous period when the Earth passed through this debris was 400–600 CE.[32]

According to Baillie, in 530 CE many 'large shooting stars' were witnessed and recorded in China and also seen across Europe. Zacharias of Mithylene notes, 'In the year of Justinian [538–539] … a great and terrible comet appeared in the sky at evening time for one hundred days.'[33] Baillie refers to a wealth of information from tree-ring data (dendrochronology), ice-core samples, folklore and legends worldwide that indicate that in certain places around the world, there is evidence of comet debris impact.

Baillie states that the name Brigid became attached to places where these events took place because of her association with fire. Irish lawyer and Celtic scholar Whitley Stokes (1830–1909) wrote of Brigid:

> 'A house within which she is staying flames up to heaven, cow dung blazes before her … a fiery pillar rises over her head; sun rays

support her wet cloak … she has according to Giraldus Cambresis a perpetual ashless fire watched by twenty nuns ….'[34]

Perhaps the name of this British goddess at the centre of Wales is associated with the destruction of the castle by fire. Alternatively, was she worshipped here as the goddess of fire since pagan times, an element used as part of the ritual ceremonies at the omphalos, like the ancient fire ceremonies on the Hill of Uisneach at the centre of Ireland?

Understandably, very few written documents survive from this tumultuous period of British history, but if you delve deep enough, you can still find historical accounts that reveal truly unbelievable events. Nigel Pennick drew on many legends and written records in the *Saxon Chronicles* for his book *Lost Cites and Sunken Lands* which reveals just how many places around the coast of Britain lost land in the 6th century due to turbulent events such as severe floods and subsidence.[35]

As we were about to leave, I remembered my friend John's quest for the mythical Excalibur or perhaps Vortigern's sword. Perhaps the High King hid the sword somewhere in the neighbourhood, having sent his trusted servants out to bury it along with his treasure, the so-called Vortigern's hoard. I pondered whether a clue to the actual location of the sword is in the name Cwmdauddwr, 'the valley of the two rivers'. Perhaps Vortigern's sword was, as John thought, 'between two rivers' and is buried a short distance away where the Wye meets the Elan, a landmark that would remain undisturbed for hundreds if not thousands of years. Did King Arthur retrieve this sword at the centre of Wales and instruct its safe return after his death? Maybe it is still there awaiting the right person at the right time to reclaim this symbol of British kingship. Magical swords like Vortigern's or Excalibur are common in Celtic lore, imbued with supernatural powers, such as the sword of Lugh, or Dyrnwyn, the flaming sword of Rhydderch Hael. Perhaps a modern 'King Arthur' will step forward to take the sword, pulling it not from a stone but out of the 'land between two rivers.'

For John, the quest for the sword inspired him to keep going during tough times as a farmer. Although he was often disappointed when the quests failed, he knew intuitively that Excalibur was still out there somewhere waiting to be found.

Abbey Cwm Hir and the Plight of the Welsh Princes

Our next quest at the centre of Wales was to search for another distinct feature found in omphalos landscapes – a religious centre of power comparable to Clonmacnoise in Ireland or Dunkeld in Scotland. However, we found that on either side of Cwmdauddwr in the 'middle lands of Gwrtheyrnion' are Abbey Cwm Hir and Strata Florida, two of the greatest religious houses in Wales (see Fig. 15).

Ruins of Abbey Cwm Hir

Abbey Cwm Hir is situated just a few kilometres to the northeast of Rhayader in the beautiful and peaceful Clywedog Valley. It was founded in 1144 by Cistercian monks, the abbey buildings having been added in 1176 by Lord Rhys of Deheubarth, a year before he rebuilt Cwmdauddwr Castle after the mysterious fire. The Victorian parish church of St Mary, about 800 m north of the abbey, was constructed close to the site of an earlier church dedicated to St Bridget. Perhaps the threat of another 'arrow of fire' from heaven that had previously threatened Cwmdauddwr was too much to risk the building of another monastery there, which may explain why important burials and ceremonies were transferred to this new abbey site close to a Bride shrine.

The gift of lands and money from various Welsh princes enabled the abbey to grow in wealth and size over the coming centuries and it would have been the largest in Wales if fully completed. However, the abbey's 14-bay nave was still longer than those of Canterbury and Salisbury Cathedrals and twice as long as that of St David's. At one point during a time of great instability in the country, the abbey was controlled by the English Knight Roger Third Baron Mortimer and First Earl of March (1287–1330). Because it was hallowed ground to the Welsh Princes the abbey endured much conflict, having been burned by the forces of Owain Glyndŵr in 1401 in an attempt to retake it, and was finally suppressed during the Dissolution of the Monasteries in 1538 when most of its buildings were plundered for stone.

The abbey is still renowned as a sacred burial ground and described as 'a tranquil place with a princely presence' – perhaps due to the many Welsh nobles that lie buried here close to the centre of their kingdom. One of them, Llywelyn the Last or Llywelyn ap Gruffudd, was the last native Prince of Wales, interred close to the high altar after he died in 1282 while fighting the English near Builth Wells. The court poet of the Kingdom of Gwynedd wrote of him:

'A man was slain for us,
a man of might,
a man for Wales was bold,
I name him:
Manly Llewelyn,
best man of Welshmen.'[36]

At the time, the abbey was under the patronage of his ancestors, the kings of Gwynedd, whose kingdom stretched at one time as far as Anglesey and Snowdonia. His grandfather Llywelyn ap Lorwerth was one of Gwynedd's greatest princes who married Joan, the daughter of King John of England.

After Llywelyn ap Gruffudd's death, the valiant resistance of the Welsh finally collapsed, leaving Wales under full control of the English throne, with Llywelyn's heirs either killed or imprisoned, their castles destroyed and their treasures taken. Llewelyn's severed head was crowned with ivy and impaled on a spike at the Tower of London, to mock the prophecy that a Welsh Prince would one day be crowned King of England.

The English further persecuted the Welsh royal line through the imprisonment for life of all the male heirs of Llywelyn and his brother Dafydd. Despite this, the Welsh continued to rebel against English rule, their sole aim being to uphold their freedom and liberty.

Owain Glyndŵr was the last native Prince of Wales from the princely line of the ancient and powerful Kingdom of Powys that once stretched from Mid Wales to the River Dee in the north. He became the last 'heart and hope of Wales' and led a revolt against the English forces of Henry IV after enduring years of high taxes to pay for the English wars in France. The Welsh also resented the privileges enjoyed by the new English landowners who dwelt in their remote castles. In 1401, Owain led his army to victory at the Battle of Mynydd Hyddgen against the English forces, on the slopes of Pumlumon.

Replica grave slab of Llywelyn ap Gruffudd, Prince of Wales, at Abbey Cwm Hir

Swords have played an important part in Welsh history and mythology and the great seal of Owain Glyndwr depicts him holding a sword like Excalibur. However, it could be the sword given to him by King Charles VI of France along with a suit of armour.

In the spring of 1402, a year after Owain's victory, a comet appeared in the sky (now known to be Hailey's Comet), which the Welsh Bards saw as an omen. They sang of ancient prophesies and victory, believing Owain to be the Welsh Prince that would be crowned on the English throne. As Owain engages in another successful assault on the lands of the powerful Mortimer family in Glamorgan and Gwent, King Henry IV with a vast army is preparing another attack on the Welsh. However, just before the advance, the English are bombarded with 'rain, then hail, and even snow, causing them to flounder. The King is almost killed by a huge tent pole as it collapses in the storm, while his men, forced to sleep in their rusting armour to stave off the cold, whisper among themselves that it was the wizard Prince Owain who must have conjured up such a 'force of nature against them.'[37]

By 1405, most of Wales was back in Welsh hands, but this was not to last. Henry retaliates and, due to heavy losses, the Welsh cause is finally lost. Meanwhile, Owain Glyndŵr evades capture and vanishes.

Helsby writes that the Bards compare his disappearance with that of King Arthur who fled to the mysterious Avalon, and, like Arthur, there were legends of Owain coming to the aid of his people after awakening from his perpetual slumber.[38] Owain was later portrayed in William Shakespeare's play *Henry IV, Part 1*, characterised as Owen Glendower, a wild and exotic man ruled by magic and emotion.

His persistent fight for independence paved the way for the young Henry Twdr or Tudor of Wales to achieve glory at Bosworth Field, which incidentally is located at the very centre of England. He was the son of Margaret Beaufort, a direct descendent of King Edward III, and Edmund Tudor of Penmynydd, First Earl of Richmond. Henry's victory against King Richard III proved the old prophecy true when finally a Welsh prince would take the throne of England, producing one of the greatest dynasties of kings and queens in British history.

There is no doubt that, if it had not been for the collapse of the royal line of Wales at the hands of the English, Abbey Cwm Hir would have become the largest and most important building in Wales and instead of being the burial ground of Princes it would be the burial ground of Welsh Kings.

Strata Florida and the Grail

From Abbey Cwm Hir, an ancient pilgrim route called the Monks' Trod, mentioned earlier, passes through Rhayader and Cwmdauddwr, and travels close to the source of the River Teifi, to another Cistercian house in this central region called Strata Florida Abbey (see Fig. 15). The Trod is one of the oldest constructed trackways in the British Isles, with its hollow green lanes running through remote valleys and isolated and ruined settlements, and is still walked by pilgrims today.

The abbey is another atmospheric ruin, set in lush meadows next to the River Teifi situated in the hills above the Ceredigion town of Tregaron. The landscape is dominated by the Cambrian Mountains, with the abbey lying in a small glaciated valley to the west.

The Norman Robert Fitz Stephen founded the first abbey in 1164 for the Cistercians, then located 3 km away by the banks of the Afon Fflur, from which Strata Florida or Ystrad Fflur meaning 'vale of flowers' takes its name. In 1184, Lord Rhys, who built Abbey Cwm Hir and Cwmdauddwr Castle, would re-establish the abbey at its present site by the River Teifi. Historians and archaeologists believe, however, that the site of the abbey was once much more extensive than the ruins we see today and may have been the largest Cistercian abbey in Britain and one of the main pilgrimage centres of Europe,

Ruins of Strata Florida Abbey

although no known shrine was ever thought to have existed there, unlike at St David's.

Like Abbey Cwm Hir, it was for a period one of the wealthiest religious institutions in Wales, with magnificent buildings and thousands of acres of land. *The Welsh Annals*, later known as *Brut y Tywysogion* (Chronicle of the Princes), one of the most controversial and historically important books on Welsh history, was thought to have been compiled here. The abbey had close ties with the House of Deheubarth, and although Lord Rhys was interred at St David's Cathedral, his brother, sons, daughters and grandchildren lie buried here, with many grave slabs from this royal cemetery still on show. Under Lord Rhys' patronage, the abbey had a great cultural influence in medieval Wales, with much Welsh scholarship in the learning of the classics and the arts centred here.

Many historians question why Lord Rhys moved the abbey to this site. Professor David Austin of the University of Wales, writing for *Wales Online* in 2012, states there is evidence that the site was already important before the abbey's foundation: 'The Abbey church, the heart of the monastery, was put over the southern edge of an ancient pre-Cistercian burial ground, with its great central crossing embracing a pre-existing holy well.' In addition, stone burial markers uncovered here were of early native kings of Wales, 'formed in the same motifs as those of the great west door.' He believes that the abbey's west entrance was 'the metaphorical place of birth and entry, and at its east end, at the point of death and transcendence, Celtic art is deployed as a marker.'[39]

However, as we have found while dowsing the serpent energies along the Belinus Line, important religious sites were often built over ancient springs or holy wells – the high altar at Winchester Cathedral for instance stands over two ancient springs that are still in the crypt below. The Cathedral precinct in Winchester was the former site of several springs and stone circles and many people wonder why the old stonemasons went to so much effort to build the grandest cathedral in the western world over such a boggy area. No doubt they were attracted by the telluric energies that exist at this site created by the fusion of two powerful male and female serpent energies and the springs, amplified by a stone building designed using the proportions of sacred geometry.[40]

The megalithic people deliberately built the stone circles upon such a site to utilise the power of the water in the same way as a stone-built cathedral. Perhaps there was a complex of prehistoric stone monuments and burial mounds at Strata Florida that once utilised the energy of the old holy well.

An archaeological survey of the area recently uncovered another holy well situated on a hill above the abbey. Although it does not appear on any map and has no recorded dedication, it is recognised as a sacred site as flowers and white quartz stones have been recently left here. The well has been described as 'beautifully made, with carefully cut slate slabs, which must have been brought from some distance away, lining the cistern and forming a broad platform and steps around it.' Even a timber pipe was installed to feed the spring water into the cistern.[41] Perhaps it was considered to have miraculous healing powers or was a place of early pagan goddess worship, similar to the St Bride wells we have encountered at power centres throughout the British Isles.

The monks may have used the water from this well while utilising the rich fertile lands on the flood plains as summer pasture for the grazing of sheep. This highly disciplined order who followed a rigid pattern of life dedicated to prayer and study also worked physically hard. They made use of other natural resources through mining and quarrying at Cwmystwyth as well as extracting peat from the boglands for fuel. They stocked the nearby Teifi Pools, the source of the Teifi River in the Cambrian Mountains, with fish for the abbey.

Henry IV's army devastated the abbey during the War of Independence led by Owain Glyndŵr, and like other abbeys throughout England and Wales, it succumbed to further destruction wrought by the Reformation. The land then passed into the hands of the landed gentry, who used intensive methods to farm the land.

As we entered the extensive ruined complex through the impressive west doorway of the abbey church, decorated with roll mouldings and spiral motifs, we noticed an unusual feature in what would have been the area of the monks' choir. It appeared to be a stone-lined basin set into the ground, which may have held water, with four steps leading down to it on two sides. Some believe it to be part of a Mandatum ritual, where, once a year on Maundy Thursday, the abbot would wash the feet of twelve poor commoners who had been specially invited into the abbey. In the covered chapels of the south transept, we came across one of the finest collections of decorated tiles, including an unusual one depicting a 'man with a mirror'.

According to legend, monks brought the Holy Grail here from Glastonbury, which was then handed down through various key families upon the dissolution of the monasteries. A local story says that in fear for their lives from Henry VIII's forces, seven monks escaped into the mountains beyond Plynlimon to a remote area before moving to Nanteos near Aberystwyth in 1539 where they kept the cup, said to be an ancient olive wooden bowl. Water given from the cup healed many people and supposedly remained in the hands of the Powells who lived there until the property was sold in the 1950s. Many believe that these seven monks lie buried in the cellar, and many ghostly 'goings-on' still occur there.

The ghost of a monk also haunts Strata Florida Abbey and appears on Christmas Eve in the area where the altar once stood. Candles are often seen alight inside the abbey. Several people we know have had deep spiritual experiences here, perhaps feeling the power of the energy where the veil between the worlds of spirit and matter is especially thin. The lights may be geoplasma released out of the region's powerful geology. Perhaps they built the abbey here because the area is haunted by the spectral lights, which they may have interpreted as spirits or even angels.

On Google Earth, I noticed that the axis of the abbey, which points slightly northeast, is directly in line with Abbey Cwm Hir, as if both abbeys are pointing towards each other. Was the intention of Lord

Rhys to create a geomantic connection between these two abbeys? If so, it is a remarkable feat of surveying.

Strata Florida was renowned for being difficult to access before the construction of modern roads. Before then, a pilgrim would have had to walk through the dense North Tywi Forest, then scramble down a steep valley, follow the bank of a stream to a place where it is shallow enough to ford, and then ascend the opposite steep slope of a mountain, before finally passing through dense rows of Sitka spruce. Perhaps it is unsurprising that it has been lost from most people's consciousness for so long in this ever-changing and fast-moving world. Luckily, it is now a scheduled ancient monument protected by Welsh Heritage.

Before we departed this navel landscape of Wales, we stood at the centre of the old ruins and sent healing light from here to Abbey Cwm Hir. We visualised the light spreading across the land along the Monk's Trod through Cwmdauddwr and Rhayader as it reconnects the energy of these old sites that have for so long represented the heart of a nation.

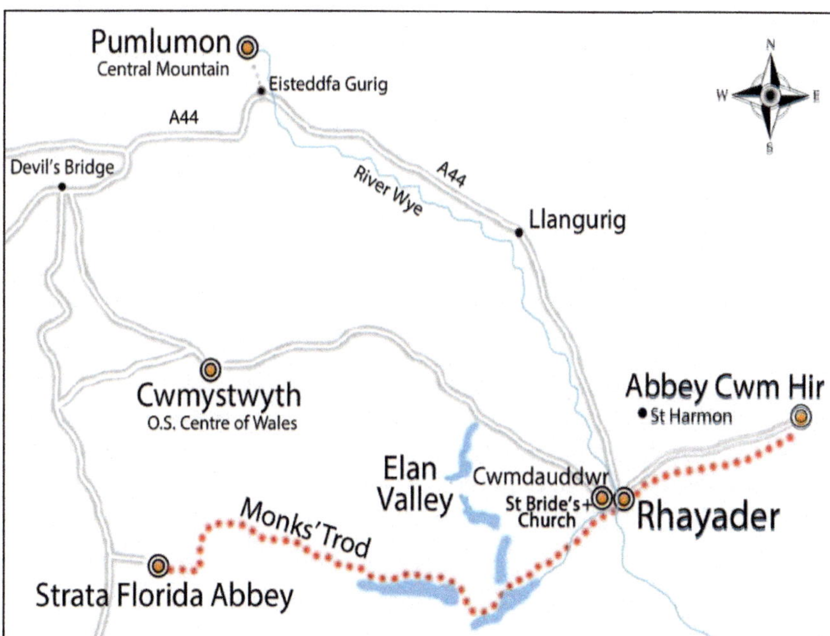

Figure 15. The centre places of Wales

References:

1. MacKillop J (2008) *Myths and Legends of the Celts*. Penguin, London.
2. Donnelly P Prof. *Welsh People Could Be Most Ancient in UK, DNA Suggests*. http://www.bbc.co.uk/news/uk-wales-18489735.
3. Bromwich R (1961) *The Welsh Triads*. University of Wales Press, Cardiff.
4. Roberts A (1975) *Atlantean Traditions in Ancient Britain*. Rider & Co, London.
5. Rees A & Rees B (1978) *Celtic Heritage*. Thames & Hudson, London.
6. Michell J & Rhone C (1991) *Twelve-Tribe Nations and the Science of Enchanting the Landscape*. Thames & Hudson, London.
7. Rees A & Rees B (1978) *Celtic Heritage*. Thames & Hudson, London.
8. ibid.
9. Morris J (1980) *'Nennius' British History and the Welsh Annals*. Phillimore, London.
10. Michell J & Rhone C (1991) *Twelve-Tribe Nations and the Science of Enchanting the Landscape*. Thames & Hudson, London.
11. Biltcliffe G (2009) *The Spirit of Portland, Revelations of a Sacred Isle*. Roving Press, Dorset.
12. Banc Ty'nddôl sun-disc. https://en.wikipedia.org/wiki/Banc_Ty%27ndd%C3%B4l_sundisc.
13. Gilbert A, Wilson A & Blackett B (1998) *The Holy Kingdom: The Quest for the Real King Arthur*. Bantam Press, London.
14. Morris J (1978) *Gildas: The Ruin of Britain and Other Documents*. Phillimore, London.
15. Morris J (1980) '*Nennius' British History and the Welsh Annals*. Phillimore, London.
16. ibid.
17. Thorpe L (Translator) (1966) *Geoffrey of Monmouth: The History of the Kings of Britain*. The Folio Society, London.
18. Roberts Revd P (Translator) (1811) *The Chronicle of the Kings of Britain*, translated from the Welsh Copy attributed to Tysilio. E Williams, London.
19. Camden William (1722) *Britannia, or a Chorographical Description of Great Britain and Ireland, Together with the Adjacent Islands, Vol. 1*. Gibson E (Translator), re-published 2017 by Forgotten Books, London.
20. Bromwich R (1961) *The Welsh Triads*. University of Wales Press, Cardiff.
21. Roberts Revd P (Translator) (1811) *The Chronicle of the Kings of Britain*, Translated from the Welsh Copy attributed to Tysilio. E Williams, London.
22. Lloyd J E (2006) *History of Wales*. Barnes and Noble, New York.
23. Thorpe L (Translator) (1966) *Geoffrey of Monmouth: The History of the Kings of Britain*. The Folio Society, London.
24. Morris J (1980) '*Nennius' British History and the Welsh Annals*. Phillimore, London.
25.https://www.jlb2011.co.uk/walespic/churches/st-harmon1.htm
26. Picknett L Prince C (2007) *The Templar Revelation: Secret Guardians of the True Identity of Christ*. Corgi, London.

27. Camden William (1722) *Britannia, or a Chorographical Description of Great Britain and Ireland, Together with the Adjacent Islands, Vol. 1*. Gibson E (Translator), re-published 2017 by Forgotten Books, London
28. Rhayader Castle.
http://castlefacts.info/Castledetails/Castledetails3?Uin=20904&Searchtex t=Rhayader%20 Castle%20(Radnorshire).
29. Cambrensis Giraldus (1188) *The Journey Through Wales and the Description of Wales*.Penguin Classics, London.
30. Morris J (1978) *Gildas: The Ruin of Britain and Other Documents*. Phillimore, London.
31. Baillie M (1998) *Exodus to Arthur: Catastrophic Encounters with Comets*. Batsford, London.
32. Clube V & Napier B (1990) *The Cosmic Winter*. Blackwell, Oxford.
33. Turney C (2006) *Bones, Rocks and Stars: The Science of When Things Happened*. Palgrave Macmillan, London.
34. Baillie M (1998) *Exodus to Arthur: Catastrophic Encounters with Comets*. Batsford, London.
35. Pennick N (1997) *Lost Cities and Sunken Lands*. Capall Bann, Taunton.
36. According to a notice board at Abbey Cwm Hir.
37. Helsby B (2004) *A Prophesy for a King: A History of Welsh Princes, English Kings, and a Prophecy Fulfilled*. The Brenin Project.
https://genyreviews.cf/public/get-ebook-a-prophecyfor-a-king-0954945603-djvu.html.
38. Ibid
39. Strata Florida Abbey. http://www.walesonline.co.uk/news/wales-news/welsh-history-month-strata-florida-2045984
40. Biltcliffe G & Hoare C (2012) *The Spine of Albion: An Exploration of Earth Energies and Landscape Mysteries along the Belinus Line*. Sacred Lands Publishing, Weymouth.
41. https://www.theguardian.com/uk/1999/nov/22/maevkennedy

Chapter 5

The Ancient Land of Kernow

The Logan Stone, Helman Tor

Cornwall is the south-westernmost county within the United Kingdom, bordered by the English Channel to the south, the Atlantic Ocean to the north and west and the county of Devon to the east. This rocky peninsular was one of the last refuges of the ancient Britons during their enforced exodus westwards by the invading Saxons and Angles. Safe in its situation, surrounded by the strong currents of the Atlantic Ocean and bordered by the great river Tamar, Cornwall and its people have maintained a degree of separateness and independence and in recent times revived their P-Celtic Brythonic language.

The land has a timeless feel where megalithic stones and ancient crosses punctuate a diverse landscape of ghostly moorlands, watery ravines and remote woodlands where occasionally you will encounter sacred springs or holy wells. Crossing the border from Devon, we often sense that we have entered a foreign yet enchanted land. Local author Paul Broadhurst explores many of Cornwall's landscape mysteries in his book *The Secret Land*, and he describes the feeling after crossing the Tamar as encountering a 'subtle shift in perception, a vague feeling of expectation and adventure in the air.'[1]

Cornwall, known as *Kernow* in the Brythonic language, has a backbone of crystalline granite intrusions and high silica Devonian shales, which generate a powerful magnetic geology and a strange feeling of otherworldliness. Dr Philip Callahan found that rocks high in silica over underground water aquifers are conducive to a 'thin veil' place, where people often experience moments of divine connection to spirit, healing, ghostly apparitions, time-slips and balls of plasma.[2]

As the powerful waves that pound Cornwall's coastline, on all but its east side, charge up the silica stones, the resulting energy affects the temporal lobe in our brain, inducing for some a dream-like or psychic state that can allow us into other dimensional levels where elementals and deities dwell. The abundant megalithic monuments across this rocky land amplify the landscape's unique energies, particularly on or near fault lines or blind springs and aquafers.

Kernow's many holy wells, half hidden in the hedgerows, are also remarkable and renowned healing places, their mineral-rich waters charged by the pressure of the magnetic rocks. One potent site called King Arthur's Hall on Bodmin Moor, is a unique rectangular stone-lined earthen water temple aligned to the north, surrounded by a curb of megaliths dating from Neolithic times.[3] Like Ireland, Cornwall is considered the realm of the goddess, her life-giving and sustaining force having been honoured by ancient peoples over thousands of years. Even its most famous river, the Tamar, is named after the goddess Tamara.[4]

As you would expect with an ancient British kingdom, Cornwall has its fair share of legends, including its Bronze Age foundation myth. According to Geoffrey of Monmouth, Corineus along with the Trojan Prince Brutus, a descendant of Aeneas, sailed with a band of Trojan immigrants to Britain after the fall of Troy around 1100 BCE. After defeating the native giants, including their monstrous leader Gogmagog, whom Corineus vanquished, Brutus became the first king to rule this ancient land, awarding Corineus with Cornwall.[5] Curiously, for many years wooden effigies of Corineus and Gogmagog were paraded as part of the Lord Mayor of London's annual show and displayed in the Guildhall in the City of London.

The cult of the fire goddess and the perpetual flame associated with the Greek deity Vesta was allegedly brought to the west by Aeneas, who survived the fires of Troy to establish a new colony at Lavinium, the sacred city of the Latins on the coast just south of Rome, known today as Practica de Mare.[6] The same goddess may have arrived in Britain with Brutus, later becoming one of the primary goddesses of the Britons, perhaps evolving into Brit, Bride or Britannia.

The Cornish landscape has been a source of mining interest since early times due to its rich mineral content, including the soft, silvery-white metal tin, which has been traded since the Middle Eastern seafaring Phoenicians arrived here around 500 BCE. Tin was vital for making bronze and the Cornish tin mines were a closely guarded secret. Julius Caesar also knew of the importance of British tin when he invaded the island in 55 BCE, and during the reign of Claudius, the Romans were in control of most of the world's tin supplies. Some antiquarians believed the tin trade existed as early as 1500 BCE and Sir Edward Creasy writes, 'The British mines mainly supplied the glorious adornment of Solomon's Temple.'[7]

Cornwall was known by the Romans as *Cornubia*, which at that time was part of the Kingdom of Dumnonia, ruled over by the High King of the Cornovii; the name Cornwall is often thought to have been derived from this tribe. In 60 BCE, the Greek historian Diodorus Siculus named Cornwall *Belerion* meaning 'shining land'. Cornwall's early medieval history, in particular the early Welsh and Breton sources, refers to the legendary King Arthur of the Britons as being a king of Cornwall. Such a hero could well have existed, as early British kings such as Belinus, son of King Dunvallo Molmutius, was reputedly King of Loegria, Kambria and Cornwall *c.* 390 BCE. Likewise, King Constantine the Blessed *c.* 542 CE was Duke of Cornwall. Geoffrey of Monmouth writes that Tintagel Castle was the reputed place of King Arthur's conception and birth and the possible site of Camelot.[8]

Another of his suggested courts was at Kelliwic or Celliweg, now Callington, mentioned in the medieval *Welsh Triads* along with Mynyw (St David's) in Wales and Pen-Rhionydd or Penrynydd in the North of England, and cited as one of the 'Three Tribal Thrones of the Island of Britain.'[9] In the Arthurian Romances, Gorlois of Tintagel, husband of Igraine before Uther Pendragon and father of Morgan le Fay, held the title Duke of Cornwall in the early 6th century. The place where King Arthur met Mordred during the decisive Battle of Camlann in 537 is favoured by some as being around the old settlement of Slaughterbridge, near the Cornish town of Camelford.

One of the first Celtic Christian missionaries to set foot in Cornwall was St Piran or Pyran (d. *c.* 480), who became the patron saint of Cornwall, although St Michael and St Petroc also have some claim to this title. Several sources have identified him as St Ciaran of

Saigir, for both of their feast days lie on the same day, 5 March. The issue of identifying this saint becomes clearer with the interchange between the Cornish and Irish languages. The Irish word for head is 'Cedd' but in Cornish, it is 'Penn', hence the translation of Ciaran to Piran.

St Ciaran or Piran's establishment of an important ecclesiastical site during early Christian times should not be confused with the saint who founded the religious complex of Clonmacnoise at the centre of Ireland and Fearnan near the centre of Scotland. According to medieval Irish manuscripts, Ciaran of Saigir's father was Lugna, a nobleman of the Dál Birn rulers of the Kingdom of Osraige. His mother Liadán, before she conceived Ciaran, had a dream that a star fell into her mouth. She related this dream to the Druids who told her that she would bear a son 'whose fame and virtues would be known as far as the world's end.' Ciaran of Clonmacnoise has a similar vision associated with him, which foretells him having a significant influence over the flowering of Christianity at the centre of Ireland, which would become one of the most important schools of ancient knowledge in Europe. Ciaran supposedly settled as a hermit at Saighir or Seir Kieran near the central Slieve Bloom Mountains, but soon disciples were attracted to him and a large monastery grew up around his cell, which became the chosen burial place for the Kings of Osraige. This important and powerful ecclesiastical centre was the burial place of Prince Diarmait, son of Ceerball, the High King of Osraige, the young prince 'soon to be king' who aided Ciaran of Clonmacnoise during the foundation ceremony of his new monastery.[10]

Cornish folklore says that St Piran arrived at these shores tied to a millstone, placed there by the Irish who, having tired of his good deeds, tossed him into a stormy sea. However, instead of drowning as was expected, the monk floated and was miraculously carried by the waves to the north coast of Cornwall at Perranporth. Here he built a stone oratory or chapel, now located on Penhale Sands about 2 km to the east of Perranporth. It was rediscovered in the late 1800s after being buried in the sand for hundreds of years and is now preserved under a rather hideous concrete building, much to the locals' dismay.

Dumgarth, Dwingarth, Donyarth or Doniert was the last recorded king of Cornwall, possibly a vassal of the Kingdom of Wessex. King Doniert's Stone, consisting of two pieces of richly carved Celtic crosses, stands at St Cleer in Cornwall, inscribed *doniert rogavit pro anima* meaning 'Doniert has asked [for this to be made] for his soul's sake.' The inscription commemorates this great king of Dumnonia, a kingdom that covered most of southwest Britain, who drowned in *c.* 875. Below here is an underground passage and cross-shaped chamber thought to be either the remains of tin workings or a possible oratory.

St Piran's Oratory, Penhale Sands

After many years fighting the incoming Saxons and Danes, the Cornish Celts finally lost their independence in 927 CE when Howel, the last King of Cornwall, was forced to swear allegiance to Athelstan, King of Wessex, alongside the kings of Northern England, Wales and Scotland. In 1337, the title Duke of Cornwall was created by the English monarchy, to be held by the king's eldest son and heir. After the signing of a treaty, the Anglo-Saxon Athelstan became the first supreme sovereign of pre-Norman Britain, dashing any hopes of a Celtic resurgence by the Cornish, Welsh and Scottish.

A. L. Rowse wrote that the Cornish were gradually 'absorbed into the mainstream of English life' between 1485 and 1700. This slow response to join the rest of Britain was possibly due to Cornwall's physical isolation, being practically severed from the rest of Britain by the River Tamar, which runs almost from sea to sea. The native Cornish are descended from the ancient Britons, and 'as late as the mid-16th century, they still possessed their own styles of dress, their own folklore, their own naming-customs, their own agricultural practices and their own games and pastimes.'[11] According to

Professor Mark Stoyle, in *West Britons: Cornish Identities and the Early Modern British State*, the indigenous peoples of Cornwall are descendants of the early British who up to 500 years ago believed themselves to be a distinctive people or 'race'. DNA studies by researchers at Oxford University have found that native Cornish people, together with the Welsh and Bretons, are indeed related to the most ancient of the Britons and the most genetically distinct of all the groups on mainland Britain.[12]

Cornwall was fully incorporated into the Kingdom of Great Britain along with the rest of England by the 18th century with much of Cornwall's language and culture in steep decline. The Industrial Revolution and Methodism brought huge changes to the county and, with the loss of many of its tin mines, mass migrations overseas soon followed.[13]

The Navel of Cornwall and the Saint's Way

The small picturesque village of Lanivet is located at the very heart of mid-Cornwall, an area now bisected by the main tourist route of the busy A30. Lanivet lies 4 km southwest of Bodmin and is renowned as the geographical centre of Cornwall. The village is situated within a bowl-shaped valley, almost mirroring the depression of a belly button or navel, with many springs running down towards the church and the main street.

The early stone crosses in the churchyard mark it as a sacred omphalos of the early Christian saints who came here to establish a religious centre. The village stands at the halfway point on the Saint's Way, an old trail that links the ancient ports of Padstow in the Camel Estuary and Lostwithiel or 'The Port of Fawi' next to the River Fowey on Cornwall's southern shores, which throughout the 14th century was its capital. Lanivet is also situated centrally along the old east-west route that runs along the spine of Cornwall, now replaced by the A30, but only if you discount the peninsular of Penwith where we find Land's End and St Michael's Mount.

A uniquely carved stone pillar and the crossroads of ancient tracks are two integral features in many omphalos landscapes. The Saint's Way is also known as the Drover's Way, used in the past by traders and pilgrims from Ireland and Wales as they made their way to Brittany and onwards to Rome or the great shrines of Spain at Compostela. They would have used this way as a safer overland option rather than risking the rocks and treacherous seas around the horn of Cornwall.[14]

Archaeological evidence from the number of standing stones and settlements along this route suggests it was utilised by early traders such as the seafaring Phoenicians, Etruscans and Greeks, who came

Figure 16. Map of Cornwall showing the Saint's Way

to this land to seek Cornwall's rich resource of metals, most notably tin used in the making of bronze. Paul Broadhurst notes that classical writers mention how the Cornish warmly welcomed these foreign traders and that Lanivet as a sacred centre was 'a great melting pot of many religions and different beliefs in a way that was unusual to the rest of Britain.'[15] Archaeologists also found early remains of Byzantine pottery from North Africa, Turkey and Carthage from a trading settlement situated at the mouth of the River Camel.

This ancient path has since been resurrected as a pilgrim trail, although its route has been changed in places to combine public rights-of-way and interesting focal points. Numerous early Celtic stone crosses can be found in hedges and on banks along this ancient route. Examples include the Reperry Cross beside the old pre-turnpike road from Bodmin to St Austell, the Fenton Pits Cross, and the St Ingunger Cross next to a chapel and holy well just southwest of Lanivet. This now-forgotten site dating from the early 6th century was home to the hermit St Congar of Congresbury, who founded a Celtic Christian settlement here.

The Saint's Way was also a safe overland route between Ireland and Brittany for the Celtic Christian missionaries during the Saxon raids of England. After the Saxons destroyed most of the early churches in England, the Britons and their old Celtic religion fled to Wales, Northern Britain, Cornwall and Brittany. Although Cornwall came under the control of Saxon King Egbert of Wessex in 883, this far-southwestern kingdom was soon ignored when his attention was diverted north towards a new enemy, the Danes. This left Cornwall free for the British merchants and religious men to use its routes for onward travel to the Continent.

Many Bronze Age markers stand at strategic places along the Saint's Way, such as the 3-m-tall Longstone on St Breock Downs called *Men Gurta* or 'the stone of waiting', which is said to weigh a whopping 16.5 tons. This whole area is sacred ground, surrounded in all directions by Bronze Age burial mounds. The prominent natural granite outcrop of Helman Tor to the south of Lanivet has the remains of a Neolithic enclosure and, on a clear day, you can see both the Camel and Fowey estuaries. Traces of an old section of sunken road lined with granite-walled hedges lead south from Helman Tor to Lostwithiel. As the Fowey estuary began to silt up in the 1500s, owing to excessive streaming for tin on the moors, Lostwithiel as a port eventually became unnavigable to sea-going ships, losing its shipping trade to the natural harbour at the medieval village of Fowey.

Lanivet's village green is surrounded by pretty stone cottages and an ancient parish church, with an old abbey, a pub and a shop close by. As we parked the car and walked towards the church we were heartened by the spring sunshine and delightful birdsong. Upon entering the churchyard, our friend who accompanied us that day announced that it was Lady Day, with Mothering Sunday the following day. Lady Day is the feast day of 'the Annunciation of the (Blessed) Virgin Mary', the Christian celebration of the announcement by the angel Gabriel to the Virgin Mary that she would conceive and become the mother of Jesus. This seemed a very

Celtic Christian cross at Lanivet Church

auspicious time considering that one of the purposes of our journeys around the sacred centres of Albion was to resurrect and honour the divine energy of the Mother goddess at such places.

The circular churchyard is indicative of its ancient origins as a pre-Christian place of worship, being the possible ceremonial sanctuary of the Druids. Lanivet translates as 'a pagan sacred enclosure or grove', *Lan* meaning 'church' or 'enclosure' and *neved* meaning 'pagan place'. However, Nicholas Roscarrock, writing in *c.*1600, believed that Neved came from St Nivet, an earlier dedication of the church, Nivet or Nevidh being the daughter of the 5th-century Welsh King Brychan.[16]

The church stands adjacent to the village green, a rare English feature in Cornwall. The early Celtic crosses in the circular churchyard and the Romano-British stones stored inside the church have led many to believe that it stands on the site of an early monastery. However, the shape of the churchyard has the same feel and dimensions as the circular Celtic sanctuary of St Bride's Church at Cwmdauddwr in Wales. A carpet of celandines, primroses and violets greeted us as we wandered around the back of the church to see the famous carved stone cross of Lanivet, which has the unique reputation of marking the geographical centre of Cornwall.

This exquisitely carved granite cross is the most decorated in Cornwall and stands in a solitary position on the higher-sloping ground with Celtic knot designs on all four sides. What makes this curious cross even more special is the additional carving of a human figure with a halo or aura around it and a spiral coming out from its waist that some believe is a tail. The cross also features several cup and ring or dot and circle marks, one on the tail and another between the figure's legs. Moreover, on one of its side panels is another cup mark encircled by two concentric rings, which may be symbolic of a geomantic centre. We wondered if the tail or spiral with the dot within the circle engraving signifies an umbilical cord connected to a symbolic centre, perhaps the centre of their kingdom or the centre of the Universe.

On the north side of the church shrouded by an enormous yew tree is another tall carved granite 'wheel' cross, said to date from the 10th century. In the porch, is a rare hogback tomb associated with burials of Norse warriors. There were once eight early crosses standing in the churchyard, which some believe were brought here from elsewhere. Similar to St Bride's Church at the centre of Wales, this atmospheric and magical site felt far older than the Norman church that stands here today and almost certainly was an important ritual centre of the old British Kingdom of Cornwall. However, one important element was missing – a holy well, the focus of goddess worship – but as we were soon to discover, we were standing only a short distance away from it.

Although records claim that Lanivet Church has no known dedication, its feast day is the last Thursday in April, curiously only a few days before the spring celebrations of Beltane. Inside the church are the tombs of the Courtenay family of Tremere in Lanivet, descendants of the Earls of Devon of Powderham Castle who were landowners in the parish during the 14th century. One of the treasures of this church is an unusual stone thought to be Romano-British called the 'Annicu Stone', dated to the 5th or 6th century and marked with a Latin inscription commemorating someone called Annicu, of whom nothing is known. More treasures, now sadly gone but recorded in 1864, included medieval frescos, one of which depicted a crowned female saint holding a sceptre said to be St Crede, Creda or Cride. Another depicts Christ cupping his hands under an open wound in his chest as if to catch the blood. The figure is also wearing an unusual headdress, with foliate decoration on his arms and torso. A third fresco showed a dragon holding or swallowing a group of naked people in its mouth. The fresco of St Crede struck a chord with me and I wondered why the name sounded so familiar.

St Benet's Abbey

While exploring the area, we chose to stay at St Benet's Abbey in Lanivet village not only because of its fabulous garden next to a trickling brook but also for its fascinating history. As soon as we arrived, we instantly noticed a large plaque depicting the black-and-white image of a Maltese-style cross adopted by the medieval order of the Knights Hospitallers. The abbey, now run as a B & B, was originally founded by Benedictine monks as a Lazar House and hospital, subordinate to the monastery at Monte Cassino in Italy.

The present house dates to 1411, although very little remains of its recorded history. However, the present owner was able to tell us that in 1430 the site included a chapel with a tower, the remains of which can still be seen in the garden behind the house. After the Reformation, it became the home of the Courtenay family.

We marvelled at the original granite fireplaces and wooden panelling as we made ourselves comfortable in the old lounge. The presence of the Knights Hospitallers was all around us, with effigies of the Templar cross adorned on the old ceiling, and we could imagine many of the local knights meeting together here to discuss the religious and political matters of the day.

Over the years, previous owners have added various unusual features to the garden, including a stone seat next to a little bridge over a cascading stream decked in quartz crystals brought here by the abbey's Victorian residents from different parts of the world. The chi of the running water beneath the bridge seemed to amplify the powerful healing qualities of the crystals, so we all took turns sitting on the seat to benefit from its curative powers. Next to the chair is a Celtic Christian cross, perhaps moved here when the old Saint's Way that passes by here was widened in more recent times to become a major road. The shape of its elegant tapering shaft reminded us of a cloaked goddess as she guards the symbolic entrance to the old abbey by the little river, the strange pattern created by the small worn wheel cross within a circle adorning the top, almost reminiscent of her eyes and smiling mouth.

However, for us, the magic of this garden was surpassed by the discovery of a secret holy well behind the abbey. To our surprise, the owner informed us that the well had been lost from sight for hundreds of years, having been completely covered by brambles and dense vegetation and only rediscovered three years ago during major restoration work. He also informed us that bamboo was once deliberately grown here in abundance to feed the pandas at the London Zoo.

An old stone lintel supports the opening to the spring, with a stone stoup above surrounded by more crystals left here in Victorian times, similar to those found on the bench by the stream. The crystals appear to have come straight from the bowels of Mother Earth and are full of powerful beneficial qualities uncorrupted by man. We could still hear the water trickling inside the well and felt sure that the water spirits must be delighted now this special site has been restored to its former glory.

During supper in a local restaurant that evening, we perused the fact that Lanivet once stood at a major crossroads of the important north-south trading route that became the Saint's Way, between Padstow and Fowey, and an ancient east-west route from Devon to Land's End that eventually became the A30. We concluded that the unusual cross in the churchyard behind the church may well be an omphalos stone placed there to deliberately mark the central crossroads of the old Kingdom of Cornwall. I was still curious about the fresco I had seen earlier that day in the church depicting the mysterious St Crede.

St Benet's Abbey holy well and chapel tower

Back at the B & B, I started to read the history of this fascinating building and discovered that according to 16th-century records, St Benet's owned the religious house of Credow or Credis near Padstow. Could this be a reference to the female saint depicted in a medieval fresco in Lanivet Church? Although very little is known of this saint, later traditions claim she was the daughter of either King Mark of Cornwall or an Irish monarch.

After breakfast the following morning, we laid our various healing stones by the well at the back of the abbey. Honouring Mothering Sunday, Caroline blessed the waters, inspired by the words of Lunaea Weatherstone in *Tending Brigid's Flame*[17], which we adapted to bless the other navel sites during our quest:

'May the Goddess Bride's blessings of these waters
be at this sacred centre of Cornwall on Mother's Day.
May we see stability in its tides and
wisdom of its depths.
Be with us this day and every day.'

As we made our way to the village, the church bells were ringing out across the landscape, calling people to prayer on a day that evolved from a far-earlier pagan celebration that honoured the mother goddess at the spring equinox. We soon discovered another old well by a small tributary of the River Camel next to the village green, now blocked up by a concrete box. Was this the site of the village well, another possible site of a holy spring? The locals appear not to be aware of any wells in their village and very little is written about its history. However, early maps indicate a well exactly at the spot where the concrete box stands by the playground next to the brook. We placed a healing stone in the bank beneath it, again blessing the waters:

'May the Goddess Bride's blessings be at this spring
at the sacred centre of Cornwall on Mother Goddess Day.
May we see stability and harmony in the land in its hills and tors,
in the rootedness of its trees,
in the abundance of its crops,
Be with us this day and every day.'

After entering the church, we felt it highly significant that the vicar gave her blessing for us to look around the church and grounds at any time during the Sunday service. We waited until the bells had stopped to mark the beginning of prayers and then made our way to the stone cross, Cornwall's axis mundi at the back of the churchyard. I picked out a serpentine green stone from Iona with unusual markings symbolically reflecting the 'eye of Bride' and placed it at the foot of the cross as we blessed the spot with these words:

'May the Goddess Bride bless this sacred navel of
Cornwall and its people.
May the encompassing of Bride protect them.
May the encircling of Bride cherish and sustain them.
May the soft hand of Bride soothe them and give them strength.
May the eye of Bride keep watch over and show them the way.
May the heart of Bride love them and provide them
with health and wellbeing.
Be with us on this day and every day.'

We then visualised the light expanding east across Cornwall to its boundary with Devon and then in all other directions to its coast, north, south and west, encompassing the county in beautiful golden energy. As we stood by the old cross I could sense a strong energy radiating through the churchyard, which I confirmed through dowsing as a major earth energy line. I also detected other smaller lines of energy connecting with the cross coming from different locations. Little did we realise that this would lead us on other adventures associated with the omphalos of Cornwall.

The Mystery of St Crede and the Centre of Penwith

It later dawned on me that the name Crede is also mentioned in Michell's *At the Centre of the World*. He refers to a tradition relating to the far-western peninsular of Penwith at the western tip of Cornwall, once a separate kingdom during Celtic times. Michell calculated the exact centre of this old region to be the church of Sancreed or Saint Creed, earlier recorded as Sancta Crida. The church was built on a raised mound within a circular churchyard, indicating a possible sacred place of assembly. It also lies upon the longest axis of Penwith from Gwennap Head in the southwest corner to Clodgy Point in the far northeast and the crossing of a line from Pendeen Head on the north coast to Carn-du near Lamorna. The parish of Sancreed is the most centrally placed in this region and the only one with no connection to the sea.[18]

Michell observed that several trackways converge at this centre, also denoting it as a place of importance in the past, although just the church, a few houses and a farm are all that remain there today. According to one source, the circular arrangement of the churchyard may be due to it once being surrounded by a collection of monastic huts or cells, housing a community of monks, manual workers and domestics possibly founded by a male missionary of St Petroc's called Creden, from which the church takes it dedication. However, this is merely a supposition by historians and therefore it could be just as likely that Sancreed derives its name from Crida, the saintly daughter of King Mark of Cornwall.

Inside Sancreed Church is a curious carving on a screen of a crowned head with three faces, possibly denoting a place of kingship. In the churchyard is a stone cross with an unusual design carved just below the crosshead showing two diagonal lines crossing within a rectangle, which Michell believed denotes the four quarters of Penwith in a place that 'may have formed the sacred ritual centre of the far western kingdom.'[19] No less than five stone crosses exist around the church, with a few carved with the equal-armed cross, some possibly dating back to the 6th century.

The Penwith region is littered with prehistoric monuments, ancient holy wells and early Celtic Christian sites, which mark this region as a special place of sanctity to the early Cornish pagans, their ritual importance remaining a mystery. Nearby is the prehistoric settlement at Carn Euny which dates back to Neolithic times.

Sancreed holy well, set in a wooded glade a short distance from the church, has been described by many who visit it as magical and enigmatic. Revd A. Lane-Davies wrote in *Holy Wells of Cornwall* that: 'The spot always seems to me to possess a greater air of mystery and sanctity than any other in Cornwall.'[20] It stands close to the remains of an early stone chapel or baptistery, built before the present parish church and restored in the 15th century, now almost entirely reclaimed by nature except for a couple of sections of stone wall made of large blocks. The well itself was lost completely at one time until the vicar of Sancreed rediscovered the spring in 1879.

It can be accessed via a footpath opposite the entrance to the church, which weaves its way around the back gardens of some cottages and then into a magical wooded grove. The well has several stone steps that lead down towards an opening almost hidden by the surrounding fauna, which many have described as being directed straight into the body or womb of Mother Earth herself. The moss-covered stone lining of the well glows with the rays of the sun as it penetrates the watery grotto. Above is a tree covered in clootie, an old custom of hanging strips of cloth or 'cloot' on branches of sacred trees which has grown more popular in recent times. The idea is that when the cloth disintegrates so does the illness.

Sancreed holy well

Cheryl Straffon mentions the discovery 'that the radiation count of the water measures nearly two hundred per cent above background radiation, and may have been used to induce trances and visions.'[21] The water here has probably been sustaining and healing the people of this area for thousands of years, but now it is only known to a few who wish to seek out these special places.

Associated with this well is the story of St Creden, who, having accidentally killed his father, became a swineherd in penance. Sancreed Church has a carving above the porch door of him holding a pig, perhaps symbolising the Celtic tradition of pigs being associated with the Otherworld. As mentioned earlier, wells and caves are often places where the Otherworld can be accessed if you have the initiatory powers to do so. Before taking the water, you have to honour the genius loci or spirit guardian here, a custom usurped by Christianity when given the dedication of a saint.

Above here is Sancreed Beacon, a sacred round-topped hill adorned with two cairns at its summit, almost certainly used for ritual and ceremony due to its proximity to the ancient holy well. Perhaps the well was part of a sacred route between the Beacon and the sacred enclosure below, now the site of the church, where the early priests processed to honour the feminine power within the land, partaking of the precious waters of the sacred well as part of a long-lost ritual at the centre of the old Cornish Kingdom of Penwith.

Very little is written about the well and the church's associations with a sacred sanctuary of the divine feminine, except for its possible connection to St Crida or Crede. I later discovered another church in Cornwall dedicated to this female saint in the village of Creed, just half a kilometre south of Grampound between Truro and St Austell. High up overlooking the gentle flow of the River Fal, the old Norman church was supposedly built over the site of a place of worship erected here by this female saint for her nuns. The establishment of a nunnery for women is reminiscent of St Brigid of Kildare in Ireland.

Having previously found the British goddess Brigid, Bride or Ffraid at the centres of Ireland, Scotland and Wales, we began to wonder whether her cult had indeed found its way to Cornwall, transferred to these old Celtic lands of the early Britons, the name Bride having transformed into Cride, Crida, Creed or Crede. In Devon, the town Crediton, whose church houses a crossing-point of the Michael and Mary dragon lines, is said to have been taken from Creed, the name of the river formerly called the Cride. There are many rivers in the West Country named after Bride, so perhaps Cride is a Brythonic version of Bride.

Unlike Ireland, Wales, Scotland, England and the Isle of Man, there is no evidence of a Bride cult of the fire goddess in Cornwall.

Cheryl Straffon and Caeia March in their article *The Search for Bride's Well* also questioned why they had not as yet found a single reference in Cornish folklore and mythology to the Celtic goddess Bride or Brigid, having themselves written many books about this British Celtic realm.[22] Many of the early Celts came to Cornwall from Ireland and Wales and several of the names found here seem to have more in common with both countries rather than anywhere else. As the Irish and Welsh Celts travelled along the Cornish trade routes they would almost certainly have brought their legends and beliefs with them, including the cult of their goddess Bride or Brigid.

However, we did find a reference to a saint venerated as Breaca or Breage, a nun who came to Cornwall from Ireland in the 5th or 6th century to establish a religious community, having been first educated at St Brigid's convent in Kildare. Her church stands in the village of Breage or Breeg, as it was once known, with two early Celtic crosses near Helston in southwest Cornwall. Breaca or Breage could well be Bride, as it sounds similar to other versions of her name found throughout Britain, including Breeshey, Bredy, Breedy and Bega.

Straffon and March discovered a St Bridget's Well on the private estate of Landue near Lezant, near the site of an earlier chapel to St Bridget – Lezant being Cornish for 'holy place' and Landue possibly meaning 'sanctuary'. The owner of the estate mentioned to Straffon and March that there were other wells in the area referred to by the local people as Bridget Wells, which is likely to be a very old folk memory of a Celtic settlement in the area.[23]

Following the Saint's Way

The Saint's Way connects significant sites to the navel centre of Lanivet, similar to the key places along An Slí Mhór in Ireland, the Monk's Trod in Wales, and Glen Lyon in Scotland. Less than 3 km directly south of Lanivet the old path passes the prominent outcrop of rocks called Helman Tor, which is also skirted on its southern slopes by the St Michael alignment. Its sculpted granite stones smoothed by the natural elements over millennia can be seen for miles around. The Tor is part of a north-south granite ridge, which overlooks the marshy ground and heathlands of Red Moor to the east and Breney Common to the west, with fertile farmland beyond settled since Neolithic times. Nearby are remains of a prehistoric henge at Innis Downs, a megalithic burial chamber called the Lanivet Quoit, and numerous

Bronze Age barrows. Centuries of tin mining have shaped the landscape around here, creating hillocks and hollows reminiscent of 'the Shires' created by J. R. R. Tolkien in *Lord of the Rings*.

One remarkable feature here is a 'Logan Stone' or rocking stone, similar to the rocking stone that tops the imposing cliffs of Castle Treryn (or Treen) near St Leven in southwest Cornwall. Such stones are famous for being rocked at the gentlest touch as they rest delicately poised on smaller boulders beneath them.

They are also considered to have magical properties as, despite their ability to rock, they are hard to remove. The Roman writer and philosopher Pliny the Elder (23–79 CE) wrote that a rock near Harpasa (in Caria, Asia Minor) could be moved with a finger, but was impossible to dislodge even with a thrust of the whole body.[24] They are found all over the world and are often associated with Druid ceremony and witchcraft. Another stone on the summit of the Tor is carved with a cross, perhaps left by the many pilgrims who must have passed through here as they travelled along the Saint's Way below.

As we ascended the hill from the car park, we mingled with a herd of Belted Galloway cows and their calves as they gently and calmly moved around the stones, as if showing a natural reverence to the site. Sitting on top of the granite boulders enjoying the panoramic views over the middle lands of Cornwall, we soon found ourselves falling into an almost trance-like state. We could sense the feminine quality of the rocks, creating a feeling of serenity and contentment within us.

I placed one of my powerful healing stones on the Logan Stone to honour this enigmatic site, recognising its once sacred role when the Druids possibly rocked it to balance the energies of the land. We also paid homage to the site as an important point near the centre of Cornwall, as from here you can see the north and south coastlines on a clear day.

We continued south along narrow ancient lanes, possibly dating to Neolithic times, until we came to the quaint village of Lanlivery and the church of St Brevita or Bryvyth, a saint sounding remarkably like Britta or Bride, of which little is known. The now sleepy little village was reputedly an important royal centre and has a holy well dedicated to St Brevita that lies hidden in a magical woodland next to a footpath at the back of the old pub called the Crown Inn.

Lanlivery's large imposing 15th-century church stands on a hill within a circular churchyard and, like Lanivet, is a possible site of pre-Christian worship. Its original foundation was Norman when it was under the Benedictine Priory of Tywardreath, and its earliest dedication, according to church records, was to a St Vorck. Inside the tower is a painted copy of a letter of thanks written by Charles I to the people of Cornwall in 1643 for their support during the Civil War. Perhaps the locals subconsciously understand this energetic connection between Helman Tor and Lanlivery as we noticed a poster advertising a Good Friday Pilgrimage from the church to the summit of Helman Tor, where 'Egg Rolling' would follow a religious service.

Here, the Mary dragon current that accompanies the St Michael alignment enters the church as it travels through Cornwall east-west, visiting numerous sites on route including Carn Lês Boel, St Michael's Mount, Roche Rock Hermitage and the Cheesewring. With her male counterpart Michael, she winds her way around the straight alignment like a caduceus infusing the land with healing and fertility.[25]

St Brevita's Holy Well, Lanlivery

We made our way to St Brevita's Well along the old holloway at the back of the pub and soon arrived at a gateway on the left that takes you into the grounds of a centre for disabled children and adults. We passed through an outdoor teaching area into woodland and turned right onto a path that led to the well house hidden behind tall ferns next to a small brook. The stones that lined this magical well seemed very old and, judging by the flowers and candles left here, this ancient sanctuary is still honoured today, the offerings gifted to the spirit deity of the well. As we sat quietly enjoying this peaceful setting, we left our Iona stone here briefly as we gave Bride's blessing, intending to raise the vibration of this once important holy well.

Suddenly, I felt a powerful energy and confirmed with my dowsing rod that we were sitting right on the Mary dragon line that passes through the well. We also sensed that this sacred place was a site to commune with the Mother goddess Bride, and we later discovered that the name Brivita is a derivation of Brigitta or Bride.

The Saint's Way continues south to Lostwithiel, set at the end of a beautiful wooded valley of the Fowey estuary where the river starts to widen before continuing out to sea. Its name in Old Cornish is *Lost Gwydhyel* meaning 'tail-end of the woodland'. However, Paul Broadhurst alerts us to an alternative meaning by Richard Carew, a member of the Elizabethan Society of Antiquaries, who states that the name derives from the old Brythonic Celtic language to mean 'Lion's Tail'.

Broadhurst believes this alludes to a cosmological association in this area where the constellations of Leo Major and Leo Minor were mirrored in the landscape in the areas of Bodmin and Lostwithiel. The lions, as totem animals, were adopted by the Normans and later Plantagenets 'to become the royal symbols for the entire English realm.' Broadhurst suggests this may have been a deliberate act to associate themselves with symbols from the old British race during a time when Cornwall was part of the ancient lands of Lyonesse mentioned in Arthurian legends.[26]

Although today the modern Saint's Way avoids Lostwithiel, it would have been a key place on the original trade and pilgrim route when it was a major port and former capital of Cornwall, possibly dating back to Celtic times. Its development as a major destination point to Europe was instigated by the Cardinhams, one of the most influential families in Cornwall during medieval times.

Records show that the town was the second busiest port in Cornwall, with its own mint. Although it is now just a minor Cornish town, there are still reminders of its former glory in the 13th-century Duchy Palace, constructed by the Earl of Cornwall, and its impressive Norman church first founded in 1190. Before the silting of the river, pilgrims would have worshipped in St Bartholomew's Church before embarking on their onward journey to the sacred shrine at Compostela. St Bartholomew is the patron saint of tanners, a key industry of this town. The church's great spire has a carving of a Catherine wheel, perhaps symbolising the Christian St Catherine, whose wheel and spindle represent the axis mundi. The Knights Templar adopted her as their patron saint; they saw her spiked wheel symbolically representing a 'sun wheel', a round table for solar or cosmic worship observing the rising and setting of the sun, moon and major constellations.

During medieval times, the church stood at the top of a triangular marketplace close to the port, linked by a stone bridge next to the Duchy Palace or Great Hall. The Palace, Cornwall's oldest non-ecclesiastical building, would have been a hive of activity, acting as a court and administrative centre of the Earls of Cornwall and a place of taxation dealing with the Cornish tin industry, later becoming a Masonic Lodge.

According to *A Concise History of The Church of St Bartholomew, Lostwithiel* written by Miss F. M. Hext in 1891, the church was built over the site of one 'which some people suppose had been built in the days of the renowned King Arthur.'[27] Its unusual 14th-century font is carved with a rare image of a Green Bishop, which is a Green Man with foliage sprouting from his mouth wearing a mitre. Another is of two serpents entwined on the head of a grotesque gargoyle, which is rather apt as it is here the Mary and Michael serpent currents cross. Miller and Broadhurst write: 'Here we have another crossing point,

Lostwithiel Palace by Samuel and Nathaniel Buck, c. 1734

this time at a Christian "holy well", or at least its equivalent, for a font is nothing less than a "well" constructed from a raw block of stone and taken inside. It is common practice to use the waters of any nearby original sacred spring.'[28]

The gargoyle also has a curious protruding forehead adorned with a spiral, now worn and discoloured from being rubbed by pilgrims for hundreds of years. Miller and Broadhurst noted that this representation of a swirling vortex is where the Third Eye Chakra point is located. Dowsers discovered that a vortex of energy is omitted from a node of earth energies especially if connecting with an underground water source. Through the Third Eye, one can access the higher consciousness of being and enlightenment, so perhaps this was once a pagan shrine next to a spring important to the ancient priesthood, who were adept at working with higher vibrational energies. The Druids may have meditated around this spot to access a higher degree of psychic communication with the ancestors and nature spirits.

The 19th-century antiquarian Dr Richard Lanyon also believes the church was constructed during the Dark Ages and mentions the font as 'sculptured in the days of Arthur, who was King of Wiltshire, Devon, Dorset, Cornwall, and Wales.' He also concludes that two lions carved on one of the font's panels are the 'armorial bearings of the Cambrian and Cornish Kings.' He further claims that a 'Royal Palace at Lostwithiel' was the residence of the Kings of Cornwall, who were also Kings of Wales until the death of Cadwallader in 689.[29]

Close to the Saint's Way a little further south of here is the Iron Age hillfort of Castle Dore, said to be the castle of the legendary 6th-century King Mark of Cornwall, father of Crida, and inside the enclosure can be traced the outline of a timber hall. King Mark is most famous for his appearance in the Arthurian Romances as the uncle of Tristan and husband of Iseult. Perhaps he was responsible for building the early church under the foundations of the present St Bartholomew's. A carved stone cross at the church may also be from that time when the Celtic missionaries founded a religious settlement here at the southern point of the Saint's Way.

At Golant is the delightful old church of St Sampson with an ancient holy well next to its main entrance. Nestled by the western banks of the River Fowey and surrounded by a glorious landscape, it stands close to a once important fording place of the estuary. The Welsh St Sampson, possibly from Llantwit Major, came here in the late 5th century to visit a hermitage, renowned as the first religious building to occupy this pagan sanctuary next to a spring near Golant Harbour. The spring, now covered by a 15th-century well house, seems timeless and perhaps has existed here for thousands of years, continuously ushering forth its healing water through the granite rock.

One of the stories associated with St Sampson is the slaying of an evil dragon, which had his lair in the cave near Golant Harbour. This reminded us of the tale of St Serf who in the village of Dunning in Scotland rescued the locals from a terrifying dragon, which he killed with his staff. Mentioned in an old manuscript, he had a vision while in his cell there that 'a dragon great and terrible, and very loathsome was coming into his township whose aspect no mortal could suffer.' Andrew de Wyntoun (1350–1420) also describes this event in *The Orygynale Cronykil of Scotland*:

> 'In Donnyng, of his devotion
> And prayer, he slew a fell dragowne;
> Where he was slain, the place was ay
> The Dragownes Den called to this day.'[30]

Dragon slaying is common in British folklore in many parts of the country, the lair of the dragon is often associated with mounds, caves and lakes, all places that attract powerful earth energies. St George and St Michael are perhaps the most famous dragon slayers, although they are largely depicted subduing the dragon rather than killing the beast. The dragon or serpent is often portrayed in ancient folklore across the world as the invisible fertilising force within the land. This symbolic 'slaying' of this earthly force may represent the fixing of its fertile qualities at a sacred place, especially at Beltane, the beginning of spring. However, when the dragon force is out of balance, it creates a negative energy that can be detrimental to our health, which we believe is symbolically portrayed in the story of Lludd and Llefelys when the whole country suffered from the effects of two dragons fighting at the centre of England. The problem was remedied by the subduing, transformation and removal of the beasts.[31]

Using these same principles, the healing of detrimental earth or 'dragon' energies can be undertaken by visualisation of cleansing, clearing and transforming them into a positive force. The practice of driving a stake in the ground to cure imbalanced earth energies, called by dowsers 'black streams', is a modern version of the dragon-slaying act.

The reformed Saint's Way continues to the picturesque Fowey Harbour with its narrow streets lined with quality gift shops, boutiques, art galleries, cafes and restaurants. Its deep natural harbour is a hub of fishing vessels and yachts, overlooked by its historic medieval and Georgian buildings. Near the harbour, among the hustle and bustle of this popular tourist town is the Norman church dedicated to the 6th-century St Finn Barr, Latinised as St Fimbarrus, the first Bishop of Cork. His name means 'shining hair' due to his exceptionally fair hair, the name given to him by the monks he served under while studying at a Priory at Kilmacchill in Kilkenny. While en route to Rome, this Irish saint sailed to Padstow from Ireland and then travelled overland to Fowey. Here he built a little sheltered church in the hills. In the 5th century, these hills were called Langurthowe meaning 'cell or church of Gurthowe'. Some believe this name refers to the Irish saint Goron, Goran or Gorran who first built a cell in Bodmin, said to have come to Cornwall at the same time as St Petroc.

In 1150, the cell was replaced by a church run by the Benedictine monks of nearby Tywardreath Priory, the lands having passed into the hands of the Norman Fitz Turnolds, who would change their name to Cardinham after their homeland Caer-Dinan. The church was later destroyed in 1328, possibly at the hands of pirates, but its delightful Norman font still survives. The striking 14th-century clerestory stained-glass windows are perhaps its greatest feature, helping to create an atmosphere of expanding light and space. One of them, over the south aisle, depicts the saints Finbarrus, Catherine and Nicholas. Others show Cornish saints Blazey, Sampson, Germanus, Dwyn and Petroc. St Catherine's Point at the harbour entrance was the former site of a chapel also dedicated to this female saint, which at one time functioned as a lighthouse.

Returning to Lanivet, we followed the Saint's Way north to the village of Withiel. The spring flowers that adorn the banks on the side of the lane that leads to the church were a glorious sight. Dedicated to St Clement, this delightful little church was first recorded in 1297. However, this is a later dedication as the name Withiel is said to derive from 'Uvel', a 4th-century Irish saint. The lands according to the *Domesday Book* belonged to the Monastery of Bodmin founded by St Petroc, although there is no mention of a church here at that time. The early 16th-century octagonal font is made of quartz porphyry, a type of volcanic (igneous) rock, and carved with foliage and spirals. One of its panels depicts St Clements, the third Pope of Rome, who was martyred on an anchor in the Black Sea.

Climbing out of the verdant valleys, we reached a high point on St Breock Downs, with its many megalithic stones, including a

Longstone called Men Gurta. The Saint's Way then brings us to St Issey, which means 'a church on a tumulus', obviously another sacred pagan site, and the partly Norman church does indeed have an ancient feel to it, as does the local pub called 'The Ring of Bells', said to be one of the oldest in Cornwall.

As we continued to the north coast, the last couple of kilometres along the Saint's Way led us past the hamlet of Credes, a former monastic house once owned by St Benet's Abbey in Lanivet. Our final destination was St Petroc's Church in Padstow, where many pilgrims began their journey along this ancient route after crossing from Ireland. We arrived on a sunny but rather windy afternoon and, after parking our car, made our way through the pretty and largely unspoilt fishing town, passing trawlers resting in the picturesque harbour. The charming narrow streets filled with craft shops, art galleries, tearooms and restaurants made this a perfect end to our fascinating pilgrimage around the centres of Cornwall. We found a delightful cafe to rest our weary feet and indulged ourselves with a delicious cream tea.

The name Padstow is derived from Petroc-stow or 'Petroc's place', after the Welsh missionary St Petroc, who in 518 reputedly landed at Trebetherick, just across the river mouth from Padstow, to preach Christianity to a largely pagan community. Much has been written about the life of St Petroc, who was born a Welsh prince, his father, according to Nicholas Orme in *The Saints of Cornwall*, was King Glywys of Glywysing.[32] After studying in Ireland, he arrived in Padstow and founded a church and monastery at the top of a hill overlooking the Camel estuary, a place already well established by St Wethinoc and St Sampson. Many tales of miracles, healing and the banishing of monsters are associated with the saint who reputedly converted the pagan King Constantine of Cornwall.

Padstow is best known for its 'Obby'Oss' festival which starts at midnight on May Day eve with the townspeople gathering outside the Golden Lion Inn to sing the 'Night Song'. By morning, the town has been dressed with greenery and the maypole is decorated with flowers. Two separate processions make their way around the town, each led by a male dancer dressed as a hobby horse. Although its origins are uncertain, many believe the procession stems from an ancient fertility rite, perhaps associated with the Celtic festival of Beltane.

The remains of two carved cross shafts in the churchyard of St Petroc's Church are possibly the first features to symbolise the coming of Christianity to this pagan settlement. Petroc's monastery built on the headland above the estuary consisted of a school, hospital, library and cells for the monks. It was destroyed during a Viking raid in 981, after which monastic control transferred to Bodmin, where the saint's relics were enshrined after his death *c.* 564. It was rebuilt in the 12th century, although most of what we see today is restoration carried out 300 years later. Inside the church is a remarkable 14th-century dolerite font carved with the twelve Apostles.

Simon Calder writing in *The Independent* newspaper in 2015 describes the Saint's Way as a 'spiritual superhighway.' He writes that the white cross on a black background on the Cornish flag could

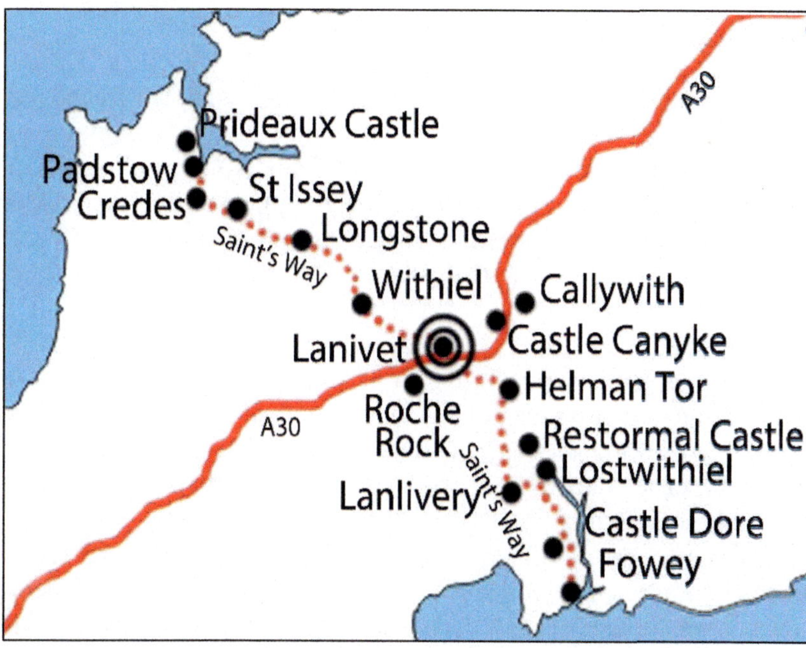

Figure 17. Map of the Saint's Way and the Centre of Cornwall

represent 'the spine of Britain's south-westernmost county' intersecting with 'an ancient holy pathway between the north coast and south.'[33] As we headed home along the A30, we realised the significance of this important east-west route that travels along the central spine of Cornwall leading to St Michael's Mount. The ancient mid-point of Cornwall is situated almost exactly halfway along this great highway, as it intersects with the old north-south trackway that later became a pilgrim route for Celtic Christian saints and their followers as they journeyed overseas to the shrines in Europe in the Middle Ages.

We feel it important to honour these ancient routes, which we have found to be an integral part of our explorations of the centres of Britain and Ireland, and will probably continue to do so as we travel to the sacred omphalos of England. So too the holy wells, the abode of the goddess, are integral to the sacredness of these ritual and ceremonial centres. Therefore, the discovery of the well at St Benet's Abbey seemed significant, being right at the heart of middle Cornwall close to the ancient crossroads of these old Cornish north-south and east-west routes.

The Grail Chapel

One last important feature found in many omphalos landscapes is a sacred religious site and a hill representing a World Mountain. Just over 6 km southwest of Lanivet is Roche Rock with its ancient chapel built into a rocky outcrop as a hermitage, a place steeped in folklore and history, and the perfect representation of Cornwall's world mountain. It stands next to the old east-west route of the A30, its tall vertical pinnacles towering dramatically on a prominent ridge on the northern edge of St Austell Downs, close to the headwaters of the Fal River, Cornwall's longest and most sacred river. Much of the surrounding landscape has been devastated due to tin mining and china clay workings, leaving it covered in 'ridges and troughs, bumps and pools.' The quarries here produce feldspar crystals used in glazes, glass and porcelain.

The power of this place is amplified by its geology, the rock is made of granite with black tourmaline crystals, and even in prehistoric times, it was revered as a special place of sanctity. In the past, seams of highly paramagnetic rock containing dolerite or 'greenstone' and underground springs lay beneath the ground here, creating a 'thin veil area' conducive to connecting with one's higher consciousness through meditation. Perhaps this is why hermits were attracted to build their cells here incorporating the bedrock in its structure to commune with earth spirits and the cosmic realms. They would have been sustained by the two known holy wells that once existed at the base of the rock along with a magical pool. A chapel was added on its summit in 1409, constructed of large squared blocks of granite and dedicated to St Michael, the guardian of high places.

John Michell suggests that one of the roles of the hermit was to keep a light burning to aid travellers as they crossed the wild moorland. One of the hermits known as St Conan or St Roche became Bishop of Cornwall and later resided at St Michael's Mount. The Mary energy current of the St Michael Line connects with the chapel here, having already visited St Michael's Mount. Her current then continues through St Brevita's Well and Lanlivery Church to St Bartholomew's at Lostwithiel on the Saint's Way. As we found while dowsing the Belinus Line, the early Christian saints built many of their cells, hermitages, churches and chapels on powerful serpent lines of energy.

The hermit Ogrin also exiled himself here and, being a leper, only allowed his daughter Gundred to fetch water for him from a hole in the rocks beneath the hermitage, known as St Gundred's or Gonetta's Well. According to legend, the well water ebbed and flowed with the tide, influenced by the cycles of the moon.

The east wall of the chapel still survives to almost its original height, with a large arched window now missing its tracery. A rather rickety metal ladder that replaced rock-cut steps leads you to the summit. It is well worth the effort, however, as glorious views greet you when you reach the topmost tiers of the outcrop. More important for us was the discovery that the old north-south and east-west routes are in plain sight as they pass close by, and we could see Lanivet

Chapel on Roche Rock

where they intersect in the distance. Below is Roche parish church, dedicated to St Gomonda or Gonand, with Norman foundations.

The ruined chapel has an eerie but timeless atmosphere and one ghost story associated with this enigmatic rock involves a 16th-century lawyer called Jan Tregeagle. After his death, he was reputedly sent to Hell for using his legal prowess to steal from his clients. However, it is said that his spirit returned to court to testify on behalf of a man who was about to be executed for a crime that Tregeagle had committed. The judge took pity on the ghost of Tregeagle and instead of forcing him back to Hell, he was sentenced to empty the water of a nearby pool with a cracked shell. Having tired of this task, he fled to Roche Rock's chapel for sanctuary, pursued by headless hounds. As he clambered up the rock, he was savagely bitten by them but was eventually rescued by a priest whose prayers drove the hounds away. Yet again, he avoided Hell, for the forgiving priest sent Tregeagle's hapless soul down to the coast, giving him the task of creating a rope out of the sand, and where, it is said, he remains to this day.[34]

The sanctuary is often described as a Grail chapel and perhaps one of its most enduring legends refers to the doomed love affair between Tristan and Isolde. Based on French medieval romances by the poets Thomas of Britain and Béroul (*c.* 1160), the tragic story tells of the adulterous love between the Cornish knight Tristan (Tristram) and the Irish princess Isolde (Iseult), which later provided the background for the writings of English author Sir Thomas Malory, who wrote *Le Morte d'Arthur.* [35]

Tristan was the nephew of King Mark of Cornwall, who accidentally shared a love potion with the King's intended bride Isolde, resulting in Tristan and Isolde falling hopelessly in love. Thereafter, they are involved in a series of adventures while escaping the wrath of King Mark. According to Béroul, the lovers took refuge in the hermit Ogrin's chapel, the description of which bears a strong resemblance to Roche Rock. A later version of the story tells of Tristan's escape from the king's soldiers by jumping from one of the chapel's windows onto perilous rocks below. Although Chapel Point, overlooking the sea near Mevagissey, is the supposed site of 'Tristan's Leap', many believe it to be Roche Rock, the folktale preserved by local storytellers, which eventually drew the attention of medieval poets. Cheryl Straffon and Caeia March's research of this Cornish myth led them to believe that Isolde may have been a localised version of the goddess Bride, Bride being the goddess of poetry.

The Grail is often confused with the Chalice of Christ, which is traditionally a jewelled golden cup that contains both the wine of the Last Supper and the spilt blood from the crucifixion. This may be a Christian attempt to adopt earlier Celtic magical and spiritual traditions of sacred objects charged with supernatural powers called 'talismans'. In Ireland, the grail can be likened to Dagda's Cauldron of Plenty, one of the four legendary 'treasures of Ireland' that provided only the worthy with an endless supply of food and drink.

The Welsh cycle of legends from *The Mabinogion* refers to Bran and his magic cauldron of rejuvenation that brought people back to life again – an attribute also given to the Christian Grail.[36] In Arthurian lore, the quest for the grail was symbolic of searching for a talisman to heal or rejuvenate the sickened land after a famine or plague.

Cornwall, with its holy wells, isolated rock formations, and Arthurian traditions has an air of Celticness about its landscape and is often referred to as the kingdom of the Holy Grail. The paramagnetic force of the county's ancient granite rocks is stronger than most other Celtic realms, and the water that passes through them to become wells and springs has a worldwide reputation for healing all kinds of ailments. Therefore, many consider the search for Cornish holy wells as representative of a quest for the grail.

We felt it important that we connect with the site of St Gundred's or Gonetta's old tidal well at the base of Roche Rock, but the large fallen boulders and tall bracken and gorse made the search difficult. So, using our dowsing rods, we proceeded to locate the whereabouts of this now elusive well by focusing our minds and asking the rods to show us its location. The rods started to twitch towards the boulder on the north side of the site near the entrance by the road. Dowsing confirmed that this was the site of the old well, but as we placed our ear to the boulder no sound of water could be heard, but then again perhaps the tide was out that day. Despite the lack of water, we still felt compelled to honour this old well, so dropped one of our healing stones into an opening under the boulder and said a blessing to the spirit of Gundred.

Another holy well dedicated to this saint can be found to the north of Roche Rock just beyond the A30. Up until the new section of this western highway was constructed, the well was accessible via a steep path by Higher Holywell Farm and Cottage that descended to a dense narrow wooded valley below. Here, within a stone surround, the well was said to have been visited by maidens before sunrise on Holy Thursday to ask the spirit of the well to divine their futures. By throwing pins and pebbles into its waters, the bubbles that rose would supposedly show forthcoming events. It is also alleged that it had curative powers for many different illnesses, especially eye complaints. The well once had a statue of a saint on its roof, but this has since disappeared along with a chapel that stood nearby.

Today, the farm and well are almost impossible to visit, the surrounding lanes having been cut off by the new dual carriageway. However, we managed to park our car on the south side of the main railway line next to the A30 and found a footpath sign that took us through a tunnel under the dual carriageway towards Holywell Farm. Although there appeared to be no access to the farm, there is a path on a bend that drops down into a hidden valley of trees where St Gundred's Well and its stone arch come into view. Here we gave our blessings and sent golden light to the spirits of this well at the centre of Cornwall.

References:

1. Broadhurst P (2009) *The Secret Land*. Mythos, Launceston.
2. Callahan P S (1984) *Ancient Mysteries, Modern Visions*. Acres, Kansas City.
3. https://national-landscapes.org.uk/news/archaeological-investigation-reveals-neolithic-date-for-cornwall-monument
4. Straffon C (2012) *Pagan Cornwall: Land of the Goddess*. Meyn Mamvro, Penzance.
5. Thorpe L (Translator) (1966) *Geoffrey of Monmouth: The History of the Kings of Britain*. The Folio Society, London.
6. Vesta (mythology). https://en.wikipedia.org/wiki/Vesta_(mythology)
7. *Britain, Phoenicia's Secret Treasure*. http://phoenicia.org/britmines.html.
8. Thorpe L (Translator) (1966) *Geoffrey of Monmouth: The History of the Kings of Britain*. The Folio Society, London.
9. Bromwich R (1961) *The Welsh Triads*. University of Wales Press, Cardiff.
10. Ciarán of Saigir. https://en.wikipedia.org/wiki/Ciar%C3%A1n_of_Saigir
11. A. L. Rowse (1988) *Cornwall: a Journey through Cornwall's Past and Present*. Weidenfeld & Nicolson, London.
12. Stoyle M (2002) *West Britons: Cornish Identities and the Early Modern British State*. University of Exeter Press, Exeter.

13. Industry in Cornwall.
http://www.cornwallheritagetrust.org/discover/industry-incornwall/.
14. *The Saint's Way*.
https://www.cornwalls.co.uk/walking/the_saints_way.htm.
15. Broadhurst P (2009) *The Secret Land.* Mythos, Launceston.
16. Orme N (Ed.) (1991) *Nicholas Roscarrock's 'Lives of the Saints': Cornwall and Devon*. Boydell & Brewer Ltd, Suffolk.
17. Weatherstone L (2015) *Tending Brigid's Flame: Awaken to the Celtic Goddess of Hearth*, Temple, and Forge. Llewellyn Publishing, Woodbury, MN.
18. Michell J (1994) *At the Centre of the World: Polar Symbolism Discovered in Celtic, Norse and Other Ritualized Landscapes*. Thames & Hudson, London.
19. Ibid.
20. Lane-Davies Revd A (1970) *Holy Wells of Cornwall*. Federation of Old Cornwall Societies. www.oldcornwall.net.
21. Straffon C (2005) *Fentynyow Kernow: In Search of Cornwall's Holy Wells*. Meyn Mamvro, Penzance.
22. *The Search for Bride's Well* (1995; http://people.bath.ac.uk).
23. Ibid.
24. *Pliny's Natural History. In Thirty-Seven Books*. https://archive.org/details/plinysnaturalhis00plinrich.
25. Miller H & Broadhurst P (1989) *The Sun and the Serpent*. Pendragon Press, Launceston.
26. Broadhurst P (2009) *The Secret Land*. Mythos, Launceston.
27. Hext F M (1891) *A Concise History of the Church of St Bartholomew,* Lostwithiel. http://
www.lostwithielparishchurch.org.uk/ConciseHistoryto1890.pdf.
28. Miller H & Broadhurst P (1989) *The Sun and the Serpent*. Pendragon Press, Launceston.
29. http://www.lostwithielparishchurch.org.uk/ConciseHistoryto1890.pdf.
30. *The Orygynale Cronykil of Scotland.*
https://archive.org/details/orygynalecronyki01andruoft.
31. Jones G & Jones T (translators) (1949) *The Mabinogion*. J M Dent & Sons, London.
32. Orme N (2000) *The Saints of Cornwall* Oxford University Press, Oxford.
33. http://www.independent.co.uk/travel/uk/cornwalls-saints-way-go-beyond-the-beach-on-this-walking-route-10476242.html
34. Legend of Jan Tregeagle. https://www.cornwalls.co.uk/myths-legends/jan-tregeagle.htm
35. Malory Thomas Sir (1485) *Le Morte d'Arthur*. Barnes and Noble, New York, published 2015.
36. Jones G & Jones T (translators) (1949) *The Mabinogion*. J M Dent & Sons, London.

Chapter 6

Search for the Centre of England

Over the centuries many landmarks and villages in the Midlands have competed for the illustrious title 'Centre of England', ranging from prominent hills, ancient trees, village ponds and megalithic monuments to pillars and crosses. In reality, England's centre is the most difficult to locate because of the country's irregular shape. In this chapter, we explore the various contenders, both ancient and modern, in an attempt to reveal the hidden and historical mystery of England's true sacred navel.

Before Saxon times, the name of the Brythonic (Welsh-speaking) territory that roughly corresponded to the borders of England was Loegria, Lloegyr or Loegres. References to this territory along with its rulers can be found in *The History of the Kings of Britain*[1] as well as earlier works such as the *Brut y Tywysogion* (Chronicle of the Princes), one of the most important primary sources of Welsh history.[2] Loegria was later converted to the name England or 'Angle-land' after the invasion of a Saxon race known as the Angles.

Mercia was the largest and most powerful of the Saxon Kingdoms, covering most of middle England, partly defined in the north by the Mersey and the Trent valleys, with its southern borders tracing the river valleys of the Avon and Thames. To the west, it reached the Welsh Marches naturally bordered by the Rivers Dee and the Wye. During the 7th century, its king, Penda, became Bretwalda, a title meaning 'overlord' or 'high king' of all the Anglo-Saxon kingdoms. As in Ireland, Scotland and Wales, Penda was fulfilling the ideal of central rule within a cosmologically arranged kingdom similar to that of the Celts before him (see Fig.18).

The name Mercia means 'men of the March', as in 'Marches', a term that defines the border lands between Wales and England. These 'men' were the Angles who supposedly came over to Britain in the 6th century from a region we know today as Denmark, settling in many parts of England including Northumberland and East Anglia. The Mercian's military might would soon come to dominate much of the British Isles over a period of 300 years (600–900 CE), known as the 'Mercian Supremacy'. By the late 7th century, Penda's son Paeda introduced Christianity to the Mercians, after inviting Bishop Finan

Figure 18. Saxon England showing the central kingdom of Mercia

of Lindisfarne from the kingdom of Northumbria, to convert their middle realm.

The majority of the Mercian High Kings had their main seat of power at the historic Staffordshire town of Tamworth, although the nearby town of Stone was also a major centre founded by King Wulfhere (d. 675 CE). Tamworth has one of the largest manmade earthen mounds in Britain, possibly dating to the Bronze Age, similar in size to Silbury Hill in Wiltshire. There is also evidence that a defensive ditch and bank enclosed the town long before the Saxons arrived.

Michell calculated that the main north-south axis through Britain runs between St Catherine's Point on the Isle of Wight and Duncansby Head, east of John o' Groats, at the most northeasterly tip of Scotland.[3] Tamworth falls precisely on this 'Main Axis of Britain', determining it as not only an important geographically but also a major centre of sovereign power within the middle kingdom (see Fig. 19). In its day, with the High King seated on its impressive mound, Tamworth was the capital of a virtually united England, and even places like London, Oxford and Winchester were subservient to this once thriving metropolis.

When Oswiu, King of Northumbria won the title Bretwalda, or high king of Britain, after slaying Penda at the Battle of the Winwaed in 655, he made St Chad Bishop of York. Chad's next task was to move the Mercian ecclesiastical seat from Repton in Derbyshire to Lichfield, a few kilometres from Tamworth, where he built a monastery. Perhaps he chose this site based on its reputation as a place of early Celtic Christian settlement, which was later desecrated by the Roman Emperor Diocletian in 286 CE. Chad's feast day, 2 March, was formerly the day dedicated to the worship of Mars, the Roman god of war, which the Saxons revered as Tiw, from which Tuesday in the English calendar is derived.

Chad spent his early years as a pupil of St Aidan at Lindisfarne who sent him to Ireland for his education. The Archbishop of

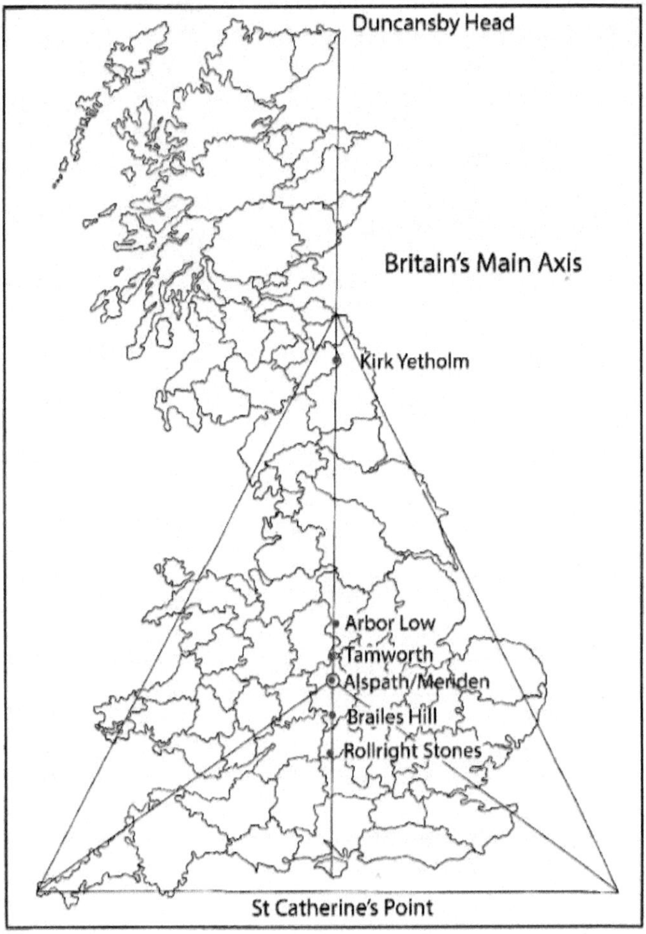

Figure 19. Britain's 'Main Axis', after John Michell

Canterbury, recognising his great devotion and character, later chose him for the position of Bishop of Mercia. He was successful in Christianising the local pagan kings and brought peace to Mercia by uniting the Britons and the Angles.

When first arriving at Lichfield, Chad built his Christian cell by a well on a low-lying swampy area, which some believe was the site of the present cathedral. Pilgrims flocked to his shrine dedicated to St Mary after his death and when miraculous cures started to occur, many more started to arrive. As a result, Bishop Hedda built a new larger church in 700 CE dedicated to St Peter to house Chad's relics and later those of Hedda and St Cedd. Soon the power of Lichfield grew, becoming not just the ecclesiastical centre of Mercia but also of the Kingdom of Wessex, now the holiest place in Saxon England.

The Venerable Bede called the area around Lichfield *Angli Mediterranei*, 'the Middle Land of England', and perhaps its status as a centre of middle England continued to be played out as part of its ancient ceremony of 'beating the bounds'. This ritual included the visiting of eight holy wells around the boundary of the town, possibly seen as symbolic of honouring the eight cosmological directions radiating from a centre.[4]

Nearby is the village of Wall and the ruins of the Roman city of Letocetum. The name derives from the Celtic *Caer Llwyd Coad* or *Caer Loit Coit* meaning 'camp in the grey woods', grey possibly referring to the colour of the lichens that once covered this area. The two major routes of Watling Street, an important route between London and Wales, and Icknield Street, from Gloucestershire to South Yorkshire, converged here, which during pre-Roman times created a significant centre of trade.

Wall was a ritual centre of the Druids, who erected a temple dedicated to the god Cernunnos, on the site of Wall's St John's Church. Cernunnos is the horned god of nature, often depicted cross-legged with an antler headdress, equivalent to the Roman god Pan, invoked by the Druids to integrate man with his natural environment. A Roman temple to Minerva also stood on the site, later transformed into a Christian monastic centre.[5]

Nennius mentions Caer Loit Coit as one of the 28 major cities of the Britons.[6] In the *Harleian MS 3859*, a warrior called Glast (*c.* 485 CE) is referred to as 'one who came to Glastening [Glastonbury] from a place called Loyt Coyt.' Glast defends Loyt Coyt against the Angles with the aid of the warrior Arthur, successfully driving them back.[7] If Caer Loit Coit or Letocetum was indeed a great spiritual centre during the Dark Ages linked to Glastonbury, as the manuscript suggests, then, like Glastonbury, it was almost certainly an important Culdee site. Although the local tribes were victorious against the Saxons in the great battle of 665, according to historical and archaeological data the town suffered severe destruction, which led to the development of the new town of Lichfield only a few kilometres away. As the present cathedral city of Salisbury replaced the ancient centre of Old Sarum, the city of Lichfield replaced the old centre of Letocetum. By the 7th century, during the time of the Venerable Bede, this area was regarded as an omphalos and Lichfield was said to mark the centre of England.[8]

It is hard to believe today that the royal centre at Tamworth and the spiritual omphalos of Lichfield were at one time the major power centres of England, like the yin and yang or even the kidneys in a beast. But they are far from the geographical centre-point of today, probably because of the vast changes to England's borders over the centuries. But other renowned places are declaring the illusive title of the navel of England.

St John's Church and Roman remains at Wall, Staffordshire

Meriden

Amongst the many claimants to the title and referred to by John Michell, is the village of Meriden, having once been part of the middle county of Warwickshire up until 1974. It is located in a green belt called 'the Meriden Gap', between Solihull and Coventry, just off the A45, a major route that runs from London to Holyhead in Wales, taking in a section of the old Watling Street.

The name Meriden is thought to derive from the Old English 'Miry Valley' or pleasant valley. However, it is also similar to 'meridian', which refers to a line on the Earth's surface or line of longitude that passes through the North Pole and the South Pole. Interestingly, having taken its name from this small English village, the US city of Meriden is located close to the centre-point of the State of Connecticut.[9]

Meriden, according to some authorities, is the most central point furthest from the sea – a claim handed down through oral tradition since the 17th century and mentioned in *Graphic Illustrations of Warwickshire* published by Beilby, Knott and Beilby in 1829.[10] A modern plaque in front of a sandstone pillar-shaped monument on the village green proudly states: 'This ancient wayside cross has stood in the village for some five hundred years and by tradition marks the "Centre of England."'

However, the cross was rebuilt on this site when the green was improved to celebrate the Festival of Britain in 1951 and there was much debate as to whether the Meriden cross stands in its original position. Local historian Doreen Agutter states in her book *Meriden: Centre of England*: 'A once famous Coventry local historian W. G. Fretton, brought up in the village, wrote in 1879 that the Cross had been moved in living memory. Finally, Mrs Frances Barton (1900–1986) of Lodge Green told me the Cross was originally opposite the Old Manor House (site between the Methodist Church and Leys Lane) according to her grandfather, a carrier and farmer, born and bred here.'[11]

An Edwardian postcard in Agutter's possession suggests that the monument has some supernatural quality by stating that it can grant wishes! She also mentions that the capstone of the cross, now lost, which took the form of a Doric capital, was perhaps symbolic of the axis mundi that marked the centres of the old Celtic regions throughout Europe.

The Bull's Head plaque proclaiming Meriden as the centre of England

Inside the village pub called the Bull's Head a brass plaque set into the floor next to the bar proclaims it as the official centre of England and a plan of Britain with lines radiating from Meriden is in the patio garden. In the past, the Bull's Head was one of several pubs in Meriden on the old coaching route from Chester to London, where many eminent travellers reputedly stayed, including the young Princess Victoria in 1832.

The village is also home to a society called the Forest of Arden Archers or Woodmen of Arden, composed of the nobility and gentry of the neighbourhood, who still hold their meetings at Forest Hall at Meriden and shoot with the traditional English longbows. In the Hall is a horn that tradition says

Robin Hood blew while supposedly competing here. The archery meetings, in their present form, were revived on the old 'Forest Ground' in 1785.

In 1822, Meriden became a key destination on civil engineer Thomas Telford's famous road from London to Holyhead (the A5). With the advent of the bicycle, it became a popular tourist attraction for cyclists, who still meet once a year at the National Cyclists' Memorial on the green to commemorate cyclists killed in the two World Wars.

Ancient cross at Meriden

Alas, Meriden's bold claim falls short when its history is examined more closely, for the original settlement was just east of here at the nearby Saxon village of Alspath meaning 'road to Al's dwelling', with its community centred on the parish church of St Laurence to the east of Meriden. According to historians, Meriden only developed as a resting place for travellers in the early 17th century after the road from London to Chester was built. Alspath stands on a hill just 1.5 km from Meriden with commanding views across the old fields and valleys of Warwickshire.

St Laurence's Church dates to Norman times, replacing one founded by Countess Godgifu (d. 1067), wife of Leofric, Earl of Mercia. She owned much of the lands around Coventry including Alspath, although her tyrannical husband failed to share her fondness for the area. She was made famous as the legendary Lady Godiva who rode naked through the streets of Coventry covered only by her long hair. Leofric was one of the most powerful lords in the land at the time and mercilessly taxed the people of Coventry to pay for King Canute's bodyguard.

When Lady Godiva pleaded with him to stop this unpopular tax, he is reputed to have said, 'You will have to ride naked through Coventry before I will change my ways.' She took him at his word and Leofric, so stunned by his wife's actions, immediately freed the town from paying the levy.[12]

The church is named after the 3rd-century Laurence of Rome or Laurence of Canterbury, who became the second archbishop in 604 CE. However, records show that its original dedication was to the Saxon martyr St Edmund, indicating a pre-Norman foundation. The church also stands on a long-distance path called the 'Heart of England Way', from Milford Common on Cannock Chase to Bourton-on-the-Water in the Cotswolds.

Just under 0.5 km southwest of the church is St Laurence's Well, now hidden in undergrowth within a copse next to a crop field. Tradition says St Laurence baptised his converts here and in later times it was visited for its curative powers, especially for the healing of eyes and legs. Followers of 'the Green Stone' quest in the 1980s placed the 'nine lights and the twelve stones' in the well at Meriden after the publication of the book *The Green Stone* by Graham Phillips and Martin Keatman. During their many psychic questing adventures, the authors along with fellow researcher Andrew Collins were led to various places of power to retrieve physical objects at sacred sites under mysterious circumstances to banish some ancient dark force inherent in the British landscape. Although their visit to Meriden is unrecorded in *The Green Stone*, it is known that they visited St Laurence's Well.[13]

The most interesting feature of this area is the village pond, located just beyond Leys Lane which connects Meriden and Alspath. The pool is fed by a larger fishpond in the grounds of nearby Meriden Hall and is situated next to a major crossroads of the old drove route to and from Wales and a north-south road between Tamworth and the south coast.

According to folklore, this body of water has two outlets – one flowing into the Humber and the other into the Bristol Channel. Indeed, many say that the area was one of the great watersheds of England, reminiscent of the waterways at the centres of Ireland and Wales.

Arthur Mee, author of *The King's England* series of books, refers to a renowned tradition that the area around Alspath was known for its health benefits, 'for when the plague came to England in 1665 few there suffered from the visitation.'[14] This was probably due to the quality of the water supplied from the pond and St Laurence's Well, possibly sharing the same underground source.

Michell's Main Axis of Britain (see Fig. 19), passes through Tamworth and also goes through the pond, once part of the old Saxon settlement of Alspath. The Axis also passes through the prehistoric centres of the Rollright Stones in Oxfordshire and Arbor Low in Derbyshire, along with Brailes Hill in Warwickshire, a renowned place of mystery. Kirk Yetholm on the Scottish Borders is also on the line, where the last king of the Gypsies was crowned in 1898. There is evidence of an ancient north-south road that followed the Axis between Alspath and Tamworth – perhaps called 'Al's path' from which the village acquired its name.

The Midland Oak

The famous Midland Oak has for at least eight centuries been the rival to Meriden as the centre of England, residing near the boundary between the old Saxon towns of Lillington and Lamintone or Leamington Spa in Warwickshire. It stood nearly 11 miles southeast of Meriden until 1967 and was thought to be eight hundred years old. It was replaced by a new oak in 1988 and next to it is a plaque that officially reinstates the site as the centre of England.

There is little evidence, however, both in geographical terms and as regards local traditions, that this area was a renowned centre of England, although Lillington's church may give us a clue as to why this area gained such a reputation.

Standing high up on a hill above the old village, the present church is built over a religious settlement dating back to 970, which came into the possession of the monks of Kenilworth Priory in 1121. The church dedicated to St Mary Magdalene is usually open for only one hour a day except on Sundays, so we were fortunate that on the day we were visiting, the church was open for cleaning. The churchwarden and her helpers were keen to chat about the church's history and its various features, including a bell cast in the churchyard in the 1400s. According to some sources, such practices facilitated the alchemical processes involved with the craft of bell foundry at sacred sites such as this, using specific metals to aid the resonance of the bell as it rang. Moreover, inscribed on the bell is 'Pray for us Katherine', a saint associated with the turning wheel on an axis or spindle, alluding to a north-south axis mundi and the wheel of the heavens.

The Oak at Morton

Oak trees are highly symbolic of the axis mundi, with their branches in the heavens, their trunk in the physical world, and their roots in the underworld. Another famous 'omphalos' oak in the Midlands was located 56 miles north of Lillington and 8 miles west of Mansfield in the Derbyshire town of Morton. Upon entering the village, its sign informs visitors that they are now at the geographical centre of England.

Using the modern boundary method, it marks the midway point along another north-south axis that stretches between Poole in Dorset and a spot near Berwick-upon-Tweed on the borders of modern Scotland. Furthermore, it is midway between Dodleston on the Welsh border and Skegness on the east coast. According to local historian Barrington Darby, during the 1800s generations of Morton residents would sit on a bench beneath the tree more or less opposite Stretton Road, believing they were relaxing at the very centre of England. After the oak's condition declined a few years ago, a replacement was planted alongside it, which also appears to have perished.

However, why the tree was ever considered to mark the centre of England is a mystery. One piece of tangible evidence comes from an article printed in *Horner's Weekly* newspaper on 1 October 1910 entitled *The Centre of England.*[15] The piece included a caption that mentions its claim as being endorsed by Ordnance Survey. Others, meanwhile, believe the parish council perpetuated the myth in the 1990s to place greater value on the town's assets and heritage. Consequently, a plaque was commissioned and placed near the tree to confirm its status as marking England's geographical centre. As the year 2000 approached, the parish council was seeking a feature to commemorate the millennium. Many ideas were suggested, but the most popular was the village sign you see today.

The Battles at the Centre of England

As we close in on the true 'omphalos' area of England, we find a place where key historical battles took place. In 2002, the Ordnance Survey officially defined the geographical centre of England to be in a field on Lindley Hall Farm, approximately 18 km north of Meriden near the village of Fenny Drayton in Leicestershire. At the edge of the field by the road is a 1.8-m tall railway sleeper with a plaque that points to the exact spot further up the field. Of great interest to us, however, is that the field is on the land where one of the most significant battles in British history took place, which ended the English reign of the Norman House of Plantagenet, its last monarch dying on the battlefield.

The Battle of Bosworth Field was the last significant conflict in the Wars of the Roses, a civil war that raged across England in the latter half of the 15th century. The battle was fought on 22 August 1485 and won by the Lancastrians, led by Henry Tudor, then Earl of Richmond, son of Margaret Beaufort of the House of Lancaster, who became the first English monarch of the Tudor dynasty. His opponent, the Plantagenet Richard III, the last king of the House of York, was killed on the field of battle. During the fight, his crown fell from his helmet, which has been worn by Plantagenet kings for over 300 years.

Geographical centre of England near Fenny Drayton

A legend says it was found on the battlefield by Lord Stanley, who supposedly betrayed the king during the last moments of the conflict. After switching sides, Stanley attacked him from behind, eventually finding the dead king's golden crown in a thorn bush. He reputedly handed it to Henry Tudor, who then immediately crowned himself king at the top of the nearby Crown Hill close to the village of Stoke Golding. Although none of the contemporary sources reported such an event, Henry VII adopted the badge of a crowned thorn tree after the battle, which was later depicted in a stained-glass window in his private chapel at Westminster Abbey.

It is interesting to note that Crown Hill is just 3.8 km from the Ordnance Survey centre of England at Fenny Drayton. A blue plaque on a brick pillar on nearby Station Road now commemorates the event. We wondered whether the battle was fought here at the centre of England as a deliberate act to maximise its effect on the English nation. Any action of such a negative nature at the navel could influence the psyche of the people across the length and breadth of the land. Had the House of York won, the Reformation may never have happened and England would have remained under Papist control.

This area has also seen historical detectives scouring the area in search of the elusive site of Boudicca's last stand against the Romans, the great warrior queen of the British Iceni tribe from East Anglia. Before his death, Boudicca's husband Prasutagas, having no male heir, willed that his kingdom should be shared between his wife and two daughters and the Roman Emperor Nero – trusting that he would have imperial protection for his family. The Romans, however, ignored this arrangement and had Boudicca flogged and her daughters raped. The outraged Boudicca organised a revolt against the Roman garrisons at London and Colchester, killing thousands. Upon hearing the news of the slaughter of the Druids on Anglesey, she then set off towards Wales to meet with General Gaius Suetonius Paulinus and his Roman legion, responsible for this famous massacre. Unfortunately, the actual site of this great battle that then ensued between these two armies remains a mystery, although, according to some experts, it took place on Watling Street in 60 or 61 CE 'somewhere between St Albans and Anglesey.'

Boudicca greatly outnumbered the Romans, having been aided by mercenary soldiers, and should have won a great victory, thereby ending the Roman occupation of Britain. At first, the regular troops stood their ground, with the Romans using the surrounding valleys as a natural defence. However, Boudicca's half-trained and poorly armed troops, recruited from all walks of life, were no match for a highly seasoned, better-equipped, well-trained and highly organised Roman Legion.

The battle was decisive, with the Britons suffering an overwhelming defeat. According to the Roman writer Tacitus who gives a more conservative estimate of manpower and losses, over 80,000 Britons died compared to only 400 Roman soldiers. Many accounts record that during the battle when defeat was near, Boudicca committed suicide.[16] If this battle had gone the way of the British it would have been one of the greatest victories against foreign repression in our nation's history, but alas it marked the beginning of a subservience to Roman rule that lasted another 350 years.

Tacitus writes that Suetonius chose a position in a 'defile' or 'narrow valley', with woodland protecting him to his rear, faced by open country with little protection against ambush.[17] Many historians believe it to be close to the village of Mancetter near Atherstone in

Warwickshire where Watling Street meets the River Anker. The Romans had a fort here called Manduessedum which translates as 'the place of the chariots', next to the present-day A5 around the Bull Inn close to Fenny Drayton, the modern OS centre.

In 1978, the late Graham Webster, archaeologist and specialist in Romano-British history made a convincing case for Mancetter as the site of the battle in his book *Boudica: The British Revolt Against Rome AD 60*. While studying the topography around the village, Webster recognised that Hartshill Ridge, just south of there on the outskirts of Atherstone, matched Tacitus' description based on the original shallow profile.[18] The area now occupied by Dobbies Garden Centre near the River Anker is thought to be the site.

Atherstone itself was deemed the centre of England by Sir Charles Arden-Close, Director-General of the Ordnance Survey in 1941. He identified the spot as being 'on Watling Street, 4 miles ESE of Atherstone, close to the railway bridge, between the villages of Higham-on-the-Hill and Caldecote.'[19] This location is just over 1.5 km away from the new OS-calculated centre at Fenny Drayton. We felt it significant that two of the key battles over the fate of the country, against the Romans and later the Plantagenets, took place close to the omphalos of England. As discovered previously, major battles for the right to control the sovereignty of a country have also taken place at the centres of Ireland, Scotland and Wales.

The Roman Axis and High Cross

Finding and marking the centre of a kingdom was not only a Greek obsession but also a sacred ritual of the pre-Roman Etruscans of central Italy, a tradition which the Romans continued after usurping their culture. Roman surveyors first came to this country in 43 CE after the successful invasion of the south under the leadership of Roman General Vespasian, with the Isle of Wight becoming a base for his surveyors to plan for the invasion of the rest of Britain.

Michell believes that the Romans later surveyed a line through Britain from St Catherine's Point on the Isle of Wight to the last fort on Hadrian's Wall at the mouth of the River Tyne (see Fig. 20). Upon this axis, they located the official centre point at 'High Cross' where Watling Street from London to Chester crosses the old Fosse Way from Lincoln to Exeter.[20] With more accurate computer mapping programs, I discovered Michell's 'Roman Axis' has a remarkable number of important historical sites along its course, including St Catherine's Hill in Winchester, a holy sanctuary of the Druids and later Christians, which at one time was the capital of the early Britons and later the Kingdom of Wessex. On top of the hill is a turf-cut labyrinth which represents the journey to the centre, or the dance around a fixed centre. The many myths and legends associated with this hill and labyrinth feature in our book *The Spine of Albion*.

The Roman Fort of Arbeia in South Shields marks the most northerly point of the Roman Axis and the Roman Empire as a whole in Britain. The fort is built over a prehistoric sacred site called Lawe Tap Hill, and a Roman seaport associated with this important military base on the River Tyne served as a gateway to this northernmost frontier of Roman Britain.

Recently, the head of a small statue of a northern British goddess was unearthed here, adorned with a mural or crown, possibly from a temple or walled enclosure. Archaeologists believe it to be the goddess Brigantia, as an altar dedicated to her was found nearby. This suggests that a shrine to this ancient goddess of the early Britons once stood within a prehistoric site usurped by Arbeia Fort. The statue has been dated to around 208 CE, during the time Emperor Septimius Severus arrived in South Shields, who possibly destroyed the native sanctuary of the great mother goddess of Britain to dominate and control the region and its pagan people.

At St Catherine's Point on the Isle of Wight, on the southern tip of the Roman Axis, there is a stone tower, formerly a medieval lighthouse, with a chapel attached called St Catherine's Oratory. There are several sacred hills as well as coastal chapels named after this female saint, who became the patron of sailors. She is often portrayed with a wheel by her side, which was said to be her instrument of martyrdom in the early 4th century at the hands of the pagan emperor Maxentius. St Catherine is also linked with dragon slaying and her wheel is associated with the omphalos – the axial representing the axis mundi; the Oratory on St Catherine's Point being the perfect representation of an axis mundi.

St Catherine is another personification of the old British goddess, a deity that has been revered at both the most southerly and northerly ends of this Roman Axis. Morton in Derbyshire with its central oak also lies upon this line, along with several major crossroads at Newbury, Banbury and Nostell Priory. More significant on this axis is the West Yorkshire village of Barwick, once part of the old Celtic

Kingdom of Elmet and the capital of the powerful Brigantian queen Cartimandua. Also precisely on the line just north of there are three megalithic standing stones called the Devil's Arrows at Boroughbridge, erected in an alignment across the A1, the old Roman road between Lincoln and Hadrian's Wall.

The Roman High Cross is situated on an area of elevated ground along the A5 east of Atherstone about 19 km northwest of Meriden and is perhaps the oldest crossroads in Britain, where Watling Street crosses the Fosse Way. A stylish 18th-century stone monument, now partly ruined in a private garden, but easily visible from the road, marks the spot said by many to be the true centre of England. Recently, archaeologists have concluded that these roads date to Celtic times, repaved by the invading Romans to stop the British

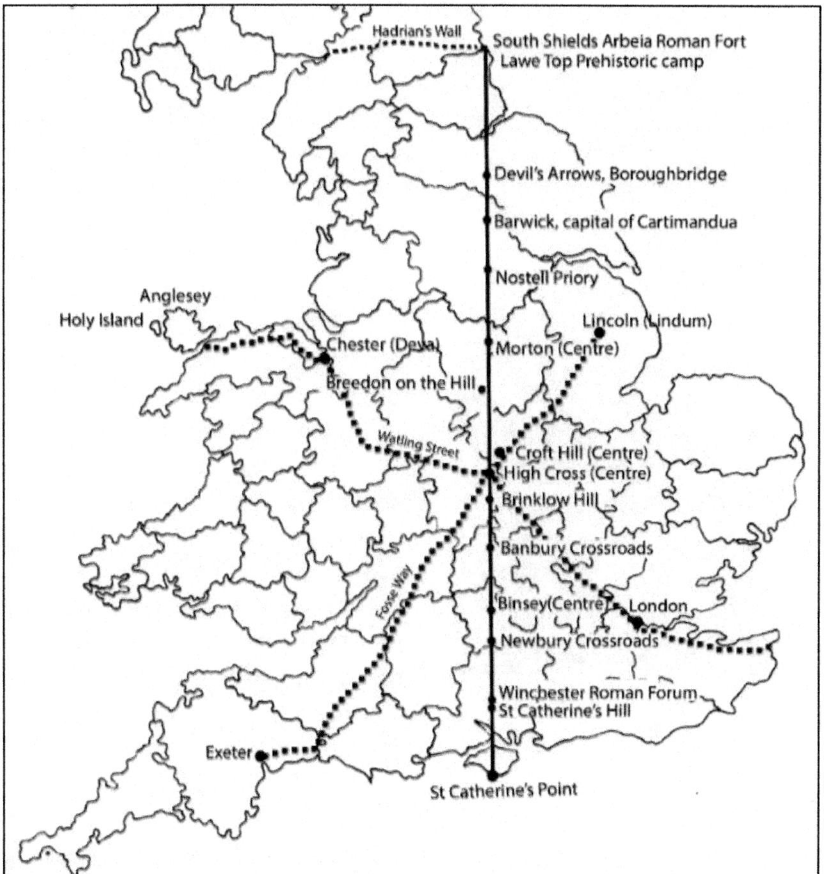

Figure 20. Britain's 'Roman Axis', after John Michell (1994)

chariots that had been so effective at compromising the progress of the Roman advance.

Geoffrey of Monmouth refers to an Iron Age system of road building instigated by King Molmutius and his son King Belinus – descendants of Brutus, the mythical founder of Britain. Belinus ruled the kingdoms of Cornwall, Kambria (Wales) and Loegria (England), from *c.* 380 to 363 BCE and 'summoned workmen from all over the island and ordered them to construct a road of stones and mortar which would bisect the island longitudinally from the Cornish Sea to the shore of Caithness and should lead in a straight line to each of the cities on route.'[21] He decreed that all the temples in the major cities and the roads that led to them were sanctuaries, where men and women were safe from attack or arrest, and that everyone should respect a Highway Code of laws laid down by his father Molmutius.

Monument at High Cross, Leicestershire

The Roman historians who documented the invasion of Britain made no claims that the Latins built great highways, and it is more likely that they paved over the chariot tracks of the Celts. Arthur Pickering in *The Roman Sites of South-West Leicestershire* observes: 'In the construction of both Watling Street and the Fosse Way the Roman engineers would have taken their sighting point from the vicinity of High Cross, this being the highest point in the district (actually 443.4 ft above O.D.). To do this two sighting points some 36 m apart would appear to have been used. This suggests the question of whether the line of one or both of the roads are partly determined by existing roads.'[22]

According to archaeological evidence, the Roman garrison built the township of Veronis or Bennonis near High Cross over an Iron Age settlement. Moreover, there are faint traces of a henge monument or sacred ditched enclosure very close to this ancient crossroads, which remains unexcavated. Antiquarian Joseph Tom Burgess observed the rise upon which High Cross sits in 1876, as being in sight of 57 church towers.[23]

In *Itinerarium Curiosum* (1776), William Stukeley described High Cross as 'the centre, as well as the highest ground in England; … for from hence rivers run every way.' The present structure replaced one erected there upon orders of the Justices of Warwickshire in 1712, recorded in one of Stukeley's drawings dated 1724.[24] An inscription on one side reads: 'The noblemen and gentry, ornaments of the neighbouring counties of Warwick and Leicester, at the instances of the Right Honourable Basil Earl of Denbeigh, have caused this pillar to be erected in grateful as well as a perpetual remembrance of Peace at last restored by her Majesty Queen Anne, in the year of our Lord, 1712.'

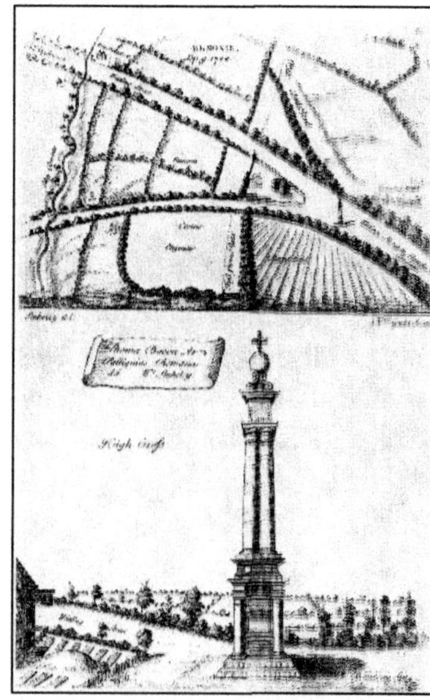

1724 engraving of High Cross by William Stukeley

The worn lettering continues on the other side: 'If, traveller, you search for the footsteps of the ancient Romans, here you may behold them. For here their most celebrated ways, crossing one another, extend to the utmost boundaries of Britain.' The stone-built monument erected by the Earl of Denbigh replaced a wooden cross that existed on the same spot for several centuries. In 1791, it was struck by lightning and what remained of it was re-erected in its present position.

As we looked up at the now neglected, overgrown and crumbling monument, it was hard to believe that it once marked the symbolic central crossroads of England. Today, thankfully, there are plans to restore this important fading symbol of our British heritage.

Although most focus their attention on the High Cross as being a Roman centre of England, it is clear from the Iron Age remnants of an earthen enclosure next to it that this was an important sacred sanctuary of the Celtic Britons positioned next to this central crossroads long before the Latin invaders came to our shores. Stukeley's drawing of the 1712 cross shows a tumulus standing near the Inn that stood next to the cross. Perhaps the Romans were aware that the prehistoric Britons and the later Celts revered this place as a sacred omphalos. Pickering cites a letter sent to Sir William Dugdale in 1657 which states: 'At High Cross … is the foundation (as I guess) of a Roman temple, about six yards long, and four yards broad; and where, they say, not long since, was a thing like a silver mace dug up.'[25]

Is it also a coincidence that only a couple of kilometres from here is Bosworth Field and Crown Hill, where Henry Tudor after his victory against the armies of Richard III in 1485 was crowned king of England? The loss of Richard III's coronet after his death on the battlefield at the centre of England may be just a myth, but it is symbolic of the enormous shift of power that took place at the time. It saw the end of the 300-year rule of the French dynasty of Plantagenet kings and the beginning of a new era when a new ruler with the blood of the old British and Welsh kings coursing through his veins came to the English throne. Henry Tudor was descended from the Welsh line of Owain Glyndŵr, the last native-born Welshman to claim the title Prince of Wales, and some people say, from the legendary King Arthur.

Interestingly, High Cross also falls on an east-west alignment 90 degrees off the Roman Axis, which runs from Lowestoft, the most extreme easterly point of England, to Pumlumon Mountain at the centre of Wales (see Fig. 21).

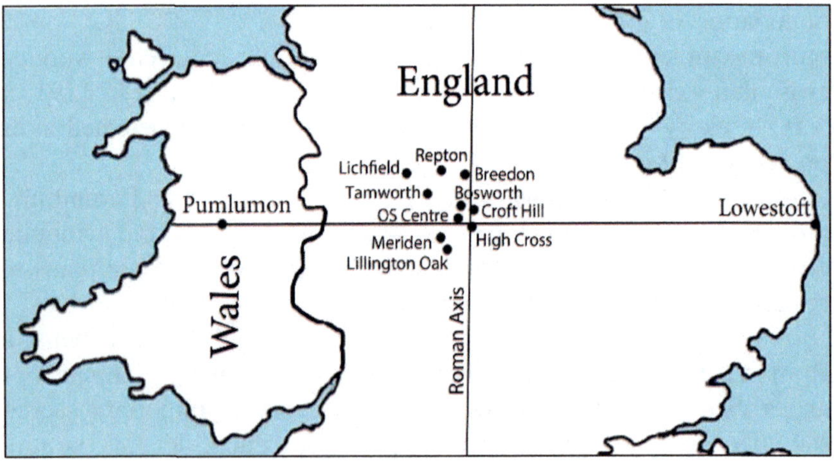

Figure 21. The centre places of England

The Celtic Omphalos of England

Just 8 km NNE of High Cross is possibly England's most central hill, or symbolic world mountain, called Croft Hill, straddling the River Soar near the village of Croft in Leicestershire. It is also one of the highest peaks in the Midlands, rising to 128 m as it overlooks the Soar flood plain. During the 1960s and 1970s, the area around Croft Hill was the centre of several UFO incidents, with hundreds of sightings reported. Many researchers would camp on the hill in the hope of experiencing and capturing 'light ball activity' referred to by Paul Devereux. In his book *Earth Lights*, Devereux describes how he drew a circle within a 16-km-radius around Croft Hill and found that 50% of the reports of strange lights fell within the circle, 25% of which fell within an 8-km-radius of Croft Hill itself.[26]

However, as we have discovered while investigating earth light phenomena at power centres on the north-south Belinus alignment, the so-called UFO sightings may have been plasma lights, which fault lines are known to discharge when under pressure especially around rocks such as granite and sandstone that have inherent magnetic qualities. Moreover, many people have witnessed this natural phenomenon in certain geological zones all around the world. Vinod Krishnan, a senior Professor and Dean of Sciences at the Indian Institute of Astrophysics says that:

> 'Nature began with plasma. Cooling of the plasma converted it into gas. Cooling of the gas converted it into liquid. Cooling of the liquid converted it into solid matter. That plasmas are the first state of matter, out of which arose the other three states of matter has been demonstrated. The ubiquity of plasmas in the Universe needs no demonstration. The phenomenal diversity of plasmas is there all over the Universe for all to see.'[27]

Plasma is highly luminous and can exist outside our space-time continuum, performing extraordinary manoeuvres, which many in the past interpreted as dragons or serpents and today UFOs. Plasma can also rearrange its molecular structure to any shape or form, allowing it to connect with our three-dimensional world in whatever form would be acceptable or known.

As mentioned previously, plasma emits strong magnetic fields that affect the temporal lobe of the human brain, and this can cause varying degrees of physiological and psychological disturbances including hallucinatory or visionary experiences. Incidentally, fourteen different leys or alignments cross at the summit of Croft Hill, which is an indication of its magnetic power and former importance. Devereux refers to a fault line at the base of the hill and a great slab of rock in the lower slopes uncovered by erosion that appeared 'so regular as to look artificial.' In *Space Time Transients and Unusual Events*, the authors Dr Michael Persinger and Gyslaine F. Lafreniere scientifically demonstrate a correlation between areas of unusual paranormal events, such as strange creatures, UFOs and time-slips, and geological anomalies that produce plasma, such as fault lines.[28] Perhaps this is why this old beacon site was chosen by the Druids of old as their 'mother mountain'.

Local historian T. L. Walker believed that Croft Hill was a lost British 'mesomphalos' and wrote in 1879 that in ancient Gaul there was a supposed mesomphalos 'where the druids met on an isolated hill in the midst of a plain in the centre of the country by the River Loire. The idea of such a mesomphalos was said to have been borrowed from Britain.'[29] Perhaps he was referring to Croft Hill?

Devereux also believed Croft Hill was a mesomphalos – 'a central sacred site at the "fulcrum" of Britain's magical Landscape.' He also mentions that the ancient church at the base of the hill, St Michael and All Angels, is a dedication often associated with locations of

Croft Hill, Leicestershire

geomantic significance and several monarchs of England surveyed their kingdom from Croft Hill's summit.[30] Around the base of the hill, there are earthworks said to be remnants of a surrounding ditch, which is unusual as most of Britain's hillforts were constructed on the top of hills or ridges. This may suggest that the ditch was not constructed for defensive purposes but as a ring of sanctuary, similar to that surrounding Avebury and Stonehenge. Devereux also refers to megaliths used as mark stones around the hill, now lost through quarrying.[31]

Early Christians also understood the significance of this hill when they chose it as a meeting place or moot for open-air courts and fairs. Royal Mercian assemblies took place here and most probably a series of synods attended by kings, bishops, abbots and other chief men to discuss important matters, called a Clovesho. In 836, the court of King Wiglaf of Mercia assembled on Croft Hill, alongside Ceolnoth, the Archbishop of Canterbury, and eleven of his bishops and three abbots, together with 'twenty-two laymen of authority and influence.' Their purpose was to witness the grant of land by Wiglaf to the monastery of Hanbury. In 1124, an assize was held here, with Lord Bassett acting as Lord Chief Justice of England for Henry I.[32]

These remarkable assemblies are reminiscent of the Irish gatherings on the Hill of Uisneach and confirmed our growing opinion that Croft Hill was the true navel of England along with the ancient High Cross a few miles away. We discovered during our quest for the centres of Britain and Ireland that many omphalos sites have been usurped by invading cultures as they seek to destroy the established sovereignty of the existing ruling dynasty. The destruction of the Pictish place of assembly at the omphalos of Scotland at Moulin near Blair Atholl is one such example, its once powerful presence in the landscape is now lost from memory. Likewise, in Wales at Pumlumon, the old beacon site with its burial mounds and stone monuments has been desecrated by battles since Celtic times.

The name Croft was first recorded in 836 CE, possibly derived from the Old English *crebre*, *cræft* or *craft* meaning a 'machine or engine', associated with the nearby Roman quarry workings. Alternatively, some believe the meaning refers to a water mill, the *Domesday Book* of 1086 having recorded two mills at Croft. However, according to Bob Trubshaw, 'crebre' was one of the few rare Celtic names in Leicestershire.[33] This led me to discover that in the Gaelic language, *cree* means 'heart, core or centre' and *bree* translates as a hill; therefore, crebre becomes 'central hill'. Cree is also reminiscent of St Creeda or Cride associated with the centres of Cornwall.

We parked the car in a layby nearby and walked towards the hill along a footpath. As Caroline and I climbed the steep path around its summit, we stopped dead in our tracks as we came to the edge of a sheer cliff. Here, a hole in the ground drops to over 91 m into one of the deepest quarries in Britain and is recorded as the largest manmade ravine in Europe.

In the 1920s, Croft Hill was a renowned picnic spot for Sunday School trips and was popular with the people of Leicestershire before quarrying destroyed most of the hill, creating this massive canyon we see today. The hill was particularly targeted by industry because beneath its slopes is a rare type of pre-Cambrian pink syenite granite, which was used as building material and hardcore filling for roads. Syenite is a form of grainy red or pink granite similar to Aswan granite in Egypt and revered by the ancient Egyptians, using it to build some of their most sacred temples and obelisks. The Romans were the first to come to Croft Hill to quarry this special stone for the construction of roads and bridges, particularly the Fosse Way.

This type of stone is highly magnetic and we found a similar type of granite in Shap in Cumbria, at the centre-point of the Belinus Line, where it was once used by the prehistoric builders to construct a megalithic serpent temple, similar to Avebury in Wiltshire. Today the quarry at Croft Hill produces 2 million tonnes of granite anually and to date has removed over 45 million tonnes of this highly valued stone.

As we walked back towards the trig point on the summit of the hill, we noticed a man picking up litter. Caroline stopped to pick up a discarded chocolate bar wrapper and a beer bottle which she then handed to him. He was very grateful and explained that he and many other villagers come to the hill regularly to clear it of litter left behind by weekend revellers who seem to be drawn here to drink alcohol and take drugs. He told us that he originally came to the area to work at the quarry, retiring in the late 1990s and had fallen in love with the hill and the surrounding landscape. We asked how long the quarrying would continue and to our surprise, he replied, 'Only another two years.' Apparently, the quarry owners wanted to continue to quarry the entire area including the rest of Croft Hill but the locals got together to save it and won their case – 'to think of them crushing up our precious hill just to lay it on our roads made us fight for its survival.'

We then asked what would happen to it when quarrying had ceased and he explained that it would naturally fill with water to become a lake. There are still large quantities of water under the hill which the quarry company has to pay British Waterways to pump out every day into the river, amounting to 10,000 gallons (45,000 litres) every hour! He also mentioned that when the mineral content of the water was analysed, it was found to be the same as water from a lake in France, although he couldn't remember exactly where. Perhaps the water does indeed flow to this area from the Continent through an underground fissure or fault.

He took pride in showing us around the hill, pointing out various features such as traces of the old earthen ditches around the base of the summit. T. L. Walker witnessed three large boulders of syenite granite at the foot of the hill to the northeast on a visit to Croft Hill in 1853. Upon closer examination of this area, he found faint traces of a ditch and bank running a full two-thirds of the way around the circumference of the hill. He too concluded that it was constructed as a sacred enclosure.[34] We believe such earthworks around the hill make it a very special ceremonial site, as, according to occult law, encircling a site in this way acts as psychic protection while performing any ceremony.

The controversial author David Icke lived below the hill in the village of Croft during his time as a BBC Sports presenter in the 1970s. He mentions in his book *Truth Vibrations* that he was led psychically to connect with many places of power as a way of awakening him to the universal consciousness – perhaps Croft helped to initiate or prepare him for this personal spiritual journey.[35]

The hill is also home to ravens, which have probably more folklore associated with them than any other bird in Britain. Welsh traditions tell us that the raven was the totem of Bran the Blessed, who was seen as a primordial deity and guardian of Britain. In Greek mythology, ravens are associated with Apollo, the god of prophecy, and were seen as symbols of good fortune.

The significance of this lonely hill has long been wiped from the memory of the English people, and its ancient heritage can now only be glimpsed at. The violation of this sacred enclosure on such a massive scale by the big business of industrial quarrying has devastated England's navel, which must have had a detrimental effect on the energy of England. We sat on the grass next to the trig point and contemplated the incredible yet sad history of Croft Hill. Over half of the hill has disappeared and much of the valley below. However, the locals have saved what is left of it, which we must be thankful for, otherwise this old sacred assembly place of the Druids and British and Saxon kings would have been lost forever.

We could almost hear the elementals and guardian spirits of this hill crying out at the damage that man has inflicted upon this precious landscape. Nature has its hierarchy of elementals, an invisible force of etheric beings or spirits that tend to the energy needs of Mother Earth. We cannot see them unless we raise our vibrations through meditation or under certain conditions when the local magnetic field increases.

Croft Hill teetering on the edge of the quarry

Such desecration can cause disharmony and imbalance within the land as it disrupts the natural flow of Earth's energies. The ancients would see this as a sickness of the land, termed by geomancers as 'geopathic stress', which comes from the Greek *geo* meaning 'of the earth' and *pathos* meaning 'suffering or disease'. It relates to irregularities in the Earth's magnetic field, which can be aggravated by a variety of natural and manmade features such as quarrying and mining. A 'wound' in the land of this magnitude so close to the Roman Axis of England would have a severe and long-lasting effect on the peace and harmony of the country.

When all was quiet and after all the dog walkers had left, we felt moved to perform a healing ceremony invoking the elementals and spirit guardian to guide us and Bride, the mother goddess of Britain whose energy also resides within this hill. We sent honouring to the Druid ancestors, who once revered this centre of England, and visualised the pure healing power of our sacred healing stones connecting with the underground water and rocks of the hill revitalising the damaged earth energy grid and seeing all the lines reconnecting to the surrounding sacred sites once more. We also visualised the great wound formed by the quarry gleaming with light as it fills with water in the future, seeing the light radiating from the hill across the landscape like sunbeams. We then buried an Iona stone near the summit to seal our intentions within the hill.

Intriguingly, the smallest chapel in Leicestershire lies just a short distance from the hill to the southwest at Potters Marston Hall, built on land once owned by the medieval Priory of St Mary in Coventry. Beyond is Stoney Stanton, a village mentioned in the *Domesday Book*, with a medieval St Michael's Church, and the historic market town of Hinckley, once an important Iron Age and Romano-British settlement next to Watling Street.

The road north from Croft Hill takes you to the ancient Danish settlement of Desford, later owned by Norman Baron Hugo de Grantmesnil after the Battle of Hastings who became Baron of Hinckley and Desford. The ancient Fosse Way runs diagonally southeast of the hill, which only reaffirms Croft Hill's former importance.

The fascinating history and folklore of this ancient omphalos most certainly qualifies it as England's central mother mountain. In its isolation, it looms above the lowland flood plains of South Leicestershire and once emanated immense telluric power throughout the land through its special granite geology. The ancient earthworks that surround it are possibly from a time when the Druids cared for and harmonised the land through a sacred ceremony using the nurturing and healing power of the goddess energy within the feminine-shaped hill. As we strolled back to the car, we began to see the remains of this pitiful hill in a different light – a bright shining one!

The Perpetual Choirs and the Whiteleaved Oak

Croft Hill is also one of ten equidistant sites on a massive landscape decagon across the heart of England and Wales that according to Michell includes Llantwit Major, Glastonbury, Stonehenge and Goring-on-Thames, where monks supposedly held 'perpetual choirs' during Celtic times. At the hub of this great landscape figure is a hamlet called Whiteleaved Oak, positioned at the southern end of the Malvern Hills where the counties of Herefordshire, Worcestershire and Gloucestershire meet.[36]

The earliest reference to the 'perpetual choirs' in Britain is by Pierre Jean-Baptiste Le Grand d'Aussy's in *Fabliaux or Tales*, published in 1796 and compiled from 12th and 13th-century French manuscripts.[37] There are several interpretations of the concept of the perpetual choirs; some suggest they were choirs of Druids or early Christian monks maintaining perpetual chanting at many key points around the country.

In ancient times, priests marked the procession of the seasonal cycles in an endless round of chanting and ceremonies. Michell refers to Plato's view of paradise, whereby colonists of a new city should 'seek out the shrines of the native gods and spirits, perpetuate their cult and hold festivals at their sites. There should, he says, be no less than 365 festivals in the country during the course of the year. This idea of an unbroken festive cycle is matched by Plato's belief in choral singing as a beneficial exercise for all citizens.'[38]

Michell states that a relic of those days may be seen in the tradition of the perpetual choirs of Britain mentioned in ancient bardic lore and recorded in *The Welsh Triads*. He names the three main Perpetual Choirs as Glastonbury, the Choir of Ambrosius or Stonehenge, and Llan Illtud Fawr, which is the old Celtic sanctuary at Llantwit Major in Glamorgan (see Fig. 22). The positioning of the three choirs are equidistant from each other by 62 km on an arc that is centred on Whiteleaved Oak in Herefordshire. Moreover, Goring-on-Thames stands almost 61 km east on the same arc from Stonehenge where ancient tracks including the Icknield Way meet the Ridgeway at the River Thames.

As well as Croft Hill, the completed circle of perpetual choirs includes Stoney Stratford, Uttoxeter, Ellesmere, Carno (12.8 km west of Pumlumon Mountain) and Llandovery. The early Christian saints who came from the Holy Land re-established traditions of perpetual choirs throughout Britain, their mystical purpose being to enchant and heal the land and spread their 'religious influence'. They were simply adapting a far older Celtic practice when governments 'were conducted through the influence of music rather than by a rigid code of law.'[39]

In contention with Michell's discovery, *The Welsh Triads* describe

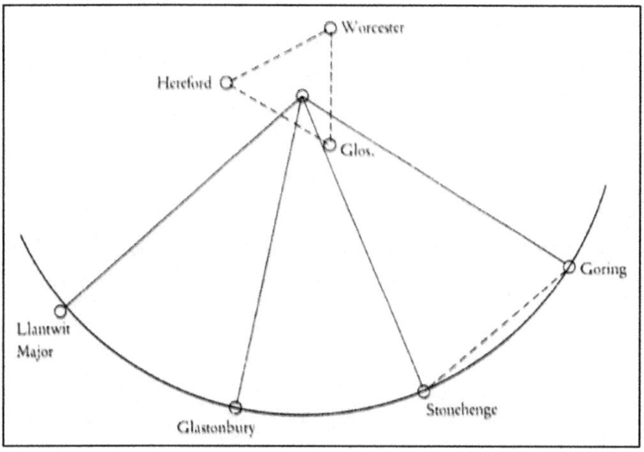

Figure 22. The three equidistant perpetual choirs with Goring, centred on Whiteleaved Oak, after John Michell's 'The Dimensions of Paradise' (1988)

in *Triad 90* 'Three Perpetual Harmonies of the Island of Britain' as being 'Bangor is y Coed', 'Caer Garadawg' and 'Innis Witrin' or the 'Isle of Afallach'; 'In each of these three places were 2,400 religious men; and of these, a 100 in turn continued each hour of the twenty-four hours of the day and night in prayer and service to God ceaselessly and without rest forever.'[40]

Some historians argue that Innis Witrin may be the Isle of Glastonbury, but Bangor is y Coed and Caer Caradoc, which translates as fortress or citadel of Caradoc, are not included in the three sites proposed by Michell. King Caractacus was a great British warrior who fought guerrilla warfare against the Roman occupation around the borders of England and Wales. Some believe this site to be a hillfort near the town of Church Stretton in Shropshire where he fought his last stand, while others claim it as an enclosure in Mid Glamorgan on a hill called Mynydd-y-Gaer. Only Geoffrey of Monmouth expressly identifies Caer Garadawg (Caradoc) with Salisbury,[41] which is close to Stonehenge. Likewise, Bangor is y Coed was a large monastery in North Wales on the River Dee where the

Saxons under Northumbrian King Aethelfrith massacred 12,000 British monks.

Despite these discrepancies, Michell's discovery by using a simple compass on a map has reawakened interest in this sacred circle of sites associated with this ancient practice of perpetual choirs, and the curious symmetry and positioning of Glastonbury, Stonehenge and Llantwit Major is still remarkable.

The Whiteleaved Oak at the very centre of the decagon is also a curious place, a hamlet in an imaginary triangle that connects the three cathedrals of Worcester, Hereford and Gloucester. These ancient cathedrals maintain an annual choral music festival at the end of July called 'The Three Choir Festival' that dates back to the 18th century and rotates between them, each city having three competing choirs. The name Whiteleaved Oak recalls a celebrated tree within its bounds that was cut down in the 19th century. *In The Forest and Chace of Malvern*, Edwin Lees writes:

> 'The "White-leaved Oak" valley between the Ragged-stone and Keysend-hills, keeps in its name the memory of an oak that existed there within memory, whose leaves being variegated with white blotches, caused it to be considered a curiosity and prodigy. Others believe it was a centre of the Druids who determined their fate by the arrangement of the blotches on the leaves. Within the memory of living men an oak existed in the little valley, intervening between the two peaks we have named, round which superstitions still lingered, which were unquestionably of Druidical origin. Its leaves were dotted over with blotches of white just as those of oaks still growing in other parts of the district are to the present hour; and their size, and arrangement, and number were taken as so many omens by the credulous rustic, of the fortunes, good or bad, which the fates had in store for him.'[42]

Although this area of England is not geographically central, the tree is symbolic of a mythological world tree or axis mundi that stands at the centre of the Nordic and Saxon worlds. Moreover, it is a rare variety of oak with white-flecked leaves, once used as an oracle, and stands below a twin-peaked hill, which is significant in itself, as peaked hills are considered by indigenous tribes all over the world to be sacred to the goddess.

Back in the mid-1990s, after reading Michell's *The Dimensions of Paradise*, my friend John and I met to discuss the perpetual choirs at his farmhouse in Dorset, where we often bounced ideas off each other. The ten sites of the decagon and its centre at Whiteleaved Oak were of great interest to us at the time and we discovered some conflicting stories about the true origins of the tree. We first investigated the mystery at the Great Malvern Library where we delved into the history and legends of the area. Several local books in the Malvern Library informed us that the Whiteleaved Oak was not as unique and mystical as first thought but was one of many native to this area for hundreds if not thousands of years. In the 1920s, other examples were recorded in Whitman's Hill Coppice northwest of Malvern.

We searched the coppice for hours looking for an oak with the unusual white-flecked leaves, but soon realised that it could take months, for the coppices around Malvern are full of oaks! Back at Whiteleaved Oak village, we decided to ask a local about the history of the original tree and approached a woman weeding her garden. 'Oh, you are looking for the oak then. It was cut down a long time ago by a farmer fed up with pilgrims coming to pick leaves from the oak which was on his land,' she said. Seeing our disappointed expressions, she continued encouragingly, 'Most people go to the great oak a couple of fields away through that gate over there.' 'Is that an oak with white leaves?' I asked. 'No, no', she replied and explained that it was not even a relation of the original. 'Where did the original oak stand?' asked John. She then pointed to a spot on the green near her cottage, she replied, 'It was located there near the post box.'

I looked across at a small treeless patch of grass, trying to imagine this sacred tree, the greatest expression of a world tree that stood at the navel of Michell's decagon of sites including Stonehenge and Glastonbury. I asked her if it had white blotches on the leaves and she said, 'There's a local elderly man who lives in the cottage down that road close to the bend; he knows about the tree, his great-grandfather lived here when it was still alive.' Excitedly, John strolled on towards the cottage indicated by the lady. 'Come on', he said, 'we must find this cottage and talk to this man.'

I knocked on the door as John stood back. The door opened and an old gentleman crooked with age peered out. 'What do you want?' he said rather abruptly. 'I understand you know something about the history of the Whiteleaved Oak,' I replied. 'Oh not that blooming oak again. I'm fed up with people asking me about that great oak', he rasped. 'It's in the field over there', pointing towards where the other woman indicated the 'replica' oak stood. 'But that is not the real

Whiteleaved Oak', I said. The man looked at me with a little more respect, straightened his back and replied, 'Yes, yes, well, the real oak fell in a storm.' 'I heard it was cut down by a farmer fed up with pilgrims honouring the tree', I ventured. 'The truth is', he said, avoiding the answer, 'the tree can't be grown from acorns. It has to be grafted from one of its sprigs to get the blotches.' 'What, like the Glastonbury thorn?' John stated. 'I don't know', he said, 'but I do know that they tried to grow new oaks in the village from cuttings of the original, but they didn't live long.'

More intriguingly, the old gentleman told us that the twin-peaked hill that overlooks the hamlet is called Ragged Stone Hill and was once sacred to the Druids. It also has an ancient holy well on its slopes, one of three around this sacred hill, probably associated with Little Malvern Priory, 3.8 km to the north, which existed in the area before the Reformation.

Ragged Stone Hill stands closest to the centre of the great decagon and is considered by many seekers of the enigmatic Grail to be the spiritual heart of England. To the pagan Celts, twin-peaked hills were symbolic of the breasts of the goddess, like the Paps of Anu in Ireland and the Paps of Jura in Scotland. While researching the area, I found a legend associated with the hill concerning its shadow, which is reputed to cast misfortune on whomever it should fall upon. I discovered that this story stems from a monk belonging to Little Malvern Priory who was condemned to crawl to the summit of Ragged Stone Hill once a day as punishment for breaking his vow of chastity. His crime was to marry a woman whom he had rescued from the advances of a dishonest knight, falsely accused of killing her father in a duel. When he could no longer bear the punishment, he cursed the hill. According to another legend, the Druids used the hill for sun worship, and it was here that they made their last stand against the Romans.

After climbing Ragged Stone Hill, Caroline and I placed some sacred stones on its summit to help with the healing of this ancient curse. After reciting a powerful blessing, the wind suddenly picked up and soon heavy rain and thunder sent us scurrying back to the car. I wondered whether we had triggered some energy release such as orgone. After the rain had stopped, we walked from the village along a footpath and through a field to the great oak with its plain green leaves, now the new focus of veneration for those wishing to connect with the centre of the perpetual choirs. Here we met a few pilgrims who were tying clooties to its branches. Although gnarled and hollowed with age, it is a quite magnificent tree, its huge trunk growing out of a rock and its branches decked with coloured ribbons and many other offerings including items of clothing, coins, jewellery, flowers and hand-written messages.

Despite having no connection with the original Whiteleaved Oak, this tree, now nearing the end of its life, has become the world tree for earth mystery researchers. A young woman, sitting inside the hollowed trunk, remarked on the powerful yet nurturing energy she could feel. She then turned to us and proudly declared, 'This is the Whiteleaved Oak, it is only one of its kind in Europe and it stands at the sacred heart centre of England.' We nodded, not wanting to shatter her illusions. 'It certainly is a special tree,' I replied politely.

The Great Oak, Whitleaved Oak Village

Sadly, the tree burned down in 2020 after a candle was left burning in the hollow of the tree. Although I resigned myself to the fact that the Whiteleaved Oak has long gone from this area, I never completely gave up my search for one. Eventually, three years later, we discovered an almost identical species in the gardens of Biddulph Grange. Now run by the National Trust, the gardens are located just north of the town of Biddulph in Staffordshire. For years, Caroline and I had been visiting this delightful place with its grand house during our research of the Belinus Line but failed to notice the white-speckled leaves of this majestic tree next to one of the footpaths.

Previously, we dowsed Elen, the feminine serpent current, passing through the spring-fed pond and one of the monuments in the gardens, styled as an Egyptian temple to Aten. James Bateman, a prolific collector of trees, created this popular tourist garden in the 1840s. Although there is nothing documented about this tree, it supposedly dates from the period when the original Whiteleaved Oak was felled below Ragged Stone Hill. It is possible, therefore, that Bateman took cuttings after the frustrated farmer cut it down, and grafted it with a young sapling from an acorn also grown from the same tree. We also discovered that Bateman was a mystic so perhaps knew of its magical properties and legend as an oracle tree.

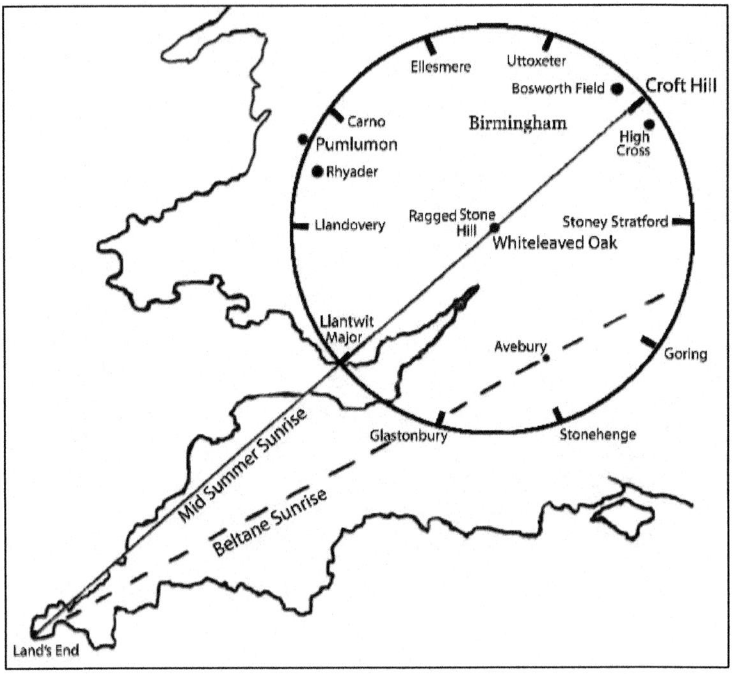

Figure 23. The circle of perpetual choirs and its solar alignments, by Madan

We had a sense that Ragged Stone Hill was the focal point of energies at the centre of the decagon and not the oak. Despite its reputation as a cursed place, it was once an important sacred heart centre of the Druids, a twin-peaked hill where they revered the goddess as well as the sun, possibly within a grove centred on a holy well. We soon discovered the existence of a covered spring called 'Lady Well', which is a name often used to Christianise a pagan site, the land having been owned during medieval times by Little Malvern Priory. After searching the base of the hill for this old well, we soon found ourselves in dense woodland on its eastern slopes. Here we noticed a wooden door set into the hillside, reminiscent of a fairy entrance to the 'Otherworld' or 'Hobbit house' featured in Tolkien's epic tale *Lord of the Rings*. The door opened to reveal a well-house made of brick with water trickling out into a culvert.

On the opposite side of the hill, facing west is another spring, now neglected and overgrown, its waters providing a nearby cattle trough. A third well is marked on old maps as located on the north side of the hill, which is now covered by a row of private dwellings.

The whiteleaved oak tree, Biddulph Grange,

Several alignments cross over this hill, the most significant being one that links it with Land's End. The alignment follows the path of the rising sun on the summer solstice and passes through the early religious centre of the Druids and early Christians at Llantwit Major. In the opposite direction, the line continues to Croft Hill, which is on several important British alignments, furthering its claim as the one true navel of England (see Fig. 23). Perhaps the Druids also knew of this midsummer solstice line, as in legend Ragged Stone Hill was a significant place of solar worship.

This decagon has now become one of the most revered landscape temples in Britain, with several articles and publications written on the subject. It seems clear to me that although there is no evidence for any historical three choirs at the sites mentioned by John Michell, he had envisioned something remarkable, a blueprint for the future. Today more people are visiting these ten sites than at any other period in their history. I believe this revival surrounding this new landscape temple will play a vital part in the creation of a spiritual renaissance, a reawakening of the hidden knowledge of old Albion.

With Croft Hill set to be restored and rejuvenated in the future, healing the land through chanting and singing at the various locations associated with this decagon at the heart of England and Wales would have a beneficial effect on the British Isles as a whole. The cessation of quarrying around Croft Hill and the return of the Earth's sacred waters to the site forming a reflective lake will bring a key component of the circle of Perpetual Harmonies to life. The sunrise at the midsummer solstice along this line of the ancient British priesthood from Land's End will fire the energies of the hill and revitalise the navel of England once again.

References:

1. Thorpe L (Translator) (1966) *Geoffrey of Monmouth: The History of the Kings of Britain*. The Folio Society, London.
2. Brut y Tywysogion. https://archive.org/details/brutytywysogiono00cara.
3. Michell J (1994) *At the Centre of the World: Polar Symbolism Discovered in Celtic, Norse and Other Ritualized Landscapes*. Thames & Hudson, London.
4. Trubshaw Bob (1991) *The Quest for the Omphalos: Finding the Mystical Middle of England*. Heart of Albion Press, Loughborough.
5. Biltcliffe G & Hoare C (2012) *The Spine of Albion: An Exploration of Earth Energies and Landscape Mysteries along the Belinus Line*. Sacred Lands Publishing, Weymouth.
6. Morris J (1980) *'Nennius' British History and the Welsh Annals*. Phillimore. London.
7. Gilbert A, Wilson A & Blackett B (1998) *The Holy Kingdom: The Quest for the Real King Arthur*. Bantam Press, London.
8. Pennick N (1979) *The Ancient Science of Geomancy: Man in Harmony with the Earth*. Thames & Hudson, London.
9. Michell J (1994) *At the Centre of the World: Polar Symbolism Discovered in Celtic, Norse and Other Ritualized Landscapes*. Thames & Hudson, London.
10. Beilby Knott & Beilby (1829) *Graphic Illustrations of Warwickshire*. Beilby, Knott and Beilby, Birmingham.
11. Agutter M K (2013) *Meriden 'Centre of England'*. http://www.meridenparishcouncil.org.uk/ wp-content/uploads/2017/08/meridenUpdate.pdf.
12. Innes A D (1913) *A History of England: From the Earliest Times to the Present Day*. G. P. Putnam & Sons, London.
13. Phillips G & Keatman M (1983) *The Green Stone: A True Story of Paranormal Adventure*. Neville Spearman, Jersey.
14. Mee Arthur (1947) *The King's England: Warwickshire*. Hodder & Stoughton, London.
15. Morton Oak. https://www.mortonparishcouncil.org.uk/history/centre-of-england
16. Trow M J (2003) *Boudicca: The Warrior Queen*. Sutton, Stroud.
17. Cornelius Tacitus, *The Annals*. http://www.perseus.tufts.edu/hopper/text?doc=Tac.+Ann.+14.34&fromdoc=Perseus%3Atext%3A1999.02.0078.

18. Webster G (1999) *Boudica: The British Revolt Against Rome AD 60*. Routledge, London.
19. *In Search of Middle England*. http://philipcoppens.com/venonae.html
20. Michell J (1994) *At the Centre of the World: Polar Symbolism Discovered in Celtic, Norse and Other Ritualized Landscapes*. Thames & Hudson, London.
21. Thorpe L (Translator) (1966) *Geoffrey of Monmouth: The History of the Kings of Britain*. The Folio Society, London.
22. Pickering A (1934) *The Roman Sites of South-West Leicestershire*. W. Thornley, Leicester.
23. Burgess J T (1876) *Historic Warwickshire*. Simpkin Marshall and H. T. Cooke, London.
24. Stukeley W (1776) *Itinerarium Curiosum or an Account of the Antiquities and Remarkable Curiosities in Nature and Art Observed in Travels through Britain*. Baker & Leigh, London.
25. Pickering A (1934) *The Roman Sites of South-West Leicestershire*. W. Thornley, Leicester.
26. Devereux P (1982*) Earth Lights: Towards an Understanding of the Unidentified Flying Objects*. Turnstone Press, Wellingborough.
27 Krishan, Vinod. (2014) *Plasmas: The First State of Matter*. Cambridge University Press, Cambridge.
28. Persinger M Dr & Lafreniere G (1977) *Space Time Transients and Unusual Events*. Nelson Hall Publishers, Chicago.
29. Walker T L (1884*) Druidical Remains at Croft Hill*. Transactions of the Leicester Literary & Philosophical Society, Vol unknown, Leicester.
30. Devereux P (1982) *Earth Lights: Towards an Understanding of the Unidentified Flying Objects*. Turnstone Press, Wellingborough.
31. Ibid.
32. Hoskins W G (1950) *Croft Hill*. Transactions of the Leicestershire Archaeological and Historical Society Vol 26, p.84, Leicester.
33. Trubshaw B (1991) *The Quest for the Omphalos: Finding the Mystical Middle of England*. Heart of Albion Press, Loughborough.
34. Walker T L (1884) *Druidical Remains at Croft Hill*. Transactions of the Leicester Literary & Philosophical Society, Vol unknown, Leicester.
35. Icke D (1991) *Truth Vibrations*. Aquarian Press, Wellingborough.
36. Michell J (1988) *The Dimensions of Paradise*. Thames & Hudson, London.
37. Pierre Jean-Baptiste Fabliaux or Tales.
https://archive.org/details/fabliauxortales04legrgoog
38. Michell J (1988) *The Dimensions of Paradise*. Thames & Hudson, London.
39. ibid.
40. Bromwich R (1961) *The Welsh Triads*. University of Wales Press, Cardiff.
41. Thorpe L (Translator) (1966) *Geoffrey of Monmouth: The History of the Kings of Britain*. The Folio Society, London.
42. Lees E (1877) *The Forest and Chace of Malvern, its Ancient & Present State:* With Notices of the Most Remarkable Old Trees Remaining within its Confines. Republished 2010. Kessinger, Whitefish, MN.

Chapter 7

Power Centres of our Collective Nations

In the previous chapters, our journey has taken us to the centre-points of individual countries such as England, Scotland, Wales, Cornwall, Northern Ireland and the Republic of Ireland, and in this chapter, we seek a centre-point of the combined lands of England, Wales and Cornwall, called Old or Celtic Briton, and the omphalos of Great Britain, consisting of England, Wales, Cornwall and Scotland. Likewise, we will visit the middle place of the United Kingdom, which includes both Great Britain and Northern Ireland. We conclude with the centre-point of the British Isles, an archipelago that includes the United Kingdom and the Republic of Ireland and their islands.

The exact centre-point of any territory is a key place to send love and healing to the land and spread divine light and positivity from the centre to its boundaries. In the past, the location was known through traditions or various surveying practices. But with today's accurate maps and Google Earth, we can find the exact spot more precisely, although we often find they are close to the traditional ceremonial centres known from ancient times.

Stratford-upon-Avon, the Centre of Celtic Briton

William Shakespeare's Stratford-upon-Avon lies in the heart of Warwickshire in the central county of England. In the words of Arthur Mee, 'Stratford is the heart of the heart of England', and there may be some truth to this saying by the author whose *The King's England* series of books enlightened many during the 1950s to the delights and mysteries of the British countryside.[1]

In his book *Powerpoints*, researcher Robin Heath refers to Stratford-upon-Avon as the centre of a combined England and Wales at the crossing of two alignments. The first stretches from Carmel Head near Amlwch, at the extreme northwest point of Anglesey in Wales, to Dungeness Point in Kent. The other connects Hopton-on-Sea, at the end of the St Michael Line on the coast of Norfolk, to Albion Sands at Marloes, near Milford Haven in Wales. [2]

I discovered that a circle drawn with its point on the Bard's town can be traced around these sites touching the coastline of the old Celtic British kingdom of England and Wales. Moreover, the town stands upon an impressive north-south meridian that begins at the most central southerly point of England at St Catherine's Point on the Isle of Wight. From here it runs up to the Forth River to a natural feature called Hanging Rocks west of North Berwick at Gullane Bay, the most northerly point of the ancient territory of the Welsh Britons (see Fig. 24).

South of Hanging Rocks, the meridian travels through the Royal Burgh of Haddington, the main administrative, cultural and geographical centre for East Lothian, which was known officially as Haddingtonshire before 1921. Continuing south, the line just misses the town's Collegiate Church dedicated to St Mary, which is the longest parish church in Scotland and the site of a medieval Cistercian abbey. The meridian also marks two very important early Celtic Christian sites overlooking the River Tweed at Old Melrose and Dryburgh Abbey. Further south in Northumberland, the line passes through the old market town of Haltwhistle, said locally to be the centre of the combined kingdoms of England, Scotland and Wales, although there is no historical evidence of it ever being considered a centre. A sacred mountain called Pen-y-Ghent in the Yorkshire Dales is also included; *pen* in the Cumbric language means 'top or head' and *ghent* possibly refers to an 'edge or border', therefore 'hill on the border'. Incidentally, this sacred mountain also features on the northern edge of the circle centred on Stratford-upon-Avon which encompasses the coastal towns of Hopton-on-Sea and Marloes.

Lichfield Cathedral, the spiritual centre of Saxon England, and Croxden Abbey are also exactly on the line; and south of Stratford, we have Chastleton House, the home of Robert Catesby, leader of the infamous Gunpowder Plotters. If the plot had succeeded, he intended to establish Stratford as the religious capital of England. Further south, the line passes close to the turf-cut figure of the White Horse at Uffington and a group of prehistoric mounds called Seven Barrows where the St Michael Line crosses the Belinus Line. We then arrive at Wherwell Priory in Hampshire, where, according to legend, a duck laid an egg in the crypt of the abbey, which, after being hatched by a toad, turned into a cockatrice, a kind of dragon. It grew to an enormous size and had an insatiable appetite. This is symbolic of the dragon that sits at the base of the world tree, the axis mundi. The meridian terminates at St Catherine's Point on the Isle of Wight, passing through the rocket-shaped oratory of St Catherine that was once an old lighthouse and chapel.

Stratford-upon-Avon is a lovely quintessential English town with black-and-white Tudor houses and is famous all over the world as the birthplace and final resting place of William Shakespeare, the celebrated and enigmatic Elizabethan playwright who Arthur Mee stated became 'better known than Caesar.' However, we also discovered a hidden history to Stratford linked with the cult of St George and that the town was once considered a spiritual centre of the Catholic Gunpowder plotters. Its natural surroundings are important too, set in beautiful countryside precisely at a spot where the River

Figure 24. Stratford-upon-Avon at the Centre of Celtic Britain

Avon widens into a floodplain, which we would later discover has cosmological significance.

We also discovered that Stratford-upon-Avon is a significant place on the Belinus Line, along with the cities of Winchester, Birmingham, Manchester, Carlisle and Dunfermline, the old capital of Scotland (see Fig. 2). Although the line misses the town by just over a mile a couple of kilometres to the west, both accompanying female yin and male yang serpent energy lines cross or node in the main church in the town very close to Shakespeare's tomb. This led to many years of dowsing and historical research of the area, which in turn revealed its fascinating hidden secrets.[3]

Stratford-upon-Avon's recorded history begins in early Saxon times when this district of the River Avon was part of the kingdom of the Hwicce that later became part of Mercia. The first Saxons utilised an important crossing of the Avon where Clopton Bridge stands today. The name of the town derives from the Roman word for road, *strat, strada* or street, and ford, which relates to the fording of the Avon at a junction of several important roads, including a Roman trade route from London to Wales. However, the settlement may stretch back further than Saxon times, as Bronze Age artefacts have surfaced near the ford as well as evidence of a minor Roman settlement. Archaeologists have recently excavated the garden of Shakespeare's old home New Place and surprisingly they found evidence of an Iron Age settlement, including grain storage pits dating from 400 BCE to 43 CE. These prehistoric pits are unique to this area, making this an important site close to the ford and far enough away from flooding of the Avon.[4]

The Hwicce built a monastery by the Avon in around 691, which became a minster during the time of Beorthwulf King of Mercia in 845. In 1192, Richard the Lionheart granted Stratford the privilege of holding a market, established further along the river from the monastic settlement next to the ford. The exact site of this religious house is unknown, although historians and traditions say that it stood on or near the site of the present Holy Trinity Church, next to a stretch of the Avon where swans have nested for over 2000 years. Swans were sacred within royal circles and protected by law, their meat reserved purely for kings and monks.

By the 14th century, the town had become an important centre for trade, bringing with it much prosperity and a thriving wool industry between the 15th and 17th centuries. During the Elizabethan period,

John Shakespeare, William Shakespeare's father, moved to Stratford to become a wool trader at a time when the industry was at its peak. Today, as a world-renowned cultural centre, the place thrives from the millions of visitors it receives every year, visiting its historic buildings and packing out the theatres to watch the famous Royal Shakespeare Company perform.

A stone-built college for a community of chantry priests founded in 1331 once stood near Holy Trinity Church, where monks would chant continually for their benefactors. Nigel Pennick mentions that chantries were 'geomantically sited chapels' built by medieval geomancers who were initiated into the secret knowledge of the Mystery Schools. The word 'geomantic' derives from geomancy, the ancient art of divining centres of energy on the Earth's surface and the artificial modification of the terrain to express their geometric relationships with other centres.[5]

Parts of the Holy Trinity Church date back to 1210, and by 1269 its welfare became the sole responsibility of the Guild of the Holy Cross, which developed most of the town in medieval times. The path from the road to the main visitor's entrance has an avenue of lime trees that, like a Druid grove, seems to initiate visitors as they enter this sacred sanctuary. According to local tradition, the twelve trees on either side of the path represent both the Apostles and the Tribes of Israel.

Just to the south of Stratford is Celtic Briton's World Mountain – Meon Hill, a visible landmark that stands at the northern end of the Cotswold chain of hills. *Meon* is the ancient British word for 'middle', similar to Meonenim in the Holy Land. Further research of the name Meon revealed some interesting results; the middle string of an ancient five-string lyre, an instrument played by the sun god Apollo, is the 'Meon' string. Like St Catherine's Hill on the outskirts of Winchester, which marks the centre of the old Kingdom of Wessex, Meon Hill has carved bank and ditch fortifications and is considered a place of power associated with strange legends of witchcraft, occult and 'devilish deeds'. This reminded us of the 19th-century house called Tigh-na-Geat close to the centre of Scotland mentioned earlier. Its original name means 'house of the harp string', the harp being similar to a lyre.

One allegorical tale linked to Meon Hill suggests that it was a hilltop shrine associated with the dead, for the Celtic King Arawyn, the lord of departed spirits, goes on a hunt around the hill at night, gathering souls while riding his pale steed accompanied by his phantom white red-eared hounds. For many years, locals have seen phantom black dogs around the hill, a portent of death to anyone who crosses their path.[6]

Between Meon Hill and Stratford is the quaint little village of Luddington, its name possibly having a connection with the legendary King Lud, who founded London or 'Lud's Town' before the Roman invasion. According to the earliest surviving records of British history, transmitted orally from Welsh and English sources, King Lud reigned in 72 BCE and built walls of lime and stone around London, adding to it a western tower and entrance called Ludgate, which survived until 1760. Is it a coincidence then that Lud (Lludd), a name associated with the search for an omphalos, also appears in the name of a village beneath Meon (middle) Hill and close to a town at the heart of England?

Ancient Whalley

According to the Ordnance Survey, there are two centres of Great Britain excluding Northern Ireland, both determined by the gravitational or centroid method and both are in my home county of Lancashire in the north of England. One is a wooden marker on a remote moorland hillside near Dunsop Bridge in the ancient Forest of Bowland, signifying the centre of Britain and its 401 offshore islands. The other, marking the centre of Great Britain's landmass, is just 18 km SSE of Dunsop Bridge very close to Whalley, a small town in the Ribble Valley near Clitheroe.[7]

The little town of Whalley, just to the northeast of Blackburn in Lancashire, still attracts many visitors to its ruined Cistercian abbey, ancient parish church and quaint tearooms set deep within the valley of the Calder River. However, very few know of its relatively new status as the most central town in the British Isles without her outer islands. The precise spot, according to Ordnance Survey, is in a field near Netherton, a northern suburb of the town, by the River Ribble just under a kilometre from the abbey, near the intriguingly named Calderstones Hospital.

The name Whalley derives from the Saxon word Walabaeg meaning 'field of wells'. In *A History of the Original Parish of Whalley* (1872) Dr Whitaker refers to this name:

> 'No term more strikingly descriptive could have been chosen, for, situated as it is upon a skirt of Pendle, and upon the face of those vast inverted mineral beds, popularly denominated the "Rearing Mine", the Earth, if drained, bleeds almost at every pore, and there are no less than six considerable springs within the immediate precincts of the village.'[8]

The town is also very close to the Belinus alignment and during our research of *The Spine of Albion*, we followed the feminine serpent energy Elen here. She passes through one of the most remarkable ancient churches we have encountered so far in the north of England. The church, dedicated to St Mary and All Saints, has the oldest religious setting in Lancashire, which Whitaker refers to as an extension of Pendle Hill, an ancient place of assembly.[9]

The Venerable Bede and the *Anglo-Saxon Chronicle* both record in the year 664 CE that Bishop Tuda visited the area west of the Pennines to oversee the submission of the Celtic Church to Roman Catholic rites. Bede states that there was a monastery at Whalley then called Paegnalaech where Bishop Tuda died of bubonic plague.[10][11] In *Journeys through Brigantia*, the authors John and Philip Dixon refer to archaeological excavations at Whalley between 1985 and 1988 that uncovered earthwork boundaries of a large monastic settlement.[12] Their excellent series of guides, sadly many now out of print, have been a great source of local knowledge to our own journeys through the old Brigantia lands over the past 20 years.

The first recorded church at Whalley dates from 628 CE during the time of St Paulinus, who according to local tradition preached here. However, the monks of Whalley Abbey recorded that St Augustine founded a church here in the early part of the 7th century dedicated to All Saints.[13] By the time the Normans arrived in 1080, the church at Whalley was the largest in Lancashire, later replaced in 1200. For 500 years, its priests held office through hereditary title, known as a dean, holding sway over a wide area. The bishop rarely visited the region due to its inaccessibility and 'the wild animals that roamed the road' between Whalley and his home in Lichfield, awarding greater power to the Dean.[14]

The first rector was Peter de Cestria (Chester) (1235–95), who built the old chapel next to the river, which also happens to mark the female serpent flow of the Belinus Line. De Cestria was a man of great 'ecclesiastical and political influence.' He was buried in the churchyard, but his tomb was removed to its present position by the font in 1950.[15]

The churchyard has three remarkable ancient stone crosses, the oldest being from the 7th century and probably dating from the time of St Paulinus; the others have stood since the 11th century. At some stage in the past, they were broken up and used for gateposts but later restored to their original sockets in the churchyard. As was customary in both Britain and Ireland, the early Roman missionaries would erect their crosses inside stone circles or ceremonial henges as if staking their authority upon the powerful terrestrial energies at these places. This suggests that the site of Whalley Church may have once been a prehistoric or Druidic sanctuary, or an earthwork similar to the Welsh 'Cors' or the 'Rounds' of Cornwall.

The largest of the crosses is 3 m tall and has an interesting piece of folklore attached to it. According to an inscription on its shaft, any person who can decipher and transcribe its hieroglyphs 'will be awarded the power to become invisible.' This story has its roots in pagan times before Roman Christianity arrived with Augustine. In one of the carved panels of the cross are two open-mouthed serpents on either side of a haloed saint with his or her arms held aloft, a stance similar to that of an Indian snake charmer. On the badly worn cross nearest the church, you can just make out two haloed figures linked by Celtic knot patterning.

Carvings on the west face of the third cross, however, caught our attention as they depict a central rounded shaft or pole with a triple spiral motif below. Some believe this represents the Celtic 'Tree of Life', while others say it is the Christian 'Tree of Calvary'. To us, it symbolised the axis mundi or 'world pillar' as it rises out of the womb of the Earth goddess whose symbol is the triple spiral. The east face depicts the tree springing from a pyramid at the base. These carvings identify this site as a significant centre of power and the churchyard its epicentre.

The Whalley omphalos cross, at the centre of the British kingdom, symbolically represents a pillar of knowledge, its carvings, if deciphered and understood correctly, may enable one to achieve a higher vibrational state. This powerful stone is reminiscent of the Lanivet carved cross at the centre of Cornwall and the Stone of Divisions at Uisneach marking the omphalos of Ireland. Perhaps the cup-marked stone fragment at St Bride's Kirk at the centre of Scotland was once part of a larger omphalos stone.

In the oldest part of Whalley Church, there is an abundance of esoteric symbolism, particularly in the finely carved wood misericords, originally made for the nearby Whalley Abbey in 1430, depicting such figures as St George slaying the dragon and a unique triple-faced Green Man. Others include the comical depiction of a

Axis mundi cross, Whalley Church

warrior with a discarded sword being beaten by his wife with a frying pan and a scene from 'the flight of Alexandra'.

Another striking feature is the oak roof, also transferred from the abbey, with beautifully carved bosses. A 1920s stained-glass window just on the edge of the Elen flow was installed to commemorate those lost in WWI and shows the legendary King Arthur with the Grail cup, St George slaying the dragon, and St Nicholas. I was delighted to see King Arthur represented at the omphalos, for although it is a relatively modern window, symbolically, like St George, this great warrior acts as a guardian and protector of Britain.

But to our surprise we came across, in the north aisle, a remnant of a Roman altar stone, showing what many believe to be the horned god Mars, though it also has the likeness of the local Brigantian god Lugh. There is also a fragment in the arch over the inside of the north door inscribed with the name 'Flavius', which some believe came with the altar stone from a Roman structure at Ribchester. However, excavations revealed a drainage system beneath Whalley Abbey made up of well-cut arched stonework, indicating a Roman origin. John Dixon, who took part in the excavations at Whalley, believes that because there is good stone available nearby at Whalley Nab, it is unlikely that the stones came from Ribchester and there is evidence that Whalley was 'a very large Roman civil settlement.'[16]

Another stone in the churchyard at the foot of the south side of the tower takes the form of a large square block of black stone, which I discovered was emanating a strong energy field. The church guidebook says it was once part of the foundations of the tower close to where it now rests and exhibits Roman tooling, although this may be later. This mysterious block with its powerful radiating energy is certainly symbolic of an omphalos stone perfectly placed at the modern centre of Britain's landmass.

The ruined abbey, just a short and very pleasant walk from the church, also holds some fascinating secrets. Its origins began with the Cistercian monks seeking a new site after Stanlaw Abbey, on the banks of the Mersey, suffered from constant flooding. Henry de Lacy (who built Killare Castle in Ireland) granted them the lands of Whalley in 1283, which consisted of a rectory and chapel belonging to the parish church built by Dean Peter de Cestria. After the Dissolution of the Monasteries in 1537, Ralph Assheton acquired the Cistercian abbey and adapted the lodgings into an Elizabethan manor house. It remained as a private residence until the Church of England took it over in 1923.

Despite the many changes to the site, the original chapel built by its founder still survives now roofless close to the banks of the Calder River, albeit restored many times. We dowsed the female current found at the church passing through the little ruin, and although there is little evidence of anything earlier on this site, we wondered whether it stood over a pagan temple connected with the worship of the river goddess. As we strolled around the ruins, we spotted a stone plinth set into the base of a table in the garden courtyard beside the abbey café, inscribed 'IHS' and surrounded by five crosses. We later discovered that it came from a chapel that once stood at Brennand Farm next to a hill called Middle Knoll in the Forest of Bowland.

Next door to Whalley Abbey, on the grounds of the Presbytery by the Roman Catholic Church, is a former monastic building called the 'lay brothers dormitory'. At the northeast corner of the building is yet another unusual carved stone of uncertain origin used as a gatepost and known locally as the 'Sun Stone'. Upon this mysterious pillar is the carving of a sun face, a human head and a spiral insignia, having possibly been unearthed or moved from the parish church or the abbey.

Altar stone, Whalley Church

We also came across a reference to a landscape zodiac discovered by Nigel Pennick and Robert Lord in the 1970s that covers this area and that of Clitheroe and Pendle Hill. There are many examples found around the country, including the famous Glastonbury Zodiac where, within a circle or ellipse in the surrounding landscape, twelve astrological signs are each outlined by rivers, roads and footpaths. The lion figure representing Leo in the Pendle Zodiac is the guardian of this landscape astrological figure, and we found that the Belinus alignment travels through its heart. The front paw of the sovereign lion figure rests upon the ancient religious centre and omphalos at Whalley.[17]

A field located 1 km away from the town, at the confluence of three rivers, the Ribble, Calder and Hodder by Mitton Wood, marks the exact centre of Great Britain's landmass calculated by OS. In the middle of the field appears to be earthworks, perhaps the remains of a Saxon settlement or medieval hall. On the bank opposite is a tumulus – quite rare in these parts, possibly a sacred mound or a burial. Furthermore, the confluence of rivers is bisected by a Roman road that runs through Mitton Wood past the 17th-century Hacking Hall, built on the site of an earlier moated manor house.

Meetings of rivers are sacred, particularly three, as they relate to the trinity in religion and symbology. In Eastern religions, the confluences of rivers were places of pilgrimage and healing to bathe. A possible reason for the sacredness of confluences is the friction caused by the clashing of three fast-flowing rivers. This can create a high level of ozone or chi which is beneficial to health.

Pendle Hill, the axis mundi of the Northern Celts

Pendle Hill. Courtesy of Immanuel Giel

Pendle Hill stands brooding over the Lancashire landscape from a height of 557 m (1827 ft), just short of 2000 ft, the official height to designate it as a mountain. The terrain consists of rough moorland grass with patches of peat exposed through weathering over the top of several geological layers of millstone grit and limestone. Although Pendle Hill was renowned for the mining of gold, rubies and lead, it was mostly significant as a place where cultures gathered over thousands of years for ceremonial worship; even the Romans came to honour their gods here.

A tradition recorded by H.V. Morton in his popular book *In Search of England* describes an ancient celebration of Beltane on Pendle Hill, the origins of which may go back to ancient times. In the early 1900s, 'Springers' would arrive at the hill on May Day and travel from village to village singing until midnight, having climbed to the top of Pendle Hill.[18] After reaching the summit, they would light a fire and face the east to await the rising sun. During Easter, the hill once attracted huge crowds of festival-goers and even today many climb the hill on Good Friday and at Halloween. I remember visiting Pendle Hill on a couple of occasions in my youth, organised by local pubs specifically to climb its slopes at midnight on Halloween. The sight of hundreds of drunken revellers trying to climb the hill at night in pitch darkness was quite a spectacle, but for some, it was an attempt to continue an age-old tradition.

In 1612, the famous Pendle Witches, who lived in the forests around Pendle Hill, were involved in one of the most famous and very public witch trials in English history, charged with the murder of ten people by the use of witchcraft. Up until then, they made their living from healing, begging from neighbours and extracting doles, a charitable gift of the church, with the threat of some terrifying spell if they refused to pay up. However, it was the great rivalry between the two witch clans that forced their eventual demise. After their incarceration in Lancaster Castle dungeons, the town witnessed the hanging of ten of the Pendle witches.

Of interest are the paranormal events experienced by many on the hill, with several people witnessing balls of light and another rare but natural phenomenon. Occasionally the pressure of water builds up inside the hill under the limestone core and, when the millstone grit above fails to contain it, water bursts through to the surface at a weak point and cascades down the hillside. Near the summit or 'Big End', as it is locally known, is a spring called Robin Hood's Well, formerly Robin Goodfellow's Well. 17th century literature describes this character as a popular trickster fairy and Shakespeare mentions him as Puck or the devil. Perhaps a ball of light or plasma was witnessed hovering over the well and became mistaken for a mischievous fairy. A round-headed cross once stood next to this old spring, marking it as a place of pilgrimage. Perhaps the stone pillar marks a geomantic centre as the hill was reputed to be the 'world mountain', a representation of the cosmic axis, sacred to the Brigantes, an Iron Age Brythonic-speaking tribe of the old North.

The Centre of Great Britain with its Outer Islands

Just north of the tiny village of Dunsop Bridge, only 18 km NNW of Whalley, is the exact centre of Great Britain if you include her 401 offshore islands. A nearby hill set within the Forest of Bowland opposite Beatrix Fell has the name 'Middle Knoll' and just to the north of there on bleak moorland are the Whitendale Hanging Stones, the nearest natural feature to mark the centre.

The dome-shaped Middle Knoll has the remains of a Romano-British camp or fort near the summit. How it received its name is a mystery, but its association with the centre of Britain goes back long before the calculations of the Ordnance Survey. Indigenous peoples in many different parts of the world regarded such feminine-shaped hills as sacred. This area was once rich in seams of silver, and the Brigantes, who held this area at the time of the Roman invasion, were the first to extract this precious metal until the Romans took over the mining.

For the long trek to Middle Knoll, we chose a fine day and set off from the car park at Dunsop Bridge. Following the River Dunsop along the designated footpath, we eventually arrived at the foot of

Whitendale Hanging Rocks marking the centre of Britain and her outer islands by Anthony Parkes

Middle Knoll, passing through Brennand Farm, which has the distinction of being the most central dwelling in Britain. According to Dixon and Dixon's walking guidebook *Journeys through Brigantia*, Brennand was a lodge for local kings in the days when Bowland Forest was their hunting ground, a place to rest after a day's chase.[19] A chapel once stood on the site of the barn housing a portable altar stone, later transferred to Whalley Abbey.

A local tradition says that a bottomless pool called Brennand Tarn to the east of the farm is the hiding place of precious gold and silver belonging to Whalley Abbey. This valuable hoard lies at the bottom of the pool, put there by the monks for fear it would fall into the hands of Henry VIII's men during the Dissolution of the Monasteries. Many have tried in vain to find the treasure over the years, but only Abbot Paslew, whose ghost haunts Whalley Abbey, knows the secret of how to recover it. The monks of Whalley must have known the significance of this area, as Brennand and Middle Knoll including the silver mines were once part of their manor.

Dixon also mentions a curious event called by locals 'the Middle Knoll Phenomenon'. Apparently during late May and early June when

Middle Knoll

the sun sets over Morecambe Bay, a minute after total sunset in the Hodder Valley a shaft of the sun's final rays strikes through one of the many ravines which bisect the Bowland Fells. The light appears to run up Middle Knoll like a forest fire until the whole west side is illuminated.[20] The Brigantes tribe must have seen this natural phenomenon as very special. However, Pendle Hill has a much stronger case for being Britain's 'world mountain' with its prominent shape, ancient history, occult folklore, and sharing a similar energy to Schiehallion and Pumlumon.

With the shrill song of a pair of lapwings hovering nearby, we continued walking around the hill, following a footpath east to arrive at Whitendale, the remotest farmstead in the county. In its grounds stands a large ash tree, which Dixon refers to as 'the greatest ash in

Bowland Forest.'[21] In Norse mythology, the world tree or *Yggdrasil* was an immense ash tree where Odin, the pagan god of the Scandinavians, found enlightenment and received knowledge of the Runes. It is also home to the serpent or dragon Nidhogg, which lurks at its base. The Norse believed that the great ash tree nourished gods, humans and animals, connecting all living things and all phases of existence.

The Whitendale Ash

This must have been an important place of assembly of the Norse clans, as they often held them under the sacred boughs of the ash, the name 'Whitendale' being derived from the Old English word 'Witan' or 'moot'. At these gatherings both kings and bishops discussed royal grants of land, church benefices, charters, aspects of taxation, defence, foreign policy, customary law and the prosecution of traitors; the Witan even acknowledged the succession of kings.

Dunsop Bridge honours itself with the title of being the most central village in Britain when calculated with the country's outer islands. The tiny hamlet lies within the beautiful Ribble Valley, 14 km northwest of Clitheroe. In 1992, British Telecom installed its 100,000th payphone at Dunsop Bridge, unveiled by Sir Ranulph Fiennes, which included a plaque to explain its significance – the plaque reads: 'You are calling from the BT payphone that marks the centre of Great Britain.' The Queen has visited Dunsop Bridge twice, once during the late 1980s and more recently in the summer of 2006. Latterly, the phone box was due to be removed, but now it has been preserved for the nation.

It is in a delightful setting surrounded by the rolling hills of the Forest of Bowland next to the confluence of the River Dunsop and the River Hodder before the Hodder flows south to join the River Ribble near Clitheroe. Nearby is the atmospheric Salter Fell Track, a pass along which the Lancashire Witches are believed to have been taken to their trial at Lancaster Castle.

The preserved phone box at Dunsop Bridge

While dowsing the male dragon current through the area during our research of the Belinus Line, we came across nearby Knowlmere Manor built by the descendants of British Prime Minister Sir Robert Peel. According to Alice Peel in *The Manor of Knowlmere*, this Victorian Gothic mansion was constructed over the site of a lost village that lay within the earthworks of a Roman cavalry station manned by Sarmatians.[22] These great nomadic warriors from the Russian Steppes arrived in this country under the banner of the Romans to garrison the region of the Brigantes at Ribchester. After the Romans left in the early 5th century, many thousands of Sarmatians remained in the area and used Whalley and the Forest of Bowland as a base to breed horses. They eventually created a territorial cavalry to protect the locals against the Saxon incursions.

Their greatest leader, known as 'The Bear', with his standard depicting the dragon, fought a great battle at nearby Bashall Brook. Some stories equate this Sarmatian leader with the legendary King Arthur, as in the old Welsh language Arthur means 'bear'. The Sarmatian warriors were notorious as 'Dracomen' or 'Dragonmen' because their standard was a silken windsock with a dragon's head made of small copper plates. As the bearer's horse charged into battle, the windsock made a frightening hissing noise, terrifying the enemy into believing it to be a real dragon.

Nennius records that Arthur fought his sixth battle on a river called Bassas.[23] This location is a mystery, but locals here believe it to be Bashall Brook. John Dixon also refers to this ancient tale that every year on the eve of the battle, Arthur's Knights rise from the grounds of Knowlmere Manor, mount their horses and, with standards streaming in the wind, charge up the side of Birkett Fell through the grounds of Browsholme Hall to meet their foes at Bashall Brook near Bashall Hall.[24]

Locals say that three ancient battles took place in the area of Bashall: one in the 6th century between the Britons under Arthur and the Saxons led by a great warrior called Tarquin. Another was the Battle of Brunanburgh, a key conflict for the supremacy of Britain fought between a Norse–British confederacy led by Constantine, King of the Scots, Anlaf of Dublin and Athelstan, King of England in 937. Although there is little archaeological evidence of these two battles, skeletons and weapons at nearby Backridge were unearthed dating from the Iron Age, which Dr Whitaker referred to as 'some place of a great engagement between the Romans and the British Celts.'[25]

Here, again, we find key battles taking place near the omphalos of a kingdom or country on lands sacred to our native ancestors. At these thin veil places, the spirit of the ancestors could be invoked to help change the fate of the battle. Perhaps a Celtic Arthur defeated the Romans here with the help of these ancestor spirits at the centre of Britain. The monks of Whalley Abbey had dominion over the lands of both OS omphalos sites during a short period of history. Likewise, Clonmacnoise in Ireland, Abbey Cwm Hir in Wales and Dull in Scotland all took over the spiritual role of the omphalos of their respective nations.

Sarmatian Warrior, a Dragoman of Arthur

The Centre of the United Kingdom

Morecambe in Lancashire is a seaside town located in the North West of England overlooking the Irish Sea. Fishing for shrimps and collecting cockles, mussels and whelks was its main industry until the introduction of the railway in 1850. The new roads and railway networks in the early 19th century linked the sleepy seaside town to cities in Lancashire and Yorkshire, and its new harbour started to attract visitors to this thriving seaside resort.

Interestingly, I have a personal connection to the town, having lived there as a child in the early 1960s. The stunning view across Morecambe Bay towards the distant peaks of the Lake District has always inspired me even today and I remember strolling along the promenade with my family, which was always beautifully adorned with summer blooms right up until the 1980s. Sadly, arson attacks and council mismanagement caused a steep decline in the town's

Morecambe Promenade Maze near the centre of the UK

prosperity, which damaged tourism and the local economy, allowing Morecambe to enter a dark period in its history.

Little did I know as a child that the centre of the UK is only 1.5 miles out to sea from Morecambe's promenade. Today Morecambe is beginning to rise from the ashes of the awful events that once plagued the town and many of its historic buildings have been restored to their former glory to become a much-improved place to visit for day trippers and weekenders. Hopefully, this newfound positivity will help raise the energy of this centre-point for the benefit of all. The Stone Jetty on the promenade has 'centre symbolism' in its maze with a little omphalos stone pointing towards the UK's exact centre out at sea.

Haltwhistle and Allendale

The OS gravitational or centroid method has proved to be similar to the boundary method when calculating a geographical centre. However, a small town in Northumbria, 112 km north of Dunsop Bridge on the A69 between Carlisle and Newcastle, also claims to mark the centre of the United Kingdom and indeed the British Isles as a whole, due to its position as the midpoint of the longest British north-south meridian.

Haltwhistle is set on the northern banks of the South Tyne River just to the south of Hadrian's Wall, at a point considered the most spectacular and complete section of this remarkable feat of human endeavour. The town is nicknamed 'the centre of Britain' based on a

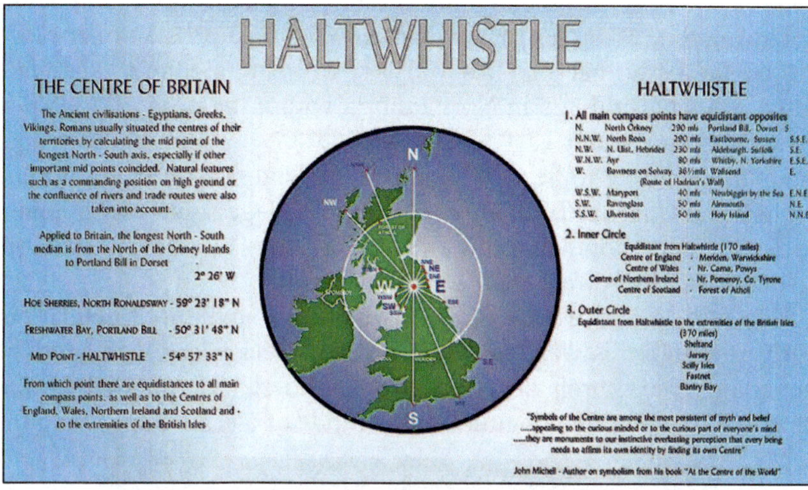

Figure 25. Plan of Haltwhistle as the centre of Britain and Ireland

calculation made by the owner of the 'Centre of Britain' Hotel, who measured it as being equidistant from the sea using the principal points of the compass at the centre of the longest meridian through Britain.

David Taylor, the owner of the hotel, describes himself as an 'amateur centrographer' and is passionate about the topic. He points out that Haltwhistle lies halfway along Britain's longest Meridian – 466 km from Portland Bill in Dorset (south coast) and 466 km from North Orkney (north). It is also 58 km from Wallsend (east coast) and 58 km from Bowness on Solway (west coast).

I also noted that Haltwhistle is on a meridian line that stretches from St Catherine's Point, the most southern tip of the Isle of Wight, to Black Rocks on the Firth of Forth, the highest point of the old boundary of northern Britain. This line also features the early religious centres of Old Melrose and Lichfield, the spiritual centre of Mercia and Stratford-upon-Avon a possible centre of England and Wales (see Fig. 24).

Taylor's findings regarding his longest longitude line are interesting as a diagram provided by him depicts an inner circle 170 miles equidistant from Haltwhistle, which incorporates the other centres of the United Kingdom, including Meridan and the Forest of Atholl. Moreover, an outer circle on the plan, 370 miles equidistant from Haltwhistle, touches the extreme points of the British Isles (see Fig. 25). Although Haltwhistle's claim is strong, it lacks any centre features and symbolism and traditions of being a historical omphalos.

During the research of Haltwhistle, we came across another place not too far away that also has a history of being a centre. Allendale Town is a small village in Northumbria within the pretty East Allen Valley, 16 km south east of Haltwhistle and 13 km southwest of Hexham, claiming to be the centre of mainland Britain including the Orkney and Channel Islands. Its charming village square with quaint tearooms and popular pubs makes it one of those desirable destinations to stop for lunch and take a stroll.

The title of the centre of Great Britain was given to Allendale in 1842, although this was later transferred to Peckriding, just south of the village. The church, dedicated to St Cuthbert, has a sundial set into the tower that records longitude and latitude of 54° 50' supporting the

Allendale New Year fire ceremony. Courtesy of Mick Borroff

village's claim. Despite Dunsop Bridge being the official centre, old traditions die hard and every year the town square is packed with revellers to celebrate the coming of the New Year. The celebrations involve lighted tar barrels that are carried on the heads of revellers called guisers – fire rituals are often found at centres of power. This tradition dates back so far that it is untraceable, although written accounts record the event from the mid-1800s.

Both Haltwhistle and Allendale are a short distance from the Cumbrian border, a county we now focus upon in our quest for the centre of Britain as well as the whole of the British Isles.

Cumbria, the Heart Centre of the British Isles

Although calculations of the various mid-points of Britain mentioned previously were carried out using the rational mind and science, there is evidence of a more mystical nature that determines the true centre-point. When science dovetails with the mystical we can find places of great power that many people feel drawn to naturally, even psychically. In my experience, one of the best examples of a magical

The remarkable pink soil and rocks of St Bees Head, West Cumbria

landscape that has enticed people of all ages and beliefs over many centuries is the Lake District in Cumbria – a land that many feel to be the sacred heart of Britain.

After attending a lecture on the mystery of St Bees Head in Cumbria by Alex Langstone, Earth Mysteries researcher and author Andrew Collins had a powerful dream showing St Bees Head as a centre of Britain and Ireland. Exploring this idea on a map with a compass point on St Bees Head, Collins found that the outer ring does indeed encompass the whole of Britain and Ireland including the Orkney and Scilly Isles (see Fig. 26).[26]

Geographically, Cumbria is indeed the most central ancient kingdom in mainland Britain, situated halfway along its central spine between St Catherine's Point lighthouse on the Isle of Wight to Cape Wrath lighthouse in Scotland.

The Lake District National Park is one of the most beautiful mountainous areas of Britain and has a vast number of megalithic monuments. Some are colossal, such as the three great circles of Long Meg and Her Daughters in the Eden Valley, Castlerigg near Keswick and Swinside near Duddon Valley. There are also remnants of two

Figure 26. The circles of St Bega and the Cumbrian omphalos, after A. Collins from Spirit Chaser by Alex Langstone

circles and a lost stone avenue at Shap and smaller Bronze Age circles elsewhere in the county, including henge monuments and standing stones, cairns and tumuli. In geological terms, Cumbria's fault lines, sandwiched between high mountains of crystalline rocks and deep freshwater lakes, create a powerful force of natural magnetism that our ancient ancestors focused on in many of their monuments and utilised for healing and spiritual purposes.

The present boundaries of Cumbria include the old regions of Cumberland, Westmorland and part of Lancashire. However, for centuries the Lake District and its mountains had their natural boundaries, formed in the south by Morecambe Bay, the Irish Sea to the west and the Solway Firth in the north. The rivers Eden, Lyvennet and Lune define the east side, together with the natural plains that form a great valley between the mountains of Lakeland and the

Pennine hills, through which many main transport routes extend. One of the major roads through here is the A6, once the 'old north road' to Scotland, passing through the frontier towns of Kendal, Shap, Penrith and the city of Carlisle, now replaced by the M6 motorway a short distance to the east with the railways in between.

The Lakeland landmass forms an irregular circle with the great mountain of Helvellyn standing near the centre overlooking Grisedale Tarn, the true mid-point of this ancient kingdom. Here we find a fascinating legend relating to Cumbria's last British king whose crown is said to lie at the bottom of the tarn, waiting for a time when he will awaken and call it forth to lead the nation once more.

Circle or ring symbolism seems most prevalent in the county of Cumbria, apparent in its many stone circles, local family coat-of-arms and features in many legends in the form of rings and plates. Moreover, several of its sacred sites are featured on ley circles rather than straight leys. Symbolically, the circle represents divine power, an archetype of wholeness and integration, used for protection in magic and occult practices. One of the most important and powerful symbols in sacred geometry and Freemasonry is a point within a circle. The point represents the centre of the Universe around which everything revolves.[27]

In Neolithic times, Cumbria was the centre of a remarkable trade in greenstone axes, carved from the scree in the hills of Great Langdale and the fells of Scafell Pike, the highest mountain in England. These stone axes were so renowned that they turned up in archaeological sites all over Europe. Some experts believe they were high-status symbols or had some possible religious significance related to this central region of Britain and the high peaks from which the greenstone came. Most were carved from stone from the precipitous slopes of Pike o' Stickle, which is a domed feminine-shaped hill with a mound-like pinnacle. Despite there being other hills in the valley where good quality greenstone could be more easily obtained, traders preferred the stone from this sacred mountain. In folklore, these axes were called 'Elfin Stones', having magical powers and associated with the elemental fairy race.

It is of no surprise that in this powerful heart kingdom, we find the old pagan worship of Brig, Brighida or Bride, the goddess of centres, which has survived longer here than in any other part of England, Scotland and Ireland. F. J. Carruthers writes in *People Called Cumbri*: 'Transmission of Brighida from Ireland into Cumbria or indeed any part of the Brigantian North Country was unnecessary; she was already the principal deity there.'[28] Cumbria is also rich in traditions and history harvested from the works of the ancient Celtic bards or poets, which it shares with Wales, Ireland, Northumbria and southern Scotland.

Cumbria during the Dark Ages attracted many Christian missionaries to a land then known as the holy Celtic kingdom of Rheged and became a springboard for them to spread the gospels into Pictland and Ireland. This assumption is as wild as the mountainous landscape itself, but in this far-flung corner of Britain, the old ways have quietly continued up until the present, although played down by the locals. Arthurian traditions are also strong in Cumbria and survive in the folklore and place names, although other contemporary figures also shared the limelight with Arthur during the remarkable heroic age of 'the Cumbri'. These warriors were Urien of Rheged, his son Owain, Dunmail (the last king of Cumbria), and King Eveling.

Eveling was a mysterious monarch whose palace stood at Ravenglass, one of the largest natural harbours on the west coast of Britain where the Romans built a large fortified town for trade.[29]

While living in Lancashire during the 1970s and 1980s, I spent much of my time exploring Cumbria's fascinating prehistoric sites, often witnessing strange natural phenomena, which I now realise was part of my initiation into the mysteries of plasma. In the past decade, I have become fascinated with the area of St Bees Head, a sandstone headland that juts out into the sea pointing towards the Isle of Man. This westerly point of Cumbria is strongly associated with the goddess Bride and, as Andrew Collins' dream revealed, is a strong contender for the omphalos of Britain if you include the whole of Ireland, the Isle of Man and the Orkney Islands.

The Shap Serpent Temple

Cumbria has many places of power, but the greatest was the Shap Serpent Temple, now unfortunately destroyed, with a 2-mile-long avenue of massive megaliths that rivalled Avebury. The now quiet village of Shap on the old A6 once held one of the most important megalithic complexes in Britain and only a walk amongst the fields around the back of the houses to the west of the main road will reveal the occasional fallen or broken remnant of it.

Today, anyone driving through here on this high plateau of land, the road lined with 18th-century grey stone houses, a handful of pubs, a shop and a cafe, will be blissfully unaware of its former sacred grandeur. Before its destruction in the 16th and 17th centuries, the Shap serpent temple consisted of possibly three stone circles linked by two stone avenues, built as an important spiritual centre for the prehistoric tribes of the North and the Brigantes, the largest Iron Age Celtic tribe in Britain and worshippers of the goddess Brig, Brigid or Bride (see Fig. 27).

Like Avebury, the megalithic ritual complex of Shap was geographically located at the most convenient place for tribal gatherings and kingship ceremonies at the omphalos of the prehistoric

The Goggleby Stone, one of the remaining Shap Avenue stones

northern tribal territories on this natural boundary between the Cumbrian Fells and Pennine Hills, a route that has existed since the Ice Age. For thousands of years, this wild and windy place has witnessed various cultures settling here, adding to its enigmatic atmosphere.

The name Shap derives from either *heape* meaning 'pile of stones' or *hep, heppe, heps* or *hips*, the fruit of the dog-rose. The rosehip may refer to the distinctive colour of the unique pink or rose-coloured granite said to be biotitic granite with large crystals of pink plagioclase feldspar that only exists in this region of Britain and is still quarried today. Just south of the village next to the busy A6, in the shadow of the industrial workings near the River Lowther, is Kemp Howe, a stone boulder circle made from this beautiful stone. The construction of a railway line destroyed most of it, cutting right through its centre in 1845, leaving just an arc of six stones to the west of the embankment, the largest being 3 m long.

Kemp Howe, according to John Waterhouse in *The Stone Circles of Cumbria*, was part of a large Neolithic complex that included a stone row known as the Shap Stone Avenue.[30] Descriptions from antiquarians who visited this site over a hundred years ago suggest that Shap Avenue was very similar to the West Kennet Avenue of megaliths at Avebury. William Camden (1551–1623), one of the very first antiquarians to explore Britain's stone monuments, noted that the northern and southern avenues at Shap consisted of large stones 'in the form of pyramids set almost in a direct line and at equal distances, for a mile together.'[31] Likewise, when Stukeley visited the site in 1725, he observed that the avenue resembled a 'megalithic serpent', and produced accurate surveyed plans, which have sadly disappeared.[32]

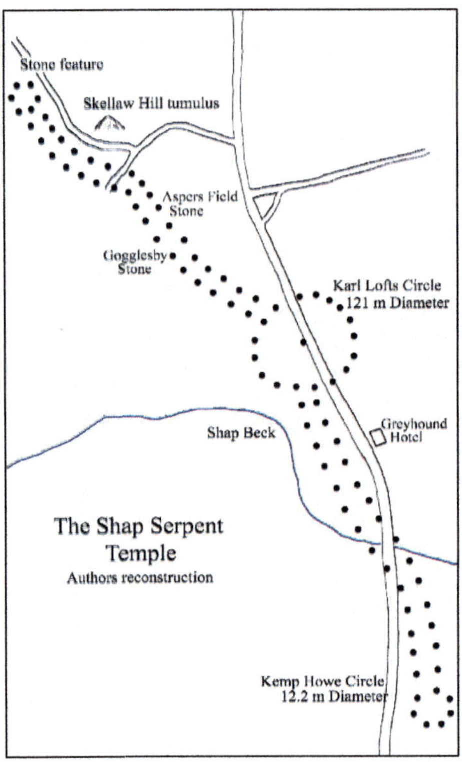

Figure 27. Authors' interpretation of Shap Serpent Temple

The width of the avenue, according to antiquarian Thomas Pennant, writing in 1769, was 27 m in the south, gradually reducing to 18 m as it passed through the village. The avenue then turned towards Skellaw Hill in the northwest, on top of which was a large barrow.[33] All that remains of the avenue today is the Goggleby Stone in a field behind a row of cottages, along with one other stone, a massive tilted megalith called the Aspers Field Stone. According to Revd J. Simpson, a local antiquarian who was also the vicar of Shap during the mid-1800s, cup and ring marks could be observed on these stones.[34]

Just north of the Greyhound Inn, an enormous stone circle stood halfway along the course of the Shap Stone Avenue, known as Karl Lofts. This remarkable ring measured 121 m in diameter and was referred to in *The History and Antiquities of the Counties of Westmorland and Cumberland* written in 1777.[35] Some of the circle's stones are still visible in the wall alongside the pavement of a row of terraced houses called Carl Lofts. If we are to assume that all these early accounts are true, then the village of Shap lies on the site of the second-largest stone circle in England after Avebury.

All that remains of this magnificent monument are a few stones scattered about in some of the fields surrounding the village or piled up like rubble beside the railway line. A painting in Burl's *From Carnac to Callanish* entitled *The Shap Avenue sketch by Lady Mary Stuart, wife of the first Earl of Lonsdale in 1775* shows the stones as stumps after they were dynamited upon orders of successive Earls of Lonsdale of Lowther Castle to make way for quarrying and the railway.[36]

During our investigation of the Belinus Line, we painstakingly pieced together a map of this great megalithic ceremonial landscape temple. I believe an avenue of granite boulders ran from Kemp Howe to the larger stone circle called Karl Lofts, with a separate avenue continuing northwest curving to the left of a large mound that once existed at Skellaw Hill to the north of the village and terminating at 'a four stone feature' (see Fig. 27).

There is little remaining of this tumulus at Skellaw Hill, just a slight rise where we found a node of the male and female earth serpents associated with the Belinus Line. Some believe the mound was a stone cairn, which may be the origin of the name Shap meaning 'heap of stones'. According to local legend, Skellaw means 'hill of skulls', perhaps derived from the many skulls discovered during excavation or the destruction of the cairn.

The hill was an important feature of the Shap temple, as from its summit looking south you can view the whole complex, including Kemp Howe, just under 3.2 km away. Similar to Silbury Hill at Avebury, this hill may have been significant as a sighting place for the priests to coordinate processions from Kemp Howe.

I also discovered an equinoctial alignment of sacred sites between St Bees Head and Whitby Abbey in Yorkshire that passes straight through the circle. Part of its route through Cumbria forms the famous Coast to Coast walking trail devised by Alfred Wainwright in the 1960s.[37]

The Thunder Stone, a massive glacial erratic boulder almost the size of a car, is located further north of Skellaw Hill, which one local tradition says may have been part of a stone circle or feature that

Remains of Kemp Howe stone circle, Shap

marked the terminus of the northern avenue as it extended from the Karl Lofts circle. Others suggest that the avenue continued for over 8 km (5 miles) northwest to the Cop Stone on Moor Divock.

Today the altitude of Shap at 304 m makes it a cold and harsh environment to live in, but in Neolithic times when the climate was equal to that of the South of France, it would have been a pleasant place for tribal festivals and ceremonial practices. In the Neolithic and Early Bronze Age periods, there were no boundaries dividing Britain and this geographically suited meeting place was considered a sacred navel site to honour the earth spirits and heavenly deities within a magnificent ritual stone temple. The fact that this area has the largest concentration of prehistoric stone circles and monuments anywhere else in Britain is indicative of its former importance as a powerful centre in the heart kingdom of Cumbria.

Psychic Centre of Britain and the Rings of Power

Even when I moved south to Dorset in the early 1990s, I was always finding some line of research connected to Cumbria, including an unexpected link with a Dorset church in the little market town of Beaminster, north of Bridport. I first visited the church some years ago while working locally. Sitting on a bench eating my lunch, I was admiring the many remarkable and rare statues set into the niches of the tower, but one eroded statue of a female saint caught my eye. In one hand she appeared to be holding a model of the church, and in the other the 'palm of peace.' I also noticed that all the other saints were staring towards the west, but this female saint directed her gaze upwards towards the northern sky as if searching for something.

As I stood to take a closer look at the stone figure, a voice from behind almost made me jump: 'Can I help you?' I turned to face an elderly man dressed in a long grey coat. I pointed towards the curious statue and asked who she was. 'That is the founder of this church,' he said. 'Her name is St Bega and the church she is holding is this very church.' My jaw dropped with surprise as he mentioned this obscure saint for I had made a strong connection with her in Cumbria many years before. 'Surely not the Cumbrian saint?' I enquired. 'Yes, the very same,' he said, rather surprised by my knowledge of her. 'But what is she doing here in Dorset so far from the Lakeland Fells?' I continued. 'It is a well-debated mystery to the locals,' he replied. 'Nobody knows for sure and many now doubt the legend.'

I moved closer to the sandstone statue that glistened in the mid-day sun, trying to understand this curious dedication. A Cumbrian legend states that Bega was the daughter of an Irish king who reigned as a Christian monarch in the 7th century. She gave her life and service to God and vowed never to marry, later affirmed by an angelic visitation. During this divine encounter, the angel presented Bega with a bracelet and spoke the following: 'Receive this mark of favour, sent to you by the lord God, since you own that you are ordained to his service, and that he has become your bridegroom. Place it therefore upon your heart and upon your arm, that you may admit no suitor but him.'

However, her father demanded that she marry the son of a Norwegian king and arranged a feast to celebrate her engagement. Naturally, Bega was unhappy with her father's decision and looked to God for help. She received a message from him to flee to the coast where a boat would be waiting to meet her. During the banquet, Bega slipped away to England, arriving on the western shores of Cumbria on midsummer's day at a promontory now named after her, St Bees Head.

After landing safely on the coast, she wished to establish a nunnery on the headland above, but in order to do this she sought permission from the local landowner, Lord Egremont. In his grand hall surrounded by his ministers and followers, he mocked her request and said, 'You can have as much land as is covered by snow on the morrow.' Being midsummer's day, the warmest time of the year, it would of course take a miracle for such an event to occur.

That night she prayed to God for help and by the following morning, miraculously, an area of land was covered in snow, and so after Lord Egremont heard the news he promptly awarded it to her. Here, the saint built her nunnery and stayed many years accompanied by six nuns, performing several miracles with her sacred bracelet. Dreading the thought of losing her virginity to the oncoming marauding Vikings, she fled, leaving the bracelet behind. According to local tradition, the bracelet became the 'magic ring' of Bega, which rested under the altar at the priory of St Bees, with many swearing oaths over it until the 13th century.[38]

Stained glass window depicting the legendary arrival of St Bega to the Cumbrian coast, St Bees Priory

Not long before my visit to Beaminster church, I attended a lecture about this obscure Cumbrian saint at the Psychic Questing conference in London. It was organised by Andrew Collins, who envisioned the 'ring' around Great Britain and Ireland including the Orkney and Scilly Isles with St Bees Head at its centre. The venue was Conway Hall, a quaint, slightly run-down, atmospheric theatre in Red Lion Square, the perfect place for the various occult and supernatural subjects discussed that day. One of the speakers was Alex Langstone who gave an inspirational talk about his strange experiences while on holiday in Cumbria in 1989 with his psychic friend Carole Young.

Having based themselves at a holiday cottage on the lower slopes of Skiddaw by Bassenthwaite Lake, their adventure began soon after their arrival on midsummer's day. Carole had a sense of a spirit presence and a calling to go outside, and after following a footpath, she was drawn to a raised area of trees gouged by a stream where she psychically encountered a ghostly monk.

St Bega's Church, Bassenthwaite

Information given by the spirit and other subsequent psychic messages led them on a journey around many important Lakeland sacred sites to heal the landscape of Cumbria. They eventually uncovered the mystery of St Bega, her ring, and the omphalos of the British Isles.[39] The monk turned out to be none other than Ciaran of Clonmacnoise in Ireland, whose guardian spirit seems to haunt many of the mid-point centres of Britain and Ireland.

Parapsychology, the Super-ESP (extrasensory perception) theory, coined in the 1950s by American sociologist and psychical researcher Hornell Hart, and the works of Carl Jung may explain such strange synchronicities and mystical events experienced by Alex and Carole. Here, the collective unconsciousness is seen as an invisible multidimensional mass of intelligence, similar to what the ancients and the mystics call the *Akashic Records*. This can act on humanity in such a way as to perceive it as an outside intelligence, such as a ghostly monk or any historical character, depending on what you as an individual find acceptable and within your frame of reference. Those with a psychic awareness can attune to this collective unconscious and experience its presence in the form of messages, images, synchronicity and mystical revelations.[40]

The Akashic Records contain the memory of the Earth and are available to the minds of humankind as a race memory to tap into and use. In a sense they are the ultimate form of telepathy and psychometry and have often been used to explain the existence of past life recalls and mediumistic qualities.

Any localised landscape has a memory of its most ancient and modern history as well as emotional experiences both positive and negative, which can collectively appear to the psychic according to their belief system. All energy requires balance and therefore the soul memory of a place may seek this equilibrium from certain individuals with the knowledge and knowhow to perform the required act of healing. This collective memory is available at certain times of the year when the magnetic field of the Earth allows contact with this higher vibrational energy. When Alex and the psychic healer Carole arrived in the powerful landscape of Bassenthwaite and Skiddaw around midsummer, the scene was set for a connection with spirit that guided them around the sacred sites of Cumbria to rebalance the energies within the old Celtic kingdom of Rheged.

A year later, Alex had become a member of Earthquest, a psychic questing group in Essex led by Andrew Collins. After Alex had given a talk on his Cumbrian adventure, Collins had a dream where he found himself by the coast next to a white signpost standing in the water pointing in all-different directions. Two of the directions were to Land's End in Cornwall and John O'Groats on the northern coast of Scotland. Instinctively, he felt that he was standing at the central point of the whole of Great Britain and Ireland. He also dreamt of a cave near Long Meg Stone Circle, later identified as Lacy's Cave on the banks of the River Eden, associated with a ring of sites that represents the omphalos of Britain; interestingly, the Eden River was the old border of this Lakeland realm. This led Collins to draw the perfect ring around Britain and Ireland, including the Orkney and Scilly Isles, pivoting exactly on St Bees Head (see Fig. 26).

An expedition to Cumbria was then organised by Collins and the Earthquest team to explore the sites previously visited by Alex and Carole and new places indicated by group meditation. The climax of this latest adventure ended with the remarkable appearance of an 'apport', the materialisation of an object or artefact by occult means, in the graveyard of St Bega's Church by Bassenthwaite Lake, witnessed by all the members of the group. This apport began as a speck of light flashing across the graveyard, which then formed into a glowing ball of light, finally settling on a gravestone as a solid object. The apport was a Russian wedding band, which consisted of three gold rings made of white, red and yellow gold linked together. I had a sense that the symbolism of the three conjoined rings was almost certainly a clue to the mystery of St Bega and the healing power of Cumbria.

Further research by Langstone uncovered a cosmic connection to St Bega; her celestial name is representative of the star Vega, one of the brightest stars in the northern hemisphere in a constellation known as Lyra. Beag in Old English means 'ring' and Bega's magic bracelet could represent the Corona Borealis, a ring of seven stars that accompany Vega, as they swoop down in front of it to the horizon and rise again. In addition, ancient Egyptians depicted Lyra as a bee; Boötes, the constellation next to it, was known as 'the Bee Keeper'.[41] Perhaps this area at the centre of Britain was also a centre of cosmic worship linked with a heavenly aspect of Bride.

When standing on St Bees Head during the winter months today, you will see in the northern skies Corona Borealis slowly descend to the horizon, set, and then rise again further east. The bright star Vega then follows the same course as it reaches the horizon, but hovers there instead of setting. However, around 400 BCE, Corona Borealis remained in the heavens and only fully set below the horizon around 700 CE. St Bega is said to have arrived on the coast of Cumbia just before its full setting *c.* 650 CE. Perhaps the ring of Corona Borealis is symbolic of the bracelet that became lost to her when she fled the nunnery in fear of losing her virginity.

The landscape around St Bees contains many megalithic sites relating to the relevant star clusters, such as a group of stone circles on a hillside near Kirkstanton 32 km to the south of St Bees called Lacra, which may allude to the stars of Lyra. Another is a group of circles above the village of Boot, perhaps referring to the stars of Boötes.

Boot lies in the beautiful Eskdale Valley 19 km southeast of St Bees, and has a tiny church dedicated to St Catherine, a saint who also has connections to the Bega mystery. Inside the church, Bega is depicted on the reredos holding a church, possibly the one she founded at St Bees or the church in which we were standing having been rededicated. There is also a holy well to the east of the church hidden among bracken, which despite its antiquity and general condition still flows with sweet-tasting spring water. This remote and enchanting circular stone-lined pool must have been the perfect place for observing the reflections of the moon and the stars and the mystical art of scrying by the ancient priesthood. Coincidently, there is also a circular spring-fed pool to the northeast of Beaminster, within the semi-circular bowl of hills. Perhaps this was also used for healing or scrying?

I wondered whether the stone statue of Bega in the tower of Beaminster church in Dorset was looking up to the northern skies in search of her bracelet. The local topography around Beaminster is interesting as it stands overshadowed by hills forming a bowl or semicircle, the rivers and streams cascading down to meet around the church, which appears to lie within the circular piece of land, like a ring within a ring. The name Bega derives from 'ring', which possibly suggests a possible Viking establishment or sacred place associated with a magic band.

Is Bega's bracelet symbolic of healing power? Bega is the cosmic or heavenly aspect of Brigid and perhaps equates to the nurturing Egyptian sky goddess Nut whose symbols represent resurrection and rebirth. She is often depicted arched across the skies with stars forming her clothing, her elongated legs and outstretched arms symbolising the four pillars of the heavens. She also represents a cow, a form she takes to carry the sun god Ra on her back to the sky, and her breasts dripping with milk over the Earth. Bride or Brigid is also associated with the cow.

According to Lunaea Weatherstone in *Tending Brigid's Flame: Awaken to the Celtic Goddess of Hearth, Temple, and Forge*, milk is a symbol of the sacred feminine and 'Brigid is a protectress of both the earthly cow whose milk sustains the body and the white red-eared otherworldly cow whose milk sustains the soul.'[42] Brigid's feast day is Imbolc, the time when female mammals secrete milk.

St Begnet

Researchers of St Bega state there is no substantial evidence to link this saint to any known royal family from Ireland or Wales. However, by chance or not, we came across a 7th-century Irish female saint with a similar name while researching the east-west An Slí Mhór and the centres of Ireland.

St Begnet the Virgin is associated with the fashionable Dalkey area of Dublin, with its quaint picturesque harbour and fine restaurants and cafés, the haunt of such Irish celebrities as Bono, the Edge, Enya and Van Morrison. It has two churches dedicated to St Begnet, one on

Dalkey Island and the sanctuary of Begnet, Dublin Bay

Dalkey Island with a holy well and the other in the town next to the castle.

Her name derives from *Beg* or *Bec*, the same diminutive form as Bega, and her story is almost identical. Begnet was beautiful and desirable but refused her suitors in favour of a religious life of devotion. She was an Irish princess said variously to have lived as an anchorite or as the abbess on a small island off the coast of England. This may well have been Preston Isle, which is now part of St Bees Head; this obscure piece of history perhaps went unnoticed by early historians who presumably failed to connect her with the Cumbrian saint.

According to the story, during her early childhood, Begnet was visited by an angel who gave her a bracelet inscribed with a cross as a mark of her vocation. Years, later, to avoid marriage, Begnet would leave her home with only the bracelet. In another version of the tale, Begnet flees to Northumbria, where Bishop Aidan receives her into the Church. After years of enduring continual raids by pirates, she moves to Cumberland, as West Cumbria was then known. Her bracelet became an object of veneration long after her death. By the 12th century, the veracity of legal testimony could be asserted by swearing on the bracelet, with the penalty for perjury being death.[43]

During the 7th century, the Kingdom of Northumbria included Cumbria, Lancashire and Yorkshire, and here Aidan acted as Bishop for the ruling Angles. It is more likely that Begnet landed on the western shores of Cumbria which was then within the Kingdom of Northumbria.

Dalkey Island, with its ruined church and holy well, sits at the southern arc of the semi-circular Dublin Bay. Therefore, I wondered if the name Begnet might also allude to a circle of sites around the bay itself, reminiscent of Bega's ring. The island is associated with healing and the growing of medicinal herbs and was undoubtedly inhabited by the ancient Druids who once practised in the area, as the nearby Druid's Hill and site of a stone circle (now lost) recall. After some experimental doodling with a compass and a map of the area, I discovered that St Begnet's Church in the town and Dalkey Island are both on the arc of a circle that encompasses Dublin Bay and passes through St Mary's Abbey on the Hill of Howth.

Caroline and I joined a guided tour of Dalkey Castle to gain access to the roofless ruin of St Begnet's Church, which was a fun experience due to the comic antics of our Irish guides. Unfortunately, almost all of the history they chose to tell us was from the period of Henry VIII, who took over the castle and destroyed the church. They also kept asking us to shout 'hail to the king' every five minutes so we replaced it by shouting 'hail to the goddess', although nobody seemed to notice. Eventually, we had our chance to connect with the old ruins of Begnet or Bega's church at our leisure. The west wall houses a stone lintel that according to the guide would bring good luck to anyone who touches it. As I put my hand upon the cold gritty stone, I sensed that this little church was the centre of healing long ago as part of a 'beag' (ring) of sites around Dublin Bay.

St Bees Priory and Isle of the Priests

St Bees Priory, West Cumbria, by Samuel and Nathaniel Buck, 1739

We picked a fine sunny day to visit St Bees Head and the Priory, to find out if there was anything to substantiate the various psychic claims that this area on the coast was a geographical centre or indeed part of a ring of sacred sites.

Geographically, the part-ruined Norman Priory of St Bees lies just to the south of St Bees Head, by a sandy inlet close to the village of St Bees on the west coast of Cumbria. There is much debate among historians as to why this site was chosen for a priory. However, reading through some of the local history books revealed that the sea reached further into the bay many hundreds of years ago, which allowed boats to embark at a port by the priory.

Evidence of Viking occupation of the site is still apparent in the 10th-century Norse cross and cross-slabs in the church. The Normans also left their mark here with the impressive west door dating from 1120, but the carved lintel opposite depicting St Michael slaying the dragon is evidently of earlier Norse design. The end of its tail forms a circle and a coiled serpent biting its tail known as an *ouroboros* next to it appears to be a clue to the importance of this sacred symbol here at this site. The carving merges Norse legends with Christian tales of St Michael, the figure slaying the dragon possibly being Sigurd, a Scandinavian archetype of this Christianised sun god.

The roofless chancel at the eastern end, restored in 1816, became a Theological College funded by the Earl of Lonsdale of Lowther Castle. Over 2,600 clergy were trained at the college during the course of its history, studying such subjects as theology and languages.

Stone lintel carved with St Michael slaying the dragon at St Bees Priory. Courtesy of Doug Sim

Inside the priory is a little museum of local history displaying magnificent medieval sepulchral slabs and showing the existence of a chapel here dedicated to St Bega. Near the west door is a stained-glass window depicting the saint wearing an armband stepping ashore at Whitehaven, a little way down the coast. She is certainly a character that lurks between history and legend, fact and fiction, although certain documents claim her armband or bracelet was housed in the new Norman church at St Bees, with many miracles attributed to this holy relic. A 13th-century manuscript records an oath taken by John of Hale 'having touched the sacred things ... and upon the bracelet of St Bega.' Other references show that the bracelet existed in the priory up until the Reformation. However, scholars today refer to St Bega not as a historical person but as a cult figure due to the many inconsistencies between medieval texts and the significance attached to her jewellery.

In the distant past, the whole of St Bees Head was part of a fertile island called Preston Isle, growing a variety of crops. The cleft valley between St Bees and Whitehaven was a flood area and an anchor found buried halfway between the towns is evidence that small ships were once able to sail a good distance up the valley.[44] The name Preston is derived from Priest, which may denote the island as a place of an early religious settlement. A chapel dedicated to St Michael once stood on the high point of the road between Whitehaven and St Bees, and just to the northwest was a cell or chapel at the tiny

Old map of Preston Isle, O.S. 1923

settlement of Rottington that belonged to the priory. A cave in the red sandstone cliffs of St Bees Head, near the steep secluded gorge of Fleshwick Bay, is where St Bega supposedly spent her first night upon her arrival, which became a popular tourist destination in the 19th century.[45]

This fertile holy island inhabited by nuns in a remote part of northwestern England seems to have parallels with the legendary Isle of Avalon, where white maidens healed King Arthur and his knights.

In legend, the whitening of the landscape by snow on St Bees Head at midsummer may be an allegory of a holy site. In earlier times, certain holy places associated with healing or holiness were painted white including rocks, standing stones, chapels and churches.

Another Arthurian-related place lies just to the south of St Bees at the picturesque ancient port of Ravenglass, which has a remarkably well-preserved Roman building still standing. According to legend, after the Romans departed our shores it became the fortress of Eveling, king of the fairies, called Lyons Garde, who lived there with his daughter Modron, later to become Morgan le Fay of Arthurian fame. W. G. Collingwood (1854–1932) believed that 'Eveling must be Evelac or Avallach, as it was spoken by the Ravenglass people, who told the tale to Camden in the days of Queen Elizabeth.'[46] In *The Welsh Triads*, Avallach is the father of Modron who became the mother of Owain, son of the legendary Urien who ruled over the northern Kingdom of Rheged.[47]

Gosforth's Axis Mundi Pillar

Although we found little evidence of centre symbolism around St Bees, the village of Gosforth, 12.5 km to the southwest, has a fine example of a 'world pillar' or cosmic axis. The spirit of the monk Ciaran guided Alex and Carole to Gosforth and conveyed a psychic message: 'It represents many things, and among these is the common ground between different faiths and cultures .... A crossroads, a meeting point. It also represents the four quarters coming together at the centre-point of the land, where the flame of knowledge is kindled.'[48]

To most visitors, Gosforth is an ordinary Lakeland village with a scattering of period and modern houses, an old parish church, a pub and a shop. However, once it was an important centre of trade and a place of learning, just as Ciaran had implied, and full of triple or trinity symbolism.

As we arrived at St Mary's Church, we looked up to see three bells exposed in the west turret. Inside there are medieval triple head carvings on either side of the capitals of the chancel arch, one of which is said to represent past, present and future, very characteristic of an omphalos site. On the opposite side of the chancel arch are the carvings of the triple head of a Green Man linked together by a chain coming from each of the mouths. A similar triple carving can be found at the centre of mainland Britain in St Mary's Church in Whalley, referred to earlier. Some authorities believe this trinity of Green Men, a symbol of the intelligence of nature, represents creation, preservation and destruction, as they wield the power or life force of the landscape.

A magnificent high cross stands between the south door and the lichgate in the churchyard and dates from the 10th century. Its socket stone has three steps and supports a 4-m-high sandstone pillar, the tallest in Britain, crowned by a four-holed cross with carved symbols of the trinity on its arms representing the creator goddess. The partly rounded shaft is decorated a third of the way up with scaly bark or leaf carvings representing the world ash or Yggdrasil that the Norse people believed supported the Universe. The upper portion of the shaft is square and carved with four panels depicting themes from *Edda* or *Sibyl's Prophecy*, classic poems of Scandinavian mythology, expressing the poet's interpretation of good overcoming evil. Others believe that this theme of good and evil is represented by the Apocalypse from the Bible's *Book of Revelation*. These images that blend pagan and Christian beliefs with shamanic practices were used to educate Christian converts to their newly founded religion.

Three more of these magnificently carved crosses stood in the churchyard in the distant past, which were broken up, although a fragment called the 'Fishing Stone' still survives in the church depicting Thor's fishing expedition for the 'world serpent', a creature said to haunt omphalos places. The geology of these unique crosses is identified as deriving from the same strata found on St Bees Head, most probably from Fleswick Bay a short distance north of the priory.[49]

Two hogback tombstones associated with the burials of Norse warriors are also on display inside the church, one labelled 'Saint's Tomb', supposedly depicting Christianity's fight over evil. These rare tombs are the best preserved in Britain and depict a house with a tiled roof supposedly symbolising the 'Houses of the Dead'. On one side of the hogbacks is a depiction of two armies in the act of truce-making, with one leader surrendering his flag to the other – one army is thought to be Viking because of their large rounded shields.

W. G. Collingwood, in his study of Norse and Anglican archaeology and Cumbrian crosses, states that 'Gosforth is the centre of a peculiar and unique school of art, spreading widely through the northern world, but nowhere in such bloom and beauty as in this quiet secluded village.'[50] This reminded me of Ciaran's psychic message to Carole and Alex which mentioned Gosforth as a 'place of learning.'

The village was once revered as an important geographical centre by the early tribes of the region, as it lies on an ancient route that links

Gosforth cross, a symbolic world ash tree

the Lakeland valleys at the centre of Cumbria to the coastal ports of Ravenglass and Whitehaven, enabling easy access to the Isle of Man and Ireland. Moreover, it lies on the direct route to Wasdale Valley and Wastwater, the deepest lake in England. This enigmatic lake also lies at the foot of Scafell Pike, the highest mountain in England. Scafell would therefore be the 'world mountain' to the Celts of this Lakeland kingdom, and a place of pilgrimage for other cultures passing through this area. Perhaps they viewed Wastwater, the deepest lake, as representing the doorway to the underworld.

During Mesolithic times and possibly later, a land bridge connected the Isle of Man and Cumbria, which according to local legend met the coast near Seascale, just 4 km to the east of Gosforth. The legend says that the bridge was built by the Devil, who, while carrying stones in his apron dropped one on the shore. A huge boulder called Carl Crag is said to be the Devil's stone, now buried beneath the shifting sands near Seascale, consisting of two white quartz seams, supposedly the marks made by his apron strings.[51]

Often these legends have some hidden truth to them, possibly a folk memory of a disastrous tsunami that severed the causeway here in prehistoric times. Many believe that one such event occurred in 2354 BCE when Hekla 4, a large volcano in Iceland erupted, and again in 1159 BCE when neighbouring Hekla 3 blew. Tree ring data and soil samples show that the coastline and lakes around Northern Ireland were flooded during those dates, affecting the growth rate of the trees. The disastrous climatic change resulting from the massive explosion of Helka 4 most probably ended the Neolithic Age in northern Europe and Britain. If the coast of Seascale was indeed part of a land-bridge, then for thousands of years Gosforth was strategically placed on a major route to and from Ireland, linking it with the axe factories at Langdale and the megalithic stone temples of Cumbria.

Also at Gosforth is a famous holy well at the top of a field just under a kilometre above the church, which can be reached by a footpath that takes you alongside Gosforth Hall Hotel, continuing through the beautiful garden of a private house. Remains of a well chapel 10 m long and 6 m wide were still evident in late Victorian times, although there is nothing to see today. C. A. Parker in *The Gosforth District* writes that medieval well chapels were rare in this area and appeared to be of the Celtic type found in Cornwall and Wales. An ugly modern metal lid now covers the well, but if you lift the lid, the original stonework that lines the well can still be glimpsed. Tradition says that on certain feast days wine was poured into the well, which the villagers would then drink as it came out of a stone spout in the village. At some time before 1901, the location of the well was lost, but it was rediscovered during excavations of the little chapel that once stood next to it.[52]

Gosforth Church and its cross are on a straight ley that also includes St Bridget's Church at Calder Bridge and St Bees Priory. This alignment links the two centre places with dedications to saints Bega, Bridget and Mary, perhaps three aspects of the same goddess energy. Gosforth's church also falls on an alignment that includes the summit of Snaefell, the highest mountain on the Isle of Man, and the summit of Scafell, the highest mountain in England.

The Goddess in Cumbria

Alex Langstone also mentions that St Bees Head, formerly Preston Isle, sits at the centre of a triangle formed by the three holy islands of Lindisfarne, Iona and Glastonbury.[53] A coincidence perhaps, although it substantiates our belief that St Bees Priory below the headland was an important centre of renown in the distant past. I also sensed that the considerable number of Bride, Brigid or Bridget churches that fall within a 16-km radius of the priory is key to the mystery; in fact, there are more sites dedicated to this mother goddess of the Britons in Cumbria than anywhere else in the British Isles and even in Ireland. This led us to believe that the St Bees area was perhaps at one time the main focal point of the worship of the old Celtic goddess (see Fig. 28).

When history refers to 'Celtic Lands' we generally think of Ireland, Wales, Cornwall and the Western Isles of Scotland. However, between the Roman retreat and the Saxon takeover of Britain 410–540 CE, certain Celtic kingdoms of the north thrived, particularly the Isle of Man and Rheged ruled by the great warrior Urien, a region that stretched from the western ridge of the Pennines in Lancashire all the way north to Galloway in southern Scotland. It is here within this well-protected region that the Celtic Church began to flourish.

The Celtic Church held a less rigid philosophy of Christian religion than the Roman Catholics and later Protestant Church. Many believe that this early faith evolved first in Ireland, and then spread to the north of England and Scotland. However, there is evidence that Cumbria and the Isle of Man may have also played a decisive role in the spread of this religion from earlier seedings.

The equal-armed crosses carved by the earliest Celtic Christians stood at pivotal centres of their faith, expressing their beliefs of interconnectedness with nature and the cosmos. The Isle of Man is geographically central to Ireland, Scotland, England and Wales and has the greatest number of the earliest examples of Celtic crosses.

In England, the nearest coastline to the Isle of Man is St Bees Head and the ancient ports of Whitehaven and Ravenglass. There is no doubt that a great trade existed between here, Ireland and the Isle of Man, which at the time allowed their religious influences to take root in Cumbria. However, there is little evidence of Cumbria's role in the early Celtic Church except in its place names, legends and outstanding collection of Celtic crosses scattered throughout its many ancient churches.

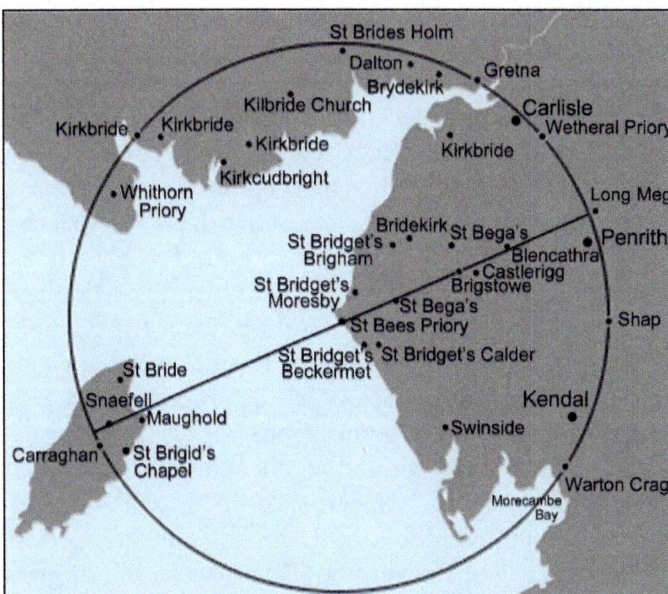

Figure 28. The Ring of Bride

Just south of St Bees Priory is the atmospheric St Bridget's Old Church, just outside the village of Beckermet. Built on a mound, this tiny 'low church' above the River Ehen dates from the 13th century and was erected on the site of a 7th-century nunnery or monastery. In the graveyard are the remains of some of the oldest crosses in England, with detailed runic and scrolled carvings. A translation by Cardinal Gasquet in 1915 reads: 'Abbot Adulf, a monk of Iona, erected this cross in honour of the Holy Virgin Bridget.'[54] The cross is cylindrical in shape, reminiscent of a pillar with a double collar moulding and identical to the Mercian 'pillars of declaration' found at many sacred places in Staffordshire, Cheshire and Derbyshire. There is also one similar at Eliseg in Denbighshire, Wales. The question as to how this style of pillar exists so far north is curious.

In his paper on *The Saxon Cross at Bewcastle*, the Revd D. H. Haig translated the runic inscription on this cross as a commemoration to the Saxon Bishop Tuda of Northumbria, who died of the plague that ravaged the whole of Britain in 664. He also states that the cross links St Bridget's with the illusive monastery that existed here recorded by the Venerable Bede as the settlement of Paegnalaech in Northumbria where Tuda was buried, denoting the importance of this little church as being greater than even St Bees Priory.[55] Curiously, Paegnalaech has also been identified as the old monastic site at Whalley, at the OS centre of Britain's landmass.

The modern name Beckermet is interesting, for although some say it means 'where streams meet' derived from 'beck', an Old English word for 'small stream', and 'met' meaning 'meeting', it is actually pronounced Bec-Kermet with the stress on the Ker.[56] As this area has strong connections with Ireland and St Bridget, the meaning may derive from Irish Gaelic. With this in mind, *bec* may translate as 'little'. The second syllable closely resembles the Middle English word *ermite* meaning 'hermit'. Therefore, Beckermet could mean 'little hermit or hermitage', probably referring to the ancient site of the church. The Place Name Society has determined that it could also translate as the 'stream of the hermit from Beck.'[57]

However, earlier maps printed in the 16th and 17th centuries, including Saxton's of 1576, Speed's of 1611, Jansson's of 1646, Seller's of 1694 and Morden's of 1695, all refer to the village as Beckarmond rather than Beckermet. This may be the original place name, with *mond* possibly referring to the mound or motte to the north of St Bridget's Church, the former site of a Norman motte and bailey called Caernarvon Castle.[58]

The mound on which St Bridget's Church sits resembles Bride's Mound in Glastonbury, which once had a similar-sized church on its summit built by Irish pilgrims and reputedly visited by the Irish St Bridget herself. The small area of land encompassing the mound on the outskirts of Glastonbury next to the River Brue is described in medieval documents as being called Beckery, a word not dissimilar to Beckermet. The Beckery mound is also known as 'Little Ireland', from the Irish Gaelic becc meaning 'little' and *ery* derived from Eire. Another church in Beckermet is dedicated to St John, built over the site of one constructed by Irish Celtic Christian missionaries, who may have erected the stone crosses here, now on display in the church, dating to 700 CE.

North of St Bees towards Cockermouth, on a windswept cliff overlooking the Solway Firth, is St Bridget's Church at Moresby. The freestanding chancel arch of an earlier church still stands in the graveyard. The site encompasses the earthwork remains of a Roman fort called 'Gabrosentum', which suggests that a church may have stood on this site from the earliest period of Christianity. According to legend, St Bridget came over from Ireland and founded a nunnery here, hence the dedication. The site has many levels of ancient history and the prominent hill opposite appears to have faint signs of ramparts from an Iron Age fort. A spring issues from out of the side of a hill at Parton below the church, recorded as having healing powers.

Ancient crosses at St Bridget's Church, Beckermet

At the town of Brigham, derived from 'homestead of Bride', we find another centre of early Christianity at St Bridget's Church. The church has Norman features, but like so many Bride sites, it has ancient foundations indicated by the presence of early examples of Celtic crosses and ancient carved stones.

To the southeast of St Bees is a remarkable healing shrine in the churchyard of St Mary's Church in the village of Cleator Moor, a replica of the grotto of Lourdes in France. This curious holy sanctuary was created at the end of WWI, during a time when the mines at Cleator were closed due to the low demand for iron ore. Local parish priest Fr Frederick Clayton conceived the idea to build a Lourdes-style grotto to boost employment and provide a spiritual focus for those unable to make the pilgrimage to France. A replica of the original statue of the virgin, as described by the visionary St

Bernadette, came from Paris and was placed in a niche in the replica grotto. In 1927 the shrine was dedicated to Our Lady of Lourdes and opened for pilgrims soon after.

Remarkably, stories of healing soon began to spread as if the power of the original shrine had somehow transferred to St Mary's at Cleator Moor. One miracle still talked about here is that of a paralysed woman who, after being carried to the grotto, recovered and was able to walk home.

Services for the sick were once a great feature of the pilgrimage, which took place each year in early September with people arriving from all over the British Isles and overseas. We visited the remarkable church designed by Pugin and were impressed by the beautiful stained-glass window of St Bride whose energy pervades this Catholic heart centre. Another window depicts St Bega in St Leonard's Church in the neighbouring village of Cleator, which is one of the oldest churches in Cumbria.

Just north of Cockermouth, and 25 km northeast of St Bees, is the village of Bridekirk with one of the most interesting churches in Cumbria dedicated to St Bridget. Overlooking the estuary of the River Wampool, a wooden church originally marking a Bride sanctuary has stood here for centuries dating from Celtic times, later replaced in 1130 and rededicated to the Irish saint Bridget.

Inside, there are two superb relics from the earlier church that stand in ruins in the churchyard. One is a spiral cross-head, probably 10th century in origin, the other a font, its fine carving comparable to that found in Rosslyn Chapel, the intricate detail being a wonder to behold. However, its date is disputed, with some saying 12th century while others believe it to be from the 10th century or earlier, even Roman. The design of the font is interesting, dividing into two roughly equal sections, which taper slightly outwards towards the top and depict runic lettering. It was carved by Richard of Durham with the description 'Richard he me wrought, and to this beauty me brought.' A panel also portrays the story of Adam and Eve and Christ's baptism.[59]

Another remarkable piece of ancient carving can be found on a stone situated on one of the windowsills. It is labelled as a Roman fragment and depicts a crowned lady with a cornucopia next to her resembling one exhibited in the Musee de St Remy de Provence in France, dedicated to a Celtic Gaulish goddess called Rosmerta, another version of Brighida. It is of great age, having been found over

1.8 m beneath the graveyard north of the old church, and therefore unlikely to be a fragment from a nearby Roman town. It may be a remnant from an early shrine built in honour of a local Cumbrian goddess or possibly Bride herself, her effigy captured in a beautiful stained-glass window inside Bridekirk Church. Outside, near the old chapel site, are numerous ancient tombstones and grave slabs.

The large number of Bride sites around this coastal region is said to be attributed to Irish missionaries. However, another reason may be due to the worship of the ancient goddess Brig or Bride having survived longer in this remote area, which experienced much less destruction by the Romans, Saxons and Normans than the rest of England and Wales. It seems more likely that the cult of Bride or Bridget originated in the British Isles and was later supplanted in Ireland by Celtic monks fleeing there from Roman persecution. Perhaps the cult of Brig, Bega and Bride has always existed in Cumbria long before it found its way to other parts of Britain and Ireland, for the land of the lakes was from ancient times an important centre of goddess worship defended by a line of illustrious kings until the 10th century, last of which was Dunmail whose crown lies buried to await the next ruler of Cumbria.

The visionary artist and designer Graham K. Griffiths saw the outline of Cumbria as the figure of the Aquarian-Phoenix, reminiscent of the landscape figures found in the Glastonbury and Preseli Zodiacs. As we are now experiencing the dawning of the Age of Aquarius, perhaps visiting the sacred sites on this fire bird of Cumbria, at the very heart of the British Isles, will help to spiritually awaken us.

Standing on St Bees Head, looking west across the Irish Sea, we could see the outline of the Isle of Man, renowned as marking the centre of the combined nations of Britain and Ireland. St Bees Head and the priory were once under the jurisdiction of the high king of the Isle of Man and from Snaefell, its highest mountain, you can see on a clear day England, Wales, Scotland and Ireland.

John Michell mentions the Isle of Man as the omphalos of the British Isles and Ireland in his book *At the Centre of the World* and points to a fifty-mile circle centred on the southern peninsular of Langness touching England, Scotland, Wales and Ireland. Moreover, by extending this circle to England's southern tip at Lizard Point in Cornwall, the circle will contain all the countries of the UK and Ireland.[60] Like, Ireland, Scotland and Wales, the Isle of Man is cosmologically divided into four districts and continues an ancient practice of parliament meetings on a tiered conical mound. Therefore, it is this ancient region that we turn our attention to next in search of the ultimate sacred omphalos of the collective Celtic nations.

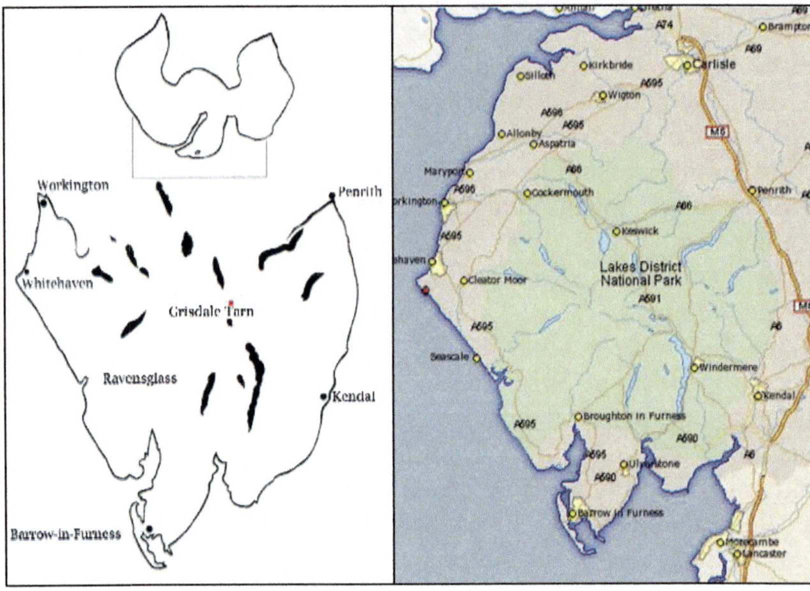

The inverted Phoenix shape of Cumbria, the Aquarian fire bird by Graham K Griffiths from his book 'Behold Jerusalem'

References:

1. Mee A (1978) *King's England Series: Warwickshire*. Hodder & Stoughton.
2. Heath R (2005) *Powerpoints: Secret Rulers and Hidden Forces in the Landscape*. Bluestone Press, St Dogmaels, Wales.
3. Biltcliffe G & Hoare C (2012) *The Spine of Albion: An Exploration of Earth Energies and Landscape Mysteries along the Belinus Line*. Sacred Lands Publishing, Weymouth.
4. *Iron Age activity, New Place*, Stratford-upon-Avon. http://timetrail.warwickshire.gov.uk/detail.aspx?monuid=WA13516.
5. Pennick N (1979) *The Ancient Science of Geomancy: Man in Harmony with the Earth*. Thames & Hudson, London.
6. Biltcliffe G & Hoare C (2012) *The Spine of Albion: An Exploration of Earth Energies and Landscape Mysteries along the Belinus Line*. Sacred Lands Publishing, Weymouth.
7. *Centre points of the United Kingdom*. https://en.wikipedia.org/wiki/Centre_points_of_the_United_Kingdom.
8. Whitaker T D (1872–76) *A History of the Original Parish of Whalley*. https://archive.org/details/historyoforigina00whituoft.
9. Ibid.

10. Dumville D (ed.), Shirley-Price L & Farmer D (translators) (2003) *Bede: Ecclesiastical History of the English People*. Penguin Classics, London.
11. Ingram, J. (translator) (1912) *The Anglo-Saxon Chronicle*. Everyman Press,
12. Dixon J & Dixon P (1993) *Journeys through Brigantia, Volume 9*. Aussteiger Publications, Clitheroe.
13. *History of St Mary and All Saints Church, Whalley*. https://sites.google.com/site/whalleyparishchurch/Home/history-of-st-mary-and-all-saints-church-whalley.
14. Whitaker T D (1872–76) *A History of the Original Parish of Whalley*. https://archive.org/details/historyoforigina00whituoft.
15. The Parish of Whalley. http://www.lan-opc.org.uk/Whalley/index.html
16. Dixon J & Dixon P (1993) *Journeys through Brigantia, Volume 9*. Aussteiger Publications, Clitheroe.
17. Pennick N, Lord R (1976) *Terrestrial Zodiac in Britain. The Nuthampstead Zodiac and The Pendle Zodiac*. Institute of Geomantic Research, Cambridge
18. Morton H.V. (1947) *In Search of England*. Republished 2002 by Folio Society, London.
19. Dixon J & Dixon P (1992) *Journeys Through Brigantia, Volume 8*. Aussteiger Publications, Clitheroe.
20. Dixon J (2003) *Dunsop Bridge: Bowland Forest*. Aussteiger Publications.
21. ibid.
22. Peel A (1913) *The Manor of Knowlmere*, privately published, Knowlmere.
23. Morris J (1980) *'Nennius' British History and the Welsh Annals*. Phillimore, London
24. Dixon J (2003) *Dunsop Bridge: Bowland Forest*. Aussteiger Publications.
25. Whitaker T D (1872–76) *A History of the Original Parish of Whalley*. https://archive.org/ details/historyoforigina00whituoft.
26. Langstone A (2012) *Spirit Chaser: The Quest for Bega*. Spirit of Albion Books, Cornwall.
27. Biltcliffe G (2022) *Mysterious Portland, Revealing the Sacred Landscape and Legacy of Britain's Masonic Isle*. Sacred Lands Publishing, Weymouth.
28. Carruthers F J (1979) *People Called Cumbri*. Robert Hale, London.
29. ibid.
30. Waterhouse, John (1985) *The Stone Circles of Cumbria*, Phillimore & Co, London.
31. Camden William (1551-1623) *Britannia, or a Chorographical Description of Great Britain and Ireland, Together with the Adjacent Islands, Vol. 1.* Gibson E (Translator), published in 1722, republished 2017 by Forgotten Books, London.
32. Stukeley W (1776) *Itinerarium Curiosum or an Account of the Antiquities and Remarkable Curiosities in Nature and Art Observed in Travels through Britain*. Baker & Leigh, London.
33. Pennant T (1771) *A Tour in Scotland 1769*. J. Monk, Chester.
34. Stone Circles & Avenue. http://www.shapcumbria.co.uk/stone-circles.htm.
35. *The History and Antiquities of the Counties of Westmorland and Cumberland*. https:// archive.org/details/historyandantiq00burngoog.

36. Burl A (1993) *From Carnac to Callanish: Prehistoric Stone Rows of Britain, Ireland and Brittany*. Yale University Press, New Haven.
37. Wainwright A (2010) *A Coast to Coast Walk*. Second Edition: *From St Bees Head to Robin Hood's Bay*. (The Pictorial Guides to the Lakeland Fells). Frances, Lincoln.
38. Wilson J (editor) (1905) *Houses of Benedictine monks: The priory of St Bees, A History of the County of Cumberland,* Victoria County History, Constable & Co, London.
39. Langstone A (1992) *Bega and the Sacred Ring: Restoring a Goddess Archetype*. The Lantern Press, London.
40. Jung C (2013) *Memories, Dreams, Reflections*. Fontana Press, London; New Ed edition (6 Mar. 1995),
41. Harris Rendel J (1928) *St Bees*. Aberdeen University Press. Republished in 1993 Lantern Press, Leigh on Sea.
42. Weatherstone L (2015) *Tending Brigid's Flame: Awaken to the Celtic Goddess of Hearth, Temple, and Forge*. Llewellyn Publishing, Woodbury,
43. St Begnet – St Bega. http://www.dalkeyhomepage.ie/stbegnet.html. https://en.wikipedia. org/wiki/Begnet
44. Williams J (1869) *The Visitor's Guide to St. Bees, Whitehaven, Egremont, Ravenglass, and the Surrounding Country Villages*. Reproduced 2017, Andesite Press.
45. ibid.
46. Collingwood W G (1930) *The Lake Counties*. J. M. Dent, London.
47. Bromwich R (1961) *The Welsh Triads*. University of Wales Press, Cardiff.
48. Langstone A (2012) *Spirit Chaser: The Quest for Bega*. Spirit of Albion Books, Cornwall.
49. Parker C A Dr (1904) *The Gosforth District: Its Antiquities and Places of Interest*. Reprinted 1986, Michael Moon, Whitehaven.
50. Collingwood W G (1930) *The Lake Counties*, J. M. Dent, London.
51. Parker C A Dr (1904) *The Gosforth District: Its Antiquities and Places of Interest.* Reprinted 1986, Michael Moon, Whitehaven.
52. ibid.
53. Langstone A (2012) *Spirit Chaser: The Quest for Bega*. Spirit of Albion Books, Cornwall.
54. Carruthers F J (1979) *People Called Cumbri*. Robert Hale, London.
55. Haig, D. H. Revnd (1822) *The Saxon Cross at Bewcastle*, Archaeologia Aeliana, N.S. vol. i., p. 149.
56. Morris J (1980) '*Nennius' British History and the Welsh Annals*. Phillimore, London.
57. Beckermet Local History Group (2009) *Beckermet: A Tale of Two Parishes, A Quarter and a Tale*.
58. ibid.
59. Carruthers F J (1979) *People Called Cumbri*. Robert Hale, London.
60. Michell J (1994) *At the Centre of the World: Polar Symbolism Discovered in Celtic, Norse and Other Ritualized Landscapes*. Thames & Hudson.

Chapter 8

The Isle of Man

The Navel of Britain and Ireland

The landscape goddess at the centre of the Isle of Man

The Isle of Man lies in the middle of the Irish Sea, some 96 km west of the Lancashire coast in Northern England, 32 km southwest of Galloway in Scotland, 51 km east of Ireland and 70 km north of Wales. The island's natural beauty is apparent in its varied terrain, including two mountainous areas divided by a central river valley that runs east-west between the main towns of Douglas and Peel. Beyond the mountains to the North are the flat plains of Andreas, leading to the tip of the island called Point of Ayre. The landscape is softer in the south, with rolling hills and valleys sheltering picturesque villages and small fishing ports. The highest mountain, Snaefell, rises to 620 m above sea level and from the summit, on a clear day, you can see the coastline of Scotland, England, Wales, and Northern and Southern Ireland.

Steeped in folklore, the Isle of Man is the epitome of a holy island and recognised as a cultural omphalos of the northern Celts and the geographical centre of the British Isles and Ireland. Manx folklore refers to a perpetual fire within the island that creates the surrounding mists, serving as a protective veil when invaders approach. Perpetual fire is said to represent the eternal flame at the centre of the world associated with goddess worship. The concept of a sacred eternal fire has echoes in beliefs, traditions and religions from all over the world, stretching back to the dawn of history.

The Isle of Man, also called Mann, lies at the halfway point along the longest north-south axis of Great Britain, from Land's End in Cornwall to Duncansby Head near John o' Groats in Scotland – a distance of 970 km. This axis, first discovered by John Michell, appears in *At the Centre of the World*, published in 1994.[1] There is, however, a longer line that can be drawn through Great Britain from the highest and lowest points on the mainland from the Lizard Point in Cornwall to Dunnet Head in Caithness, which is 976 km, and remarkably, its halfway point is also marked by the Isle of Man.

Our visit to Mann coincided with the island's Tynwald Day celebrations, an annual event held on 5 July at the village of St John's, near the coastal town of Peel. The festivities focus on its primaeval four-tiered earthen mound called Tynwald Hill – a rare modern remnant of an ancient ritual landscape ceremony surviving in isolation. We also planned to review the claims that refer to this mound as a symbolic navel of the combined nations of Britain and Ireland.

Virtually every square mile of the island has tales of fairies and unearthly creatures, and as we have previously discovered, such stories are typical of axis mundi places. Here, the veil is thin between Earth and other spiritual dimensions, enabling elementals to access the Earthly realm at certain times of the year.

The History and Mystery of Mann

The natural beauty of the island is apparent in its varied terrain featuring rolling hills littered with ancient monuments such as holy wells, Celtic chapels, ancient crosses, standing stones, hillforts and spectacular waterfalls, glens, cliffs, sandy beaches and charming harbours – a wonderful vibrant blend of natural features and sacred sites for such a small island. North to south, the island measures 53 km (33 m) long and 21 km (13 m) at its widest. In the past, Mann was known variously as *Mona*, *Mana*, *Mannin* and *Ellan Vannin*, all of which derive from the name of an ancient sea god called Manannan Mac Lir, meaning 'son of the sea'. Over 8500 years ago, the Irish Sea was dry land and the Isle of Man was a hilly region within green valleys between Ireland and England. After sea levels began to rise from the melting Ice Age glaciers, the hills of Mann formed an island with a land bridge or causeway to West Cumbria in the area of Seascale.

This final link to the mainland of Britain submerged around 2310 BCE when the Hekla 4 volcano in Iceland exploded with a force calculated to be three times greater than that of Thera (modern-day Santorini), which destroyed the early Minoan civilisation in 1629 BCE. Many experts now believe that the incredible destructive force of Hekla and its dust cloud aftermath may have brought the Neolithic Age to an end in northern Europe. Not only was the land devastated by the tsunami that followed the eruption but also the poisonous cloud of ash emitted by the volcano blocked out the sun and contaminated the lakes, streams and springs for many years to come. With no harvest or clean drinking water, the inhabitants of Britain had little choice but to migrate to Central Europe and the Mediterranean.[2]

Many of the islands that satellite Britain, such as the Isle of Wight, are considered otherworldly places with a history of hauntings and supernatural occurrences, but according to the famous researcher Jenny Randles, the Isle of Man has the most paranormal activity.[3] However, few people get to know the sanctity of Mann or hear of its mysterious side because the main focus for tourists is its famous TT Race – the ultimate challenge for speed warriors on their motorbikes for the last hundred years. Like the chariot races of the Greeks and Romans in great stadiums risking life and limb, today the stadium is the island around which the high-powered superfast motorcycles encircle to cheers of the thousands of spectators watching their incredible skills as they negotiate the most dangerous course in the world.

We soon discovered after visiting the island's Heritage Centre that very little written history of Mann has survived from before the 19th century, except for a few medieval religious manuscripts such as the *Chronicle of the Kings of Mann and the Isles*[4] and a few 16th-century songs that tell of Mann's ancient past. What has survived are fantastic legends that stretch the imagination, for the island is considered a veritable fairyland in which the Irish gods and heroes occasionally resided, including Manannan Mac Lir, a magician and navigator of the seas who became its High King.

Manannan is described as wearing chainmail armour with a breastplate and cloak that made him invisible at will. On his helmet were two jewels that 'shone like the sun', and he possessed magical spears, swords, and a boat called 'Wave Sweeper' that could glide by volition. His mighty steed, 'Enbarr of the flowing mane,' could gallop over land or sea. The tales of Manannan are the equivalent of one of today's Marvell superheroes.

In *The Atlantis Researches* by Paul Dunbavin, the author gives a scholarly account of an earlier catastrophe caused by a pole shift around 3000 BCE during Britain's Neolithic Age and claims that it caused a dramatic rise in sea levels around Britain. He states that the Irish Sea north of Anglesey between Ireland and England was a vast level plain before flooding, which fits with Plato's description of the plain of Atlantis, and that the submerged mountains of Atlantis became the Isle of Man, with its city somewhere at the foot of the Irish Sea south of Mann. Furthermore, Poseidon, the great god of the sea who ruled Atlantis, could be equated to Manannan, the Celtic god of the sea.[5]

Academic historians believe that Irish migrations to the island began in the 5th century CE and formed the basis of the modern Manx Gaelic language. However, Mann had a considerable Celtic population long before this, where their priesthood, the Druids, founded a great school of learning. According to Mann historian Joseph Train, 'the head of the Druid order, the Arch-Druid, had his residence and college on Mann. What is more, the children of the great Celtic rulers from all over the British Isles were sent here to be taught astronomy, astrology, philosophy, alchemy and metallurgy, as well as Gnostic, Arabic, Greek and early Christian doctrines.'[6]

During the Roman invasion of England, some sources suggest that Mann became a haven for the Druids and other refugees from Anglesey after the Romans sacked the island in 60 CE. There is an area of land on the Isle of Man still called Druidale and a site called 'Druid's Circle' exists near Ballaugh in the North of the island.

The geographical central location of Mann in the middle of the Irish Sea, with sheltered natural harbours equidistant from England, Wales, Scotland and Ireland on sea routes from Scandinavia to Europe, attracted many traders and settlers over thousands of years. However, being free from British law enticed those who sought to share or control the rich trading between the nations, particularly the Norsemen of Scandinavia, who were no different to the earlier Phoenicians of the Mediterranean. At the end of the 8th century, they forcibly settled on the island and inter-married with the Manx people, siting their burials in pre-existing graveyards of the old Celtic churches.

Many of the most sacred Celtic sanctuaries in Ireland, Scotland and Wales lie within sight of Mann from the coast across the sea, including Downpatrick in Co Down, where St Patrick, St Columba and St Bridget are buried; the holy sanctuary in Whithorn in Dumfries and Galloway, where St Ninian established the first Celtic Christian settlement in England North of Hadrian's Wall in 397 CE; Holyhead Island on the Isle of Anglesey in Wales, anciently called Mona and the healing sanctuary of St Bees in Cumbria.

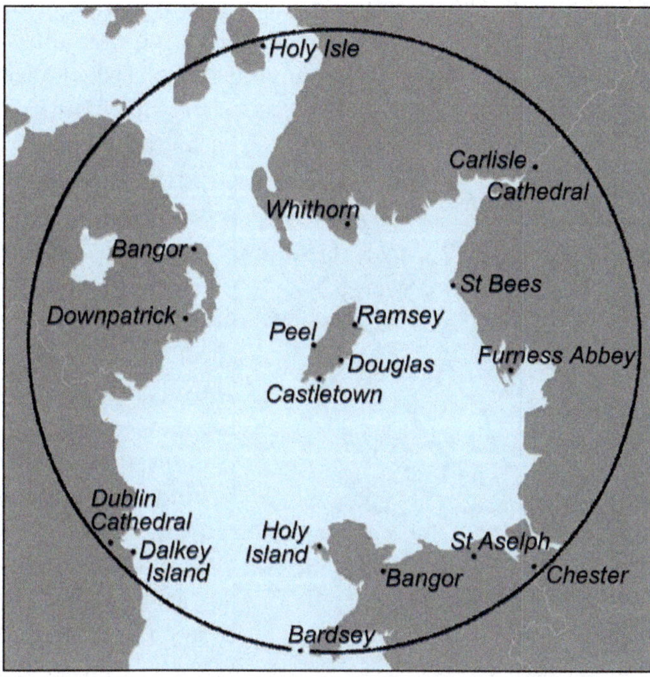

Figure 29. Ring of holy sites around Mann

A circle can be drawn to include the holy sites pivoting on the centre of Mann with its circumference touching the northwest coast of Bardsey Island, the alleged Avalon of Wales, this approximately 100-mile diameter circle also touches another Holy Island on the east coast of the Isle of Aran in Ayrshire, also described as an 'Avalon' (see Fig. 29).

Certain traditions state that Celtic Christianity spread from Ireland into Scotland and Wales, and the first Christians on the Isle of Man were Irish missionaries known as Culdees who arrived around 447 CE. Interestingly, there are a surprising number of Celtic stone crosses on Mann, and according to the Heritage Centre in Douglas, there are hundreds stored around the island, because the museum was unable to display them all. In fact, the Isle of Man has more Celtic crosses than Ireland and Britain put together. This has led some to believe that it was the epicentre of Celtic Christianity, where it was first taught and then spread to other parts of Britain and Ireland.

Michell revealed ancient Celtic cosmology in the early divisions of Mann, similar to Ireland, Scotland and Wales, having four provinces or kingdoms called North, East, South and West, which eventually encompassed a central fifth called Marown. The Celtic Christian Church eventually reformed these regions into sixteen parishes or Norse 'sheadings', each having four parishes.[7] However, in the 14th century, Santon parish was further divided into two and a new landlocked parish was formed called Marown, making seventeen districts in all. Each of the four divisions had its own main town or regional capital – the East kingdom had Douglas (now the capital of Mann), Peel was the former capital of West, the North had Ramsey and the South, Castletown (also a former capital) (see Fig. 30).

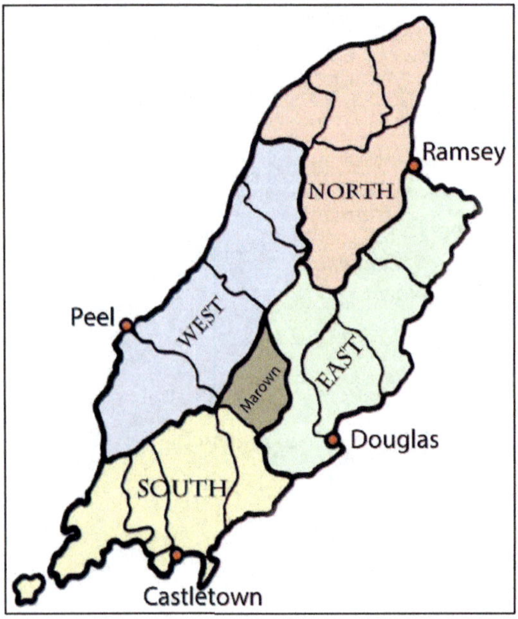

Figure 30. The ancient divisions of the Isle of Man, adapted from a map by Christine Rhone in 'At the Centre of the World' by John Michell

Michell also refers to two main axis lines on Mann, both extending from the Point of Ayre at the most northerly point of the island. One stretches to the Calf of Man, an isle off the southwest tip, and the other to Dreswick Point in the far southeast. Furthermore, there are two east-west axes – both pivoting on the kingship site of St Patrick's Isle at Peel in the west to two points on the east coast, namely Clay Head and Douglas Point. Here, we can see a harmonic blend between the sacred places of the island and its geometry, with the lines connecting with many ritual centres of Mann including Old Tynwald, the Tynwald Mound, St Bridget's Church and its holy well in the parish of Bride, St Luke's Church at Baldwin built over the site of a 6th-century stone chapel and the parish church of Marown dedicated to St Runius also the site of an ancient keeill (see Fig. 31). But which culture was responsible for the island's geometry and the establishment of its ritual centres?

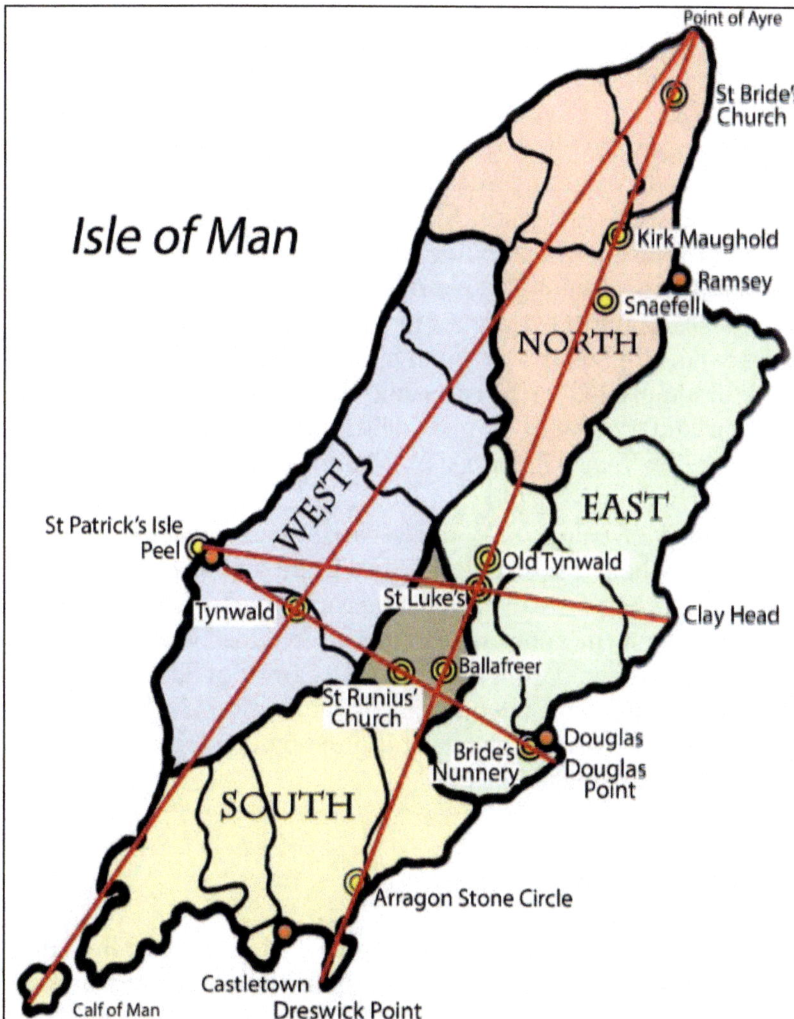

Figure 31. Map of the Isle of Man with its main alignments

Very little is known of Mann's history before the Vikings invaded in the 8th century and gradually took over its ritual centres, crowning

Magnus Heraldson their first King of Mann in 967. Magnus was also 'King of the Isles', ruling over the Western and Hebridean Isles of Scotland. We later discovered that these Viking islands were also divided into four regions, which included Lewis, Skye, Mull and Islay, and modern representatives from these islands still attend the midsummer Tynwald ceremonies on the Isle of Man today.

The division of these islands into four, follows an age-old Eastern ritual of cosmology, whereby the four provinces mirrored the quartering of the sky for divination purposes. This practice dates back to 3000 BCE, with the Sumerian and early Indus Valley civilisations, later adopted by the Phoenicians, Greeks, Etruscans and Vikings. The Vikings may have been descendants of the ancient Phoenicians who escaped the Roman Empire. Many historians today argue that they followed the northern sea routes, eventually settling in Iceland.

Godred Crovan, the greatest Manx king, was a native of Iceland and after escaping the Norman invasion, settled on Mann with his descendants, founding a royal dynasty there around 1079, which lasted for almost 200 years. His seat of power was on St Patrick's Isle on the island's western shores, which became the main religious house for the four kingdoms of Mann. The Manx affectionately referred to him as 'King Orry' and during their height of power, these Norse Kings of Mann held thirty-two separate islands. However, invasions by the Norse-Gaelic warlord Somerled in 1156, who ruled from Argyll, took many of them back under Scottish control, including Mann. In 1266, when the native dynasty of kings ended, control of the island passed briefly to the Crown of Scotland and then to England. Although independent of the United Kingdom and the European Union today, Mann is still ruled by the British Crown, and its people are British citizens.

The Supernatural Realm

We were soon to discover that the whole island had all the ingredients of an omphalos landscape, and Snaefell, the holy mountain of Mann, would qualify as the 'world mountain' or navel of the British Isles and Ireland. The name of this distinctive mountain derives from the Norse meaning 'snow mountain' and, according to an old island saying, 'you can see six kingdoms from the summit: Mann, Scotland, England, Ireland, Wales and Heaven.'

The rolling mists that drop down from the mountain into the valleys and shroud the island like an ethereal cloud are called the 'cloak of Manannan', which the sea god uses to protect his island from invaders. The mists also touch a superstitious nerve in Manx people, for these veils of fog are associated in folklore and legend with portals into another world through which mythical creatures and the souls of the departed emerge into the physical world.

One well-known Manx otherworldly story associated with the fog is based on a true-life event that happened during a TT (Tourist Trophy) Race. It involved one of the marshals, Jim Quayle, who was inspecting the track on the 'Verandah' section of the course at a sharp left-hand corner of the road near the 'Graham Memorial' on the side of Snaefell. Suddenly, a thick mist descended all around him, which caused him to stop what he was doing and proceed further along the mountain road to a point of safety to wait for the fog to clear. Suddenly, he heard what he thought was the unmistakable roar of a BMW Kompressor, one of the great iconic machines of the 1930s, followed by the sound of footsteps coming towards him. Feeling unsettled and disturbed, Jim stared ahead into the gloom and could just make out the dark eerie shape of a man emerging from the thick mist. Not sure what to expect, the old marshal was relieved to be greeted by a man clad in black and wearing an old-fashioned crash helmet. He was unsurprised by the man's attire, as many motorcycle enthusiasts who attend the TT event often rode in the vintage bike race wearing specific clothing of the period.

The motorcyclist turned out to be German and seemed unsure about where he was. Luckily, Jim understood the language and heard him say, 'I have been lost for a long time. Please help me.' The marshal introduced himself and the German, after a minute or two, remembered that his name was Pete. He then said a rather strange thing: 'Now that I remember, I need to go home. I have been here for a long time and my family are missing me.' He then shook Jim's hand and said, 'I have been waiting for so long for someone to find me. Thank you for finding me, Jim. I just needed someone to find me.' When the marshal suggested that he would help him find his bike, the German simply said, 'I will be all right now,' and then turned into the mist and disappeared. Eventually, it dawned on Jim that he had seen a ghostly apparition from the past and, after a bit of research, discovered that a German motorcyclist called Peter had indeed been killed in an accident on that stretch of the track back in the 1930s.[8]

I believe Peter's spirit, due to the traumatic nature of his death, had become attached to the area and perpetually lost, walking the roads around Snaefell until the right conditions manifested for him to appear to mortals. His encounter with Jim triggered his memory and confirmed that he was still alive in some ghostly form.

At the end of May and throughout June the famous TT races are the island's main focus, a prestigious annual international two-week event. During this time, the island's 85,000 inhabitants are subjected to over 500 motorcyclists racing at speeds of up to 325 km per hour (200 mph) along a circuit that courses through the streets and main roads of their towns and villages. Tens of thousands of fans from all over the world flock to the island to watch this event, which has been held here since 1907. Dubbed the 'Road Racing Capital of the World', the island's sharp bends and treacherous mountain passes become the ultimate test for competitors and machines alike. All year round, spectator grandstands remain as does the safety padding on numerous stone walls, gateposts and telegraph poles, a constant reminder of this gruelling and dangerous race that spoils the beauty of the island.

However, there is a certain level of honour attributed to the Isle of Man circuit among the racers, and to end their days here on their motorcycle on this hallowed island is comparable to a warrior's death in battle, like the chariot races of ancient Roma and Greece. However, as we were about to discover, the island has much more to offer those who are fascinated and intrigued by things more sacred and magical. In our experience, a violent act of death or intense emotional trauma occurring at certain places in the landscape, leaves behind a detrimental energetic stain, especially around areas of powerful geology. This can reverberate through the natural energy veins of the Earth, which dowsers often detect as 'black streams', which can create imbalance and disharmony in the land.

Manx folklore is full of tales of fairies, bugganes, witches, giants and black dogs appearing and disappearing all over the island. There seemed to be a tradition that the locals never called these tiny elementals by any name, believing it unwise to speak of them outright, and so referred to them as 'themselves'. Sometimes, fairy music lures or bewitches people wandering the hills and valleys. Margaret Killip in *The Folklore of the Isle of Man* relates one such story: 'Bill Pheric was coming home late one night across the mountains from Druidale, and heard the fairies singing, just as he was going over the river by the thorn tree that grows there. The tune they had was Bollan Vane, and he wanted to learn it from them, so he went back three times and stayed until dawn approached, for fairies always go before sunrise. He came home whistling the tune, and since then it has been popular and much played on the fiddle. Many people say that Bill Pheric invented the tune, but he always maintained that he got it from the fairies.'[9]

According to locals, one of Mann's key energy sites is Sky Hill overlooking Churchtown near Ramsey. The tree-shrouded dome-shaped hill is said to be the starting point of King Orry's Road and supposedly where the great warrior defeated the Celtic Manx in a battle. From a distance, the giant mound radiates a powerful presence in this part of the island and marks the start of an ancient north-south route called the Millennium Way, once known as King Orry's Road. The path travels down the spine of the island around the north side of Snaefell to the Old Tynwald circle mound at Baldwin and the old capital of Castletown on the south coast. Another name for King Orry's Road was the 'Milky Way' because 'when Orry came to Mann he landed at the Lhen Beach in the northwestern shore on a bright starry night. Those gathered on the shore asked him whence he had come, and pointing upwards the Milky Way, he said, "Yonder is the road whence I came, and along that star-spangled dome is the way that leads to my country."'[10]

Travelling to the island before or after the TT races allows the visitor to experience a more relaxed atmosphere and a fuller appreciation of its remarkable landscape and beautiful coastline. During our week's exploration of Mann, we based ourselves at a delightful cottage by the River Sulby in the beautiful Sulby Glen, located in the northern part of the island set below Mann's highest mountain, Snaefell. After chatting to the charming couple who owned the accommodation, we asked about the 'dragon in the landscape' which they first mentioned to us when initially booking the cottage. They pointed towards the wooded ridge behind us and said, 'Can you see its eye?' We stared intently in the direction they were indicating and, sure enough, we could see the sun lighting up a rugged escarpment of sandstone exposed among the trees that looked just like the eye of the dragon. In fact, the hillside from a distance resembles a dragon's head, and as the sun disappears behind a cloud, the dragon gives the impression of closing its eye, as if settling down to sleep.

That evening, I read about the fascinating creation myths, folklore and mysteries of the island from an excellent collection of local books provided at the cottage. I could hardly believe the number of paranormal occurrences around the island including mysterious balls of light, fairy abductions and strange beasts terrorising the locals. During our research of the Belinus alignment, we often found that certain places made famous by their stories of hauntings are located on or near unusual geology and fault lines.

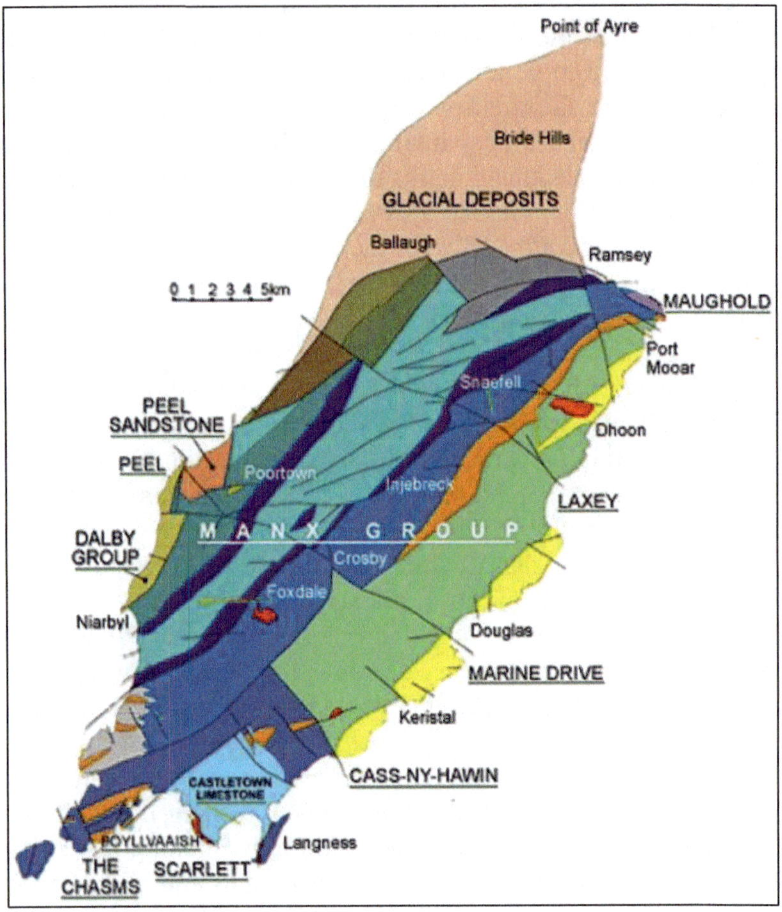

Figure 32. Geology of the Isle of Man. Courtesy of Dave Quirk

A fault is a fissure between two landmasses, and when seismic or cosmic activity takes place, the friction between the rocks creates a high magnetic field and this can be amplified by underground water aquafers. This affects the temporal lobe region of our brain, which can stimulate psychic abilities or the imagination, often subconsciously. Where there are large fault lines in strata containing silica, such as sandstone or granite, you will often experience ghostly apparitions, strange lights and time-slips. These events are found to occur under specific conditions, particularly when the faults are under stress either by the passage of the full moon, solar flares, slight earth movements or after a period of heavy rain.

In *The Spine of Albion*, we mention the mystical Isle of Wight and its long history of paranormal events, which include ghostly encounters, time-slips and sightings of strange lights that may be due to its powerful geology. An east-west ridge of hills, also a geological fault, runs from Bembridge Down on the east coast to the chalk stacks called the Needles at the west end of the island. This ridge has a geological layer of Upper Greensand, consisting of hard crystalline iron-bearing sandstone, otherwise known as firestone because of its fiery colour. We found that some of the Isle of Wight's most haunted places are situated on this firestone layer.

The Isle of Man also has a rich diversity of geology including limestone, quartz sandstone, granite and glacial deposits. The bulk of the island, however, consists of geological layers called the Manx Group, comprising a mixture of sedimentary and volcanic rocks, folded and faulted by millions of years of tectonic pressures as far back as 480 million years ago. They gave the island its mountainous spine and spectacular rocky coastline.

I believe that Mann's highly magnetic geology, fault lines and atmospheric conditions opened a portal in the area below Snaefell, allowing Jim, the race marshal, to communicate with Pete, the ghostly German motorcyclist. The shock of his sudden death along with a disbelief in an afterlife kept him suspended in a spirit world close to our own Earth plane. His release came after meeting Jim and remembering who he was and what had happened to him.

St Patrick's Isle and the Royal Citadel

We awoke the next morning to be greeted by rather unsettled weather, but alas, that is the nature of the Isle of Man. Its mountains lure the clouds that sometimes linger all day or just stay for an hour or two, eventually giving way to the warmth of the sun. While reading *Supernatural Isle of Man* by paranormal investigator Jenny Randles, I was intrigued by the author's reference to an ancient east-west route between Douglas and Peel following a central valley.

This 24-km-long valley divides the island's two mountainous regions of Snaefell and South Barrule along a major fault line (see Fig, 32). With the melting of glaciers after the Ice Age, the force of the water gouged out the valley, creating its rivers including the Dhoo, Greeba and Neb. Randles states that the valley experiences a great number of paranormal events, recorded in much of Mann's folklore and mythology.[11]

During the Dark Ages and before, the flat lands north of Sky Hill were flooded to form great lakes before being drained to create the arable lands in the districts of Bride and Jurby. Therefore, prior to the draining of the land, the road between Ballaugh, Sulby and Ramsey marked the old northern island boundary making this central valley, mentioned by Randles, geographically the middle route through Mann similar to An Slí Mhór in Ireland.

We have found previously that a key ingredient of many omphalos landscapes is a centrally located crossroads of north-south and east-west historic routes. I discovered on a detailed map of Mann that the old north-south Royal Road between Ramsey and Castletown now called Millennium Way, crosses the east-west central valley at a village called Crosby. These two ancient paths connect the island's four main towns like a giant cross. Interestingly, before the draining of the lakes in the North that shortened the landmass, Crosby was the most central settlement on the island (see Fig. 34).

A little research on Crosby revealed that surrounding it are some interesting ancient monuments including the remains of a Celtic keeill dedicated to Vreeshey or St Bride, as she is known on Mann. Thus, as in Wales, Scotland and Ireland, we find Bride at the centre of a kingdom and close to a crossroads of major routes. It now seemed important for us over the next few days to investigate the sites along the central valley fault including Crosby, and the Millennium Way.

Today, the busy A1 between Douglas and Peel follows the central valley, although it is difficult to navigate by foot and, during May and June, it is part of the TT race course. However, you can still walk part of the fault line via a footpath along a disused railway line called 'The Heritage Way'.

At the western extremity of the valley fault, at the mouth of the River Neb, is St Patrick's Isle, the ancient royal seat of the Lords of the Isles and Kings of Mann. Like St Michael's Mount in Cornwall and Mont St Michel in Brittany, they are geological centres of power separated from the shores by an 'umbilical' natural causeway, a symbolic sanctuary for the living and the dead. The Neb is one of the island's principal rivers, rising in the Michael Hills and continuing through St John's and Tynwald Hill before joining the sea at Peel. The well-preserved ruin of Peel Castle on St Patrick's Isle occupies most of the island, which includes an Irish-style round tower, St Patrick's Chapel and the remains of St German's Cathedral. This 'isle within an Isle' juts out into the Irish Sea, a steep rocky outcrop of Silurian

St Patrick's Isle, Peel

stones consisting of fossils and mudstones.

Based on archaeological evidence, this tiny but strategic island has been inhabited since Mesolithic times, around 8,000 years ago. The Manx name for Peel is *Purt-ny-Hinshey* meaning 'harbour of the island'. According to C. W. Airne in *The Story of the Isle of Man*, St Patrick's Isle was the principal stronghold of the Iron Age Picts from where they governed the whole island, being a natural defence against invaders by sea and land.[12] Whereas Cubbon, mentions a 13th-century Irish author who states that St Patrick's Isle was the 'Tara of Mann.'[13] In the 1980s, excavations uncovered post-holes from circular dwellings dating between 650 BCE and 600 CE, the same period when Tara in Ireland was at the height of its power.[14]

St Patrick's Isle became the holiest Christian centre on Mann focused around St Patrick's Chapel where the Irish saint supposedly first set foot. William Sacheverell wrote in *An Account of the Isle of Man* that St Patrick when returning from Liverpool to Ireland in 444 CE with a band of thirty followers, 'found the people, at least the rulers, given to magic. But being overcome or convinced by his preaching and miracles, they were converted or else expelled from the island.' St Patrick stayed on the island for three years, 'converting the people by means of his preaching and his miracles.' He is said to have blessed the Isle of Man 'from end to end', freeing it from toads, snakes and 'venomous beasts, visible devils and a multitude of magicians.' He drove out the Druid priests including Manannan Mac Lir and his followers, 'who fled across the sea.'[15]

In *The Life and Acts of St Patrick*, the 12th-century Cistercian monk Jocelin wrote: 'Saint Patrick placed as Bishop over the new church of this nation one of his disciples, a wise and holy man named Germanus, as Bishop … in a certain promontory which is yet called St Patrick's Isle, because he used to reside there from time to time.'[16] St Germanus or German, is thought to be St Garmon of Wales who pursued King Vortigern to his tower at Cwmdauddwr.

The historian Joseph Train (1779–1852) recorded that St Patrick obtained 'fire from heaven to consume nine wizards clothed in white vestments, feigning themselves to be saints.'[17] This resembles the story of 'fire from heaven' that supposedly destroyed King Vortigern's Tower at the centre of Wales, which possibly alludes to a time in the Dark Ages between 400 and 600 CE when, according to Welsh manuscripts, meteor showers bombarded the Earth. These extraordinary events may have been the result of comet debris, which has been woven into tales of the exploits of saints to aggrandise their power and reputation.

St Patrick's Chapel is the most sacred spot on this rocky isle, built over a keeill site that some sources believe was part of a 5th or 6th-century Celtic monastery. The low walls of another tiny chapel, possibly a second keeill, at the very centre of St Patrick's Isle, appear to have been built into a wide bank that surrounds an artificial mound, today marked with a flagpole. Excavations in the 1920s and 1940s revealed no evidence that the mound was earlier than the 15th century. However, if the early chapel dates from the 11th century and was built into the earthen ditch and bank, then the earthworks would appear to predate the chapel. We had a sense that it was an Iron Age mound perhaps erected for a royal burial or ceremony during the time of the Picts.

We have discovered all over the British Isles that certain mounds when excavated revealed no signs of interment, but instead, layers of organic and inorganic materials were found such as earth and chalk or stones and peat. Renowned Austrian scientist Wilhelm Reich (1897–1957) revealed that raising a mound formed of such layering

The chapel and mound at the centre of St Patrick's Isle, Peel

attracts a cosmic energy he called orgone. This exists in all living things and accumulates in the upper atmosphere. Reich suggested that the ancient races around the world who built these mounds knew how to amass this beneficial energy from the atmosphere by making layered mounds to draw it down. The mound then gradually stores the energy until it becomes overcharged, releasing it across the landscape and magnetising the soil, which creates a healthier and more fertile crop.[18] Often these mounds were located on high ridges near or on fault lines. We noticed on the geology map of the Isle of Man a fault line passing close to St Patrick's Isle where a ridge of slate meets with sandstone (see Fig. 32).

As we continued to explore the ruined buildings and earthworks, we had a strong sense of two earth energy lines flowing through the site, similar in nature and vibration to the Elen and Belinus earth serpents. Although it was not our intention to follow the flow of these lines of energy from here at the time, we later encountered them at other sites along the Central Valley including the Tynwald mound at St John's.

The Tynwald Mound

A National Day of Celebrations is held once a year in mid-summer at an enigmatic mound called Tynwald Hill in the village of St John's. Interestingly, situated 4.5 km to the east of Peel, the mound lies precisely where the longest axis from the Calf of Man to the Point of

Ayre crosses with the alignment between St Patrick's Isle at Peel and Douglas Head. The four-tiered circular pyramidal earthen structure is located on the village green and has represented the independent parliament of Mann since the time of the Norse rulers and perhaps earlier to the 1st century CE. The artificial mound is conical in shape and is 25 m in diameter at the base and 3.7 m high. Each tier decreases in height to the top and is made up of stones and soil from each of the island's seventeen ancient parishes. The mound's tiered design represents the hierarchy of the ruling body, with the king or highest dignitary seated on its summit.

Locals still attend an annual open-air meeting of the parliament on the mound every year on 5 July – the old midsummer's day when the sun starts its precession to the winter solstice position. In 1752, when Britain switched from the Julian to the Gregorian calendar, eleven days were removed, making midsummer's day 24 June. The people of Mann, however, refused to acknowledge this new date and continued to celebrate this ancient ceremony on 5 July. The rest of the year, parliament meets at the Council Chambers in Douglas.

Just 115 m from the mound is St John the Baptist's Church, also

Tynwald Hill, St John's, June 1937

known as the 'Royal Chapel', linked with this ancient ceremonial site by a processional way orientated east-west towards the rising and setting sun at the equinox when the hours of day and night are equal. There were once earthen walls or banks encircling both the church and the mound, symbolising the divine (church) and the physical realms (mound) connected by a sacred pathway. Old photographs clearly show a maypole on top of the mound, a symbol of the world tree or axis mundi.

When the English Baron Sir John Stanley I (*c.* 1350–1414) became titular King of Mann, his descendants, the Earls of Derby, curtailed the stronghold of the church over island customs by reinstating the Tynwald Parliament that had fallen into misuse. During their reign, however, they encouraged greedy and unscrupulous English nobles to settle on the island who increased land rents and questioned through the force of the law the ancient tenancy agreements of the Manx farmers, forcing many of them off land worked by their ancestors for generations.

The powerful Dukes of Atholl, who reside at their stately home Blair Castle within the central province of Scotland, inherited the island from the last Baron Stanley. Sadly for the Manx people, their rule was equally draconian, having eventually handed over their island's precious sovereignty to the English government. In *Island Heritage*, William Cubbon writes: 'The statutes which had rapidly passed through Parliament … inflicted an irremediable wound on the well-being of the Manx people. They also struck a fatal blow at their cherished independence.'[19] Spencer Walpole also wrote: 'For centuries the Isle had preserved the appearance of independence, it had been left to regulate its own affairs and to make its own laws. It had the mortification now to see that the Parliament of Great Britain was disposing of its sovereignty, and imposing new and heavy burdens on its trade.'[20]

Although Tynwald Hill at St John's is some distance from the island's omphalos, it is a modern ceremonial centre of power. Michell refers to an older Tynwald site very close to St Luke's Church north of Baldwin that is closer to the geographical centre and its church stands on the site of an ancient stone chapel called Keeill Abban.

The island has many Celtic churches called keeills or cells, the remains of which are still evident in many places around the island, their construction similar to the small rectangular stone chapels seen in Ireland and Scotland. Evidence of Bronze Age finds in their foundations proves they were built over pre-Christian sites, often positioned near a sacred holy well or stream, indicative of securing a pagan sanctuary and using the holy spring water to administer as a sacrament. Today, only thirty-five keeills remain out of two hundred recorded in the past. They were simple in design, having no division between the nave and chancel, with a narrow door situated in the western gable and a single altar placed against the eastern wall. Often the keeill was built upon a natural or artificial elevation or mound with an attached burial ground, reminiscent of the Celtic 'raths' in Ireland.

Michell believes that the Baldwin Tynwald enclosure 260 m along the old Royal Road northeast of St Luke's Church is the true omphalos of Mann, which would also mark it as the actual centre of the whole of the British Isles and Ireland. He came to this conclusion after noticing the site lies upon the Dreswick Point to Point of Ayre axis and close to the St Patrick's Isle to Clay Head axis (see Fig. 31).

Today, the old Tynwald site resembles an old sheep pen with a low drystone wall enclosing a mound. But according to Michell, it was the original meeting place of royal assemblies until Tynwald Hill at St John's replaced it.[21]

The 5 July is a public holiday on the Isle of Man and we awoke that morning to an island readying itself for the historic event and pageantry that is Tynwald Day. Gone were the cloudy skies that shadowed us during the last couple of days, the sun now illuminating the landscape and warming the moods of the swarms of visitors that were now making their way to the village of St John's. This is the most important day of the year for locals and is not to be missed. It has taken place since the Vikings established their open-air law court at the mound, which happens to lie over the major fault line that follows the Central Valley.

In an article called *Tynwald, Symbol of an Ancient Kingdom* published in the official Tynwald Day magazine in 1986, David Craine writes that wherever the Norse invaders settled they brought with them the Icelandic principle of creating an open-air assembly place for freemen: 'where the old laws were recited, new laws submitted for approval, judgment given on lawbreakers and punishment immediately following.'[22] However, Michell states that these men of the North adopted some of the existing laws and traditions of the Celtic Manx, including their custom of kingship long after it was abolished in Norway, the Icelanders having abandoned theirs in 1800.

The original Nordic name for a place of assembly was *Alþingi* or *Al-thing* meaning 'assembly fields' or 'parliament plains.' The word Tynwald derives from the Norse *Ting-Völlr* meaning 'field of the thing'. Interestingly, Al-thing reminded us of Alspath, the old name for Meriden, the proposed centre of England. A tiered Ting Mound also exists in Langdale in Cumbria at the foot of Wrynose Pass, which is similar but less grand than the Manx Tynwald Hill. It was located at the heart of the Lake District next to a Roman road, which made it accessible from all directions.

As we sat outside a pub overlooking the historic mound, we could see the vast array of tents and stalls covering the large green behind the church already filling up with people arriving from the makeshift car parks in the surrounding fields. The weather continued to stay warm and sunny, and soon the welcoming sound of a brass band filled the air along with a commentator announcing the day's events over the loudspeakers. A group of people arrived and sat at the table next to us dressed as Vikings with horned helmets and plastic replica weapons and ordered coffee. The event was truly a unique spectacle with a great carnival atmosphere.

According to the *Prehistoric Sites in the Isle of Man*, the settlement of St John's is much older than the time of the Vikings and some believe that the mound dates to the Bronze Age and is surrounded by an earthen ditch and bank.[23] It may have been a gathering place for the island's ancient tribes where new kings were inaugurated, with perhaps a sanctified stone like the Lia Fáil at Tara or the Stone of Destiny of Scone standing on top of the mound. It was the custom for the rulers to stand on mounds with their heir apparent, known as the Tanist, presented for the approval of the gathered assembly – tanistry was a Gaelic system for passing on titles and lands. This custom continued on the Isle of Man until 1392, when Sir William le Scrope (1350–99), First Earl of Wiltshire and King of Mann, stood on the hill with his son Stephen.

The Lord of Mann, or their representative, still oversees the Tynwald ceremony – the present Lord being King Charles III, having inherited the title from his mother Queen Elizabeth II. After a church service, the court members make their way along the processional way between St John's Chapel and the mound, led by the scarlet uniformed figure of the sword-bearer carrying the Sword of State displaying the Manx triskelion. The sword was supposedly made for Sir John Stanley II (*c.* 1386–1437), whose father was granted the tenure of the Isle of Man by Henry IV.

In the past, the majority of the Lords of Mann that presided over the ceremony were British monarchs or aristocrats who were not resident on the island, namely the Duke of Atholl in 1736 who lived at the centre of Scotland. Thirty years later, he sold the Lordship of Mann to the British Crown, and due to the upheaval that followed there was no Tynwald ceremony for five years, resuming in 1770. George VI was the next notable Lord of Mann, who presided here in 1946, as did Elizabeth II in 1979 during the millennial anniversary of Tynwald's establishment and again in 2003; on two occasions she allowed her sons the Prince of Wales and Prince Edward to represent her.

The traditional Tynwald Fair, held alongside the pageantry, has numerous craft and food stalls, live music, dance displays, heritage exhibitions and of course fireworks. As more and more people gathered around the mound and causeway leading to the church, we realised that the religious service attended by all the dignitaries in St John's Chapel would soon be ending. Although the present church was built in 1849, this site has seen many temples of worship over the centuries. The structure is made from Isle of Man crystalline granite, having been built over an ancient keeill and a shrine dedicated to the Norse god Thor; excavations found several burials of Viking warriors in the vicinity.

In the porch is an old stone cross inscribed with ogham script. Having a reputation of being a sacred isle of the Druids, we wondered whether a stone circle or a grove once existed here. Numerous churches around Britain and Ireland are built over ancient pagan sites including circular ceremonial henges and stone circles.

Prehistoric burials lie scattered around the village including the remains of a Neolithic chambered tomb called the Ballaharra Stones opposite St John's Chapel dating to 2300 BCE, one of only ten known Neolithic tombs to have survived on the Isle of Man. Its remaining four stones were re-erected here as part of a garden ornament within a small manicured park. A post on the *Modern Antiquarian* website suggests that one of the stones 'was possibly cupmarked', which we failed to notice.[24] However, many chambered cairns throughout the British Isles have cup and ring-marked stones, so this observation may well be correct. The stones originally came from the Ballaharra Sandpits about a kilometre away along the Central Valley towards Peel.

Another group of ancient stones belonging to a Bronze Age burial mound called the Giant's Grave lies in a bank about 27 m to the West of Tynwald Hill next to the road to Tynwald Mills. They were exposed during road building that cut right through the site, originally having been covered by a circular mound of Earth.

Perhaps summer solstice festivals were celebrated at St John's by the early pagans when fires were lit in celebration of the sun god Lugh and the old sea-god Manannan, the Norse kings seeing it as a perfect place for their midsummer parliaments. Even today, the laying of rushes on the processional way between the mound and the church is a survival of the old Celtic midsummer tradition when people offered bundles of green bent grass to their gods.

Two important hills overlook Tynwald Mound – to the east is the sphinx-like Greeba Mountain that commands the pass through the Central Valley, and to the immediate south is the high hill peak of Slieau Whallian, also called 'Witches Hill', which has a grisly tale associated with the punishment of witches.

We made our way towards the mound to find a good spot to view the procession but soon found ourselves surrounded by more Vikings and kilted Scottish Highlanders, just two of the many nationalities represented here today whose ancestors have had links to the island in the past. From the 1820s, many Manx families left for the colonies during a time when English barons subjected them to crippling taxes,

The Tynwald ceremony

leaving many of Mann's inhabitants destitute, forcing them off the island and abandoning their culture and traditions. Many more moved away after the enclosure of the common land in the 1860s, which continued up until the early 20th century. David Craine's article also mentions the diary entry of crofter Thomas Kelly, who emigrated to America in 1827. Kelly wrote: 'This morning, before daylight, I stole away to St John's, for to see one last time the ancient ceremonies on Tynwald Hill, and secretly to take from its lowest round, one little handful of that earth which has seen and heard more history than any other spot on the island.'[25]

Soon we could see the feathered hat of the Lieutenant-Governor bobbing towards us as he walked down the processional way followed

The Tynwald Avenue ceremonially linking the Tynwald Mound with St John's Chapel

by various members of the State and Church. As he made his way to the top tier to sit on a throne-like chair, his entourage took their seats on the lower terraces below him. According to the mound's information board, the earliest written account of the Tynwald ceremony was in 1471 – 'the King of Mann (as the Lieutenant-Governor still does) sits in royal state on the top of Tynwald Hill, facing East, his sword held point upright before him.'

They had been processing along the joining causeway between the chapel and the mound since 11am and we noticed, with all the dignitaries settled and ready for the proceedings to begin, that it was precisely noon, when the sun on midsummer's day is at its highest zenith. How appropriate that at this powerful time of the year the ruler of the Isle of Man, the symbolic sun god, proclaims his authority over his land and people as has been the practice here for over a thousand years.

We were curious to hear as part of the ceremony the words 'fence the Court' directed by the Lieutenant-Governor. The full Declaration goes as follows: 'I fence this Court of Tynwald in the name of our most gracious Sovereign Lady the Queen. I charge that no person do quarrel, brawl or make any disturbance and that all persons do answer to their names when called. I charge this audience to witness this Court is fenced,' which is then said twice more. We felt it was a way of placing protection around the hill before parliament commences. Of course, today, the words would reflect the nation's new sovereign, Charles III.

After the ceremony when all the dignitaries and islanders had dispersed, we stood next to the mound and after calling upon Mann's spirit guardians and elementals, we visualised it shrouded in healing energy, sending light, love, unity, balance and harmony from this point to all the navel sites of the British Isles and Ireland. We then spent the rest of the day browsing the many craft tents and sampling the delights from the various food stalls. Of particular interest to us was a tent featuring written studies of the island's rich history, geology and folklore, which enabled us to gather a great deal of fascinating information for our research.

We returned the following day and dowsed the dragon energy currents, first detected flowing through St Patrick's Isle, connecting

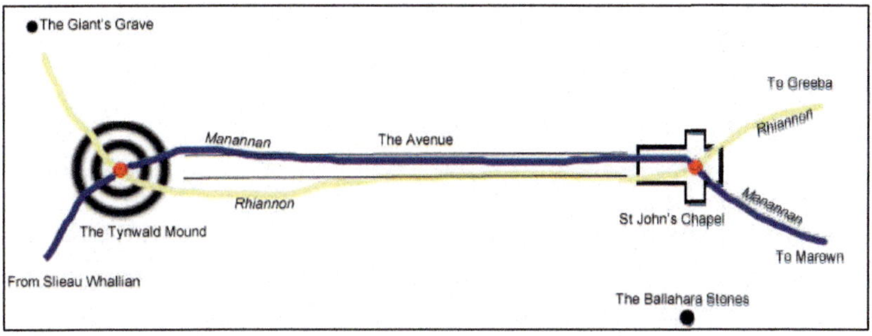

Figure 33. The dragon lines at Tynwald, St John's

with Tynwald Hill. We found the male and female lines crossing or forming a node on its summit, before flowing eastwards side by side along the processional way, reminiscent of a sacred marriage. They cross again inside St John's Chapel just before the high altar, where members of the island's parliament sit during the Tynwald Day service (see Fig. 33). The discovery of these two node points, one at the mound and the other at the church is quite remarkable and energetically linked to the ancient Tynwald ceremony.

The Old Royal Road and Tynwald

After honouring Tynwald Hill at St John's, we felt compelled to visit the other Tynwald site north of St Luke's Church at Baldwin, which Michell believes was the original assembly place marking the present omphalos of the Isle of Man and the sacred navel of the British Isles and Ireland.[26]

St Luke's Church stands directly on a crossing of the axis that links Dreswick Point with the Point of Ayre and the St Patrick's Isle to Clay Head axis. Therefore, it is quite possible that the keeill upon which St Luke's stands and the Old Tynwald site were at one time honoured as marking the centre of the island. Parking alongside St Luke's Church to access the Old Tynwald site, we decided to have a look around the churchyard. On the east gable over the main entrance to the church, we noticed a square block of sandstone carved with a cross, said to be from the old Keeill Abban that once stood on this site. According to an old church guide by T. S. J. Cowell, a local farmer removed the stone in the 1830s along with other stones from the keeill to use in the building of a new cowshed. After it was completed, the farmer started to experience ill luck. All his animals became sick and died, and when his wife fell ill he decided that the sandstone block should be returned to the church. He later helped to build the new church that you see today.

From the church, we headed north along a stony track, part of the Millennium Way, until we noticed a gate on the left. Passing through the narrow opening, we approached the Old Tynwald site which had a dry-stone wall encircling a slight elevation. The location commands glorious views across this picturesque but extremely remote part of the island. We sat down inside the walls of the mound to connect with the site, the central Carraghan Mountain behind us and Snaefell, Mann's holy mountain to the east, placing our sacred stones at various positions around us. We visualised the Millennium Way from Sky Hill bathed in a beautiful cleansing light passing through to the great crossroads at Crosby where it meets the central valley fault. From there, we sent the light to the Tynwald site at St John's, the sacred isle of St Patrick's and Douglas, the capital.

Despite the Old Tynwald's notoriety as an omphalos, there is no actual evidence of its former importance. Its earlier name was Killabane although it is also known locally as Cronk Keeill Abban, 'cronk' meaning hill. The earliest reference to a court or assembly site here is in 1429 although its exact location is unknown and the present circular dry-stone enclosure near the church was constructed in 1929 in commemoration of the original Tynwald. Some believe that the original assembly place was a tumulus constructed for ritual purposes or as a burial. Local history states that parishioners of Braddan would every year walk around the site giving three cheers. The mound may

Tynwald Monument built in 1929, Baldwin

have served as a regional Tynwald assembly for the southern sheadings of Garff, Middle and Rushen.[27] However, some believe another possible location for this larger mound is further north along the Millennium Way where the road seems to divert around an invisible feature in the landscape aligned with the ancient track.

Michell maintains that the Old Tynwald site close to St Luke's was the true ritual centre of the island because King Orry ceremonially processed to this point along the old road, now the Millennium Way, upon becoming the new ruler of Mann: 'the newly arrived king followed the same route to the centre of the realm. He ascended the Sky Hill [near Ramsey] and followed the old Royal Road, which in legend he identified as the Milky Way, which leads straight to the Keeill Abban [site of St Luke's Church] sacred sanctuary … This means it was a sacred path, a processional and pilgrimage road leading to the "pole star" of a central sanctuary, the omphalos of the Isle of Man.'[28]

The old royal road was re-opened in 1979 as the Millennium Way after it was pieced together from fragments of ancient paths from Ramsey to Castletown to celebrate a thousand years of independent government from England. The road was first recorded in the *Chronicle of the Kings of Mann and the Isles* (1261–62) by the monks of Rushen Abbey at Castletown. In this document, the old Royal Road is called 'Via Regia'.[29]

By walking these celestial pathways, pilgrims believed they were close to the gods or their ancient ancestors, and partaking in a heavenly journey among the stars to the very source of creation. The foundation of the old Royal Road and ancient mound on the Isle of Man that hosted the royal courts possibly stretches back before the time of the Norse kings, perhaps constructed by the same race who created Uisneach in Ireland as a royal centre.

Interestingly, other cultures have sacred roads associated with the Milky Way. In an article called *In Heaven as on Earth, Royal Roads and the Milky Way,* Penny Drayton cites Jacob Grim who writes that Watling Street, one of the oldest roads in England, reflects the pathways of the stars. The Welsh call it *Hynt St Ialm* meaning 'St James' Way' and *Heol y gwynt*, 'the way of the wind.' Similarly in Spain there is 'the road to St Iago' or as we know it today the Camino de Santiago, an ancient and popular pilgrimage route to St James' Shrine at Santiago de Compostela; Compostela, derives from campus stellae meaning 'field of the star'.[30]

William Cubbon, one of the most respected Manx historians, says that *Raad Mooar Ree Gorree,* which means 'the great road of Orry', refers to the great north-south line of stars that forms the Milky Way. This is because when Orry arrived on Mann at Lhen Beach [on the Land's End to Duncansby Head line] on a bright starry night, those that had gathered on the shore to greet him asked him where he had come from, and he pointed up to the Milky Way as his home.[31] However, the author does not claim that Orry was ever associated with the Old Tynwald site near Keeill Abban. We soon discovered that the old Tynwald site and Tynwald Hill at St John's were two of many that once existed around the island.

The Manx National Heritage website says there are four known Viking assembly sites or Tynwald Hills – St John's near Peel, Castle Rushen in Castleton, Kirk Michael near Ballaugh and Keeill Abban near Baldwin.[32] I believe these Tynwald mounds represented the old parliaments for each of the four regions, North, South, East and West.

Further research revealed that the coastline of Mann was altered when the flooded region at the North of the island was drained and the land reclaimed. The land beyond Ballaugh, Sulby and Churchtown was almost at sea level and covered with lakes and bog at the time of the Viking invasions – probably flooded by the cataclysms that changed the coast lines of Northern Ireland in 1159 BCE. Therefore, when King Orry arrived, the village of Crosby marked the geographical centre of the island until the draining of the lakes in the north created a new omphalos in the area north of St Luke's Church, possibly close to the Tynwald memorial.

The Royal Crossroads

The Millennium Way, the old Royal Road from Sky Hill, meets the east-west Central Valley Way, between Peel and Douglas, near the village of Crosby, the name meaning 'town of the cross or crossing' (see Fig. 34). The modern Heritage Trail that runs parallel to the central valley follows the disused narrow-gauge railway line from Douglas to Peel, which was closed in 1968. However, remnants of the original royal route still follow the contours of the surrounding hills, avoiding the waterlogged valley floor, and passing through the northern boundaries of Crosby near Keeill Vreeshey.

Vreeshey is the Manx word for Bride or Brigid and just to the south of the keeill is a hidden holy well, which was still in use in the 20th century, when people from all over the island came to receive its healing properties. According to one local, the field in which the keeill and holy well are located was called 'the Breesh', possibly a corruption of 'Breeshey', also derived from Brigid or Bride.

When travelling to the various centres of Ireland, Scotland and Wales, we discovered that each of their centres has a powerful and vital connection with the ancient fire goddess Bride or Brigid, who nurtures the land at its navel. So, it was no surprise to us that at the very centre of the combined lands of Britain and Ireland, she also features strongly. According to Manx tradition, St Brigid travelled from Ireland to the Isle of Man with three virgins to receive the veil from Bishop Maughold, similar to the legend at Uisneach where she received the veil from St Patrick.

The Isle of Man has many sites associated with Bride or Brigid and two of them lie close to the central valley fault. In the north of the island, St Brigid founded a monastic site and a church at the village of Bride, formerly known as Kirkbride; in fact, the whole region is named after her. In *Brigid: Goddess, Druidess, Saint*, the author Brian Wright, writing of the Isle of Man, mentions that:

> 'In the past St Brigid, known as St Vreeshey in Manx Gaelic, was strongly venerated, with seven ancient Keeills or chapels, a nunnery and a parish church along with the parish of Kirkbride in the northern part of the island. There are three wells dedicated to St Brigid and these are found in the parishes of Braddan, Bride and Patrick. In Manx Bride's feast day is known as Laa'l Breeshey and on that day, the lady of the house placed rushes by the hearth as a bed for the saint, then called out, "Bride, Bride, come to my house, come to my house tonight. Open the door for Bride and let Bride come in."'[33]

Although today ugly metal railings surround the keeill and only rubble remains of the low walls, it is probably one of the best preserved on the island. Over the years, antiquarian societies and local newspaper reports have mentioned this site as being the most frequently visited sacred place on the island and people travelled here from many parts to be healed.

Marking this possible national omphalos was a standing stone, now destroyed, described in Shaw's 1871 *Tourist's Picturesque Guide to the Isle of Man* as standing by the wall of the chapel, 'one of several stones inscribed with various designs and inscriptions.'[34] Shaw shows the standing stone as having two concentric circles or cup and ring marks, similar to many stones found all over the north of England and Scotland at ceremonial sites dating from the Neolithic to Early Bronze Age periods. This led us to believe that perhaps this stone was a remnant of a prehistoric sacred enclosure, burial mound or stone circle. Curiously, a 7th-century cross was also recorded here, and like the cup and ring marked megalith, also disappeared almost as if there was a deliberate attempt to diminish the importance of this site.

We could find no evidence of the sacred holy well mentioned as existing just south of Keeill Vreeshey until Caroline located it in a nearby hedge using her dowsing rods. As we both peered down towards where the rods were pointing, we could just make out the faint sound of trickling water. With our hands and boots, we peeled back the bramble and vegetation to reveal traces of a stone-lined well, which the farmer has since used to pipe water to a nearby water trough for his livestock.

We sensed that the well and the keeill needed to be reconnected with each other, so instinctively we placed our healing stones at the well and the site of the keeill's old high altar and visualised a line of divine light connecting the two sites through the healing stones. We then said a blessing to Bride at this central focal point of the island and called in the ancestors of Mann to send honouring and light into this once magical place of the goddess and special sanctuary of

Keeill Vreeshey

healing. Like in Ireland, Scotland and Wales, we find a sanctuary of Bride, the goddess of fire, creativity and healing close to a crossroads of ancient routes at the centre of a nation, whose role here is to tend and nurture the navel of Britain and Ireland.

Masculine energy has dominated the island as far back as the Norse invasions, celebrated through the honouring and recognition of the mighty and legendary King Orry. Today, this warrior energy is epitomised in the TT race, a new focus of worship here for thousands of devotees from all over the world.

The longest north-south line through Britain, from Land's End to Duncansby Head discovered by John Michell, also passes through

Crosby and the old parish church of Marown dedicated to St Runius, south of the village (see Fig. 34). The axis first enters Mann in the far southeast through the sacred St Michael's Isle on the Langness Peninsular. This island, like St Patrick's Isle, has a causeway and a sanctity reminiscent of St Michael's Mount in Cornwall and Mont Saint Michel in Brittany. Like these sacred isles, St Michael's Isle has an ancient religious sanctuary in the form of the now ruined 11th century Celtic-Norse St Michael's Chapel, built over the site of a keeill dating to the earliest period of Celtic Christian settlement. This important sacred sanctuary was the scene of two great battles between England, Scotland and the Manx when fighting for control of the island in 1250 and 1275. The Manx won the first battle, but 25 years later they surrendered their island to the Scots.

The line then passes close to the famous Fairy Bridge, situated on the A5 between Rushen and Douglas, which has a custom whereby anybody crossing must first greet the fairies before continuing their journey; otherwise, bad luck may befall them. This superstition probably stems from the bridge's location on the boundary of nearby Rushen Abbey. It was the tradition long ago to cross oneself at the sight of a crucifix marking a boundary of monastic land. The line leaves the island through the old airfield at Jurby and Lhen Beach on the northwest coast, where the great King Orry is said to have landed on his journey from the stars.

Greeba and the Sleeping Warriors

Only a mile west of Keeill Vreeshey within this omphalos landscape is Greeba Castle nestling at the base of Greeba Mountain. The castle is a grand Victorian villa that was for a time the home of Sir Thomas Henry Hall Caine (1853–1931), the famous Victorian novelist and playwright who at one time acted as secretary to the Pre-Raphaelite artist Dante Gabriel Rossetti. On the grounds of the castle is a house called Greeba Towers built upon an earthen mound called *Cronk ny Bingagh*. Cubbon explains its meaning as 'hill of the jury' and believes the hill or mound was an important 'place of assembly' in Celtic times. Greeba or Gnebe is derived from the Scandinavian *gnipa* meaning 'peak', and Cubbins further states: 'However much we study Greeba Mountain, its Sphinx-like riddles defy a solution. It has a weird mystery that no other place on the island possesses.'[35] One local man told us of a Manx legend that places the mountain as the abode of Merlin, the magician associated with King Arthur.

On the slopes of Greeba Mountain is a promontory of rocks shown on the map as *Gob ny Creg*, also known as St Patrick's Chair; confusingly, another monument by that name is not far away on the south side of the valley near Old Marown Church of St Runius. According to Cubbon, Gob ny Creg consists of a huge outcrop of rock, with spots of quartz, fashioned by man in the past like a seat. Before the dense tree growth that surrounds it today, it would have overlooked the low-lying fields around the ruined church of St Trinian's below, a most impressive outlook in days gone by. It lies close to a cave called *Garey Feeyney*, which has steps leading up to a grassy platform above. The name means 'garden of the Feni', a place where the Feni or Fianna once resided, a band of early Celtic legendary warriors whose leader was Fin or Finn MacCool. Fin was a hero warrior associated with the Irish Celts and the various adventures and stories of valour surrounding him and his band of nine warriors known as the Fianna are very similar to those of King Arthur and his Knights. Richard Crowhurst in *The Search for Answers on the Isle of Man* mentions a curious local legend that Merlin used a cave on Greeba Mountain.[36]

Like Arthur, Fin and his warriors lie sleeping in many caves in Ireland and Scotland, only to wake when their country is in its greatest hour of need. Inland caves are rare on the Isle of Man and so this grotto, set in the Central Valley, would have been considered a very special place indeed. Although all mention of it has been lost, Cubbon refers to the remains of a stone wall that once protected its artificially carved entrance, with flooring inside made of large slate.[37]

We located the footpath leading to the summit of Greeba Mountain off the main A1 close to the entrance to Greeba Castle. We followed the track through woodland called the King's Plantation until we spotted a metal gate on the left just after a sharp bend. Beyond the gate, another path led us deeper into the woods. After a few metres, we looked up towards the steep bank and there, just peeping out of the leafy undergrowth, was a rock plateau. After clambering further up the steep bank, we soon realised that we had found Gob ny Creg, although the cave was nowhere in sight. The lush woodland now obscures the panoramic view observed by the Druids in the distant past as they sat on the chair to observe the stars or moon as it appeared on the southern horizon.

The sunken track to the stone and cave seemed ancient, one of those old hollow-ways that may date from the Iron Age or even earlier. As I sat on Gob ny Creg I could feel the power radiating from the crystalline structure of the rock as it surged through my body, the energy raising me to a higher state of consciousness. It reminded us of similar outcrops of rock revered by the ancient peoples of the area such as St Cuthbert's Cave in Northumberland, an ancient place of initiation Christianised by the incoming missionaries from Iona.

In a field below we find the roofless 14th-century chapel of St Trinian's. Originally, the church was dedicated to the 4th-century Scottish St Ninian, later changed to Trinian. It too stands on the site of a keeill with its ancient burial ground dating from the 6th to 10th century called Keeill Brisht meaning 'broken church'.

The atmospheric ruin is the scene of one of Mann's most famous legends concerning a fierce goblin-like creature called a buggane that lived on Greeba. One night, having disliked the sound of ringing bells, he ripped off the roof of the newly built church, leaving the locals puzzled the next day. A new roof was promptly constructed, but yet again, they came the following morning to find it removed. After the

St Trinian's Church, Greeba

roof was replaced a third time, Timothy the tailor decided to lock himself inside the church overnight to find out who was behind this wanton destruction to prove there was nothing to fear. Later that night, the buggane emerged through a gaping hole in the floor and terrorised the man before chasing him to nearby Old Marown Church. Luckily for the tailor, the sanctity of this ancient building saved him, for the terrorising goblin found that he could not cross its holy bounds, and so it ripped off his own head and threw it at the frightened man, where it exploded among the gravestones.

This is reminiscent of the many stories of plasma light ball phenomena, their often erratic and curious behaviour witnessed by people all over the world throughout the ages. One incident includes a sighting on the night of 21 October 1638, when a great storm hit the

Figure 34. The ancient tracks of Mann crossing at Crosby

Dartmoor village of Widecombe-in-the-Moor in Devon. Witnesses described an 8-ft (2.4 m) ball of fire entering the church and causing severe damage. The fiery globe then divided into two, one exiting through a window by smashing the glass, and the other imploded, leaving the church with a foul sulphurous odour and dark, thick smoke. Because of the smell of sulphur, superstitious locals believed the 'devil' had entered the church – this was later blamed on two people playing cards in the pews during the sermon.[38]

Curiously, some of the capitals of St Trinian's Church show ugly carved human heads, perhaps placed there to frighten or commemorate the buggane! There are also several incised stone cross-slabs from the 10th to the 11th century. The church and lands were once the property of the Priory of Whithorn in Galloway founded by St Ninian, hence its dedication here.

St Runius' Church

A short distance south of Crosby village is the ancient parish church of Marown dedicated to St Runius representing Mann's symbolic religious centre at the omphalos, similar to Clonmacnoise and Strata Florida Abbey. Here we find ancient foundations of an early chapel or keeill where three of the island's most important Celtic Christian bishops lie buried. Marown is the only parish that has borders not connected with the coast, making it the only central ward on the island, Mann's middle province. St Runius still has its original medieval stonework, unlike the majority of Manx churches that were heavily restored in Victorian times. The sanctity of this place is revealed through the existence of some of the finest early Christian crosses on the island, many dating from the 7th century. Stepping inside you feel as though you have entered the 18th century, the interior having changed very little in the last 300 years.

The church lies at the centre of Great Britain's main axis from Land's End to Duncansby Head, and the Millennium Way or old Royal Road passes alongside it on its way to Castletown (see Fig. 34). Major crossroads seem to be a prominent feature of this area of Crosby as an ancient east-west track called the 'Rocky Road' intersects here.

As we entered the enchanted graveyard with its wonderful old trees and wild flowers, we sensed it had been the site of an ancient ceremonial enclosure, perhaps part of a much larger ceremonial complex at the centre of the island.

The first recorded vicar at St Runius' Church dates back to 1187, and locals still attend services here. The three island bishops buried here are an indication of the reverence attached to this important central sanctuary. At the altar, we lit a candle and said a blessing in honour of the mother goddess Bride or Vreeshey.

Just south of the church we visited St Patrick's Chair, a muddle of old stones in the middle of a field with the feel of a megalithic site, later adapted by early Christian missionaries. The original monument

St Runius' Church, Marown

had five granite standing stones, but only three remain with smaller boulders piled up around them. Two of the stones are etched with crude Christian crosses, perhaps carved when St Patrick himself came here in the 5th century to bless the pagan stones and curtail their ancient power. Long before the stone keeills were built, conversions by Christian missionaries were performed at roadside crosses, so perhaps this was one of their outdoor preaching sites or moot hills.

The stones of St Patrick's Chair stand on a mound, so they likely date from at least the Bronze Age. Cubbon also refers to a story that in the 19th century, locals revered this place as a healing shrine.[39] At the southern end of the field is a holy well called Chibber y Chairn or 'well of the chair', also known as St Ronan's Well. We could see no obvious signs of this holy spring so again used our dowsing skills to locate it in the southeast corner of the field.

Like Vreeshey's Well just north of Crosby, it too was hidden from sight, and wire fencing placed right across the face of the well prevented us from getting close to it. After the well-blessing, we managed to drop one of our white quartz healing stones into its waters, hearing a loud 'plop'. We visualised healing light pouring through this neglected and desecrated site, honouring its protective spirit guardian. With that, the shrill and haunting sound of a curlew pierced the silence as if to acknowledge our ceremony.

As we walked back to St Patrick's Chair, we noticed on the northern horizon that the central hills in the distance form a perfect reclining feminine-shaped figure. Standing at the monument, we could see the high conical-shaped peaks of Carraghan and Beinn-y-Phott, also known as Penny Pot, resembling female breasts, with Injebreck Hill forming a swollen belly symbolic of the procreation and fertility powers of Mother Earth. In Ireland, the two prominent peaks of the Paps of Anu were also celebrated as a place of the old pagan goddess, as were Scotland's Paps of Jura and the Maiden Paps near Hawick. It seemed apt that at the centre of Britain and Ireland lies the majestic landscape figure of the reclining mother goddess, perhaps it is Bride herself looking up towards the heavens and the source of all creation.

We were delighted to see that the old Royal Road or Millennium Way passes straight between these two breast-shaped hills, symbolic of a twin-peaked world mountain of the British Isles. As mentioned in the previous chapter, the circumference of the ring of Bega or Bride, centred on St Bees Priory, also passes between Carraghan and Penny Pot, the 'Paps of Mann.'

I also noticed that a stretch of straight road from the old St Runius church aligns precisely to a gap between the 'Paps of Mann' on a compass heading 36.8 degrees east of North. This aligned road is significant, for it points directly to the summit of Snaefell Mountain beyond. I later checked this direction with my Stellarium computer program and found it to be where the moon would rise at its widest arc on a 'major standstill' during the Bronze and Iron Ages. Therefore, viewed from St Runius' Church, the moon at the standstill would rise out from between the breasts of the goddess. Archaeologist Alexander Thom was the first to introduce the term 'lunar standstill.'

This unusual extreme movement of the moon is similar to the sun's varying declination during the summer and winter solstices – solstice meaning 'sun standstill', although in neither case do these celestial bodies stand still, but appear to rise and set in the same place for three days.[40] Unlike the sun, which reaches its most northerly rising in June and most southerly in December, the lunar standstills follow an 18.6-

year cycle, with the moon's 'major standstill' reaching its highest and most northerly rising in the east and most northerly setting in the west. The 'minor lunar standstill' indicates its least northerly rising and most southerly setting.

St Patrick's Chair aligned to the central peaks of Carraghan and Beinn-y-Phott

The Neolithic and Bronze Age Celts, who were seemingly obsessed with cosmology, must have seen this event as most auspicious and perhaps aligned their stone monuments towards this lunar standstill. Later I discovered a perfectly straight alignment to this major standstill that includes St Patrick's Chair, St Runius' Church, the centre of Crosby and Bride's shrine at Keeill Vreeshey.

Also, in this omphalos landscape and a short walk from the crossroads at Crosby is a standing stone mentioned by Cubbon near Glen Vine. In a narrow lane, we came across the remarkable 2-m-tall white carved standing stone called the 'White Lady of Ballafreer'. Cubbon wrote:

‘It has been an object of reverence, of wonderment, of admonition and of fear for many centuries. In view of the fact that Ballafreer was reckoned holy ground – the genesis of the name is “the home of the brethren” – it may have had a blessed significance, there was certainly a belief that it shed especial protection over women folk .... A girl about to be wed would fill her mouth with the water from Chibbyr Pherick, “St Patrick’s Well,” which flowed only a few yards away. She would then walk three times around the pillar, and this must be done jesh-wise or sun-wise, and then swallow the sacred water, saying in Manx: Ayns yn Ennym Yee, as y Vac, as y Spyrryd Noo, “In the Name of the Father the Son and the Holy Ghost.” Child-bearing women also did this ritual. And, in order to be effective, it must be performed before sun rising.’[41]

The White Lady of Ballafreer

This extraordinary 'goddess' stone also stands precisely on the Dreswick Point to Point of Ayre axis which connects the site with St Luke's Church, the old Tynwald site and St Bridget's Church and its holy well in the parish of Bride in the north of the island.

Today, locals hardly give the standing stone a second glance, except for one old gentleman, born on the island, who now lives near the monument. He informed us that he often tends to the stone, washing it down, repainting it white and pruning the hedge. Believing the stone to be made of white quartz, we gave him a quizzical look, at which he continued, 'It is well known that stones are painted white to imbue them with an air of holiness.' We could imagine it gleaming as the rays of the full moon cast themselves upon it. He then announced that there is a tradition that this white 'lady' has been here for 6,000 years.

As we examined the stone more closely, we wandered whether the white paint was obscuring an ancient megalith. Caroline then suddenly announced that from a certain angle, the head and long neck looked more phallic-like in shape and further offered, 'perhaps the women encircling and touching the phallic part of the stone mentioned by Cubbin were taking part in some sort of fertility ritual, believing that the energy of the stone and the water from the nearby holy well would enable them to be successful in conceiving a child.' The old man nodded his head: 'Maybe that is why the locals believe it was erected there to a god.' Was it Manannan Mac Lir we wondered? 'I don't know about that', the man continued, 'but I remember when people placed a hat on it similar to Napoleon's.' We both looked at each other with the thought that this monument was getting more intriguing by the minute!

Caroline dowsed around the stone to see if she could detect an energy line at the stone and instantly questioned why a male energy current was flowing through the White Lady of Ballafreer. I replied, 'Perhaps you are right and that this stone is not a "lady" but a male "fertility" stone!'

The old well dedicated to St Patrick also mentioned by Cubbin was reputedly located in a field just a few metres to the south of the stone, which is now completely waterlogged, indicating that the holy spring has long since been abandoned, its waters having spewed across the field, creating an area of marshland and bog.

The old man mentioned another object of devotion lying in a field nearby, called *Lhiabbee Pherick* or St Patrick's Bed, also said to have certain magical powers. Later we spotted the landowner walking across the yard of Ballafreer Farm and decided to approach him to ask permission to access his land to search for St Patrick's Bed. He was friendly and chatty and informed us that an inscribed stone lies by a stream reached via a footpath just beyond the White Lady. Unfortunately, despite owning the land he knew little of the history of Ballafreer, its monuments or St Patrick's Keeill located at the back of his garden in a small copse dating to the 7th century.

After thanking him for his help, we followed the footpath sign through a small copse, its floor gloriously shrouded in wild garlic and bluebells, to a field. Just to the left we passed through a gate, and there next to a small trickling brook was a huge megalith lying flat on the ground, said to have been Christianised by St Patrick when passing through this area. Gorse had partly obscured the stone, but with a little pressure from our boots we managed to move it away to reveal the inscription on the stone – 'Lhiabbee Pherick' and underneath 'St Patrick's Bed'.

Cubbon quotes from a Kirk Marown document called *The Book of Ballafreer* under the subheading 'Tradition', written c. 1760 by the Revd John Kewley:

> 'As Saint Patrick passed through the flat of our farm east side of the Haggard, it is said that a briar caught hold of his foot, so that he was a little passionate and said, Let not this field produce any kind of grain that will make a man drunk; that he may be sober to avoid thy briars and to take care to keep his feet from thy dented prickles. This was about the year 444. He at that time was going with his disciple Saint German to appoint a place to build a chapel therein: which said chapel was built there, and the ruins of it remains to this day.'[42]

Being remorseful for his show of 'passion', Patrick repented and spent the night, recumbent on this slab, with a white quartz rock for his pillow. Like St Patrick, I lay down on the stone, but unfortunately, the quartz stone was too far away to make a successful pillow.

In a neighbouring field close to the farm and surrounded by trees are the low earthworks of St Patrick's Keeill. Approaching it with our dowsing rods, we discovered the same male energy line detected at the nearby Ballafreer stone passing through the remains of this old stone structure. Just across the main road from the entrance to Ballafreer Farm is another keeill on the grounds of Glenlough Farm known as Cabbal Druiaght meaning 'Druid's chapel'.[43] I felt that the ancients might have used this place as a way of connecting with the Earth Mother and that Ballafreer, being close to the centre of the island, was once a very special place of sanctity. Perhaps St Patrick knew this too, having supplanted Christianity within what was once a huge prehistoric ceremonial complex at the former omphalos of Mann

St Patrick's Bed, Ballafreer

overlooked by the reclining landscape goddess imbuing the island with her life-giving force.

St Bridget's Church and Well

Mann's triskele is composed of three bent armoured legs with golden spurs, said to be 'running clockwise towards the sun', adopted in the 13th Century as the royal coat of arms, having been adapted from a motif on coins minted during the time of the 10th century Norse King Analaf Cuaran. Further research into the origins of the triskele led us to discover that the four-armed Bride cross was originally three-armed, consisting of three interlocking spirals around a central point and found throughout many ancient cultures of Europe right up to Celtic times. Some claim it was originally a symbol of the sun, 'the seat of power and life.' However, it may represent the triple aspect of the goddess whose ancient symbol is the spiral, seen in the famous megalithic tomb of Newgrange in Ireland. Therefore, Mann's emblem of the three bent armoured legs may be a masculine representation of the feminine triskele.

Remarkably, if you place the three-armed Bride cross over a map of the British Isles, its centre lies on the village of Bride within a northern region of the Isle of Man also called Bride, linking the omphalos sites of Scotland, England and Ireland.

With this in mind, we felt it important to visit this northern region of Mann with its St Bridget's Church and holy well. We believe that worshipping and honouring Bride, who nurtures the divine power within the land at the navel, is integral to inducing healing and spiritual harmony. We carried her blessing with us during our various adventures around the centres of the British Isles and Ireland, including her temple site and holy well at the base of the Hill of Uisneach.

St Bridget herself supposedly founded the church in the parish of Bride, formerly known as Kirkbride. This ancient church stands on the Dreswick Point to Point of Ayre axis, which connects it to the old Tynwald site, St Luke's Church and the White Lady of Ballafreer fertility stone near Crosby. The church nestles in a picturesque valley, opposite the quintessential village teashop. To the northeast is Ramsey Bay, which is now a marine nature reserve. Its beaches run continuously from Ramsey to the Point of Ayre where you can experience spectacular views of the Scottish and Cumbrian mountains. In the churchyard is a Viking cross and the 'Adam and Eve' stone. The water from nearby Chibbyr Vreeshey or Bride's Well was once used for the baptismal font in the church.

We arrived to find the church full of delightful floral arrangements as part of the island's annual Flower Festival. The Victorian church you see today replaced one built in 1200, next to a 6th-century keeill. However, despite the array of beautiful blooms, the stone crosses displayed there soon took our focus. One dated to the 10th century is known as the 'Thor Cross', discovered when the old church was demolished in 1869.

Thor is the Norse god of thunder and seafaring and it is thought that a figure of him is depicted on the cross, carrying the head of an ox as bait 'for his mortal enemy the sea serpent Jormungand.' On its reverse, he wrestles with the world serpent, which researchers Aya van Renterghem and Heidi Stoner, writing in *Viking Myths and Rituals on the Isle of Man*, suggest is the 'Midgardserpent who encircles the Earth.'[44]

This unique stone portrays omphalos mythology, perfectly representing this centre of centres and depicting the control of the serpent, similar to St George and St Michael. In Chinese mythology, only a hero with a pure heart can tame or destroy the dragon.

Alternatively, the dragon represents the dark force that creates a harsh lesson here on Earth for souls to experience to achieve enlightenment and a higher spiritual existence – a belief held by many ancient religions including Dualism of the Cathars and Buddhism. Perhaps the dragon is our demon that we have to slay for us to ascend to a higher vibrational world.

As we stood pondering on the concept of dragon or serpent slaying, we noticed a stained-glass window depicting St Bride, with the perpetual flame above her head symbolic of the perpetual flame of the heart that never dies. This tradition is also found in Ireland and introduced here by Irish settlers. Bride's keeill once stood in the churchyard under a weeping elm, at an important crossroads that took pilgrims to all parts of the island. St Bridget may have deliberately placed her church in the North of the island, as this direction represents the season of winter, her feast day being Imbolc on 1 February which marks the end of winter and the beginning of spring. There were once seven keeills on the island dedicated to the goddess Bride, including Keeill Vreeshey near Crosby and a chapel at the old Nunnery near Douglas.

Viking cross, St Bridget's Church, Bride

During a conversation with one of the guides in charge of the flower displays, we told her of our interest in the saint and asked if she knew of the whereabouts of a holy well called Chibbyr Vreeshey or Breeshey. She pointed towards the main road and told us to follow it in the direction of Ramsey, where we would find it next to the road by a sharp bend. We walked along the busy main road and soon, to our delight, encountered the old spring preserved within a well-house, its waters still ushering from the bank. Unfortunately, a locked metal gate decorated with the three-legged Manx symbol prevented us from getting any closer.

Bride is also the goddess of water, her instrument of healing. Holy wells and springs dedicated to Brigid, Bride or her Christianised counterpart Bridget can be found all over Britain and Ireland, many of them blessed on her feast day with the lighting of a candle.

Adapting a blessing in Lunaea Weatherstone's *Tending Brigid's Flame*, we lit a candle and said the following words:

> 'I bless this well in the name of the goddess Brigid
> May these waters be filled with power, light and grace.
> As with her holy well in Kildare, so shall it be
> in the waters of this land.
> May all who touch these waters be filled
> with healing for mind, body and spirit.
> May the waters of this well be filled with the
> blessings of the goddess Brigid.
> By the power of Earth, air, fire and water,
> I name this well Brigid's Well.
> May her loving energy bless and preserve us
> with her healing, protection and grace.
> As I will it, so shall it be!'[45]

We then honoured the spirit of Bride by throwing an Iona green stone through the bars into the well to ignite her light here once more.

As we turned to leave, we suddenly came face to face with a woman who exclaimed, 'Oh thank goodness, I thought I'd missed you!' It seems that having been told by the flower arrangers of our interest in the goddess Bride, she felt compelled to seek us out to let us know of another very important well that we needed to connect with. She explained that Bride was her favourite goddess and she showed us the pagan Brigid's Cross pendant necklace around her neck.

She then announced that there was another hidden well associated with her we should visit, now dedicated to St Ciaran of Clonmacnoise. Our eyes widened as she continued to say that it was located next to a keeill within a Bronze Age circular earthwork above Sulby Glen. Our eyes widened even more as we realised Sulby Glen was the location of our holiday cottage and were delighted that we had been sleeping within the energy of one of Bride's shrines. We were also thrilled at hearing of St Ciaran's connection with the Isle of Man as he had been so important to our journey around the centres of Ireland, Scotland and Cumbria.

Cross 92, Onchan Church

Before we said our goodbyes, she surprised us again with one more nugget of fascinating information. 'There is an ancient cross in a church near Douglas at a place called Kirk Onchan where a cross-slab depicts the earliest form of a Bride cross.' Indeed, when we visited the church there was a cross labelled 'Cross 92' showing the dragons of the Earth with the cross of duality. Halfway down the shaft is a carved image of Bride's staggered cross with spirals connecting each arm. This has to be an amalgamation of the Neolithic and the Phoenician/Viking culture, as spiral motifs such as the triple goddess spirals are depicted on Neolithic monuments all over Europe and the Mediterranean. Here we have the earliest amalgamation of the mother goddess and Celtic Christianity.

Kirk Onchan has a surprising number of the earliest known Celtic crosses, and according to the Heritage Centre in Douglas, there are hundreds more stored around the island.

The Sacred Well of Ciaran

Following the instructions to St Ciaran's Well or *Chibbyr Karrin*, we soon found ourselves in a field below the mountain of Snaefell, overlooking Tholt y Will in the Sulby Valley opposite Sulby reservoir. Here, at the end of our exploration of the island, we encountered the remains of St Ciaran's keeill and well located on land called the Corrody, a name derived from 'Corrony' which is a corruption of Ciaran. The field is known as *Cronk y Keeillee*, which translates as 'hill of the keeill', built over the remains of a Bronze Age burial site, remnants of which still survive. Having encountered St Ciaran at the centre of Ireland, Scotland and Cumbria, we believe he embodies the male aspect at sacred centres, while the goddess Bride symbolises the feminine.

As we approached the stone-covered well, we were disappointed to see it blocked with stones, a common practice by farmers to protect their livestock. We noticed on the map that opposite this site on the western side of the reservoir is Druidale, the place where a local man

St Ciaran's Well, Corrody

experienced hearing fairy music. All around this area are ancient cairns and hut circles, clearly a region once highly populated within the shadow of the great Snaefell Mountain.

Chibbyr Karrin, located below Snaefell, the central mountain of all Britain and Ireland, suggests that it once drew its water from deep within the skirt of the mountain, and therefore must have been an integral part of this sacred centre and an important place for healing. We placed our sacred stones here to help restore its healing power and to heal the wounds of Mann's past. We then uttered blessings from Bride at this central shrine.

We later met with a local researcher into Mann's sacred sites and he mentioned a peculiar tradition that, even in recent times, kings and queens of England have come to Mann to stand on a huge quartz rock called Creg Bedn ('White Rock') near the summit of Slieau Managh ('Monk's Mountain') to survey their entire domain of Scotland, Wales, England and Northern Ireland. He pointed to this rock on the map and, to our surprise, we noticed that our holiday cottage was situated on the lower slopes of this hill. The rock was also known to have healing powers and in the past sick people were taken there in the hope of a cure.

We returned to our delightful cottage to enjoy our last evening on the island and sat outside to watch the sunset. We discussed the goddess Bride's connection with many of Mann's centres particularly the discovery of the breast-shaped hills, an ancient central crossroads, the healing shrine of Keeill Vreeshey, and the Tynwald ritual sites. But, one question remained, which of these sites is the true navel of the Isle of Man?

As we said farewell to our guardian dragon on the hillside under its watchful eye, we wondered if the entire island and all its energy points represented the sacred omphalos of Britain and Ireland. As the sun dipped below the horizon, we looked towards the eye of the dragon and for a moment, I felt sure it gave us a wink.

References:

1. Michell J (1994) *At the Centre of the World: Polar Symbolism Discovered in Celtic, Norse and Other Ritualized Landscapes*. Thames & Hudson, London.
2. Baillie M (1998) *Exodus to Arthur: Catastrophic Encounters with Comets*. Batsford, London.
3. Randles J (2003) *Supernatural Isle of Man*. Robert Hale, London.
4. Broderick G (1995) *Chronicle of the Kings of Mann and the Isles. 2nd ed.* https://books.google.co.uk/books?id=q7YJAQAAIAAJ&source=gbs_book_other_versions.

5. Dunbavin P (1992) *The Atlantis Researches: Earth's Rotation in Mythology and Prehistory*. Third Millennium, Nottingham.
6. Train J (1845) *An Historical and Statistical Account of the Isle of Man, from the Earliest Times to the Present Date; with a View of its Ancient Laws, Peculiar Customs, and Popular Superstitions.* https://archive.org/details/historicalstatis01trai.
7. Michell J (1994) *At the Centre of the World; Polar Symbolism Discovered in Celtic, Norse and Other Ritualized Landscapes.* Thames & Hudson, London.
8. The Lost German on the Isle of Man TT Course: A Ghost Story from the Isle of Man. www.transceltic.com/manx/lost-german-isle-of-man-tt-course-ghost-story-isle-of-man.
9. Killip M (1975) *The Folklore of the Isle of Man*. B. T. Batsford, London.
10. Cubbon W (1852) *Island Heritage: Dealing with Some Phases of Manx History*. George Falkner & Sons, Manchester.
11. Randles J (2003) *Supernatural Isle of Man*. Robert Hale, London.
12. Airne C W (1949) *The Story of the Isle of Man*. Vol 1. C. W. Airne, Southport.
13. Cubbon W (1852) *Island Heritage: Dealing with Some Phases of Manx History*. George Falkner & Sons, Manchester.
14. Airne C W (1949) *The Story of the Isle of Man. Vol 1*. C. W. Airne, Southport.
15. Sacheverell W (1702) *An Account of the Isle of Man: Its Inhabitants, Language, Soil, Remarkable Curiosities, the Succession of its Kings and Bishops, Down to the Eighteenth Century*. Manx Society, Isle of Man, 1859.
16. *The Life and Acts of St Patrick.* https://archive.org/details/lifeandactssain00jocegoog
17. Train J (1845) *An Historical and Statistical Account of the Isle of Man, from the Earliest Times to the Present Date; with a View of its Ancient Laws, Peculiar Customs, and Popular Superstitions*. https://archive.org/details/historicalstatis01trai.
18. Callahan, P.S. (1984) *Ancient Mysteries, Modern Visions*. Acres, Kansas City.
19. Cubbon W (1852) *Island Heritage: Dealing with Some Phases of Manx History*. George Falkner & Sons, Manchester.
20. Walpole Spencer (1893) *The Land of Home Rule: An Essay on the History and Constitution of the Isle of Man*. http://www.isle-of-man.com/manxnotebook/fulltext/sw1893/index.htm.
21. Michell J (1994) *At the Centre of the World: Polar Symbolism Discovered in Celtic, Norse and Other Ritualized Landscapes*. Thames & Hudson, London.
22. Craine D (1961) *Tynwald, Symbol of an Ancient Kingdom. The Government Property Trustees for the Isle of Man*, Douglas.
23. Manx National Heritage (2005) *Prehistoric Sites of the Isle of Man*, The Manx Museum, Douglas.
24. https://www.themodernantiquarian.com/site/4403/ballaharra-stones

25. Craine D (1961) *Tynwald, Symbol of an Ancient Kingdom*. The Government Property Trustees for the Isle of Man, Douglas.
26. Michell J (1994) *At the Centre of the World*: Polar Symbolism Discovered in Celtic, Norse and Other Ritualized Landscapes. Thames & Hudson, London. www.isleofman.com
27. Johnson A & Fox A (2017) *A Guide to the Archaeological Sites of the Isle of Man up to AD 1500*. Manx Heritage Foundation, Isle of Man.
28. Michell J (1994) *At the Centre of the World*: Polar Symbolism Discovered in Celtic, Norse and Other Ritualized Landscapes. Thames & Hudson, London.
29. Broderick G (1995) *Chronicle of the Kings of Mann and the Isles, 2nd ed.* https://books.google.co.uk/books?id=q7YJAQAAIAAJ&source=gbs_book_other_versions.
30. Drayton P (1995) *In Heaven as on Earth. Royal Roads and the Milky Way*. http://www. indigogroup.co.uk/edge/Royalrds.htm.
31. Cubbon W (1852) *Island Heritage: Dealing with Some Phases of Manx History*. George Falkner & Sons, Manchester.
32. https://www.visitisleofman.com/blog/read/2024/11/the-history-of-tynwald-the-isle-of-mans-1000-year-old-parliament-b415
33. Wright B (2009) *Brigid: Goddess, Druidess, Saint*. The History Press, Stroud.
34. Shaw G (1871) *Shaw's tourist's picturesque guide to the Isle of Man: with excursions to all parts of the Island and instructions requisite for sea and freshwater fishing.* The Graphotyping Company Ltd, London.
35. Cubbon W (1852) *Island Heritage: Dealing with Some Phases of Manx History*. George Falkner & Sons, Manchester.
36. Crowhurst R (2012) *The Search for Answers on the Isle of Man*. http://gatekeeper.org.uk/ product/gkt-news-issue-29/.
37. Cubbon W (1852) *Island Heritage: Dealing with Some Phases of Manx History*. George Falkner & Sons, Manchester.
38. Warden, J. L. 1895. *An Exploration of Dartmoor and its Antiquities (4th ed.*). Seeley & Co Ltd, London.
39. Cubbon W (1852) *Island Heritage: Dealing with Some Phases of Manx History*. George Falkner & Sons, Manchester.
40. Thom A (1967) *Megalithic Sites in Britain*. Oxford University Press, Oxford.
41. Cubbon W (1852) *Island Heritage: Dealing with Some Phases of Manx History*. George Falkner & Sons, Manchester
42. ibid.
43. *List of Manx Antiquities 1930*. Isle of Man Natural History and Antiquarian
44. Van Renterghem A & Stoner H (2014) *Viking Myths and Rituals on the Isle of Man*. G Leszek & C Larrington (eds). Centre for the Study of the Viking Age, University of Nottingham.
45. Weatherstone L (2015) *Tending Brigid's Flame: Awaken to the Celtic Goddess of Hearth, Temple, and Forge*. Llewellyn Publishing, Woodbury, MN.

Chapter 9

Sacred Cities of Britain

The Oxford Skyline by Andrew Gray

The influence of cosmology, symbolism and metaphor can be seen in the foundation plans of many ancient cities around the world, from the Olmec, Maya, and Aztecs in Central and South America to the cities of Sumer and the Indus Valley. Archaeologists fail to comprehend the meaning behind the orientation of the streets, buildings and shrines and why the same cosmological layout is seen across the world. Scholars believe the motive has to be religious or superstition and ignore the divine practices of the ancient peoples who were more at one with nature and the cosmos than we are today. Their advancement was not through material and physical success but through mysticism and spiritual practices. Moreover, to live in harmony and balance with nature and the Earth, they had to create equilibrium in their buildings and towns.

Several cosmological and mythological systems portray four corners of the world or four quarters of the globe corresponding approximately to the four points of the compass or the two solstices and two equinoxes. This type of cosmology is represented in the division of the land into four provinces around a central fifth as shown in the Celtic divisions of Ireland and smaller landmasses such as the Isle of Man. We can also find it in microcosm within the foundation plans of some of the oldest cities which generally had roads leading from a central crossroads to gates in the north, south, east and west. The surrounding walls then contained four city quarters and a form of shrine or religious building close to a central crossroads. This harmonious structure gave the city a cosmic integration and connection with the solar stations governed by the gods and therefore each quarter had distinct influences suitable for four different aspects of society.

The northeast was considered the realm of the sky gods favourable to man and the best place for good fortune, while the northwest was the dominion of the underworld gods and spirits where only the priests and nobles would reside to control and determine fate. The southeast quadrant was the jurisdiction of earth and nature spirits that nurture man, and in the southwest is the abode of the underworld where elementals dwell, such as water deities, and therefore a place of wells and pools, which supplied the local population.

Beneath the streets of Mexico City in the Historic Quarter, are the ruins of an island city called Tenochtitlan, built over 600 years ago by the Aztecs on what was then Lake Texcoco in the Valley of Mexico. The foundation plans of the old city reveal the same north-south-east-west streets around a central shrine seen in earlier Middle Eastern cities as if this knowledge was widespread in the ancient world.

One of the earliest European peoples to practise quartering cosmology in the foundation of their cities are the pre-Roman Etruscans of Northern and Central Italy. The Romans later usurped the Etruscan empire using the 'Etruscan Principle' to establish new cities throughout their empire, having assimilated Etruscan engineers and augers into their society. Rome became their capital, thought to have been originally founded by Etruscan King Lucius Tarquinius Priscus in c. 575 BC.[1] The Etruscans ruled over a region of Italy called Etruria (Tuscany) between 900– 300 BCE, which covered the area from the River Po in the north to central Campania.

This mysterious advanced religious culture worshipped the Earth Mother and created shrines to the goddess at the centre of their magnificent cities. Only in the last two hundred years have their secrets come to light revealing mysterious pyramids, rock-cut temples, ceremonial passages and tombs. Their origins are a mystery and over the centuries their history has been largely ignored, historians and archaeologists having relied on accounts by ancient Greek and Roman writers of Italy's ancient past. This perhaps is partly due to the lack of authentic and detailed written records as the Etruscan chronicles were destroyed long ago.

The Romans adopted many aspects of Etruscan culture including their advanced farming, mining and building techniques. The Romans utilised their military routes and built over their great cities, desecrating tombs and looting their precious gold, silver, bronze, jewelled and ceramic artefacts.[2]

The Etruscan augur or priest operated like a Chinese geomancer surveying the surrounding landscape for favourable elements like wind and water and ensuring mountains or hills were situated to the north. The exact position of the centre was often determined by divination – for instance, looking for portents in nature or the unusual behaviour of an animal or lightning bolts.

As mentioned in Chapter 1, the centre-point or 'mundus' was established through divination in order to locate the pole star. Then followed the marking of a north-south 'cardo 'and east-west 'decumanus' and the construction of a deep shaft or well where the two lines intersected, symbolically connecting the surface world with the 'underworld'. Then a grid system of streets was laid out from the mundus spanning both sides of the cardo and decumanus to a given distance where gates were built and a wall was erected between them (see Fig. 1).

Many cities in the ancient world display cosmological division around a central shrine, including one of the oldest – the mysterious Harappan city of Mohenjo-Daro in the province of Sindh in Pakistan. This incredible stone and brick city was an administrative centre for the Indus Valley civilisation and had a population of 35,000 around 2500 BCE until it was devastated by a searing heat from above that caused vitrification and the sudden death of its inhabitants. A sunken water tank called 'The Great Bath' lies at the centre of the city and roads lead outwards from here to the cardinal points creating the quartering seen in later cities.

In the ancient East, Bagdad was rebuilt in the 8th century CE by the caliph al-Mansur using cosmological principles and enormous manpower, comprising architects, engineers, surveyors, carpenters, blacksmiths and over a hundred thousand labourers from across the empire. He also consulted astrologers, who advised him to lay the first ceremonial brick on 30 July 762. The caliph established the circular city of Bagdad as the main capital of the Islamic empire under the Abbasids.

The Celtic city of Braga built in 290 BC on the Iberian Peninsula was also founded using cosmic proportions and, like Mohenjo Daro, had a central shrine, later marked by the tomb of Henry, Count of Portugal who ruled this region around the time of William the Conqueror. This is one of many examples of how invading cultures destroy or change the sacred omphalos and we began to see a familiar pattern of ownership of key cities and kingdoms by an initiated few.

In many cases, we found that 'the centre of power' was manipulated or destroyed to regulate the kingdom. In sociological terms, whoever controls the omphalos of a city or kingdom, physically and psychically influences the heart and the soul of the people.

Another example of an inauspicious use of the omphalos is at the medieval city of Neubrandenburg, in North West Germany, first founded by a tribe of the West Slavs in the 10th century and divided into four districts with four city gates. Today, a modern complex of ugly commercial buildings marks the old square, out of keeping with its medieval plan and heritage. We have discovered that when towns and cities alter their original quartering or remove or build over the site of a former sacred shrine or monument without any thought to its important ceremonial past, they no longer thrive and the health and prosperity of the locals suffer.

In 2007, we visited a town in Croatia that many of the locals described as 'disconnected' and out of balance. While investigating their concerns, we discovered that the local authorities had constructed a huge building across the central square, cutting off one of its main thoroughfares. The effect of blocking the flow of energy at the heart of a town or city diminishes the power of the omphalos and reduces its positive influence.

In England, one city that still maintains its original cosmology is Oxford, a city that in ancient times was said to mark the centre of the British kingdom. After the Roman invasion in 43 CE, many changes were made to Britain, one of which was the building of towns. Gone were the enclosed settlements of the Celts and in came stone and brick buildings that were so well constructed that their remains can still be seen today all over the British Isles. Not all were designed in the same way due to their complex topography, but many included the Etruscan principle with a grid system of streets built around a central forum and temple. A good example is 'Venta Icenorum' in Norfolk, a name that means 'central place of the Iceni'; The Iron Age Iceni tribe were infamous for their various uprisings against the Romans led by Queen Boudicca. Other examples are Silchester in Hampshire and Chichester in West Sussex.

The city of Bath in Somerset on pre-Georgian maps *c.* 1697, shows traces of a circular walled city with four streets radiating from a central crossroads leading to gates and the cardo staggered. Today, only remnants of the north, south and west gates survive. At the omphalos was the church of St Mary de Stall (now destroyed), one of Bath's most important places of worship particularly for the city's ruling body. Inside was a chapel dedicated to the city's patron saint, St Katherine. Remnants of this church survived up until the first half of the 17th century when it was used as shops and later workshops.

England's capital city London has undergone many changes over the centuries and so it is a challenge to find any defined boundaries or cosmological plan to locate an omphalos. However, a well-known centre-point from which distances were measured is near Trafalgar Square at the King Charles I statue, now on a mini roundabout. A plaque there declares 'On the site now occupied by the statue of King Charles I was erected the original Queen Eleanor's cross, a replica of which stands in front of Charing Cross station. Mileages from London are measured from the site of the original cross.' Nevertheless, this site could never be considered a sacred or ceremonial centre of power and influence.

The best historical boundary of London is the old city walls built by the Romans. The route of the old Roman walls and the gates can be traced on old maps and today information boards around the City of London display where sections of it can still be seen and visited. However, according to a foundation myth, the walls and gates of London were built by Celtic King Lud and refortified by the Romans and later Normans. Saxon monk Nennius in *Historia Brittonum*, written in around 828 CE[3], and the 12th-century chronicler Geoffrey of Monmouth in his *Historia Regum Britanniae*[4], write that Brutus of Troy, the first king of Britain, founded 'New Troy' on the banks of the River Thames *c.*1100 BCE, which would become the great city known today as London. It was only later that it was associated with his descendant King Lud.

A legend also states that the centre of old London was marked by the 'London Stone', a small megalith of oolitic limestone, its mythology denoting it as an omphalos stone. Many believe the Romans surveyed London from this pillar, although it lies nowhere near the centre of their ancient city. The stone was moved a few yards from its original position on the south side of Candlewick Street when the road was widened to become Cannon Street. Its reputation was well-known in medieval London and was revered with superstitious respect often given to that of a coronation stone. In 1450, when Jack

Cade, leader of a rebellion against the corrupt government of Henry VI, entered the city with his men, he struck his sword on the London Stone and claimed himself 'Lord of this city.'

Today the stone is set into a wall opposite Cannon Street Station and many speculate whether it was used as a marker stone of several leys that radiated from this spot rather than as an omphalos stone. Several books now quote the famous verse attached to this stone like a 'stone of fate'; 'So long as the Stone of Brutus is safe, so long shall London flourish.' Another legend states that all milestones on Roman roads leading away from London measured their distances from the London Stone.

The London Stone, 111 Cannon St.

The actual centre-point of the old city of London is Bank Junction, where nine main streets converge, including Mansion House Street, Threadneedle Street, Cornhill, Princes Street, Queen Victoria Street, and Cheapside. The number nine is symbolic of divine wisdom and power and at this junction, we find the Bank of London, the Royal Exchange and the Mansion House (the home of the Lord Mayor). Is this a coincidence or is there a governing body that is aware of the hidden centre-point being fortuitous?

Figure 35. The thirty-three Boroughs of London with the City of London in red

The city of London is a world renowned centre of Freemasonry, which reveres the number 33. Today, the city has thirty-two local government boroughs and at the centre is the City of London Borough, located within the old walls which adds up to 33 (see Fig. 35). In Masonic circles, this number represents the highest degree and the pinnacle of Masonic knowledge and spiritual development.

When calculating London's exact centre-point of the 33 London boroughs on a large map using the boundary extreme method, we find one of the city's biggest landmarks, the London Eye. The huge Ferris wheel that faces the Houses of Parliament was once the largest in the world when it was built in 1999 in time for the new millennium. The wheel has capsules numbered 1-33, one for each of London's boroughs, but the 13th was left out for superstitious reasons, or was it? The wheel is supported on one side by an A-frame that is reminiscent of a Masonic compass. The lights around the rim are also suggestive of another masonic symbol – the point within a circle.

The London Eye at the centre of the thirty-three boroughs

Oxford: The Cosmic Division of a Sacred City

The legendary 'ivory towers' and 'dreaming spires' of Oxford nestled between the Rivers Cherwell and the Thames have a timeless air of antiquity unaffected by modern times. For over a thousand years, its ancient colleges of honey-coloured stone surrounded by green lawns and fine gardens have been a sanctuary of learning for our finest scholars and statesmen. In the ancient Celtic tale of Lludd and Llefelys from *The Mabinogion*, Oxford was said to be at the centre of the kingdom according to calculations given by the king's surveyors.[5]

Lludd and Llefelys were the sons of the British Iron Age King Beli the Great (117–42 BCE). After Beli's death, Lludd (also referred to as Lud) inherited Britain as eldest son, and set about rebuilding the walls of London (Lud's Town), erecting houses of great splendour equal to no other in the land. His brother Llefelys became the King of France after marrying the heir to the kingdom.

Later, three plagues befell the Isle of Britain, the second of which was a scream that arose every night on Mayday over the hearth of every house in the land. Such was the menace of the scream that it pierced the hearts of every man, woman and child and struck them with such terror that it made men weak and women barren and the land and animals sick.

Lludd set sail to France to meet with his brother, a wise and intelligent man who had already received news of the plagues affecting his brother's kingdom. He told Lludd that the cause of the second plague was the fighting of two dragons, one representing the Britons and the other a foreign race, which was striving to overcome the other on Mayday, and the deadly scream was from the rage and distress of the British. To heal this sickness, he instructed Lludd to measure the length and breadth of the island to find its exact centre. Once done, a pit must be dug and a tub full of the best mead covered by a piece of linen should be placed at the very bottom.

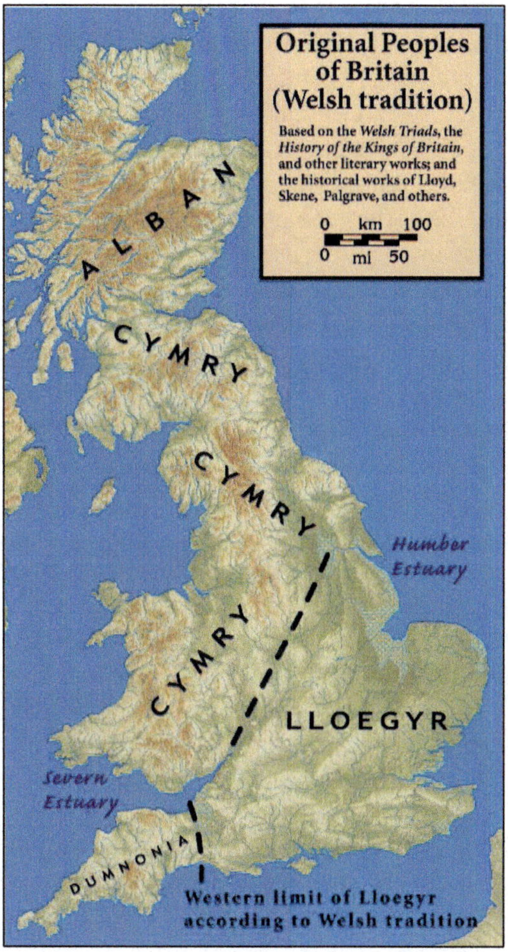

Lludd was then told to keep a solo watch over the pit on the evening of Mayday, where he would witness two dragons fighting in the air in the shape of hideous creatures. Over time, they would transform back to their dragon shape, and after growing weary of fighting each other, they would fall into the pit and change into two little pigs. As they fell into the vat of mead the linen covering would wrap around them, dragging them to the bottom whereupon they would drink all the mead and fall asleep. Lludd was to then take the linen-cocooned pigs or dragons to the strongest place in his kingdom and bury them in a stone coffin.

Llefelys assured him that as long as they stayed entombed in that place, no such plague would ever blight the island of Britain.

When Lludd returned home, his surveyors measured the land, found the exact centre to be Oxford, and so dug a pit there as instructed. As predicted, two fighting dragons appeared to Llud on Mayday and eventually fell into the vat, transformed into two pigs and fell asleep at the bottom of the tub. The king then transported them to *Dinas Emreis* (Dinas Emrys in Snowdon) and buried them in a stone coffer. As foretold, this course of action did indeed stop the screaming over all the hearths in Britain, thus ending the second plague.[6]

Although this story is based upon myth, it may be an allegorical tale, for some elements of the story relate to the site of a pre-Roman centre or shrine that once existed in Oxford. At the time of Lludd, the land we know today as Britain was divided into four separate kingdoms called Alban, Cymry, Lloegyr and Dumnonia. Lludd ruled over the kingdom of Lloegyr and at its omphalos was Oxford. According to the Welsh Brut, 'Ynys Prydein' (the Isle of Prydain or Britain) had three realms, Cymri, Alban and Lloegyr. Geoffrey of Monmouth wrote that these realms were divided between the three sons of Brutus of Troy. Locrinus was given land that covered the area we know today as England, called Loegria, Albanactus ruled over Alba or Alban, now Scotland, and Kamber Cymry was given Cymry now Wales, which he called Cambria.[7]

The P-Celtic Welsh-speaking race of Britons ruled Cymry, an area stretching as far north as the Forth and Clyde and included the whole of Wales and lands west of a border between the Rivers Humber and Avon.

King Lludd or Lud appears in many early manuscripts and genealogies as ruling over the Britons for 11 years from 72 to 61 BCE and his capital was London. His final resting place was at the old east gate to the city of London, which his people renamed Ludgate in his honour. Three statues of King Lludd and his two sons Androgeus and Theomantius were erected at Ludgate *c.* 1586 and eventually moved to the vestry porch of St Dunstan-in-the West in Fleet Street, when the city gates were demolished, where they can still be found today.

In the earliest versions of the saga of Lludd and Llefelys, there seems to be some confusion concerning the name of the fortress where Lludd entombed the sleeping pigs. The name Dinas Emrys means 'fortress of Emrys or Ambrosius' which refers to Emrys Wledig or Ambrosius Aurelianus, who seized the fort after Vortigern's downfall. However, some sources believe the name refers to Myrddin Emrys or Merlin. Although Ambrosius and Merlin lived hundreds of years after Lludd, excavations at the hillfort show evidence of occupation in the Iron Age, contemporary with this old British King.

The rocky and wooded hillfort of Dinas Emrys, standing aloft overlooking the River Glaslyn in the province of Gwynedd in northwest Wales, also has a story of fighting dragons associated with it, which the young boy Merlin prophesied was causing problems with its foundations. Some versions name the stronghold visited by Lludd as *Dinas Ffaraon Dandde*, 'fortress of the fiery pharaoh', which alludes to Vortigern's fortress or tower located at the centre of Wales. Legends say it was destroyed by 'fire from the sky' in the form of a meteorite, which killed the king. Religious people would have seen this at the time as God's divine vengeance, like the Biblical flooding of the Red Sea that swept away the evil pharaoh and his army. Although Vortigern was innocent, many believed he had betrayed his people and conceded the destiny of Britain to the invading Saxons under the leadership of the infamous mercenaries Hengest and Horsa.

When Lludd ordered his surveyors to find the centre of the land and construct a pit, he was in fact following the cosmological principle used by the Celtic Etruscans by creating a 'mundus' pit or omphalos, as mentioned earlier. Whether this story is a myth or merely symbolic, we were intrigued as to where in Oxford this pit or shrine could have been located. Was it at the centre?

An old layout of Oxford shows streets aligned north-south and east-west radiating from a central crossroads called 'Carfax', and clearly defines four quadrants and four city gates. The curious name Carfax is said to derive from the Latin *quatour furcae* meaning 'four segments or quarters', formed from the meeting of roads contained by walls. However, there is no history of a well at Carfax, for drinking water had to be channelled into the city via a conduit to a central fountain.

We were interested to discover that each of the four gates of old Oxford had churches built into them, such as the church of St Michael at the north gate on the corner of North Street and Ship Street. All that remains today is its Saxon tower, one of the oldest stone structures in the city. St Michael's is mentioned in the *Domesday Book*, as having considerable wealth. The church at the south gate spanning St Aldates was also dedicated to St Michael, demolished in 1525 to make way for what is now Christ Church College. The church at the east gate of the city was St Peter's in the East, now the library of St Edmund Hall, and at the west gate was St Peter le Bailey's Church, a medieval building that collapsed in 1726. Its replacement on the same site was demolished in 1874 as part of a road widening scheme and is now Bonn Square. These four remarkable churches are recorded in an old Oxford rhyme:

'At North-Gate and at South-Gate too
St Michael guards the way,
While o'er the East and o'er the West
St Peter holds his sway.'[8]

It is both significant and symbolic that St Michael, the Archangel of the Heavens, guards the north and south and the earthly St Peter, the rock of Christianity, guards the east and west gates of the equinox sun.

During our visit to St Michael's tower and its little museum, we discovered that long ago, there was a sheela-na-gig fertility goddess carved into a stone plaque set into the masonry overlooking those who entered the city. The symbolism of her open legs and vulva refers to an opening into the sacred place of the Great Earth Mother and to place it at the main north entrance as you enter the sacred city may reflect early Celtic traditions, where north equated to the Earth, home, security and fertility. This pagan carving at the main gate of this ancient city is also a clue perhaps to a cult of the goddess being practised here at the pre-Christian centre of Lludd's kingdom.

Oxford's history before the 10th century is rarely mentioned, its illustrious past eventually becoming the source of myth and legend, so we thought it important to dig a little deeper into the archives. The foundation stories of Oxford are as obscure and fantastical as the Lludd and Llefelys story, with tales of political intrigue, superstition, bloody sieges and tragic encounters. It is a mystery why *The Saxon Chronicles* record nothing of the city's history before 911 CE when it was one of the largest and most important towns in Saxon England. According to the Chronicles: 'This year died Aethered ealdorman of the Mercians, and King Edward [the Confessor] took possession of London and Oxford and all the lands which owed obedience thereto.'[9] This last statement implies that Oxford was already well established and important enough to be taken possession of by the then King of England.

However, local oral history tells us that the city was destroyed by the Danes with fire on more than one occasion but rose again like a phoenix out of the ashes. There is also an ancient tradition once told throughout its universities that King Alfred rebuilt Oxford in the year 886 by constructing three new university halls and re-erecting many older academic buildings. So how far back does the history of Oxford extend?

Over the centuries, renowned Oxford historians researching the antiquity of their city tended to agree that there is tentative evidence for an early foundation long before the Saxon period. The 15th-century chronicler John Rous ascribed the town's foundation in *Historia Regum Angliae* to a mythical king called Mempric who supposedly ruled during the time of the prophet Samuel of the Old Testament, having lived during the reign of King Saul (1050–1020 BCE). He also stated that this place of learning succeeded one established earlier at the nearby town of Cricklade by Greek philosophers who accompanied the Trojan Prince Brutus to Britain in *c.*1185 BCE after the fall of Troy.[10] In a topographical poem describing England and Wales by Michael Drayton called *Polyolbion*, published in 1612, the earliest name for Cricklade is 'Greeklade'.[11]

This picturesque sleepy Cotswold town lies at a strategic location on Ermin Way where centuries ago there was a fording of the river Thames. Ermin Way was an important Roman thoroughfare that linked the port of Chichester to Winchester and Caerleon in Wales, although it was most probably an earlier prehistoric trackway. A ley from the centre of Stonehenge and the great Avebury stone circle passes to the west of the village.

When Saint Augustine came to Cricklade, he successfully converted the local Anglo-Saxons to Christianity, paving the way for the authority of the Roman Catholic Church to be accepted. The well-preserved Saxon town was important as it had a royal mint producing thousands of Saxon coins. Even the main church was owned by Westminster Abbey and the town's motto 'In a pleasant place' may reference the old legend that it was the chosen settlement of the Greek philosophers mentioned by Rous. Cricklade also had four gates, a central crossroads and traces of medieval walls creating a square, which can still be seen in earthworks around the town. It was one of thirty 'Burhs' built by King Alfred to protect England from the Vikings and the Danes. Many of these fortified settlements had four gates and a central crossroads like the town of Wareham in Dorset, Bath in Somerset, Winchester in Hampshire, Chichester in West Sussex and Wilton near Salisbury.

Eventually, these learned Greek men became unhappy with the location of their new school, preferring a site further up the Thames where it meets with the River Cherwell. Here the philosophers discovered a perfect feng shui site on an elevated piece of land encompassed by rivers to its east, west and south that became the Oxford we know today. Once more, this ancient Chinese principle copied by the Celts was taken into account, seeing the surrounding meadows within an amphitheatre of hills as good protection against detrimental winds. A section of the River Thames that flows through Oxford from the Saxon settlement of Dorchester-on-Thames is called the Isis, from its earlier name 'Tamesis' – although some believe it was named after the goddess Isis, first worshipped by the ancient Egyptians and then by the Romans, perhaps dedicating this upper section of England's longest river to their mother goddess.

Rous possibly obtained his theory from Geoffrey of Monmouth who mentions that King Memphric, the great-grandson of Brutus, chose this enchanted place to build a town in 1009 BCE, probably on the site of the Greek philosophers' college. The town was known then as *Caer Memphic*, which means in old Welsh 'Memphric's stronghold, fortress or citadel'.

The legendary Brutus was a royal immigrant from the Trojan War who arrived with a vast fleet in Britain *c.* 1100 BCE and eventually ruled the island as its first king after defeating the local population of giants. However, Memphric became a despotic king, having killed his political rival and his brother – he even violated the royal Trojan code of honour by betraying his queen with his lust for younger men. In 1009 BCE, while out hunting in a forest, Memphric was eaten alive by wolves after being abandoned by his hunting party.[12] The Oxford suburb of Wolvercote perhaps recalls this macabre tale.

When the Romans arrived in the area, they called the town *Bos Vadum*, a Latin name meaning 'a fording of oxen.' Under the command of Emperor Claudius, Aulus Plautius entered the old citadel when it is said to 'have suffered its most terrible downfall and reduced to a small settlement serving only the ford to survive.'[13]

This deliberate sacking by the Romans was unusual, generally preferring negotiation to wanton violence, therefore avoiding any sudden uprisings and unnecessary loss of life. Perhaps the locals angered them in some way, or was it their intention to destroy an important pagan temple or shrine in the city?

We do know from history that such Roman ferocity was meted out to the Druids and early Christian sects, particularly on Anglesey in Wales, Wall in Staffordshire and St Albans near London.

Did the Romans desecrate an already existing Druidic shrine in Oxford which possibly marked its omphalos? Certainly, the topography in and around Oxford with its encompassing rivers would indicate the possible setting for a sacred place of goddess worship.

Oxford's Pre-Roman Shrine

Author and researcher Bob Trubshaw states that 'the earliest history of Oxford reveals that the long peninsular of land at the confluence of the rivers Cherwell and Thames was used as a barrow cemetery in Bronze Age times – a linear barrow cemetery being situated on what is now the University Parks cricket ground, with other barrows throughout the town.' He also mentions the possibility that the peninsular during the Iron Age was a boundary or 'no man's land' between three Celtic tribes – the Dubunni, the Atrebates and the Catuvellauni. The priesthood of these tribes were the Druids and so it is certainly possible they worshipped at a shrine here.[14]

Proof of pre-Roman occupation of this peninsular arrived with the archaeological excavations of St Antony's College 1.3 km north of Oxford's centre, along Parks Road passing Wadham's College. Evidence here revealed buildings belonging to the Iron Age and Romano-British period, possibly a settlement. Unfortunately, there is little mention of another highly important monument, discovered just under a kilometre north of Carfax. In March 2008, archaeologists excavated a prehistoric ditch identified as being part of a very rare and vast Neolithic henge-like structure (*c.* 2300 BCE). The curving ditch was 8 m across and at least 2.5 m deep and, based on the small part of the plan so far recovered, it would have enclosed an area of at least 150 m in diameter, encompassing both Keble College and the Pitt Rivers Museum. This impressive henge monument possibly consisted of standing stones, and if so, it would have eclipsed that of Avebury.[15]

Situated at such an important boundary of Iron Age tribes, this long peninsular of land with a mound cemetery and a ceremonial monument as sizable as Avebury, may have received national recognition in prehistoric times. Perhaps this is why Oxford had the legendary reputation of being a kingship and religious centre, the

Druids possibly using the henge monument as a national Gorsedd or meeting place. This could account for the lack of Roman settlement here, as, despite their reputation, they tended to avoid building on native ceremonial centres unless highly provoked. There is a long-standing legend that the University of Oxford was founded by British Christian King Arviragus under the reign of Emperor Domitian in 81–96 CE.[16] Therefore, it is quite likely that the Romans under Aulus Plautius targeted Oxford for destruction in revenge for an uprising.

Many antiquarians believe that after this initial destruction of Oxford, the town was quickly rebuilt, becoming once more a place of great splendour during the later Roman occupation of England when Christianity was the accepted religion.

In the 5th century, during the time of the fabled King Arthur, Oxford was known as *Caer Bosso*, similar to its Roman name Bos Vadum. Bosso was the local chieftain who reputedly attended the coronation of King Arthur at Caerleon in 516. Despite no written evidence, a local tradition still recalls that Oxford became a university town a few decades before the Roman Catholic missionary Augustine arrived in Britain in 595.

Castle Mound, Oxford

After the Saxon invasions and the gradual disappearance of Oxford's sacred monuments, its fame as a centre of power and learning declined and the pages of its history became silent. The only tradition to survive refers to St Frideswide (650–735 CE) establishing a priory in the town. Another local tale says that when King Alfred the Great (849–899) arrived in Oxford, he was so appalled at the damage inflicted upon the town by the wars between the Danes and the Saxons that he rebuilt it, constructing new halls of learning, including University College.

Alfred was one of the most celebrated kings of England and, out of respect for its former glory and its splendid situation, he moved his royal court to Oxford. He lived in the town for many years with his three sons and established a mint, its coins stamped with the name of the town, *Ocsnafordia*, and revived its status as a centre of learning once more. King Alfred ended his days at his monastery in the English capital of Winchester, handing the crown to his son Edward the Elder. However, despite successive victories against the Danes, Edward finally relinquished England to this unrelenting invading force and Oxford was once again burned to the ground.

The fortunes of Oxford revived when in the 10th and 11th centuries it became a royal seat with a palace and parliament. Such was the importance of this royal centre that it became a constant battleground between the Saxons and Danes, with the dreadful slaughter of many Danes taking place within the walls of Frideswide's Priory. Alfred's descendant King Edmund Ironside resided in Oxford until he died in 1016, with some versions of history reporting the event as being at the hands of an assassin while others say it was through receiving wounds during a battle with the Danes. The Danish King Canute took the throne and held court at Oxford for many years, and later King Harold Harefoot would make it his chief residence.

When the Normans arrived with William the Conqueror, the gates of Oxford were closed to him, the locals having denied him entry. William would later hand the city to his kinsman Robert de Oilgi, granting him the right to build a castle on a large grassy mound. Here, Empress Matilda was besieged for three months by the armies of her cousin King Stephen but escaped by crossing the frozen Thames at night dressed in white accompanied by three knights. Within the motte and bailey castle, de Oilgi built a chapel dedicated to St George. Excavations show that the mound on which the castle was built was 18 m high and 12 m wide, constructed of layers of material similar to the prehistoric mounds found all over the country. Seemingly unique in Britain, there is a subterranean hexagonal well chamber inside the mound with a 13th-century vaulted ceiling, extending 6 m down from the surface.

At the centre of the chamber, the 16-m-deep well reaches down to the water level beneath the mound, supposedly built in the event of a siege. Although some believe the well to be the one dug by Lludd, nothing is left of any pre-Saxon archaeology that might have proved this to be the case, having been destroyed by the numerous settlements constructed on the site of the mound since the time of King Alfred.

Helen Fulton, Professor of Medieval Literature at the University of York and an expert in Arthurian literature, reveals that Geoffrey of Monmouth wrote *Historia Regum Britanniae* (The History of the Kings of Britain) while serving as a canon in the castle's St George's Chapel.[17] His writings were regarded as the origin of the legends of King Arthur and Merlin. Monmouth also believed Oxford marked the centre of Britain; perhaps he had discovered some early documents that referred to Oxford as being an omphalos site and the well below the mound was the legendary pit of the dragons.[18]

The grid-like street layout of old Oxford with its four gates at the cardinal points and a central crossroads is similar to other late Saxon walled towns and cities in England built by King Alfred called Burhs as mentioned earlier. It is known that Alfred resurrected the earlier Cambrian laws and customs of the ancient British people, which he discovered within old manuscripts found in the libraries of

The well chamber in the Castle Mound, Oxford

Winchester and Oxford, possibly dating back to the time of the Iron Age King Dunvallo Molmutius the Law Giver (434–394 BCE).

During his 39-year reign, Alfred resurrected the 'Molmutine Laws', a code of laws translated from those set down by King Molmutius himself, which according to Geoffrey of Monmouth were still adhered to in the 12th century. Molmutius reputedly rebuilt and enlarged the Iron Age settlement of Winchester, the old capital of England. E. O. Gordon refers to Winchester as Winton and 'the supreme seat of civil government in Britain under Molmutius, a king recognised as sovereign paramount by the voice of the British people.'[19]

Perhaps King Alfred utilised the ancient geomantic practice of town design from old books and manuscripts hidden away in the libraries of his royal seat in Winchester that recorded earlier teachings from the legendary Greek philosophers who supposedly first settled Oxford.

Beaumont Palace in Oxford was a Plantagenet royal house built by Henry I on land situated by the north gate. His grandson Henry II frequently stayed there and it is here that Richard the Lionheart and the notorious King John were born. Today there is no trace of this grand palace except for a mention on a plaque on a wall in Beaumont Street, near the Ashmolean Museum. The old custom of locating royal houses in the northern quarter of a town or city was a practice used by the ancient Roman and Egyptian surveyors. Revolutionary Egyptian pharaoh Akhenaton, when building his new central city of Akhetaton, also placed the royal accommodation in the northern quarter. The quartering of a city is part of a divine plan to mirror the cosmos. The construction of Beaumont Palace adhered to divine principles handed down by the ancient Etruscans and Romans, the north being representative of the realm of the sky gods, much suited to the Plantagenet dynasty who were said by tradition to have descended from these divine deities.

Many historical experts tend to ignore this fantastical history of Oxford, believing it to be an invention to prove to their rivals Cambridge the city's illustrious antiquity. However, the fact that so many kings from different cultures and countries resided in Oxford, a town that supposedly had no ancient foundation, is fascinating in itself. Perhaps it is due to the strategic location of Oxford, between the Thames and the Cherwell, making this long peninsular of land a safe refuge for kings and their parliaments during times of plague and war. At the time of the English Civil War, when Charles I was expelled from London by Oliver Cromwell's Parliamentarian forces,

Oxford was the temporary capital of England. The University was a strong supporter of the Royalists and was delighted to accommodate the King between 1642 and 1646 when his Parliament would assemble in Christ Church Hall.

There is also the urban legend that Hitler intended to make Oxford his capital if he succeeded in capturing England. His plan was to inhabit Blenheim Palace, and even a document in the Bodleian Library states that Hitler's mission was to move his troops into the ancient city. Many researchers say there was an agreement between the Fuhrer and the Allied forces not to bomb Britain's university towns.

St Martin's Tower, Carfax

Symbolically marking the omphalos of Oxford like the axis mundi, is the 11th-century tower of St Martin's at Carfax. The English antiquarian Alfred Watkins discovered two ley lines crossing at Carfax that, linked several churches.[20] St Martin's stands on the highest point in Oxford on a gravel bank marking the traditional meeting place of assembly for council, justice and markets. Watkins also mentioned that the roads were later altered in such a way as not to interfere with the old church layout of sites that feature on both of these remarkable leys or alignments that more or less follow the north-south and east-west streets and their gates crossing exactly at Carfax (see Fig. 36). Perhaps Oxford's surveyors knew of these ancient alignments and deliberately constructed the town's religious establishments on them to amplify their divine power.

The chapel at Christ Church College could also be referred to as a centre, for it was deliberately built over a geomantic place of power once occupied by St Frideswide's Saxon Priory. Today it is considered the most sacred site in Oxford, being the place of the female saint's reconstructed medieval shrine. The monastery's cemetery now lies beneath the famous Tom Quad, Christ Church's main square, with a statue of Mercury designed by Christopher Wren at its centre. This alchemical figure stands within a pool of water from which run two diagonal paths extending to an outer circular path, creating the astrologer's symbol for earth, another representation of a centre. Cardinal Wolsey suppressed the Priory of St Frideswide at the height of his powers in 1525 and founded Cardinal College on its lands. When Wolsey fell from grace, Henry VIII re-founded the college as Christ Church, creating Oxford Cathedral out of the remains of the priory church.

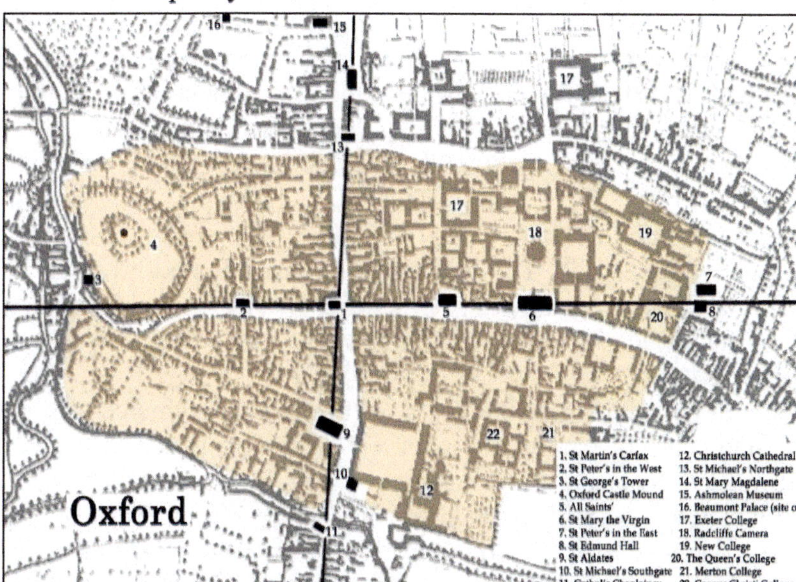

Figure 36. Old plan of Oxford showing the four quarters, churches and Watkins leys over a map engraving by Barak Longmate, 1773

St Frideswide and the Holy Well at Binsey

Unlike many cities in England, with their male patron saints, Oxford's saintly guardian is female, personified as the 8th-century English princess Frideswide. The legend of Frideswide is typical of many female saints, which describes her as the daughter of a sub-king, gifted at reciting the psalms and destined to serve God. After her mother's death here in Oxford, Frideswide was bequeathed the church built by her father in honour of his queen, where she lived as a nun along with twelve female companions. When her father died, the young princess received a message from the evil King Algar of Leicester demanding her hand in marriage. Having responded with 'I am already betrothed to the King of all kings,' Algar sent an envoy to Oxford to take her by force, but as they passed through the city gates, they were struck blind. The miracle so shocked the citizens of Oxford that they fell at Frideswide's feet, begging her to pity Algar's men.

She then prayed to God to restore their sight 'so that the people of Oxford may know his mercy.' As the soldiers replied 'Amen', suddenly their sight returned and they too fell at her feet, begging forgiveness and praising God. King Algar was so enraged upon hearing of Frideswide's miracle that he immediately set off for Oxford with his henchmen in the belief he was mightier than her magical powers. However, as Frideswide prayed that night, an angel appeared with the promise of Christ's protection and directed her to go with her companions to the Thames where a boatman provided by God would be waiting to sail her to safety. Thanking God, she took two of her monastic sisters to the river where, as predicted, a boat and boatmen were waiting. The wicked Algar reached Oxford intent on capturing Frideswide and destroying her monastery, but as he entered the north gate he too became blind. However, he was never to recover his sight.[21]

This story is known as the 'Curse of Frideswide', which condemns any king who enters Oxford with violent intent to never prosper. Many kings and princes who have ignored this curse have met a grisly end, which is why perhaps William the Conqueror stayed outside of the city when he first arrived there after the Battle of Hastings. Later, Henry III would ignore the curse at his own peril, believing that, as a divine ruler, he was above such superstition. After rallying his troops in the city before the Battle of Lewes, he and his son Edward would later suffer a terrible defeat, resulting in their imprisonment. Edward I was a wiser man and took heed of the curse when he visited Oxford, having decided to lodge outside the gates; from there he went on to defeat Wales and Scotland and become overall ruler of Britain. To this day, kings are still wary of entering Oxford less they suffer ill fortune or even death.

After her escape, Frideswide and her two companions eventually disembarked at a place called Binsey, just a few kilometres upriver from Oxford. Here they found a secluded spot to hide on the estate of Thornbiri, protected by thorn trees. Soon after, Frideswide built a small chapel or oratory out of a ruined ivy-covered pigsty where she retired in quiet seclusion. When the nuns had difficulty in drawing water from a nearby stream, Frideswide prayed to St Margaret and St Catherine for their assistance. With that, a spring suddenly appeared. A holy well still exists in the churchyard of Binsey Church dedicated to St Margaret, said to be the miraculous spring divined by Frideswide.

Carving on Frideswide's shrine, Christ Church College

When the danger was over she returned to her priory in Oxford, where her body was interred after her death on 19 October 735. Soon miracles occurred at St Frideswide's shrine and the holy well in Binsey, drawing many pilgrims from far and wide. Many were healed by drinking the well water and praying at her shrine and thereafter was honoured as a saint.

The day of her passing, 19 October, became her feast day and 12 February was the day of the translation of her relics; in Christianity, the translation of relics is the removal of holy objects from one locality to another. If the old Julian calendar had not gained 11 days, St Frideswide's translation would have occured on 1 February, the day of the Celtic festival of Imbolc, St Bride's or Brigid's Day. This story may allude to an ancient goddess shrine at Binsey that gave Oxford its notoriety in earlier times, and perhaps Frideswide is synonymous with Bride or Brigid, as in Old Welsh, Fraed or Fride means Bride.

As regards the pit or well mentioned in the tale of Lludd and Llefelys, dug at the centre of the kingdom at Oxford, if such a story was indeed true then this site's location and survival remain a mystery. We believe that rather than it being the well beneath the castle mound, it is more likely that such a well or pit would have been constructed at the recently excavated prehistoric henge, within the northern precincts of the city.

At one time, Oxford had many springs around the town, with eighteen recorded as holy wells, some known for their healing powers. One such well is in the Oxford parish of Holywell, from which it takes its name, but sadly most have been lost to the ravages of time. It is unlikely that a sacred well would have existed at the centre of a busy city, for fear of polluting its potency, but like the prehistoric henge, it may have stood some distance from Carfax for its protection and ease of access. Two wells still stand outside the city walls: one in the grounds of St Bartholomew's Chapel and old leper hospital on Cowley Road, about 3 km southeast of the city, and the other at Binsey, about 3 km to the northwest.

The well at Binsey dedicated to St Margaret and associated with the legend of Frideswide dates from at least Saxon times. This remote and hidden place may have been the new religious focus, possibly replacing one destroyed within Oxford's walls during the Roman sacking of the ancient town.

Binsey is a small village nestling next to a remote spot of the 'Isis' or River Thames. However, before the 18th century, it was a thriving settlement when the main road between Eynsham and Oxford passed right through the village. Recent historical surveys of the site revealed traces of an ancient semi-oval earthwork, which formed a boundary

St Margaret's Well, Binsey

surrounding the church and holy well still extant on the southwest side. Moreover, Iron Age artefacts from Lludd's time were also found here.

Binsey's original name was Thornbiri or Thornbury meaning 'thorny fort' derived from the thorn bushes that once surrounded it. There are many examples of hillforts in Britain and Ireland that used thorn bushes as impenetrable natural walls of protection. Eventually, its reputation as a holy sanctuary gave it the name of Binsey meaning 'island of prayer'. Close by was Seacourt, a thriving town built to house pilgrims visiting the healing well and oratory of Frideswide, with 24 inns for their accommodation and sustenance.[22] John Michell's Roman Axis passes through Seacourt woods only 2.2 km east of Binsey Church, which clips the grounds of Blenheim Palace. As mentioned in Chapter 6, this remarkable line connects many local and national centre places.

Some researchers believe that the name Frideswide is typically Anglo-Saxon and has little meaning. However, Fride is found in many Welsh names such as St Winifred and St Fride's Well, an ancient stone monument southwest of Ystradmeurig, near Treffynnon, Ceredigion. This well also has the name Ffynnon Sant Ffraed. Here we see a corruption of Fride from Ffraed or Ffriad, the Welsh word for Bride pronounced Fride. Another instance of this comes from the name of an ancient abbey in Wales called Llanfride, between Aberaeron and Aberystwyth, also in the county of Ceredigion. St Ffraid is the present dedication of the church that now stands on the site of the abbey.

When the Welsh-speaking Britons ruled over much of Cymry and Lloegyr in pre-Roman times, Oxford was a spiritual centre, the name of their Earth goddess Ffraid still surviving at the sacred shrine where she was honoured at the navel of their realm. In keeping with other major omphalos sites, people in pagan times would consult the well as an oracle to ease their burdened souls and to obtain healing by bathing in the waters. Interestingly, the legend refers to Frideswide praying to St Margaret and to St Catherine, who holds the wheel and spindle representing the axis mundi. On the wooden pulpit inside Binsey Church, we find a depiction of St Margaret emerging from the mouth of Satan in the form of a dragon. According to the church guide, the first incumbent of Binsey Church was Nicholas Breakspear, the first and only British Pope. Perhaps he was initiated here at the legendary symbolic centre of Britain before becoming Pope Adrian IV in 1154.[23]

When Caroline and I arrived in Oxford to research its various sites, we visited Christ Church Cathedral and the shrine of St Frideswide and were amazed at its beautiful carvings, three of which depict female faces peering out of foliage. This may represent Frideswide and her two companions at Binsey, but it also reminded us of a carving at Wells Cathedral that depicts Bride as a 'green woman.' The three identical faces we see here on the shrine may allude to the triple aspect of this goddess, representing intellect, creativity and fertility.

Stained-glass window of St Frideswide, Binsey Church

Inside Binsey Church is a heraldic shield on the pulpit depicting the emblem of Oxford in the form of three crowned female heads, another possible representation of the triple goddess, along with an ox crossing a ford. It also has a stained-glass window by the Pre-Raphaelite artist Edward Burne-Jones showing scenes of Frideswide's life, including one of the sleeping pigs encountered by Frideswide at Binsey. This reminded me of the Lludd and Llefelys legend when the fighting dragons fell into the pit and transformed into pigs, who then succumbed to a deep sleep after drinking the mead. Burne-Jones was an artist of great renown, initiated into the Mystery Schools, and possibly knew Binsey as an important sacred omphalos site where our ancestors openly worshipped the goddess in the land.

Bristol

Like Oxford, the city of Bristol has mythical foundations from pre-Roman times and old maps clearly show quartering cosmology, with a north-south cardo and east-west decumanus line, a central crossroads within circular walls, and four gates. The High Cross once marked the old omphalos, erected in 1373 to commemorate the granting of a charter by Edward III. It gave the city its own status, separating it from the neighbouring counties of Gloucestershire and Somerset, and its own sheriff ruling over its legal and civil affairs. In return, the town provided the king with ships and men for his wars in France.

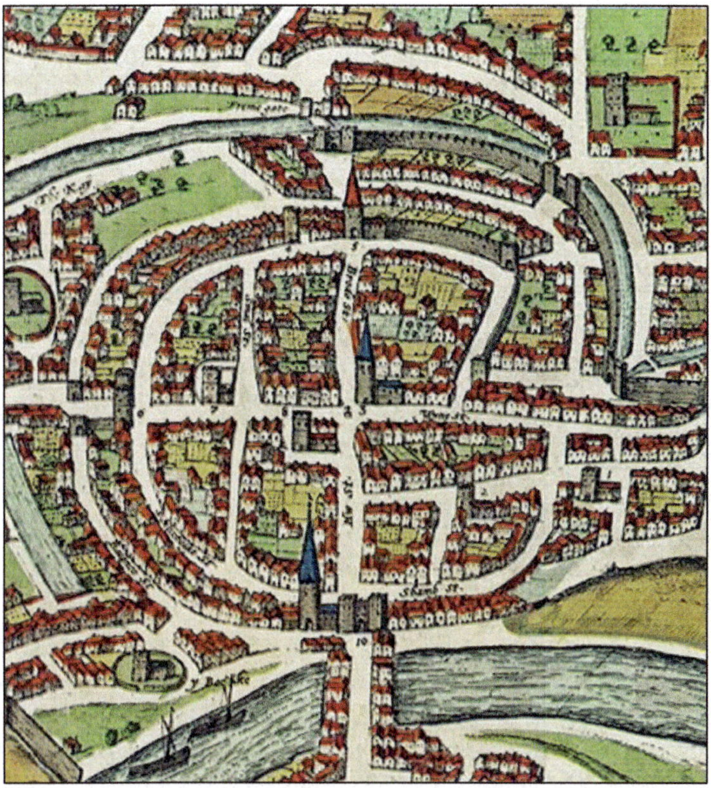

Map of the city of Bristol by Braun and Hogenberg 1575

According to John Corry in *The History of Bristol*, the founder of the city was Brennus, son of King Malmutius, who jointly ruled Cymry and Lloegyr with his brother Belinus 380–374 BCE. He is credited with 'enlarging and improving' Bristol, which indicates that it must have existed as an important town earlier in the Iron Age.[24] Old stone statues of them can be seen today on either side of St John's Gate in the north of the old city.

There is evidence of a Roman port at Bristol in an area called Seamills, where the old tidal limit of the river Trym met with the Avon and Iron Age hillforts stand on either side of the Avon near Clifton. Although there are scattered remains of a settlement from the period of Brennius in the area, most of the legendary city lies under the Saxon foundations of a town they named *Brycgstow* or *Brigg stow*, which means 'the meeting place at the bridge'. Here at a fording of the River Avon a wooden bridge led travellers to the entrance gate of a wooden stockaded town surrounded by earthworks. By the 10th century, Brycgstow had grown into a sizable and bustling city, possibly one of Alfred's royal burhs. To the north of the town was another vital river called the Frome, a tributary of the Avon, both waterways aiding the success of this settlement as an essential trading port by 1051. However, from 1239-1247, diverting the Frome made for easier navigation.

According to the *Anglo-Saxon Chronicle*, in 1063, Harold Godwinsson, three years before he met his end at the Battle of Hastings, had his ships fitted out in Bristol harbour before setting sail to battle with the Welsh. After William the Conqueror claimed Bristol as his own, Harold's sons crossed from Ireland in an attempt to raise support from the town to oust the Normans, Unfortunately, the townsfolk resisted his request, leading to Harold's invasion plans to fail.[25]

One of the earliest mints was established in Bristol in the 11th century signifying its growing importance. As a major trading town, exporting such goods as wool and leather, a weekly market probably took place drawing people from all over the west of England.

A motte and bailey castle with a tower was soon constructed by the Normans made from stone taken from nearby Brandon Hill. It was the seat of Geoffrey de Montbray, Bishop of Coutances, one of the knights who accompanied William the Conqueror at the Battle of Hastings. In 1135, Robert, Earl of Gloucester rebuilt it in Caen stone with a great Keep five stories high. The Earl also founded the Benedictine Priory of St James in 1137, which today is situated off Lower Maudlin Road next to James Park. The town also included several friaries, monastic hospitals, St James' Priory and St Mary Magdalene nunnery, all dissolved during the Reformation.

Over the centuries, Bristol has made its name as a great Maritime trade centre and by the 14th century was trading with Spain, Portugal and Iceland. Ships also left Bristol to establish colonies in the New World. Its most famous mariner was John Cabot, who set sail from Bristol in 1497 on an exploration of North America sponsored by Henry VII.

By the mid-18th century, Bristol had become England's second biggest city during a time when it was receiving goods such as sugar cane, tobacco, rum and cocoa, products of the slave trade. Bristol's rather shameful reputation for slave trading thrived in the 15th century and renewed growth peaked between 1730 and 1745, when it became the leading slaving port during the rise of England's American colonies. Over 2,000 slaving voyages were made by Bristol ships bringing with them over 500,000 Africans between the late 17th century and the abolition of the slave trade in 1807, carrying an estimated half a million people from Africa to the Americas in brutal conditions. The trade of goods from the Avon Valley to the Americas continued during the Industrial Revolution, including ores from the Mendips and coal from the North Somerset coalfield.

Much of old Bristol was destroyed during three bombing raids during WWII, the German's main target being Bristol's factories manufacturing aircraft and shipping in the port. Two bombed churches, St Peter's and St Mary le Port, still stand at the centre of Bristol in Castle Park. Sadly, what followed during the post-war years was the building of concrete office blocks and shopping arcades. Since 2006, some of these blocks were torn down and replaced with more tastefully designed buildings and houses, although there are still areas to improve in Bristol.

Today, the walls that circled the city are no longer apparent and the crossroads is devoid of anything of significance. The High Cross was removed in 1733 having once stood on a high point at the exact centre of old Bristol. It was removed by deputy chamberlain Mr Vaughan, who lived nearby, claiming 'his life and house were in danger from it every time the wind blew.' But a more likely explanation is that this ornate and historic carving impeded the flow of the busy streets in the 18th century.

The monument had niches containing the statues of Kings John, Henry III, Edward III and Edward IV, all of whom presented Bristol with charters that contributed to its expansion and trade. In 1633, the cross was repaired and altered to include the statues of Henry VI, Elizabeth I, James I and Charles I, who had further endowed privileges on the city. It must have been quite a sight when it was later painted vermilion, blue and gold.

It was re-erected on College Green, an area of parkland between the Council House and the Cathedral. However, it soon started to annoy passers-by who complained that it hindered their promenading and was 'a ruinous and superstitious relict.' Thereafter, it was dismantled and left in pieces in the cloisters of Bristol Cathedral until the cross was rescued by the Dean and given away to his friend Henry Hoare of Stourhead in Wiltshire to use as an estate ornament where it still stands today.

The centre of Bristol is marked today by the 18th-century Baroque Christ Church. It was one of two churches that marked the omphalos of Bristol, the other was St Ewen's, founded in the 1100s and demolished in 1786. Christ Church is rarely open, but fortunately, we arrived just before a service was about to start and were warmly

Bristol High Cross and the four gates by Robert Ricard c.1479

welcomed to look around. Inside, we noticed a wonderful plaque showing St Michael and the dragon and a banner depicting his counterpart St George slaying a dragon. The banner originally came from St George's Church on Brandon Hill, now converted as a concert venue. However, another banner drew our attention showing a sleeping dragon with a winged St Michael hovering above it, perhaps symbolic of harmonious energy.

Apart from the 18th-century Christ Church, there is little to recommend the modern pilgrim to Bristol's omphalos as sadly, just a few yards to the south are two of the most unsightly concrete structures you would ever wish to see. They belong to the Norwich Union Building Society and the Bank of England, which now stand derelict and vandalised. The buildings were constructed in 1962, arranged around the bombed-out ruined Saxon tower of St Mary-le-Port Church in Castle Park. We instantly felt that these abandoned architectural eyesores at the heart of such a historically important city create imbalance and disharmony for Bristol's economic and psychological well-being.

Bristol's northern city gate, with the statues of its founding father Brennus, is the only one remaining from the medieval city. Long ago, Bristol had seven fortified gateways, some incorporating churches like Oxford; at one time there were eleven places of worship within the city walls. Miraculously, the north gate still has its 14th-century church dedicated to St John the Baptist, also known as St John on the Wall. It is incorporated into the only major surviving part of the old city walls, complete with a vaulted crypt dedicated to the Holy Cross. It was originally joined to the church of St Lawrence, which stood to the south and shared the same tower. St Lawrence was closed in 1580 and demolished soon after. A conduit exists next to the main entrance of St John's on Quay Street, which supplied water piped from Brandon Hill since 1374.

Alongside the statues of Brennus and his brother Belinus, are the arms of Charles II, the City of Bristol, and the Society of Merchant Venturers, which date from the 17th Century. The statues are thought to come from a much older gate, possibly one that existed in Norman times.

Much of the interior of St John's was renovated in recent times, but the real gem is its underground crypt. Much of its original 14th century masonry remains including the fine ribbed vaulted ceiling. It felt like a church within a church and on the ceiling we spotted an unusual 'double' green man carved as a ceiling boss depicting two faces mirroring each other.

Chichester

The history of the town of Chichester in Sussex seems to originate with Cogidubnus, a local Celtic king of the Iron Age Atrebates tribe, who ruled the area between *c.* 43 and *c.* 80 CE during the Roman invasion. Rather than resisting the Romans, Cogidubnus cooperated with the Latin invaders becoming one of their puppet kings. He was given a sumptuous palace at Fishbourne near the coast and controlled the nearby town of 'Noviomagus Reginorum', now Chichester. A damaged marble slab found in Chichester in 1723 has a Latin inscription which translates as 'To Neptune and Minerva, for the welfare of the Divine Temple, by the authority of Tiberius Claudius Cogidubnus, great king of the Britons, the guild of smiths and those in it gave this temple at their own expense ...ens, son of Pudentinus, presented the forecourt.'

The name Noviomagus Reginorum is intriguing, possibly meaning 'new marketplace' of the Regni Tribe, the pre-Roman sub-tribe of that area. This may indicate that the Romans built on or over an earlier Celtic town.

Like Oxford, Chichester has four principal streets that still follow the original 'cardo' and 'decumanus' plan founded nearly two thousand years ago or before. Moreover, the city walls have remnants of Roman masonry in the foundations. Unlike many other Roman

Map of Chichester by John Speed 1610

towns in Britain, its symmetrical quadrants, creating a cross and central crossroads, survive intact, despite its long history and occupation by Saxons and Normans. An elaborate medieval market cross marks the omphalos today at the crossroads reminiscent of Oxford and Bristol. We believe by preserving this fortuitous cosmological plan, the city has continued to flourish, unlike those that have destroyed their central shrines, crossroads and quartering. The city even survived severe bombing by the Luftwaffe during WWII.

References:

1 Keller W (1970) *The Etruscans*. Book Club Associates, London.
2. Ibid.
3. Morris J (1980) '*Nennius' British History and the Welsh Annals*. Phillimore, London.
4. Thorpe L (Translator) (1966) *Geoffrey of Monmouth: The History of the Kings of Britain*. The Folio Society, London.
5. Jones G & Jones T (translators) (1949) *The Mabinogion*. J M Dent & Sons, London.
6. Thorpe L (Translator) (1966) *Geoffrey of Monmouth: The History of the Kings of Britain*. The Folio Society, London.
7. ibid.
8. Oxford History: City Wall. http://oxfordhistory.org.uk/city_wall/index.html
9. Anglo-Saxons.net. http://www.anglo-saxons.net/hwaet/?do=get&type=chron&from=880&to=927.
10. Rous (1480) *Historia Regum Angliae*. https://archive.org/details/joannisrossiant00rousgoog
11. Drayton M (2001) *Polyolbion: The Complete Works of Michael Drayton, Now First Collected: Volume 1*. Adamant Media Corporation, Delaware, MA.
12. Thorpe L (Translator) (1966) *Geoffrey of Monmouth: The History of the Kings of Britain*. The Folio Society, London.
13. Sullivan P (2013) *The Secret History of Oxford*. The History Press, Stroud.
14. Trubshaw B (1991) *The Quest for the Omphalos: Finding the Mystical Middle of England*. Heart of Albion Press, Loughborough.
15. Now you see it … Now you don't: The Oxford Henge. https://ellisctaylor.com/2015/10/23/now-you-see-it-now-you-dont-the-oxford-henge/.
16. Sullivan P (2013) *The Secret History of Oxford*. The History Press, Stroud.
17. Fulton H (2009) *History and Myth: Geoffrey of Monmouth's Historia Regum Britanniae*. Wiley-Blackwell, Oxford.
18. Thorpe L (Translator) (1966) *Geoffrey of Monmouth: The History of the Kings of Britain*. The Folio Society, London
19. Gordon E O (1932) *Prehistoric London: Its Mounds and Circles*. The Covenant Publishing Co., London.
20. Watkins A (1925) *The Old Straight Track*. Methuen Publishing, London.
21. Headlam C (1872); Railton, Herbert (1857–1910), illus (1907) *The Story of Oxford*. J M Dent, London.
22. Carr L (2014) *Binsey: Oxford's Holy Place: Its Saint, Village, and People*. Archaeopress, Oxford.
23. Morris J (2001) *Oxford*. Oxford University Press, Oxford.
24. Corry, J (1816) *The History of Bristol Civil and Ecclesiastical; including Biographical Notices of Eminent and Distinguished Natives*. W. Sheppard, Bristol.
25. Ingram, J. (translator) (1912) *The Anglo-Saxon Chronicle*. Everyman Press, London.

Chapter 10

Honouring and Healing the Centres

We believe that connecting with the centre or navel of our landscape re-activates the natural telluric power and the goddess healing energy that once existed at these places, which our early ancestors utilised long ago to create balance and harmony for their kingdom and its people. This will help us reach higher realms of consciousness and heighten our experience of the healing and nurturing 'Mother' earth goddess, allowing us to receive sacred knowledge, inspiration and wisdom. The place you choose to do this can be high up on a mountain, within a sheltered valley or at a crossroads in the centre of a town or village. It could even be in the middle of your home such as the hearth or under the stairs.

Caroline and I have created hand-drawn maps at the end of each chapter to guide you on a modern pilgrimage to all the places featured in the centre-landscapes whether it be on foot or by car. We believe that connecting with the sacred trees, wells, hills and manmade features such as megaliths and churches can be spiritually beneficial if done mindfully.

We are all born with a unique energy that operates at a different frequency. Likewise, each of the many centres discussed in this book has its own special vibration and unique frequencies. Consequently, the individual needs to visit and experience their local centre in a way or sequence that feels right for them, to maximise the healing benefits of that site. The timing of any ceremony carried out at the centre is also significant as the telluric energy at these places is at its most potent during the full moon or new moon and at certain solar festivals such as at the spring and autumn equinoxes and the winter and summer solstices.

The sequence of any pilgrimage to the centre, whether it be in Wales, Oxford or the Isle of Man, is also important to consider. Again, it may be your personal or group preference as to where you begin and end the journey and which sites you choose on the way. You may first wish to connect with a holy well, symbolic of the underworld connection, before visiting a crossroads, religious shrine or central mountain or vice versa. If you have difficulty in deciding, use divination, by pendulum dowsing over a map or diagram of the sites, asking which site to visit first, then second and so on. Alternatively, you can choose the sequence of sites by literally 'pulling them out of a hat' after writing the name of each place on separate pieces of paper, folding them and placing them in a container – similar to picking the runes; that way you are not allowing the rational mind to determine the outcome.

The integration of folklore and the geographical significance of these sites allows us to understand why these centres have such power and influence over the landscape and the people who live there. Similar to the art of acupuncture, which focuses on certain points of the body to stimulate balance and healing of the body, finding the right spot in the landscape and using the appropriate remedies, whether it be crystals, invocation, chanting, song or blessings, at the right time is the key to its healing and can open a doorway to knowledge. The healing vibrations will be carried through to all the other sites connected with the particular centre you are honouring, as they travel along the east-west and north-south pathways that lead to it, interconnecting with powerful telluric earth energies and underground watercourses. Any words you choose to say at your special centre are key to finding a connection with it and it is important to speak them clearly and from the heart, without any negative emotions interfering with the process.

The modern pilgrim encounters a new experience when they walk these ancient pathways in the open landscape for the first time, losing the insulation and protection of cars. The loss of such physical barriers can be liberating for many, allowing for inner reflection and a connection with their higher consciousness. From time immemorial, people have travelled on foot to sacred destinations as a way to escape their humdrum lives, to express religious devotion or to do penance for some wrongdoing. In medieval times, Britain had hundreds of pilgrimage routes to religious shrines until Thomas Cromwell under Henry VIII banned them during the Reformation to eradicate Roman Catholic practices.

They remained closed for over 300 years, until the resurgence of the Camino de Santiago, or the Way of St James, the highly popular pilgrimage route across Europe to northwestern Spain ending at Santiago de Compostela. In 1984, only 423 pilgrims completed the final 100-km stretch of the Camino, entitling them to an official certificate. By 2006, the figure was 100,377 and by 2016 it had exceeded 278,000. The number walking this trail currently stands at over 300,000, of those, 6000 were from the UK – a fourfold increase in a decade.

The modern pilgrim still searches for a community of sorts, but religion is often not the main motivation. It is the experience of having a spiritual connection with a holy place that people seek, but this may not necessarily be a church or cathedral, but perhaps a stone circle, cave, well or spring. Often it is a natural place of power such as a hilltop, a confluence of two rivers, a meeting of trackways or an ancient tree. Ley lines are also beginning to appeal to the modern pilgrim, such as the north-south Belinus Line and the east-west St Michael Line has become an established walking route along certain sections.

The British Pilgrimage Trust has opened up walks to include sacred landscapes and re-established old ones, including a medieval 350-km pilgrims' route from Southampton to Canterbury, which they hope will one day rival the Camino Trail. Guy Hayward, co-founder and treasurer of the Trust, states: 'Lots of people simply want to connect with the natural world at a pace at which you can appreciate it. In "normal" life, our minds are speeding up while our bodies are staying put. Here, the mind and the body can meet up.'[1]

Many of our fellow Earth Mystery researchers have noticed over the years a growing trend among modern pilgrims to achieve spiritual enlightenment while visiting sacred sites. National Geographic photographer and anthropologist Martin Grey, has spent 35 years studying and photographing hundreds of sacred sites in more than 150 countries. His observances have led him to speak about something he calls a 'Gaian Age of Pilgrimage'.

In the past, Grey has observed two types of visitors to sacred sites: traditional religious pilgrims and tourists visiting places of monumental architecture (Stonehenge, the Great Pyramid and Machu Picchu, for example). The new pilgrims, however, are also committed to the restoration of the environment and the development of new greener and more spiritual socio-political enterprises. Grey believes that during the coming decades, there will be an enormous number of people visiting sacred sites around the world, particularly the non-traditional spiritual pilgrim, who has 'transcended', or risen above, the limited views of particular religions to become part of a global community of highly conscious beings. As a result, these sacred sites in the coming years will function on a higher level of vibration and become for those experiencing them places of empowerment, seeing them as planetary acupuncture points. They will also be viewed as destiny activation sites and as energy transducers for spiritual illumination and the evolution of new ecological, social and political consciousness.[2]

Few of us may ever fully understand the true potential of the human mind, let alone the power of its directed thought. Nevertheless, as we break free from traditions and rituals and evolve spiritually, we will begin to glimpse our true essence. From a very early age, I learned that the landscape of our Earth with its wonderfully varied rocks, mountains, lakes and rivers has great healing powers, not only for the body, but also for the mind. The Neolithic and Bronze Age peoples built their almost indestructible stone monuments in special places of telluric power to help humanity in its darkest hours, to lift them from the depths of materialism to achieve a measure of enlightenment.

When visiting these remarkable centre places of power, Caroline's connection with the Earth goddess has helped to re-capture her own goddess energy. She believes that this experience is vital to enable one to reclaim a sense of feminine and personal fulfilment, which has lain dormant and unfulfilled.

Likewise, one can experience at these centres a connection to the source of creation at the centre of our galaxy, a universal consciousness linking the intelligence of the cosmos and with Mother Earth and all that she provides. This will help us reconnect with our inner centre – our core being, where we can find our internal flame or light that awakens us to our 'inner landscape'.

Yuri Leitch, whose artwork graces the front cover, writes that 'within our inner landscapes the sacred tree, or axis pole, that connects matter to spirit, is our spinal cord. We are, all of us, mobile centre-points.' He also reminds us that we are transitioning from the Age of Pisces to the Age of Aquarius', which for the Celts was represented by Imbolc, the time of the goddess Bride/Brigid. She is here for us now, waiting to be recognised once more as the life-giver and nurturer, emanating her three-fold energy, as both the sky goddess and land goddess, at the centres of power within the British and Irish landscapes.

We hope this guide to the sacred centres of the British Isles and Ireland will help you to comprehend these remarkable and special places of healing, and of course how to find them. We believe that by walking these sacred routes, communicating with the mother goddess and spirit guardians at the centres, and appreciating their mystical relationship with the heavenly or cosmic realms, we will receive healing, wisdom and knowledge to help us with our spiritual growth. More importantly, it will encourage us to love and care for our landscape rather than exploit it, thus, like our ancient ancestors, we can promote fertility, prosperity and well-being

The countryside is alive and intelligent and responds to our emotions and thoughts, therefore honouring the land with focused love and positive intentions, as Colin Bloy once taught us, will once more restore the grail archetype, which has been lost to us for so long.

References:

1. British Pilgrimage Trust. http://britishpilgrimage.org/the-bpt/
2. https://sacredsites.com/martin_gray/purposes.html

Appendix A

Centre-points of the English Counties

Those intent on healing towns and communities may find our list of English county centre-points important for your quest. Locating the centre and directing healing from there will create balance and harmony in the landscape. Many of the English counties have well-known centre-points, but when boundaries change the geological centres change too. Many of the newly calculated centres may have no monument or landscape feature and may even be a spot in the middle of a private field, lake or quarry. Therefore, we have listed the following suggestions for the nearest sacred site in each English county and the most auspicious place to connect with the omphalos.

Sadly, the knowledge of working with geographical centres has been misused by certain occult groups over the centuries, but many others seek to heal these places behind the scenes. As Colin Bloy founder of the Fountain Group demonstrated, the detrimental energy of polluted places can always be positively transformed through love and healing.

Bedfordshire	Church of the Holy Ascension, Littleworth village
Berkshire	Reading Cathedral
Buckinghamshire	Church of St Mary the Virgin, Aylesbury
Cambridgeshire	St Mary's Church, Bluntisham
Cheshire	Site of Bostock oak tree, Darnhall Abbey
Cornwall	Lanivet Church cross
Cumberland	St Kentigern's Church, Caldbeck
Cumbria	Grisedale Tarn/Helvellyn
Derbyshire	Nine Ladies Stone Circle, Stanton Moor
Devon	Celtic Sanctuary, Bow
Dorset (formerly Middleton)	St Catherine's Chapel, Milton Abbas
Durham	The Devil's Stone, Crook
Essex	Chelmsford Cathedral
Gloucestershire	Cooper's Hill, Brockworth

Hampshire	Winchester Cathedral, Winchester
Herefordshire	Hereford Cathedral
Hertfordshire	Oaklands near Woolmer Green
Huntingdonshire	St Andrew's Church, Abbots Ripton
Kent	Lenham Memorial Cross
Lancashire	Longridge Fell summit
Leicestershire	Leicester Cathedral
Lincolnshire	St Margaret's Church, Waddingworth
Norfolk	All Saint's Church, Mattishall
Northamptonshire	St Peter's Church, Walgrave
Northumberland	Harwood Forest
Nottinghamshire	St Radegund's Church, Maplebeck
Oxfordshire	Carfax, Oxford
Rutland	St Andrew's Church, Hambledon
Shropshire	Cantlop Cross, Shrewsbury
Somerset	Burrow Mump, Burrowbridge
Staffordshire	St Rufin Church, Bursford
Suffolk	Coronation Oak, Middlewood Green
Surrey	Oak Hangers Bridge, south of East Horsley
Sussex	Yew Tree at Chailey Windmill on Red House Common
Warwickshire	Lillington Oak, Leamington Spa
Westmorland	Orton stone circle
Wiltshire	Etchilhampton Water
Worcestershire	Worcester Cathedral
Yorkshire	Ash Tree at Barkston Ash

Appendix B

Centres of Europe and the EU

The location of the first-ever official 'centre' of Europe was declared in 1775 by the Polish royal astronomer who calculated it to be in the town of Suchowola in Poland, marked by a stone monument. Due to boundary changes, the centre of Europe in 1815 became a hill that forms the water division between the basins of the Baltic Sea and Black Sea next to St John the Baptist Church near the mining town of Kremnica in Slovakia, marked by a megalithic style stone.

In 1887, geographers from the Austro-Hungarian Empire constructed a stone to mark the geographic centre of Europe, located in Transcarpathia in what is today a region of Ukraine. The French National Geographic Institute in 1989, calculated the centre-point of the European landmass as Girja in Lithuania marked by a stone pillar surmounted by a crown of golden stars.

The leaders of the European Union (EU) created an omphalos 'shrine' to mark the centre of the combined lands of all their member states; between 2004–2007 Kleinmaischeid in Germany marked the centre of their 25 European states, recalculated as Geinhausen in Germany when the EU expanded to 27 member states; between 2013–2020 the EU consisted of 28 member states, and its 'centre' was recalculated as Westerngrund in Germany, 40 km from the headquarters of the European Central Bank. Post-Brexit, the centre of the EU is marked by a large plaque near the town of Gadheim in Bavaria, Germany.

Appendix C

Sicily, the Navel of the Mediterranean

Map of Sicily with Enna marked in red

Sicily is a three-cornered island that traditionally marks the centre of the Mediterranean Sea. Goethe wrote: 'Sicily is the key to everything' and according to author John Julius Norwich, it is 'the stepping stone between Europe and Africa, the gateway between the East and the West, the link between the Latin world and the Greek.'[1] It is also the land of gods and heroes, their characters woven into the island's folklore along with monsters and mystical adventures.

Sicily is renowned for its beauty with historic picturesque towns and villages and green fields, particularly around the island's most prominent feature, Mount Etna, the tallest volcano in Europe, and one of the most active in the world, standing at 3,357 m (11,014 ft) above sea level. Indeed, it is the height of Etna that gives Sicily its unique all-year-round fertility, as in the summer when most other Mediterranean countries and their islands are parched, Etna releases her water from the melting ice and feeds her landscape.

Over the centuries, Sicily's central position has made it a strategic place of trade and conquest, attracting occupation by the

Phoenicians, Carthaginians, Greeks, Romans, Arabs, Goths, Normans, Germans, French and Spanish, all having left their cultural mark in the island's food and architecture.

The omphalos of this island is the historic town of Enna, which has been described by several ancient authors as one of the most remarkable places in Sicily, said to be a day's journey from the nearest point on all three of its coasts. The ancient settlement lies on the level summit of a gigantic hill, with precipitous cliffs on all sides. Enna's natural supply of water and impregnable situation made it one of the world's greatest natural strongholds. However, archaeological excavations have revealed artefacts dating back to Neolithic times and settlements from before the 11th century BCE, which some historians believe were established by the *Sicanians* and the *Sicels*, a tribe that gave Sicily its name.

The sacred focal point of the hill is the 'Rocca di Cerere', or Rock of Ceres, a vast limestone slab that overlooks the fertile plains surrounding Enna. It was the site of a temple shrine and grove in honour of the ancient Greek goddess Demeter, sister of Zeus. The Romans knew her as Ceres and at one time her temple was a famed site of worship.[2] The shrine was known as the *umbilicus Sicilae* or

Rock of Ceres

'Navel of Sicily' – the 'womb of the Mediterranean.' Here we find a shrine to the goddess at the omphalos, and like the Celtic Bride,

Brigid, Friad or Freeshey, Demeter was the Greek goddess of fertility. Demeter's temple was described by contemporary historians as a unique and divine place of worship until it was vandalised by Roman soldiers who stole her bronze statue. Sicily's omphalos town has been at the centre of many battles and massacres and the Rock of Ceres, like the Temple Rock in Jerusalem, has been seized by various powers over the centuries, from which they would exert their control over the island and the Mediterranean as a whole. The Rocca di Cerere was also a renowned centre of pagan magic and occult activities, typical of an axis mundi site.

Like the High Kings at the omphalos of Ireland, we have a royal palace neighbouring the sacred rock built by King Frederick II in the early 1200s called Castello di Lombardia. At the time of building, Frederick was Holy Roman Emperor, King of Jerusalem and Sicily, a veritable king of the Western world. His castle at Enna became an important example of military architecture in Sicily and once comprised of twenty towers.

The powerful Rock of Ceres, on which the Demeter's temple stood, is also pointing to Mount Etna in the distance. This still active volcano serves as the 'mother mountain' of Sicily – and symbolically the 'world mountain' of the Mediterranean, the rock drawing its power from the volcano. According to ancient myths, Etna is associated with Zeus, who imprisoned the monstrous Typhon beneath the mountain after a battle for supremacy. The volcano's eruptions are often attributed to Typhon's struggles to break free. Even today, many Sicilian residents regard Mount Etna as a sentient being and leave offerings there during eruptions such as bottles of wine, hoping to appease the volcano.

Just 5 km southeast of Enna is a sacred and mysterious lake called Lake Pergusa, said to be the mythological location of the Rape of Persephone, Demeter's daughter, having been carried off by Hades, God of the Underworld into nearby caves. According to the legend, Demeter's loss caused the earth to be barren, until eventually Persephone was allowed to return to spend two-thirds of the year with her mother, which once again caused the crops to ripen and the flowers to grow. Like her mother, Persephone was a goddess of agriculture, fertility and the seasons, therefore this myth is an allegorical tale related to seasonal fertility rituals.

Incredibly, Lake Pergusa is encompassed by a modern motor racing circuit, similar to the TT motorcycle course that circumnavigates the Isle of Man, making these sacred waters impossible to access. Unfortunately, like the Manx island, the old myths and legends of goddess worship on this beautiful island no longer hold sway over this once enchanted omphalos site.

The symbol of Sicily is the three-legged Trinacria, also known as a Triskelion, very similar to the emblem of the Isle of Man. The Sicilian version relates to the three-cornered island and the triple aspect of the goddess at the centre, in contrast to IOM's masculine aspect formed by the legs of an armoured knight complete with spurs.

Sicily's Trinacria symbol

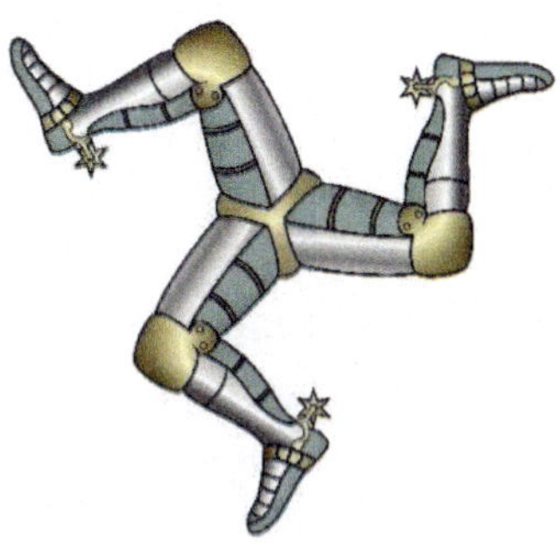

Isle of Man's Triskelion

Incidentally, Easter Island in the southeastern Pacific Ocean is another three-cornered island, which claims to be the navel of the world. This title originated from the 19th-century French ethnologist Alphonse Pinart, who based it on a translation of the island's original name *Te pito o te henua.*[3]

References:

1. Norwich, J J (2015) *Sicily, A Short History from the Ancient Greeks to Cosa Nostra*. John Murray Publishers, London.
2. Spaeth, B S. (1996). *The Roman Goddess Ceres*. University of Texas Press, Austin, USA.
3. Pinart, A (1877). *Voyage à l'Ile de Pâques (Océan Pacifique)*. Le Tour du Monde; Nouveau Journal des Voyags. 36: 225.

Acknowledgements

We would like to give special thanks to those who have helped us with our research and exploration of the centres of Britain and Ireland, including Claire Heron and Mark Barker for accompanying us around various sites in Cumbria and sharing their insights and research over the years. Ronnie and Rebecca Neilson for their help, hospitality and photos of Scotland. Janice Howdle and Brian Wills for their inspiration and knowledge of the ancient royal site at Tamworth, Boudicca and the centres of England. Celia Thomas for her perceptions at the centre of Cornwall. Richard Crowhurst for his help with the Isle of Man chapter. Brian Cowper for his hospitality and local knowledge of Cumbria.

Thanks also go to the inspiring staff at St Audeon's Church in Dublin who guided us to the Esker Riada and Kildare Heritage Centre for information on Dún Ailinne. The staff at Clonmacnoise for their help and enthusiasm, and the helpful librarian at Rhayader for assisting us in the discovery of the illusive well. Louise Coe and the Gatekeeper Trust for their support, advice and interest, and for showcasing our concepts at their conferences and talks. Alex Langstone and Carole Young for their Cumbrian adventure that has inspired and influenced many to discover their Cumbrian quest. Not forgetting the mysterious lady who sought us out at Bride's Well on the Isle of Man, to inform us of the St Ciaran connection and guide us to magical places at the climax of our island adventure.

I would also like to pay tribute to my late friend John Beasley for his support and guidance during my early psychic quests around the British Isles, which inspired some of the research in the book.

We are also indebted to Yuri Leitch for his artwork, insights, and knowledge, and his perspective on the 'Power of Centres'. Rob Wildwood for the Cat Stone photo at the centre of Ireland, and Ronnie Neilson for his photo of the Clan Stone.

Finally, we would like to acknowledge Christine Rhone and the late John Michell for their inspirational work *Twelve-Tribe Nations*, Michell for *At the Centre of the World*, and Michael Dames for *Mythic Ireland*, all of which have encouraged our own quests of the British Isles.

About the Authors

Gary Biltcliffe was born in 1960 and brought up in Lancashire. He has dedicated the last 30 years to historical research and investigation of earth mysteries, dowsing ancient sites, uncovering lost knowledge and early folklore. He has appeared on radio and television and has lectured widely in the UK and North America. Gary has also led international groups around Britain's sacred sites and written articles for journals and magazines. He moved to Dorset in 1993 and researched much of its ancient history culminating in his first publication *The Spirit of Portland, Revelations of a Sacred Isle* in 2009 (republished in 2022 as *Mysterious Portland*), *The Spine of Albion* in 2012, *The Power of Centre* in 2018, and *The Holy Axis* in 2023.

Caroline Hoare was born in 1958 and brought up on a farm in the heart of the Dart Valley in South Devon. She started her working life in a Fine Art auction house and later transferred to the world of publishing and bookselling. Caroline moved from London to Dorset in 2003 and trained as a Geomancer, Feng Shui Consultant and Holistic Interior Designer. She has also spent the last twenty years alongside Gary travelling to lost cities around the world, researching history and ancient civilisations and has a keen interest in the mythology and folklore of Britain. Caroline continues to research and write alongside Gary and co-authored *The Spine of Albion*, *The Power of Centre* and *The Holy Axis*.

Picture Credits

European centre (p ii) Juliux, CC BY 3.0 <https://creativecommons.org/licenses/by/3.0>, via Wikimedia Commons

Asian Centre (p ii) Agilight, CC BY-SA 4.0 <https://creativecommons.org/licenses/by-sa/4.0>, via Wikimedia Commons

Geographical Centre of USA (p ii) Alamy stock photo BM56j4

Our Spiral Galaxy ESA/Hubble & NASA, Public domain, via Wikimedia Commons

Nordic world tree called the Yggdrasil by Olfusen Bagge (1847). PD Art from Northern Antiquities. Prose Edda, Helios.

Mount Kailash. Jean-Marie Hullot, CC BY-SA 4.0 <https://creativecommons.org/licenses/by-sa/4.0>, via Wikimedia Commons

Figure 1. Etruscan or Roman Augur. Courtesy of Erdmann Barbara (adapted by Author), CC BY-SA 3.0 <http://creativecommons.org/licenses/by-sa/3.0/>, via Wikimedia Commons

Babylonian omphalos stone with coiled serpent by George Rawlinson (1880). The seven great monarchies of the ancient eastern world, p. 166. J. W. Lovell Company, New York.

A replica of Delphi's omphalos stone (Delphi Archaeological Museum). Yucatan (Юкатан), CC BY-SA 3.0 <https://creativecommons.org/licenses/by-sa/3.0>, via Wikimedia Commons

Chinese Dragons. Detail above entrance to Mandarin Building from Chinatown Bridge, Winnipeg, Manitoba. Ccyyrree, CC0, via Wikimedia Commons

British goddess Brigantia found at Birrens, Scotland. Courtesy of Yuri Leitch

Fig. 3 and Fig. 7 templates by Nilfanion [CC BY-SA 3.0 (https://creativecommons.org/licenses/by-sa/3.0)], Wikimedia Commons.

Fig. 4 and Fig. 6 (adapted by author) by Colm O. Lochlainn (1940). Roadways in Ancient Ireland. In: Ryan, John (ed.), Féil-sgríbhinn Eóin Mhic Néill: Essays and studies presented to professor Eoin MacNeill on the occasion of his seventieth birthday, May 15th 1938, Dublin.

Fig. 5 template by Andrein via Wikimedia Commons (Own work) [CC BY-SA 3.0 (https://creativecommons.org/licenses/by-sa/3.0) or GFDL (http://www.gnu.org/copyleft/fdl.html)].

Ptolemy's map of Ireland by Nicolaus Germanus (www.polona.pl) (Public domain), via Wikimedia Commons.

Fig. 8 template Ireland_location_map.svg: NordNordWest derivative work: Nilfanion.

St Ciaran and King Diarmait performing the foundation ceremony at Clonmacnoise. Courtesy of Ali Isaac, author and blogger

The Turoe Stone uploaded to Wikimedia Commons by author Dirk Huth.

The O'Neill's Stone of Destiny at the centre of Northern Ireland. QuartierLatin1968, CC BY-SA 4.0 <https://creativecommons.org/licenses/by-sa/4.0>, via Wikimedia Commons.

Dunkeld Cathedral by Frank Zweers
Sketch of the original Stone of Destiny by Nigel Tranter (Oct 1981). Scotland: A Very Personal Review. Richard Drew Publishing, Glasgow.
Schiehallion. Courtesy of David Cowan
Pumlumon, the central mountain of Wales. Courtesy of https://stevehynd.com.
Rhayader Hoard by Jononmac46, CC BY-SA 4.0 <https://creativecommons.org/licenses/by-sa/4.0>, via Wikimedia Commons
Fig. 14 Rhayader's central crossroads. template by http://dmaps.com/pays.php?num_pay=1694&lang=en.
*St Pirans's Oratory, Penhale Sand*s by Jowaninpensans, CC BY-SA 4.0 <https://creativecommons.org/licenses/by-sa/4.0>, via Wikimedia Commons
Eighteenth century engraving of High Cross by William Stukely published in John Nichols History of Leicestershire (Guthlaxton) 1807. William Stukeley, CC BY-SA 4.0 <https://creativecommons.org/licenses/by-sa/4.0>, via Wikimedia Commons
Pendle Hill. Courtesy of Immanuel Giel. CC BY-SA 4.0 <https://creativecommons.org/licenses/by- sa/4.0> via Wikimedia Commons
The Whitendale Hanging Stones. Courtesy of Anthony Parkes. CC BY-SA 2.0 <https://creativecommons.org/licenses/by-sa/2.0>, via Wikimedia Commons
Sarmatian Warrior Artist's rendition of a Sarmatian cavalryman with a dragon windsock standard, taken from an image engraved on a stone found at Ribchester. From the research by Dr Dan Robinson, Keeper of Archaeology at the Grosvenor Museum, Chester.
Allendale Fire Ceremony. Courtesy of Mick Borroff. Allendale Town Tar Bar'l Wikimedia Commons
The St Bees Dragon. Courtesy of Doug Sim. Uploaded to Wikimedia Commons.
Fig. 33 Geology of the Isle of Man. Courtesy of Dave Quirk https://manxgeology.com/geological-map/
Fig. 35 template design based on geography map of the Isle of Man from http://www.iomguide.com/geography.php.
Fig. 36 Roman London by Fremantleboy, Drallim (translation), CC BY 2.5 <https://creativecommons.org/licenses/by/2.5>, via Wikimedia Commons
Fig.37 The thirty-three Boroughs of London with the City of London in red. TUBS, CC BY-SA 3.0 <https://creativecommons.org/licenses/by-sa/3.0>, via Wikimedia Commons
London Eye by User: Diliff - Taken by user, CC BY 2.5, https://commons.wikimedia.org/w/index.php?curid=690130
Map of Original Peoples of Britain - my work, CC BY-SA 3.0 <https://creativecommons.org/licenses/by-sa/3.0>, via Wikimedia Commons
Map of Sicily with Enna marked in red by Cattette, CC BY-SA 4.0 <https://creativecommons.org/licenses/by-sa/4.0>, via Wikimedia Commons

Index

T

Also available from the Authors

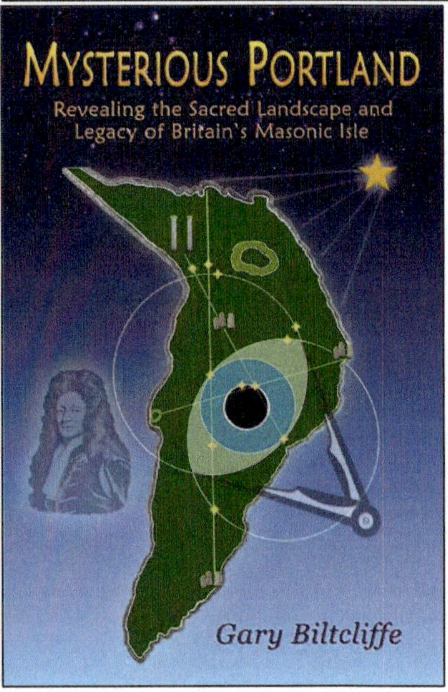

www.belinusline.com

Printed in Great Britain
by Amazon

60875380R00228